RATIONALITY, INSTITUTIONS AND ECONOMIC METHODOLOGY

ECONOMICS AS SOCIAL THEORY
Series Edited by Tony Lawson
University of Cambridge

Social theory is experiencing something of a revival within economics. Critical analyses of the particular nature of the subject matter of social studies and of the types of methods, categories and modes of explanation that can legitimately be endorsed for the scientific study of social objects, are re-emerging. Economists are again addressing such issues as the relationship between agency and structure, between economy and the rest of society, and between inquirer and the object of inquiry. There is renewed interest in elaborating basic categories such as causation, competition, culture, discrimination, evolution, money, need, order, organization, power, probability, process, rationality, technology, time, truth, uncertainty and value etc.

The objective for this series is to facilitate this revival further. In contemporary economics the label 'theory' has been appropriated by a group that confines itself to largely a-social, a-historical, mathematical 'modelling'. *Economics as Social Theory* thus reclaims the 'theory' label, offering a platform for alternative, rigorous, but broader and more critical conceptions of theorizing.

ECONOMICS AND LANGUAGE
Edited by Willie Henderson, Tony Dudley-Evans and Roger Backhouse

Forthcoming titles
WHO PAYS FOR THE KIDS?
Gender and the structures of constraint
Nancy Folbre

RATIONALITY, INSTITUTIONS AND ECONOMIC METHODOLOGY

*Edited by Uskali Mäki, Bo Gustafsson
& Christian Knudsen*

London and New York

First published 1993
by Routledge
11 New Fetter Lane, London EC4P 4EE

Simultaneously published in the USA and Canada
by Routledge
29 West 35th Street, New York, NY 10001

© 1993 Uskali Mäki, Bo Gustafsson and Christian Knudsen

Typeset in Baskerville by J&L Composition Ltd, Filey, North Yorkshire
Printed and bound in Great Britain by Biddles Ltd, Guildford and King's Lynn

British Library Cataloguing in Publication Data
A catalogue reference for this book is available from the British Library

ISBN 0–415–07571–8 Hbk
ISBN 0–415–09208–6 Pbk

Library of Congress Cataloging in Publication Data
has been applied for.

ISBN 0–415–07571–8 Hbk
ISBN 0–415–09208–6 Pbk

CONTENTS

CONTENTS

IV Institutions and Their Evolution

V Conclusion

CONTRIBUTORS

Bruce Caldwell, University of North Carolina, USA

László Csontos, University of Connecticut, USA

D. Wade Hands, University of Puget Sound, USA

Geoffrey Hodgson, University of Cambridge, UK

Christian Knudsen, Copenhagen Business School, Denmark

Richard Langlois, University of Connecticut, USA

Brian Loasby, University of Sterling, UK

Uskali Mäki, Academy of Finland, Finland

Douglass North, Washington University, USA

Viktor Vanberg, George Mason University, USA

PREFACE

Practitioners of any specific scientific discipline usually pay little attention to problems of methodology. They often have the attitude towards such problems that the distinguished biochemist L.J. Henderson once expressed thus: 'It is ordinarily far more useful to get to work on the phenomena and so acquire familiarity with things than to spend time talking about methodology or even to pay too much attention to the analysis of actual methods'. There is a considerable amount of pragmatic truth in this. General methodological discussions do not solve problems by themselves. It is one thing to lay bare problems and weaknesses within a discipline. It is quite a different thing to solve them, elaborate new approaches and then put them to work. This is usually done in connection with research on some specific problem and if the effort is successful it convinces the practitioners of the discipline of the power and usefulness of the new approach.

Yet methodological discussions have a rightful place in ordinary scientific discourse within any discipline. In the first place, they may enhance the awareness of and track down underlying problems and, thus, prepare the ground for new scientific advance. Second, during its growth any discipline now and then gets stuck or becomes so differentiated that it is necessary to take a new look at the foundations in order to provide new foundations or provide new unity in the diversity.

Whatever value these observations may have, it remains a fact that the discipline of economics during the last two decades has experienced developments that may motivate a confrontation between the discipline and theories of science and methodology. In the first place, the methodology of economics has become a new subbranch of the discipline. Second, problems concerning the role of institutions as well as of rationality have been widely discussed. The principle of rationality or of rational behaviour as well as the role of institutions are both of fundamental importance to economics, because the issue of rationality has a bearing upon the fundamental behavioural assumptions while the issue of institutions concerns the constraints and the outcome of choice.

ix

Even if the assumption of rationality certainly is no necessary pre-condition for the coherent working of an economy – it could be governed by habit, norms, fiat or whatever, if generally internalized by economic agents – it is a fact that rational behaviour looms large within economic theory both as prescriptive principle for individual behaviour and as a descriptive principle for individual-cum-collective behaviour. It is in this last respect that the principle of rationality becomes really interesting as testified already by Adam Smith in his famous dictum about the invisible hand mapping rational individual behaviour into rational collective outcomes. With Smith and other founders of political economy the principle of rationality essentially implied an assumption that individuals prefer more to less, although Senior formulated the maximization hypothesis in its prescriptive sense applied to individual behaviour. Only in the modern theory of a perfectly competitive equilibrium there is a marriage between individual maximization behaviour and collective optimality as expressed by the Pareto criterion, namely that every perfectly competitive equilibrium under certain assumptions achieves Pareto optimality.

But this triumph of the rationality principle was won at a high price. The general perfectly competitive equilibrium is about economics rather than about economy, partly because of the necessary assumptions (no externalities or economies of scale and all individuals having the same utility function, etc.) and partly because it cannot really exist due to the insuperable costs of gaining information. This indicates that the rationality principle by itself is weak and needs some complementary principles in order to create rational individual-cum-collective behaviour. It is at this point that the issue of institutions comes to the fore. When Mandeville asserted that public benefits was the outcome of private vice and Smith likewise claimed that it is the butcher's self-interest and not his benevolence that supplies us with (good) meat, they expressed the fundamental identity between individual and collective optimality and the importance of relying on self-interest in achieving collective optimality in large groups of anonymously interacting individuals. But this observation did not rule out the operation of socially imposed codes of conduct in large groups, partly because large groups are made up of smaller groups and partly because individuals in large groups (society, nation) consciously create norms and rules of behaviour and enforcement in the shape of laws, police, courts, educational and religious systems, cultural codes and philosophical principles as frameworks for individual choice.

Already John Stuart Mill was convinced that the collective economic behaviour under the rule of private property was 'the result of two determining agencies competition and custom' and in his system of logic he was groping for 'one great case of intermixture of laws' for the explanation of social behaviour.

This broader approach to economics was, of course, still more elaborated in Marx. The missing links for a general theory of economic behaviour were searched for in theories of group and class behaviour, of vertical relations between men, of interaction and conflict between individuals and groups, of organization and of historical change. Veblen put the problem neatly with respect to the institution of property: 'While the institution of property is included . . . among the postulates of the theory, and even is presumed to be ever-present in the economic situation, it is allowed to have no force in shaping economic conduct, which is conceived to run its course to its hedonistic outcome as if no such institutional factor intervened between the impulse and its realization'.

But these early forerunners of modern institutional economics had little chance of success, as long as the full implications of the theory of supply and demand had not yet been investigated and spelled out. When this had been done and it became possible, as testified by the theory of general perfectly competitive equilibrium, to see what could be achieved as well as what was missing, time was mature for a broadening of the perspective. But neo-institutional economics is still in its infancy and it is far too early to hope for a synthesis between general equilibrium theory and neo-institutional theory. Terms have to be clearly defined, theorems in delimited areas of investigation should be elaborated and relations between various entities must be established before consistent and meaningful general theories could be established. If neo-institutional economics applies the method of isolation and goes into depth in selected areas of economic behaviour and if it succeeds in attracting the best brains of the profession, we could expect interesting new results in the decades ahead. If this volume, dealing with the methodological foundation of neo-institutional economics is a step in this direction, it has served its purpose.

In conclusion I want to thank all those who have contributed to this volume and, especially, Dr Uskali Mäki and Dr Christian Knudsen for their efforts to bring it out. The Bank of Sweden Tercentenary Foundation, which sponsors thematic studies at SCASSS, generously provided financial support for the project.

Bo Gustafsson
Director of the Swedish Collegium for
Advanced Study in the Social Sciences (SCASSS)

Part I

INTRODUCTION

1

ECONOMICS WITH INSTITUTIONS
Agenda for Methodological Enquiry[1]

Uskali Mäki

ECONOMIC METHODOLOGY AND THE INSTITUTIONALIST REVIVAL

This book grew out of an attempt to marry to each other two growing currents in economics, namely the specialized work on the general methodology of economics and the resurgence of theoretical interest in the character and role of institutions. It was the idea that both parties would benefit from such an alliance. On the one hand, research in economic methodology is clearly in need of reorientation and conceptual development inspired by concrete issues involved in substantial economic theories and approaches. Institutionalist economics, with its several varieties, might provide generalists in economic methodology with a source of inspiration and a test ground for such developments. On the other hand, the recent rehabilitation of theoretical study of institutions in economics raises lots of issues of a methodological character. Although institutionalist economists have traditionally been inclined to engage themselves in methodological reflection, there is a lot of room for sophistication. Philosophically informed general methodology might be of help here.

It is much more legitimate now than, say, twenty years ago to take institutions as a serious research problem in economics. This problem is no more the sole speciality of the followers of Veblen, Commons, Mitchell, Ayres, and others in the old US American tradition. There now exists widely respected new attempts to theorize about the logic of collective action (e.g. Olson 1965), property rights (e.g. Furubotn and Pejovich 1974), law (e.g. Posner 1973), political rule systems (e.g. Brennan and Buchanan 1985), economic history as institutional history (e.g. North and Thomas 1973; North 1981), the institution of the business firm (e.g. Alchian and Demsetz 1972; Williamson 1975, 1985; Aoki *et al.* 1990), and many more. The theoretical approaches and frameworks adopted range from evolutionary approaches (e.g. Nelson

3

and Winter 1982) to the principal-agency theory (e.g. Jensen and Meckling 1976), from game theoretical perspectives (e.g. Schotter 1981; Sugden 1986) to transaction costs frameworks (Williamson 1975, 1985; North 1990). Some of the contributions adopt a literary style (e.g. Demsetz, North, Williamson), while some others employ formal techniques (e.g. Schotter, Stiglitz, Holmström). Some of them are 'closer' to standard neoclassical theory, while others are more heterodox.[2]

Given these new developments, it is no wonder that the introduction of institutions into the agenda of theory formation constitutes a major issue in economics. It is also entirely natural that the new agenda with institutions necessitates methodological reflection on the part of both those few who may object to it, those who try to do it by incorporating the notion of institution into the established body of theory, and those who pursue a theorization of institutions free from the constraints imposed by received economic theory. In order to justify a position about this issue, one needs to understand what is at stake: what the most fundamental conceptual, theoretical, and empirical problems are and how to steer one's course among them in a reasoned way. Methodological enquiry serves this need perfectly.[3]

More generally, the landscape of economics today is much richer than it was some two decades ago. The variety of rival or complementary schools and approaches may strike one as confusing. The situation makes it difficult for economists to give convincing arguments for their favoured approach as against other available options and for the newcomers to the field to make cognitively rational choices among the alternatives. Such a situation creates a natural propensity to methodological scrutiny. Characteristically, methodological enquiry may help clarify issues that are vital for orientation in this landscape, namely, it may provide analyses of the explicit or implicit commitments, the root assumptions and fundamental concepts of the alternative approaches. These concern their underlying world views, including views of human capacities and behaviour, of social structure and process, their research goals and explanatory structures, and also the more general principles of epistemic justification. These cosmological and epistemological principles serve as standards of assessment, the grounds of choice or mutual adjustment between theoretical alternatives.

Institutionalist economics in its many guises, provides a rich array of interesting topics for detailed methodological analysis. Some of the meta-theoretical commitments of the institutionalist traditions built upon the ideas of, for example, Veblen, Commons, and Ayres have been discussed, such as 'pattern-modelling' (e.g. Wilber and Harrison 1978), holism (e.g. Ramstad 1986), and pragmatism (e.g. Mirowski 1987). The economics of institutions based on the Austrian heritage of Carl Menger and Friedrich Hayek has been examined with some thoroughness in regard to its structure and philosophical premises (e.g. Vanberg 1986, 1989; Barry 1979; Gray 1984; Mäki 1990b, c). Much less work has been done on the methodological and conceptual foundations of the theories and approaches of, say, Ronald Coase, Oliver Williamson, George Akerlof, Richard Nelson, Sidney Winter, Robert Axelrod, Mancur Olson, Douglass North, or James Buchanan. This concerns matters such as the principles of appraisal and the structures of explanation as well as such fundamental categories as institution and process.

It is well known that the methodology of economics has recently progressed in leaps and bounds, both quantitatively and qualitatively. The number of books and articles published since 1980 or so exceeds the achievements of any other, earlier period. New outlets have been established, such as the journal *Economics and Philosophy*. The amount of sophisticated work on the foundations of economic theorizing has increased to such an extent that our understanding of many aspects of economics is at a far higher level than ever.[4] There are reasons for praise, but it has to be qualified.

The recent general methodology of economics has to a large extent been preoccupied with questions of epistemic appraisal, that is, epistemological questions concerning the rational acceptance and rejection of economic theories. The main concern has been the critical role of negative empirical evidence in the dynamic context of testing and progress, allegedly devoid of inductive inference. The meta-theories of Karl Popper and Imre Lakatos have provided many, if not most, economic methodologists with a framework of regulative categories and questions, even though not all of them have been committed Popperians or Lakatosians in epistemological matters. A *Popperian dominance*, a kind of Popperian mainstream in economic methodology has prevailed. It has been a dominance of certain questions and categories, such as whether economic theories are falsifiable and whether economists critically pursue falsifications, whether a given proposition belongs to the irrefutable hard core or to the revisable protective belt of a research programme, whether this or that episode in the history of economic thought is or is not progressive in the sense of providing increasing corroborated excess content, etc. Such a dominance of questions formulated in Popperian terms has not necessarily meant a dominance of answers favourable to Popperian views. Chapter 3 of the present volume by Wade Hands, is an indication of this. Hands has worked within the Popperian framework for many years, and many of his important contributions to the literature are critical of the applicability of both Popper's and Lakatos's methodologies to economics. The same can be said of Bruce Caldwell's work. Indeed, it has been established by recent research in economic methodology that the Popperian principles do not hold in economics – descriptively, prescriptively, or both.[5] Still, there are many of those who find, for instance, some of Lakatos's categories such as the hard core, protective belt and heuristics useful for some purposes. Chapters 6 and 11 by Christian Knudsen are examples of this.

Even though Popperian falsificationism – the methodology of bold conjecture and critical refutation – is not practised or even practisable in economics, it (or a loose and more or less obscure version of it) nevertheless enjoys wide popularity in the meta-theoretical commentaries by economists. This phenomenon ranges from the introductory chapters of many standard textbooks to the attempts of some new institutionalists to legitimize their endeavours in terms of 'refutability'. For instance, Douglass North provides something like a criterion of demarcation in writing that 'in order to make a contribution to knowledge, the theory must be potentially refutable' (North 1981: x). This principle is carried over to his characterization of the concept of explanation: '"explanation" means explicit theorizing and the potential of refutability' (ibid. p. 4). Another example is Oliver Williamson. He seems not particularly concerned about the fact that transaction cost economics does not involve an 'accurate view of human nature' in representing agents as 'highly calculative' and as lacking 'kindness, sympathy, solidarity, and the like', because it 'nevertheless generates numerous refutable implications' (Williamson 1985: 391–2). More strongly, he insists on 'more attention to refutable implications (and less to rhetoric)' in the study of economic organizations (Williamson 1986: 196). Of course, phrases like these do not yet imply a commitment to strict falsificationist methodology. The question that the methodologist has to face then is this: what message do such phrases convey? Given the unavoidable problems with strict falsificationism, could talk about refutable implications and the like be something else than empty methodological rhetoric? There is some work to be done here by methodologists. This also means that further research on falsificationism is not entirely futile.

In any case, I believe that the Popperian dominance has led to a misallocation of intellectual resources in economic methodology. Armed with Popperian questions and tools, economic methodologists have had little to say about many relevant issues in economics, such as the actually effective grounds for holding beliefs, the kinds and roles of inductive reasoning, the structure of explanations, the perennial issue of realisticness, and the nature of metaphysical commitments involved in actual research practice. The obvious way of improving on the situation is to adopt new conceptual tools and to engage oneself in examining descriptively the elements, structures and conditions of the theories, methods, and practices prevalent in economics, institutionalism included. Many contributions to this book exemplify this approach.

Some of the actual characteristics of economics are accessible using approaches adopted from of the sociology and rhetoric of science. Unfortunately, it is no exaggeration to say that the sociology of economics is an almost non-existent field of study. (For exceptions, see the references in Chapter 4.) The situation is somewhat better in the case of the rhetorical approach, focusing on the rhetorical devices used by economists, as exemplified in the studies by Donald McCloskey (1985), Arjo Klamer (1983) and others (see also Klamer *et al.* 1988; Samuels 1990; Henderson *et al.* 1992). The notion of rhetoric in a narrow sense is defined by the idea of eloquence. In a more general sense rhetoric is a matter of persuasion, independently of whether the language used for communicating ideas satisfies this or that standard of eloquence. Veblen is certainly a prime example of an eloquent writer. This does not however guarantee that he is found persuasive by all relevant audiences, i.e. that his rhetoric is successful. Studies of rhetoric as persuasion might help us understand why Williamson has been found more persuasive than Veblen, or more accurately, why Williamson has been found more persuasive than Veblen by certain audiences, most notably by academic economists, and why Veblen has perhaps been found relatively more persuasive by some other audiences, such as some other social scientists and lay people. Such findings are most likely not exemplifications of the Popperian canons of epistemic justification.

Some of the work on the rhetoric of economics and the sociology of science is hostile to the idea that the aspects of the world that appear as the objects of scientific theories exist independently of those theories and that those theories are true or false partly in virtue of what the world is like. In other words, many rhetoricians and sociologists of science reject scientific realism. In Chapter 2, Bruce Caldwell discusses the realist philosophy of science as an option in economic methodology. Again, in this role, realism is in need of scrutiny and development, and institutionalist economics might provide some of the necessary inspiration.[6] Chapter 6 by Christian Knudsen contains a brief discussion of the opposition between realism and instrumentalism in the context of rival conceptualizations of economic rationality.

Most if not all institutionalist economists hold that standard neo-classical theory or its particular constituents (such as the rationality assumption) are 'unrealistic', that their own alternative is at least more 'realistic' and that being realistic is a scientific virtue of a theory. This is one theme in Chapter 7 by Viktor Vanberg. Furthermore, various institutionalists take issue with each other's assessments of theses matters. In Chapter 5, for instance, Langlois and Csontos provide arguments about the desirability of realisticness in one's picture of the agent in explanations of economic phenomena. This is, no doubt, one of the most important if not the most important methodological issue in economics, but the recent methodology of economics has had little to offer that would be of help in clarifying this perennial controversy. The Popperian dominance has led methodologists to examine appraisal in terms of predictive implications of theories even though in practice a large portion of many economists' judgements seems to be based on assessments of the realisticness of the premises of theories. Since these questions are particularly pressing in debates about the economics of institutions, the institutionalist endeavours would provide excellent materials for developing and testing ideas about realisticness.

Such work would also help us form opinions about whether realism is an adequate philosophy – as distinguished from realisticness as an attribute of representations[7] – for this or that variety of institutionalist economics. Some institutionalists regard themselves as pragmatists, which, in many cases at least, implies that they cannot hold realism at the same time. Again, this does not preclude the likely possibility that the theories they hold are realistic in many senses of the term, such as being relatively comprehensive, plausible, or practically relevant. However, such attributes are not conceptually connected to realism. Something else is needed to meet the challenge of the viability of realism in economics. I have a few more words on these questions towards the end of this chapter.

There are many other methodological topics that are in need of careful analysis. The idea of explanation is one topic the study of which benefits from the investigation of institutionalism. The traditional complaint has been that institutions play no role in standard economic explanations, either in the role of *explananda* or in the role of *explanantia*. Today the explanatory ambitions of economics have been stretched beyond the traditional limits. This gives rise to several methodological questions. What, precisely, is the structure of the economic mode of explanation (or the alternative economic modes, if such exist)? Does it (or they) manage to meet the promises it (they) make(s)? What is the role of human intentionality in such explanations? What should it be? Are functionalist explanations legitimate? Chapter 5 by Langlois and Csontos discusses questions related to one particular method of explanation in economics, the method of situational analysis. The final chapter by Christian Knudsen also discusses issues of economic explanation.

I have pointed out that institutionalist economics offers many interesting topics and challenges to methodologists which should prompt them to develop their tools and views. In addition to such indirect inspiration, the contribution of institutionalist economics to economic methodology might be more substantial and more direct. I have in mind the two key concepts of this volume, those of rationality and institution. The concept of rationality is a fundamental notion in the study of both science and society. It is central to economics as well as to economic methodology. It is a major issue in these fields of study whether and in what sense economic agents on the one hand and economists on the other may be assumed or prescribed to make rational choices among alternatives or to act rationally as rule-followers. Since the traditional theories of scientific rationality have been challenged, it is necessary to search for a new understanding of what makes scientific activity rational. Institutionalist thought might be of some help here. It suggests that science, too, should be analysed as a social institution. Science does not happen in a social vacuum. All cognitive pursuits are embedded in social rules and relations. It is here that economic methodology might benefit most directly from a study of institutionalism in economics and elsewhere. In this volume, the contributions by Loasby (Chapter 8) and Mäki (Chapter 4) can be read as exemplifying this spirit.

What once was the received view implied that while scientific rationality is exclusively the concern of the philosophy of science, the study of the institution of science lies within the purview of the sociology of science. Such dichotomies, however, are much less popular now than they used to be. It is no longer unusual to attempt a fusion of the two perspectives and thereby to examine the rationality and institutionality of scientific activity within one and the same framework. The development in the theory of science parallels that in economics.

VARIETIES OF INSTITUTIONALIST ECONOMICS

Institutionalism in economics is more than an attitude but less than a school or a research programme, Lakatosian or otherwise. This does not preclude the existence of institutionalist schools or research programmes, or approaches or theories or what have you. It is my opinion that there exists such a great variety of approaches in economics which might deserve to be called 'institutionalist' that we had better avoid too restrictive a characterization of institutionalism in general. All such characterizations are based on specifications of what it is that makes a theory (school, stream, etc.) institutionalist. Let us take a look at a few of them.

On the opening page of his *Markets and Hierarchies*, Oliver Williamson coined the term, 'new institutionalist economics', and described its object in two ways. First, characterized genetically in terms of its intellectual background, the new institutionalist economics draws upon 'mainline microtheory, economic history, the economics of property rights, comparative systems, labor economics, and industrial organization'. Second, characterized in terms of three fundamental beliefs of its advocates, the new institutionalist economics is based on the view that (1) 'received microtheory . . . operates at too high a level of abstraction', that (2) 'the study of "transactions" . . . is really a core matter', and that (3) 'what they are doing [is] complementary to, rather than a substitute for, conventional analysis' (Williamson 1975: 1).

It is clear that this characterization fits well with Williamson's own version of transaction cost economics. It also seems clear that tenets (1) and (3) are shared by most of those who have been labelled as new institutionalists. Tenet (2), however, makes the characterization too restrictive to capture all such economists. No wonder then that on a later occasion, Williamson admitted that 'transaction cost economics is *part of* the New Institutional Economics research tradition' (Williamson 1985: 16; emphasis added).

There exists another major line of economic thought which has traditionally been called institutionalist and which involves a critical stance towards Williamson's version. Following the lead of Veblen and Commons, William Dugger (1990) characterizes what he regards as genuine institutionalism in terms of six tenets. First, institutionalists place special emphasis on the role of power in the economy. Second, they share a reformist scepticism towards the institutions of their own economies. Third, they subscribe more or less to the old dichotomy between serviceable and predatory (or technological and ceremonial, or industrial and pecuniary) activities and institutions. Fourth, institutionalists are unified by an 'evolutionary' approach, a study of the economy as a process of ongoing historical change, not in terms of optimum states. Fifth, institutionalists are holists in that they consider the economy, and the acting individual, as part of an evolving cultural whole. Sixth, institutionalists are typically instrumentalists in the special sense that they conceive of ideas, both positive and normative, as revisable instruments in the ongoing discretionary adjustment of institutions to the benefit of humankind. Dugger then argues that Williamson subscribes to none of these six tenets, and therefore is not eligible to be characterized as an institutionalist.

Here we face the tension between what have been called the 'old' versus the 'new' institutionalism in a particularly strong form.[8] An advocate of the old institutionalism denies that a major representative of the new variety is an institutionalist at all. Such an approach may be unnecessarily restrictive. What appears as a struggle over rights to labels is perhaps not the most fruitful line of argument. It would be more rewarding to proliferate the labels, each designating a specific version of institutionalism, and to decide on the minimum requirements that any version has to satisfy to count as institutionalism. Those requirements would have to be more permissive than either Williamson's or Dugger's. This would be accompanied by the additional acknowledgement that both the old and the new institutionalisms are far from being internally uniform. Supporters of each version could then concentrate on developing substantial arguments in favour of their own version and against others. Struggles over rights to labels could then be given up.

One possibility for a permissible and yet useful formulation of the minimum requirements for any approach counting as institutionalism runs as follows. Let [MinI] stand for 'minimal institutionalism'.

[MinI] Any economic endeavour pursuing explanations which involve institutions in the role of either *explanantia* or *explananda* or both, constitutes a case of institutionalist economics.

Institutionalist economics in this minimal sense is economics with institutions in the role of either explaining entities or explained entities or both. Different versions of institutionalism could then be understood as being based on different specifications of [MinI], such as specifications of how institutions are conceptualized; how institutions are explained; which aspects of institutions are explained; how institutions are invoked in explaining something else; what this something else consists of, etc. This would give us a whole variety of institutionalisms. The dividing line between the old and the new institutionalism becomes relativized, as it is only one among many others which cut across both of these aggregated categories internally.

Let us then take a look at Richard Langlois's characterization of the new institutionalist economics in terms of 'themes' and as a more specific 'research programme'. He distinguishes three shared themes and the corresponding items in the new institutionalist research programme (Langlois 1986b, c). I summarize them as follows.

1 Common theme: abandonment of narrow maximizing rationality in favour of rationality 'in a true sense'.
  Item in the programme: practice the method of situational analysis with 'a kind of bounded rationality assumption'.
2 Common theme: economic explanation should be dynamic or evolutionary.
  Item in the programme: construct invisible-hand explanations, i.e. explain economic phenomena as unintended consequences of individual action.
3 Common theme: besides market prices, economic activity is co-ordinated by several other institutions which should also be studied theoretically.
  Item in the programme: on the one hand, include various kinds of institutions as parts of the agent's situation, and, on the other, explain social institutions theoretically by the invisible hand process. This is the dual role of institutions in the programme.

As can be seen, the three common themes are very general, while the respective items in the programme are their specifications. It appears that the themes in the above characterization come very close to constituting the set of shared minimum requirements for any version of

11

institutionalism. Indeed, it is difficult to see why any old institutionalist could not accept them (Langlois has a reservation on this, related to the idea of the study of institutions being 'theoretical' as part of theme 3, but I will come back to that). If this were the case, Langlois's themes would be common not only to the new institutionalist economics but to much of the old institutionalist economics as well. They would not help distinguish the new from the old.[9]

On the other hand, it seems obvious that the other part of Langlois's formulation, namely that of the new institutionalist economics as a 'programme' is too restrictive to capture all versions of the new institutionalism. For example, not all versions subscribe to the notions of bounded rationality and invisible-hand explanation. In later sections I discuss the items of Langlois's list in the context of the tension between the 'new' and the 'old' lines.

It is notable that Langlois characterizes the new institutionalist economics as sharing the spirit of Carl Menger's economics, not that of his contemporary opponents, the German historicists and American institutionalists, i.e. the old institutionalists. 'Menger has perhaps more claim to be the patron saint of the new institutional economics than has any of the original institutionalists.' (Langlois 1986b: 5.) An even stronger tie between the new institutionalist and modern neoclassical theory can be suggested: the new institutionalist economics has grown, 'not via a re-emergence of traditional institutionalism, but mainly through developments in the heart of modern orthodox theory itself. The irony, of course, is that the original institutionalism of Veblen and others emerged largely out of a critique of orthodox assumptions' (Hodgson 1989: 249–50). This is compatible with Williamson's point cited above that the new institutionalist economics is not to be taken as substituting for but as complementing standard neoclassical theory.

While the formulation of the distinction in terms of the 'old' and the 'new' has an historical import and is excessively aggregative in nature, I suggest considering some of the differences in more systematic and disaggregated terms. The rest of this chapter discusses varieties of institutionalism on a number of methodological dimensions. They include the notions of rationality, institution, and explanation, the very idea of theory and the related notion of ad hocness, storytelling, individualism and holism, and the issues involved in what may be called the method of isolation. These discussions will hopefully reveal interesting topics for further methodological enquiry.

INSTITUTIONS, RATIONALITY AND EXPLANATION

The explanatory pursuits of institutionalist economics are varied. They differ in regard to both their *explananda*, *explanantia*, and the explanatory relation between the two. For instance, some versions are oriented towards explaining either the genesis or the persistence of existing institutions, while some others are engaged in accounting for different outcomes as behavioural consequences of different institutional regimes. In these accounts, the meanings of the concept of institution vary. The same can be said about the concept of rationality which plays a decisive role in the new efforts to theorize institutions.

It is much easier to insist on taking institutions seriously as belonging to the domain of economics than to provide a precise, unambiguous and at the same time both sufficiently rich and restricted definition of the concept of institution itself. What is it that we should take seriously as a theoretical problem? How should we transcend the various intuitive notions of institution? Unfortunately, no completely satisfactory definition of the concept of institution is available in social science literature.

No doubt this applies also to the definitions that the classics of the institutionalist tradition have provided. One of Veblen's formulations reads like this: 'An institution is of the nature of a usage which has become axiomatic and indispensable by habituation and general acceptance' (Veblen 1924: 101). In the words of Commons, 'we may define an institution as Collective Action in Control of Individual Action. Collective action ranges all the way from unorganized Custom to the many organized Going Concerns' (Commons 1934: 69). In most cases, habits and customs serve the role of *definientia* in the old institutionalist definitions of the concept of institution. Institutions are conceived as being based on habits and customs. A similar view is put by Geoff Hodgson in Chapter 9 of the present volume. In Chapter 7, Viktor Vanberg defines institutions in terms of routines: institutions are 'systems of interrelated and mutually stabilizing routines'.

In a modern game-theoretic context, we encounter the following definition: 'A social institution is a regularity in social behaviour that is agreed to by all members of society, specifies behavior in specific recurrent situations, and is either self-policed or policed by some external authority' (Schotter 1981: 11). Langlois cites this definition approvingly[10] and goes on to say that 'social institutions are made up of rules' of the form 'always react in manner X to event Y' (Langlois 1986b: 17–18).[11,12] There is a problem here. An institution is defined in two ways, first as a regularity of behaviour and then as normative rules underlying such behaviour. It is not clear whether what is meant is that institutions consist of conjunctions of regularities and the related rules or that there are in fact two concepts of institution here. It would be advisable to adopt the first option that institutions comprise both rules and regularities of certain kinds.

In addition to rules and regularities of action, something else is needed, namely reciprocal beliefs and expectations held by the people acting. In his more elaborated definition, Schotter (1981: 11) includes as necessary for a regularity of behaviour to constitute an institution the condition that 'everyone expects everyone else to conform to' the regularity. This element is more or less explicitly incorporated in two other definitions that are worth citing. Nicholas Rowe, an obvious advocate of some version of the new institutionalist economics, writes that 'what we call social institutions are in fact nothing more than agents rationally following rules of action, and being believed by other agents to do so' (Rowe 1989: 5). Walter Neale, more closely in the old institutionalist tradition, characterizes institutions similarly in terms of three elements, namely 'people doing', 'rules', and 'folkviews . . . explaining or justifying the activities and the rules' (Neale 1987: 1182). An incorporation of the idea of reciprocal beliefs into the notion of institution gives it a more clearly social content.

There is yet another question that can be raised about Langlois's discussion of institutions. He discusses the difference between general social norms and particular corporations, both conceived of as institutions (Langlois 1986b: 19). However, it may be asked whether particular corporations are institutions in either of the senses adopted by Langlois; they seem to be neither regularities of behaviour nor normative rules of conduct even though they involve both. Another possibility would be to conceive of particular corporations as organizations exemplifying general organization forms. All of these ingredients are incorporated in Geoff Hodgson's definition of the concept of institution: a social institution 'is here defined as a social organization which, through the operation of tradition, custom or legal constraint, tends to create durable and routinized patterns of behaviour' (Hodgson 1988: 10).

Hodgson's definition provides a composite concept which is narrower in extension than the sum of the extensions of its elements. Such a composite concept is unable to encompass all concepts of institution in use in different versions of institutionalist economics. Since it seems that there is no single concept of institution shared by even all the new institutionalists, we might have to live with several such concepts. For example, in an early contribution, Lance Davis and Douglass North suggested a distinction between 'institutional environment' and 'institutional arrangement' (Davis and North 1971: 6–7). Their characterization of this distinction is not entirely clear but it appears to have some affinities with Ludwig Lachmann's distinction between 'external' and 'internal' institutions (Lachmann 1971: 81). While institutional environments or external institutions are akin to sets of basic rules of behaviour, institutional arrangements or internal institutions are akin to established organizational structures within the frame of the basic rules. Williamson has recently appealed to this distinction and announced that 'transaction cost economics is predominantly concerned with institutional arrangements, normally referred to as governance structures' (Williamson 1990b: 9). We may add that other branches of institutional economics are primarily preoccupied with institutional environments or external institutions, that is, basic rules of conduct.

In Chapter 10 of the present volume, North makes a similar distinction between 'the basic institutional framework' and 'the organizations that arise in consequence of the institutional framework'. Another conceptual puzzle may be observed here: while North sees organizations as 'arising in consequence of' the basic framework, in Hodgson's definition it seems to be the other way around, a social organization 'creating' stable patterns of behaviour. Whether this puzzle can be resolved by terminological adjustment or whether it reflects substantive difference will not be discussed here.

The notions of institution and rationality of conduct are connected. The important fact to notice at the outset is that any attempt to theorize institutions is dependent on rejecting the extreme form of the rationality assumption which involves the idea of perfect knowledge on the part of economic actors. This is included in the message delivered by the first 'common theme' in Langlois's list characterizing the new institutionalist economics, the one calling for the concept of rationality 'in a true sense'. His programme item goes on to specify that this true sense is given by 'a kind of bounded rationality assumption'. This is not very specific, though. The attribute 'a kind of' leaves much of the import of the suggestion open.

In Simon's early and vague definition, bounded rationality can be attributed to behaviour which is 'intendedly rational, but only limitedly so' (Simon 1947: xxiv). The implications of the two attributes of rationality in this characterization are relevant to us. First, the element of intentionality or conscious goal-directedness precludes unintentional habits, customs, and routines from the scope of boundedly rational behaviour and thereby restricts the set of versions of institutionalist economics. In particular, those versions of the old institutionalist economics which build upon the notion of habitual behaviour are excluded. The notion of routine in Nelson and Winter's version of the new institutionalist economics also raises questions from this perspective.[13] Second, the element of being limited or bounded has often been interpreted as a matter of limited cognitive and computational competence. Since the agents are unable to gather and process the information required for attaining the maximum outcome, they will be satisfied with less. The recognition of this opens the connection to the notion of institution or organization: 'It is only because individual human beings are limited in knowledge, foresight, skill, and time that organizations are useful investments for the achievement of human purpose' (ibid., p. 199). It is true that many new institutionalists endorse the assumption of bounded rationality. Williamson, for example, has made this clear in the case of his transaction cost version of the new institutionalist economics.

Not all branches of the new institutionalist economics subscribe to the above interpretation of the Simonian notion, however. Williamson says that while his version uses the idea of bounded rationality, Austrian theory and Nelson and Winter's evolutionary theory employ the notion of 'process or organic rationality' (Williamson 1985: 46–7). Furthermore, Langlois's own formulation of the rationality principle seems not to be Simonian. In Chapter 5 of this volume he and Csontos suggest that situational analysis – to which they subscribe – involves the idea of rationality as reasonableness and that reasonableness is an ability of an agent to give reasons for his or her actions (p. 122). However, reasonableness in this sense is neither synonymous nor coextensive with bounded rationality in Simon's sense.

There is another aspect in Simon's suggestions about rationality that is of special relevance to institutionalist economics. It is his notion of *procedural rationality*, the idea that rationality pertains, not to the outcomes of action as in standard neoclassicism, but to the procedures of action (Simon 1976). A related way of putting this is to say that rationality pertains to rules of action rather than to actions themselves directly (see Rowe 1989). In Chapter 6 of the present volume, Christian Knudsen presents an argument in favour of procedural rationality and against what might be called *outcomes rationality* (Knudsen follows Simon by calling it 'substantive rationality'). This distinction is also the theme of Chapter 7 by Viktor Vanberg. He distinguishes between rationality as neoclassical 'case-by-case-maximization' and rationality as rule-following. Neoclassical rationality is a matter of separately assessing each particular choice situation as unique and choosing the option that gives the highest payoff. Rationality as rule-following is a matter of behaving similarly in similar situations. The agent does not take each particular situation as unique but as similar to some others, as exemplifying types of situation, and behaves regularly in regard to such types, i.e. follows rules. These suggestions have the feature that, in a sense, we may say that *rationality becomes attributed to institutions*, given a specific conceptualization of institution as people acting according to rules.

In any case, the above remarks imply that Langlois's programme item attributing bounded rationality uniformly to the new institutionalist economics is problematic. In defence of Langlois's suggestion, we might perhaps argue that each of the several versions that can be found is '*a kind* of bounded rationality assumption'. Yet, in this case we would end up with several kinds of such assumptions, while Langlois talks about one kind.

Let us next briefly discuss the question of the explanatory relation.

Langlois's programme item (1) prescribes that economists should practise the method of *situational analysis*. Here we meet Popper in another role, namely as a formulator of situational analysis as the method of explanation in economics and other social sciences. By using this method, phenomena are explained as consequences of individual actions constrained or determined by the 'logic of the situation' in which the actors find themselves. Situational analysis invokes rationality as an attribute of the actors: the actors are assumed to act rationally, or to use Popper's ambiguous phrase, 'appropriately' with respect to their situations (Popper 1983: 359). One possible reconstruction of the structure of situational explanation is as follows, call it [SA] (Koertge 1979: 87).

[SA1] *Description of the situation* Agent A was in a situation of type C.
[SA2] *Analysis of the situation* In a situation of type C, the appropriate thing to do is X.
[SA3] *Rationality principle* Agents always act appropriately to their situations.
[SA4] *Explanandum* (Therefore) A did X.

It is notable that [SA] does not cite the agent's aims and beliefs explicitly. This is due to the peculiarity of the concept of situation in Popper: in addition to the 'external' environment of action, [SA1] also encompasses the goals and beliefs of actors.[14]

In a seminal paper, Spiro Latsis employed a variant of [SA] for an examination of the neoclassical theory of the firm and its behaviouralist rivals. He interpreted neoclassicism as being committed to what he called *situational determinism*, where the behaviour of actors is conceived of as entirely determined by the 'logic of the situation' so that there is only one course of action available to them. He contrasted the situationally deterministic 'single-exit' models of neoclassical economics and the 'multiple-exit' approach of Simon's behavioural economics and argued for the latter (Latsis 1972).[15] There is a tension between these suggestions by Latsis and programme item 1 in Langlois. Whereas Langlois suggests that the new institutionalist economics combine bounded rationality and situational analysis, Latsis takes behaviouralism and situational determinism as rival approaches. In Chaper 5, Langlois and Csontos attempt to resolve this tension. They level a criticism against Latsis's conception of situational analysis, charging him for mistaking situational analysis in general for the neoclassical version of it. They argue that situational analysis does not require the thin neoclassical notion of rationality and that behaviouralist versions of situational analysis also exist.

Consider next Langlois's tenets (2) and (3) for the new institutionalist economics, especially the respective items in the allegedly shared programme. They suggest that the new institutionalist economics provides

17

invisible-hand explanations of economic phenomena and institutions (see also Rutherford 1989: 306–12). This would seem to suggest an important difference between the old institutionalist economics and the new institutionalist economics concerning the respective conceptions of the origins of institutions, even though Langlois does not explicitly comment on the old institutionalist economics position. Using Menger's distinction between 'organic' institutions (as unintended consequences of individual actions and interactions) and 'pragmatic' institutions (as results of intentional design), the difference would appear as that between the advocates of the organic view and those of the pragmatic view. Such a generalization needs some qualification.

It may be admitted that many advocates of the old institutionalist economics are in favour of viewing institutions as discretionary. For instance, Commons writes that the attention of institutional theories 'is directed towards *intended* or *purposeful* changes, and to a *managed* equilibrium instead of an *automatic* equilibrium' (Commons 1934: 120; see also, for example, Tool 1979 and Bush 1987). Such statements, however, typically concern the suggested *normative* tasks of economics. As a *descriptive* idea, the notion of unintended consequence is not alien to the old institutionalist economics. Witness Wesley Mitchell: 'Coordination within an enterprise is the result of careful planning by experts; coordination among independent enterprises cannot be said to be planned at all; rather it is the unplanned result of natural selection in a struggle for business survival' (Mitchell 1913: 38). It is because actual coordination among independent enterprises is perceived as generating 'waste', and as conducive to business cycles and other harmful effects (ibid.) that these institutionalists take the normative interventionist stance.

Another important qualification results from recognizing that the new institutionalist economics stream is itself divided about this issue. Some members of the stream are consistently in favour of practising invisible-hand theorizing about institutions, most uncompromisingly the Austrians, following the paradigm of Menger's theory of the spontaneous genesis of money and Hayek's Fergusonian dictum about phenomena and institutions as 'results of human action but not of human design'. Within the game-theoretic wing, Schotter (1981) and Sugden (1986) have provided models which conform to the invisible-hand mode. For example, in Schotter's approach, 'institutions are outcomes of human action that no single individual intended to occur ... they emerge or evolve spontaneously from individual maximizing or satisficing behaviour instead of being designed by a social planner' (Schotter 1986: 118). On the other hand, there are institutions and aspects of other institutions which are theorized by some wings of the new institutionalist economics as discretionary. For instance, in the public choice approach by Buchanan,

18

Tullock and others, one of the research problems has been the design of sets of rules that guarantee optimum outcomes; and in the contractarian approach of Williamson, North, and others, institutions are typically $\times$ considered as direct outcomes of intentional contractual design.

However, even this generalization is in need of qualification because of ambiguities, for example, in Williamson's position. Three different views have been or can be attributed to him. First, Schotter includes Williamson among those who view the emergence of institutions as an organic or spontaneous process generated by individual purposive actions (Schotter 1986: 118). None of these purposive actions is supposed to involve the specific purpose of creating those institutions. Second, as pointed out on an earlier occasion (Mäki 1987: 371), we can find in Williamson formulations which seem to imply a position which is diametrically opposite to that attributed to him by Schotter. This is the idea of a visible hand, as it were, with a specific purpose of bringing about the institutions to be explained. For instance, Williamson postulates the existence of 'an institutional-design specialist' whose task is 'not merely to resolve conflict in progress but also to recognize potential conflict in advance and devise governance structures to forestall or attenuate it' (Williamson 1985: 29, and 1986: 172). Due to bounded rationality, however, comprehensive *ex ante* planning is not possible (Williamson 1985: 30–2). Third, it is possible to argue plausibly that the structure of Williamson's theory implies a commitment to functionalism. To explain the existence of social institution X by suggesting that it serves function Y, i.e., that it has Y as a consequence of its operation, amounts to a functionalist mode of explanation. In Williamson's case, his alleged functionalism is implied in the explanation of a given governance structure by suggesting that it is efficient in economizing on transaction costs. No mechanism of mediation between existence and efficiency, either of an invisible-hand type or a visible-hand type, is or can be systematically theorized in Williamson's framework. (For this interpretation of Williamson, see Dow 1987, and the final chapter of the present volume by Christian Knudsen. Chapter 9 by Geoffrey Hodgson also offers a criticism of Williamson's views, based on the functionalist interpretation.)

While the above discussion relativizes the validity of Langlois's suggestions, it also indicates some tempting challenges to a methodological analyst. The explanatory structures actually in use in economics call for a deeper understanding.

THEORETICITY AND *AD HOCNESS*

It has been argued by Ronald Coase that 'the American institutionalists [i.e. representatives of the old institutionalist economics] were not theoretical but anti-theoretical . . . Without a theory, they had nothing to pass on except a mass of descriptive material waiting for a theory' (Coase 1984: 230). In the same vein, Langlois maintains that the old institutionalism of Veblen and his followers represents a 'non-theoretical' version of institutionalism: 'they wanted an economics with institutions but without theory; the problem with many neoclassicists is that they want economic theory without institutions; what we should really want is both institutions and theory', this last option being the new institutionalist one (Langlois 1986b: 5). This suggests that the distinction between the new institutionalist economics and the old institutionalist economics is coextensive with that between *theoretical institutionalism* and *non-theoretical institutionalism*. This seems to be one of the most popular ways of viewing the matter amongst those who identify themselves as new institutionalists.

In the context of such judgements, the very notion of theory has usually remained unanalysed. Any judgement of whether this or that variety of economics has pursued or has been able to produce theories presupposes a clarification of the concept of theory itself. Typically, this is not done by those who hold views about the matter. Given the radical ambiguity in the use of the term 'theory', such a clarification is not an easy task, and it will not be attempted here. Suffice it to make a few general remarks of immediate relevance to institutionalist economics. I use the notion of *ad hocness* for this purpose.

To begin, it may be admitted that the new institutionalists are not alone in their judgement of the old variety. This is evidenced by a recent statement by Allan Gruchy, a representative of old institutionalism. He classifies different (old) institutionalist approaches into three categories:

1 The 'miscellaneous or topical' approach which 'draws attention to economic problems that are ignored by orthodox economists [. . . but] lacks theoretical cohesiveness, since economics is said to have no precise boundaries and the doors are kept open to any topic or project that may engage the attention of the institutionalist investigator';
2 The 'thematic' approach which focuses on 'various well-established basic themes' but still lacks 'an overall framework of interpretation into which the basic themes . . . can be fitted in a general unity';
3 The 'paradigmatic' approach which seeks 'an overall analytical framework of analysis'.

(Gruchy 1990: 361–3)

Gruchy then admits that 'the majority of institutionalists [apparently of the old institutionalist type] adhere to the miscellaneous or topical approach to the study of institutional economics' and that even those few (such as Veblen, Mitchell, Commons, Ayres, and Galbraith) who have pursued developing a theoretical framework for institutional analysis have not got very far (ibid., 363–4). Elsewhere, Gruchy admits that (old) institutionalists 'have become engrossed in the analysis of limited issues rather than in an exposition of the theoretical foundations of their economics' (Gruchy 1982: 225).

Let us approach the issue theoreticity from the perspective of the notion of *ad hocness*. The traditional Popperian idea of *ad hocness* refers to the various immunizing stratagems by means of which scientists modify some of their auxiliary assumptions with the sole purpose of defending their hypotheses against negative empirical evidence: those modifications do not generate independently testable statements or novel predictions (e.g. Popper 1959: 80–2). Popper's methodology denounces the employment of such *ad hoc* stratagems. It has been pointed out, however, that Popper's own treatment of the rationality principle in the context of situational analysis appears to be in sharp contrast with this falsificationist rule (e.g. Koertge 1979, Hands 1985a); that is, he admits that the method of economics involves a crucial assumption which is false but still should not be rejected. Popper writes as follows:

> 'Now if a theory is tested, and found faulty, then we have always to decide which of its various constituent parts we shall make accountable for its failure. My thesis is that it is sound method-ological policy to decide not to make the rationality principle accountable but the rest of the theory . . .'
>
> (Popper 1983: 362)

Evidently, this is reminiscent of Lakatos's account of the scientific endeavour, based on the idea of unshakable core claims. Accordingly, the rationality assumption would be construed as one of the hard core propositions.

This is related to Lakatos's notion of *ad hocness*, according to which a move is *ad hoc* if it does not conform to the hard core and heuristics of a research programme. While the traditional idea of *ad hocness* retains the criticist spirit of Popperian methodology, the Lakatosian idea is rather conservative: *non-ad hoc* moves are conservative of established frameworks or research programmes. It has been pointed out by Wade Hands (1988) that whereas methodologists of economics have mostly employed the criticist notion of *ad hocness*, mainstream economists use the conservative notion in their own assessments of research. In the normative Lakatosian framework, there is no need to worry about this usage in mainstream economics, since Lakatos acknowledges 'the ration-ality of a certain amount of dogmatism' (Lakatos 1970: 175). He even suggests this as a demarcation criterion between mature and immature science: mature science consists of research programmes with inviolable hard cores, while immature science consists of 'a mere patched up pattern of trial and error'. Lakatos says that 'good scientists' call the latter '*ad hoc*' (ibid.). *Non-ad hocness* in this sense is a guarantee of theoretical unity and continuity.

Thus, at least the usage of '*ad hoc*' among mainstream economists accords with the Lakatosian canons. The economic substance of this notion is well-known: a piece of research is said to be *ad hoc* if it is not based on modelling involving the constrained optimization assumption. This may be called *neoclassical ad hocness*. Neoclassical *ad hocness* is a special case of conservative *ad hocness*. On the other hand, neoclassical *non-ad hocness* may be accompanied by criticist *ad hocness*: the continuity of the neoclassical endeavour may involve employing *ad hoc* stratagems to protect a certain version of the rationality principle, for instance.

Now it is obvious that all of the three institutionalist economics approaches (1) to (3) in Gruchy's list above are guilty of neoclassical *ad hocness*. In this regard they are on the same footing with the classical Keynesian assumptions of wage and price rigidities and behavioural propensities, which cannot be derived from the assumption of rational individual optimizing behaviour. On the other hand, much of the new institutionalist economics attempts to avoid neoclassical *ad hocness*; it tries to guarantee a theoretical continuity with standard neoclassical economics by adopting some of its most basic assumptions or their modifications. Similarly, the early expressions of the so-called new Keynesian approach strove for neoclassical *non-ad hocness* in attempting to reduce Keynesian outcomes to neoclassical first principles.

It seems to me that, to some extent at least, the claim of the untheoretical character of the old institutionalist economics is based on the identification of 'having a theoretical character' with 'being neo-classically *non-ad hoc*'. According to this idea, any piece of research which does not conform to some of the fundamental assumptions of neo-classical economics, or their modifications is, by definition, untheoretical. On the other hand, since many versions of the new institutionalist economics comply with them, they are said to be theoretical in character. Furthermore, it follows that if one pursues a replacement of the theoretical foundations of neoclassical economics by a different set of theoretical foundations, the endeavour is doomed to untheoreticity in the sense of neoclassical *ad hocness*. For such reasons it should be clear that the notion of neoclassical *ad hocness is* too restrictive to provide us with an adequate notion of theoreticity.

A tempting option is the loosening of the strict neoclassical restrictions on the substance of the candidates for theoretical status. This seems to be what Langlois and Csontos suggest in passing in Chapter 5. They say that the introduction of an institutional background (rules, habits, customs) against which individual choices are made is perhaps *ad hoc* from the point of view of standard neoclassical theory, but not from that of situational analysis. Here, too, *ad hocness* is not theoretically neutral, since it is characterized in terms of specific restrictions on theoretical substance.

A general and substantively neutral notion of *ad hocness*, having close affinities with Lakatos's more specific concept, might still be useful for a characterization of the idea of theoreticity. Lack of logical and conceptual unity, integration and coherence provide one legitimate sense of *ad hocness*. This may be called *theoretical ad hocness*. Furthermore, we might say that the more theoretically *ad hoc* an endeavour is, the less it has a theoretical character. It seems obvious that the old institutionalist economics approaches (1) to (3) are more or less theoretically *ad hoc* and thus non-theoretical. However, they are not equally so, but in descending extent: while (1) is entirely theoretically *ad hoc*, (3) is close to being theoretically *non-ad hoc*.

The pejorative use of the expression '*ad hoc*' has many edges, as witnessed by Herbert Simon's recent assessment of the new institutionalist economics. He first remarks that 'the new institutional economics is wholly compatible with and conservative of neoclassical theory' (Simon 1991: 27). This is to say that the new institutionalist economics is neoclassically *non-ad hoc*. Simon then says that the new institutionalist economics has incorporated a number of auxiliary exogenous assumptions to the neoclassical corpus, such as those concerning moral hazard and the incompleteness and asymmetric distribution of information. He concludes with the following statement: 'Since such constructs are typically introduced into the analysis in a casual way, with no empirical support except an appeal to introspection and common sense, mechanisms of these sorts have proliferated in the literature, giving it a very *ad hoc* flavor' (ibid.). It is not completely clear which of the two senses of *ad hocness* Simon has in mind: he may think that *ad hocness* is a matter of missing empirical support or else that it is a matter of violating something like a principle of parsimony or theoretical unity. In the latter case, he would appear to imply that the new institutionalist economics, too, has the 'flavour' of being theoretically *ad hoc*.

The lesson of all this is that there is a need for clarity in the use of the concepts of *ad hocness* and theoreticity. The methodologists of economics would do a useful favour to their fellow economists and to themselves by analysing these notions with care.

STORYTELLING

Institutionalist economists, though far from uniform on this question, have traditionally rejected the idea of theory as a formalized and axiomatized system of propositions. Economists are rather understood as 'storytellers'. 'Storytelling is an attempt to give an account of an

23

interrelated set of phenomena in which fact, theory, and values are all mixed together in the telling' (Ward 1972: 180). It is the coherence of the story, the way its parts fit together, that increases its persuasiveness. Ward's characterization of economics is not restricted to institutionalism: this is how economists of all persuasions 'do in fact behave; this is, roughly speaking, the methodology that we actually use in establishing our professional beliefs' (ibid., p. 190). A more recent statement estimates that '90 per cent of what economists do is such storytelling [telling the story of the Federal Reserve Board or of the industrial revolution]. Yet even in the other 10 per cent, in the part more obviously dominated by models and metaphors, the economist tells stories' (McCloskey 1991: 64).[16] Oliver Williamson, too, writes that his variety of institutionalism purports 'to tell plausible causal stories' in order to answer the question, 'What's going on here?' (Williamson 1990a: 65).[17]

In a much cited but somewhat obscure article, Wilber and Harrison argue that 'institutionalists have engaged in a systematic form of storytelling' called 'pattern modelling' (Wilber and Harrison 1978: 71).[18] In their understanding of pattern models they follow the lead of Kaplan (1964) and Diesing (1972). Pattern models are comprehensive or 'holistic' representations of complex networks of phenomena in which the wholeness, uniqueness and evolutionary character of the object is emphasized. The structure of such models is 'concatenated' rather than 'hierarchical' (Kaplan 1964: 298). This means that pattern models 'are composed of several relatively independent, loosely linked parts, rather than of deductions from a few basic postulates' (Diesing 1972: 222).

There are several features of storytelling by means of pattern models that make them unamenable to falsificationist testing. First, from a pattern model 'one cannot deduce specific predictions of future behavior in novel circumstances' (Diesing 1972: 164). Second, a pattern model 'is rarely if ever finished completely. The model builder always has loose ends to work on, points that do not fit in, connections that are puzzling' (ibid.). No wonder then that Mark Blaug complains that 'because storytelling lacks rigor, lacks a definite logical structure, it is all too easy to verify and virtually impossible to falsify. It is or can be persuasive precisely because it never runs the risk of being wrong' (Blaug 1980: 127). Yet, as was pointed out, storytelling is an indispensable part of all of economics and is not restricted to institutionalism. Again, it follows that falsificationism does not help us understand what goes on in economics.

The blame is not only on the Popperian dominance. Given the distinction between 'formal theory' and 'appreciative theory' as introduced by Nelson and Winter (1982), we may say that the methodologists of economics have typically examined economic theory in its 'formal' variety, theory with a well-defined deductive structure connecting 'assumptions' and 'implications' (e.g. Boland 1989) or as a set of definitions or a set-theoretic structure with separate application statements (e.g. Hausman 1992; Hands 1985b). However, much of economic theorizing has not yet reached, will not reach, or does not aim at reaching such a theory – and even if it has reached it, is not reduced to it. Methodologists would do well to start studying 'non-formal' forms of economic theorizing.

INDIVIDUALISM AND HOLISM

It has been suggested by many commentators that the representatives of the new institutionalist economics are committed methodological individualists, while the members of the old institutionalist economics category subscribe to holism of one variety or another, often of a functionalist kind (e.g. Langlois 1989; Rutherford 1989; Hodgson 1989; Hejdra *et al.* 1988). This suggests another distinction, that between *individualist institutionalism* and *holist institutionalism*, and the claim is that it is coextensive with that between the new institutionalist economics and the old institutionalist economics.

Methodological individualism in the context of economics is thought to be the thesis that the explanations of economic phenomena and institutions should be formulated in terms of the properties of individuals. Methodological holism not only denies this but also prescribes that such explanations be phrased in terms of collective entities. Functionalism is often mentioned as a prime example of holism. Before proceeding further, I would like to claim that this issue is one of the least understood in the methodology of economics. Both 'individualism' and 'holism' appear in the literature in a number of unanalysed meanings, and sophisticated case studies are not available.[19] No good analyses exist, but none will be attempted here. A few remarks may suffice to indicate that some caution is needed when attributing individualism and holism to the two aggregated institutionalisms.

The thesis of the coextensionality of the two distinctions – between the new institutionalist economics and the old institutionalist economics on the one hand and individualist institutionalism and holist institutionalism on the other – can be questioned simply by pointing out that there are unquestioned members of the new institutionalist economics category who are not consistent methodological individualists. For instance, it has been pointed out by Viktor Vanberg and others that in invoking group selection mechanisms in his theory of cultural evolution, Hayek has failed to live up to his stated individualist methodology (Vanberg 1986). Also, if it is the case that Williamson's theory is functionalist in that it explains characteristics of governance structures by their functional effects, not by any detailed mechanism of individual action and interaction, and given that functionalism of this sort is not compatible with methodological individualism, then another major representative of the new institutionalist economics would appear as a methodological non-individualist.

In passing, let us point out a link of the present issue to that of Popperian falsifiability. In their defence of the alleged individualism of the new institutionalist economics against the alleged functionalism of Marxist theory, Hejdra et al. (1988: 309) argue that functionalist explanations suffer from 'inherent untestability'. This, they seem to think, is a fatal defect, since 'most economists have, after all, come to adopt some variant of the Popperian "demarcation principle", whereby only those theories that are able to yield refutable propositions are regarded as "scientific"'.[20] The problems of falsificationism are also problems of this judgement. To begin, it is not at all evident that methodological individualism is any better in providing unproblematically refutable implications. Furthermore, the point by Hejdra et al. also raises questions of the character of Williamson's appeal to the notion of refutable implications, mentioned above. If Williamson is a functionalist and if Hejdra and his co-authors (and Jon Elster whom they cite) are correct about the incapacity of functionalism to yield refutable implications, then Williamson would have run into contradictions. Evidently this issue calls for greater clarity on a number of methodological fronts.

As suggested above, among the key notions in need of clarification are those of individualism and holism themselves and the underlying issue dividing them. The issue is sometimes formulated as that of the proper relation between 'wholes' and 'parts', sometimes between the 'micro' and the 'macro', some other times between 'agency' and 'structure'. Sometimes the issue is construed as that of the ontological status of social things (such as corporations, central banks, markets, nation-states) or social properties (such as being a business manager, having a property right, having purchasing power) or what Durkheim called social facts (e.g. the fact that OPEC raised the price of oil in 1973). Sometimes it is understood as a semantic issue concerning the linguistic reducibility or translatability of expressions of such social items into expressions of human individuals. Sometimes it is taken to be a clash between two notions of explanatory priority.

No wonder then that the very terms 'individualism' and 'holism' are desperately ambiguous. For example, some usages of 'individualism' appear to imply what is often called 'atomism' or the idea of individuals devoid of social attributes, or the idea that individuals' properties are uninfluenced by their social surroundings. This and other such narrow usages should not blur the fact that there are many other, also non-atomistic, forms of individualism. To add to the conundrum, some of these forms are forms of holism on some other dimensions. For instance, a new institutionalist economist, even though identifying him or herself as an individualist, is often a holist about social properties. Furthermore, ontological and methodological commitments do not always go together. For example, a methodological individualist of some sort may be an ontological holist of some sort without contradicting him or herself.

For further illustration, consider the following usages of the term 'holism', also found within the institutionalist discourse. First, 'holism' is being used as a name for the view that social entities (such as groups, organizations and institutions) or social properties (those involving social relations) have an independent existence (ontological holism) and/or should be referred to as the fundamental *explanantia* in social scientific explanations (methodological holism). Second, the term is used to refer to an approach which is directed to large 'wholes' so that it is comprehensive or encompassing. Such an approach avoids focusing on narrow fragments of economic reality separate from wider social structures and processes or from the whole of surrounding culture. Hence the insistence on studying the economy in intimate relation to political, social cultural, and moral aspects of society in the sense that statements concerning these latter aspects may be and often have to be used as *explanantia* when explaining economic phenomena. To create a terminological contrast to the first usage of 'holism', this view might also be called 'comprehensivism' or an 'overall viewpoint' or the like. Third, according to yet another meaning of 'holism' the world is composed of integrated wholes or organic unities akin to living organisms. It is the task of enquiry not to separate the elements of such organisms from one another but rather to study them as essentially interlinked. The elements of such organic wholes are tied together by internal relations between them: the essential properties of the elements are dependent on such interrelations. This third usage of 'holism' often goes together with one or both of the other two usages, but is conceptually distinct from them. It is sometimes called 'organicism'.

Given such a plurality of meanings of the term, the precise variety of the alleged or self-proclaimed 'holism' of the old institutionalist economics appears unclear. It seems that all three notions of holism (and more, due to their internal variation) have been advocated by these institutionalists. Their 'holism' sometimes appears as nothing more than comprehensivism, a call for breadth or an overall approach in selecting one's explanatory factors. Sometimes the thesis is stronger, that of their obtaining collective entities or organic unities as the objects of study. The advocacy of pattern modelling is a case in point. These remarks bring us to the idea of isolation in economics.

ISSUES OF ISOLATION

Any theory involves an *isolation* of a limited set of entities from all other ingredients in a total situation. Some theories are more isolative than others. Both the Walrasian overall approach and the Marshallian partial approach involve isolations of various sorts, but the former is less isolative (and more 'wholist') than the latter in that it encompasses all markets of the economy. Isolations are often accomplished by using *idealizing* assumptions such as 'information is perfect' or 'there are no transaction costs' or 'tastes are fixed' or '*ceteris paribus*'. In such assumptions a factor is mentioned but it is assumed that it or a related feature has zero impact on the object under study. On the other hand, in *omitting* a factor one simply refrains from mentioning it. Omissions are ubiquitous means of effecting isolations. Examples of omission in standard economic theories range from the omission of the role of gender and corporate culture to the omission of the age and size of the universe. The method of isolation is a poorly understood but crucial aspect of economic theorizing and controversy. The analysis of this method and its applications gives us an access to some of the roots of the theoretical endeavour of economics, something that is closed to the Popperian framework focusing on the deductive implications of theories. This is also directly linked to the issue of realisticness in economics: in an important sense, the more isolative a representation is, the more unrealistic it is, and vice versa. (For a framework for analysing various aspects of the method of isolation in economics, see Mäki 1992a).

We have already cited Williamson's (1975: 1) statement that 'received microtheory . . . operates at too high a level of abstraction'. We may now ask what this statement means. It seems that one obvious idea delivered here is that standard neoclassical theory is too isolative in that it does not encompass the reality and efficacy of transaction costs. Williamson says that the standard theory is similar to physics which studies friction-less planes, friction being the analogue of transaction costs (Williamson 1985: 19). Both poles of this analogy employ an idealizing assumption of the form, $p(x) = 0$, which serves to exclude the impact of friction and transaction costs, respectively, from consideration. By excluding trans-action costs standard theory also excludes institutions from considera-tion. On the other hand, the inclusion of transaction costs in the theory makes it capable of dealing with institutions and decreases its level of 'abstraction'. The issue between Williamson and standard neoclassicism is that of isolation.

A major issue between Williamson and much of the older branch of institutionalism is that of isolation as well. Among other things, this has to do with how economic agents are depicted. Williamson admits that, compared to orthodoxy, even though the agents of transaction cost economics 'correspond more closely with human nature as we know it', the theory 'is plainly a narrow prescription. It makes little provision for attributes such as kindness, sympathy, solidarity, and the like' (Williamson 1985: 391). Some such excluded attributes are included in some of the more traditional institutionalist analyses. Perhaps even more relevantly, Williamson's theory excludes the influence of factors such as technology and power. Again, in some other institutionalist approaches, these are supposed to have a major impact on institutional structure and economic performance. Hence the suggestion that here, too, the issue is that of isolation. (For a more detailed account, see Mäki 1992c.)

Put in terms of the idea of storytelling, it may be revealing to hear Williamson say that the research objective of transaction cost economics is 'to tell plausible causal stories with the help of a few central principles' (Williamson 1990a: 65). The result of such an approach is supposedly more isolative than pattern modelling, to which some of the advocates of the old institutionalism subscribe. As characterized above, pattern models are not derivations from a few basic principles, but instead are composed of a large number of loosely connected, more or less equal parts. Such comprehensive representations are less isolative than representations based on a few key principles.

To give an interpretation of the discussion by Langlois and Csontos in Chapter 5: they connect the issues of rationality and institution directly to the issue of realisticness and isolation. This connection is mediated by the notion of explanation. Simply put, the idea is that the more the explanatory burden is put on the situational constraints, the less the picture of individual agents has to be 'realistic': the situational logic accounts for what takes place in the economy, provided that agents act rationally. This Machlupian idea is, no doubt, an important insight. In future work, it should be developed by carefully analysing the kinds of and detailed grounds for unrealisticness defended on these lines. At this stage it is easy to see that what is at stake is one variety of isolation: the internal organization of actors, the mechanisms of gathering and processing information and the like are excluded from consideration. The theory isolates the capacity of actors to react 'rationally' to changes in circumstances from their other properties.

The notion of isolation can also be used to suggest a general idea of what makes a piece of tradition of research theoretical. We might say that an endeavour is theoretical if it involves a systematic use of the method of isolation. Of course, the consequences of this suggestion depend on the precise specification of the attribute 'systematic'. One such specification would give us the definition of theoreticity in terms of neoclassical *ad hocness*. But there are a number of others which would give us more liberal notions of theoreticity that would apply to many instances of the old institutionalist economics, for example.

In general terms, the main issue is the precise location of the boundary line between the included and excluded factors drawn by an isolative theory. I mention the final but very important problem related to the method of isolation, namely that of dealing with states and processes. On what conditions is it permissible to isolate states of the economy from the processes that produce, reproduce and undermine them? What should we think of a theory based on such an isolation? Is it an attempted description of something real, or is it just an exercise in logic? Many institutionalists are inclined to think that it is the main task of economics to theorize about processes and that the standard neo-classical preoccupation with equilibrium states does not advance our understanding of the causal mechanisms of the economy. It can be argued that this is a key issue regarding the prospects of realism in economics: it is theories of process that deserve to be treated as hypothetical, potentially true or close-to-the-truth representations of the economy. They, too, are isolative in many ways, but they at least try to avoid excluding what are conceived of as the key elements that keep the world going. (For a detailed argument of this kind, see Mäki 1992b. In Chapter 11 of this volume, Christian Knudsen makes briefly a similar suggestion, but leaves it unargued.)

THE CONTRIBUTIONS

In addition to the opening and concluding chapters by two of the editors, the contributions to the book are divided into three parts. The first part, 'Approaches to economic methodology', contains three chapters focusing on alternative methodological images of economics in general. The second part, entitled 'Broadening the notion of rationality', provides three perspectives on the conceptualization and explanatory role of the very idea of rationality from an institutionalist perspective. The third part on 'Institutions and their evolution' contains three chapters dealing with different ways of theorizing the role that institutions play in the economy and the mechanisms which generate institutions and their change.

Part II provides general perspectives on economic methodology. In Chapter 2, Bruce Caldwell accomplishes three things. First, he provides responses to some of the ordinary criticisms or suspicions that economists have against methodology as a specialized field of enquiry. He corrects some mistakes by showing that, for example, methodologists today do not pretentiously and arrogantly tell economists how to do economics; that methodology is not the province of heterodox groups, since every economist is bound to make methodological decisions; and that practising economists are not able to tell good economics from bad on good grounds. Second, Caldwell discusses some recent contributions to the study of economics and their relation to philosophy. These are the philosophy of realism, the study of the rhetoric and sociology of economics, understood moderately as complementing rather than substituting philosophical perspectives, and an anti-philosophical scepticism. Of these, the sociological approach is represented in Chapter 4 of the present volume. Third, he records three topics that deserve further study in economic methodology. They are the rationality assumption, the idea of prediction, and the role of ethics in the economy and in economic reasoning – all of them highly relevant to the institutionalist agenda. The notion of rationality is the subject of several contributions to this book.

Chapter 3 by Wade Hands gives a concise assessment of the Popperian tradition in economic methodology. He summarizes Popper's falsificationist methodology of bold conjecture and severe testing and lists some of the major problems in falsificationism, such as the Duhemian problem of the involvement in testing of a great number of uncontrolled auxiliary assumptions; the impossibility of testing severely the qualitative predictions prevalent in comparative statics; Popper's failure to develop a theory of truthlikeness to ground his falsificationist rules; and the inappropriateness in economics of Popper's idea of scientific progress, defined in terms of the notion of novel facts. Hands concludes that 'strict adherence to falsificationist norms would virtually *destroy all existing economic theory* and leave economists with a rule book for a game unlike anything the profession has played in the past'. No wonder then that falsificationism has not been practised in economics. Hands then explains why Lakatos's methodology of scientific research programmes has been more popular among economists: it allows for conservatism about a set of key presuppositions without giving up the notion that empirical evidence matters for the development of theory formation. However, Lakatos shares much of Popper's inadequate idea of scientific progress and is therefore as incapable of providing much guidance to economists in their search for progressive theory choices. Hands concludes that the Popperian tradition is not of much help to economists in the endeavour to make rational decisions about the fate of alternative theories – for instance, about the relative merits of various institutionalist theories.

Chapter 4 tries to give an impression of an entirely different perspective on studying science. Science is depicted as a social institution, as having an irreducibly social character. An analysis of recent social studies of science suggests three ways in which 'science is socially conditioned'. First, scientists may be understood as maximizers who pursue social goals such as academic credibility. Second, the justification of knowledge-claims and competence-claims may be viewed as a social process of rhetorical persuasion and negotiation. Third, some have suggested that the contents of knowledge-claims are causally produced by social interests and structures. These three approaches are then used for generating speculative explanations for the presumed fact about economics that a ranking order obtains in which standard neoclassicism ranks highest, the new institutionalist economics ranks next, while the old institutionalism ranks lowest. Without a commitment to the particular contents of these speculations, they are offered as reminders that there is more to scientific rationality than traditional simplistic methodologies, Popperian or otherwise, suggest. The moral is that whatever rationality (and non-rationality) remains in science, it should be analysed at least partly in institutional terms. The notion of scientific rationality – not only that of economic rationality – needs to be broadened.

Part III is devoted to the concept of economic rationality and to efforts to broaden the standard notion. Each of the three chapters in this part provides a perspective on standard neoclassical rationality and its 'institutionalist' rivals. In Chapter 5, Richard Langlois and László Csontos offer a reconciliatory point of view on two lines within the new institutionalist economics, namely those of neoclassical optimizing and behavioural satisficing or rule-following. For this purpose they use the idea of situational analysis, arguing that both the optimizing neoclassicals and the satisficing Simonians may subscribe to it as a mode of explanation. They argue that situational analysis should not be equated with constrained optimization involving the standard neoclassical notion of rationality. They suggest that this combination gives only one possible version of situational explanation and that rule-following, with suitable interpretation, can also be accommodated by situational analysis. Langlois and Csontos suggest that these apparently rival conceptions of economic rationality in fact exemplify the same ideal type at two different levels of generality and realisticness. They follow Fritz Machlup in arguing that there is a trade-off between generality and realisticness in assumptions. An assumption with wide applicability is in some sense typically more unrealistic than an assumption which applies to one case or few cases only. The former depicts an 'anonymous ideal type'. The use of such simplified assumptions presupposes that most of the explanatory burden is carried by what Langlois and Csontos call a 'system constraint'. More realistic ideal types are needed when a relatively larger portion of the explanatory work is accomplished by recourse to the details of agents' behaviour. Langlois and Csontos conclude by formulating arguments for situational analysis and against its behaviouralist rival understood as the assumption of pre-programmed behaviour. They argue that situational analysis is less *ad hoc* and has more explanatory power than behaviouralism.

Chapter 6 by Christian Knudsen presents an argument to the effect that it is impossible to formulate a coherent and *non-ad hoc* process story of how equilibrium states emerge as results of substantively rational activities of economic agents (that is, activities characterized by what was above called outcomes rationality) and that therefore the adoption of the notion of procedural rationality is ultimately unavoidable in economics. He provides two characterizations of this impossibility, one methodological, the other substantive. The methodological characterization amounts to recognizing the alleged failure of the notion of substantive or outcomes rationality as an internal conceptual problem within standard neoclassical economics. Knudsen rightly points out the inability of Popperian and Lakatosian methodologies to incorporate the decisive role of conceptual problems in theory development. The substantive characterization of this failure amounts to regarding it as an example of the general problem of self-reference, briefly discussed by Langlois and Csontos also. This problem is often generated by attempts to introduce optimization costs to the optimization calculus based on the notion of substantive rationality. Once we try to incorporate the idea of optimizing on the costs of optimization, we are led to an infinite regress: to make decision A is costly, therefore decision B has to be made whether decision A is worth making, but since B is costly too, decision C has to be made as to whether B is beneficial, and so on and so forth. This regress can be stopped only by dogmatic interruption or by a vicious circle. An optimal, substantively rational, solution to the decision problem is impossible. This observation on the level of the individual decision maker can be used as an argument for adopting the notion of procedural rationality. Knudsen then argues that the self-reference problem provides an even stronger argument on the level of systems of interdependent decision makers. He points out the manifestations of the problem in the cases of the theories of perfect competition, oligopoly, rational expectations, and non-cooperative games. In each case, the respective theory is unable to show how equilibria emerge out of substantively rational actions by individual agents.

In Chapter 7, Viktor Vanberg presents a lucid discussion of the relationship between two conceptions of the rationality of individual behaviour, namely the standard rational maximization approach and the rule-following approach. While the former is based on the idea of case-by-case maximization, the latter invokes routines and habits. Vanberg argues that the latter provides a notion of rational choice which retains both the methodological individualism and the self-interest assumption of the former. These two models provide different accounts of regularities in individual behaviour. The case-by-case maximization model depicts each choice as a deliberately maximizing response to unique situations where the chooser's past experience has no effect on present behaviour. A behavioural regularity consists in the person making the same maximizing choice in each of a set of recurring situations after having assessed each single situation separately. The rule-following approach pictures individual choices as responses to situations perceived not as unique but as exemplifying a more general type of situation, as similar in some respects to other situations in a larger class. A behavioural regularity is generated on the basis of the chooser's past experience of following one and the same course of action in recurring and relevantly similar situations. As different exemplifications of the rule-following approach Vanberg reviews Heiner's theory of imperfect choice, Simon's notion of bounded or adaptive rationality and Hayek's argument from the limits of reason. Vanberg then suggests that in order for the rule-following approach to gain more adherence, it has to provide a unified theory of human behaviour which conforms to our common experience of its functionality and adaptiveness. He next outlines a generalized model of evolutionary learning which might satisfy these requirements. This model provides a framework for studying the processes of generation and selection of rules in a variety of contexts and levels, including biological evolution, individual learning, and cultural evolution. Evolutionary learning or adaptive rationality is backward-looking, based on past failures and successes, whereas case-by-case maximization is forward-looking, based on purposeful calculation and design.

Part IV provides three different perspectives on institutions and their evolution. Chapter 8 by Brian Loasby covers a variety of relevant topics from several perspectives. He experiments with and develops Kelly's idea of treating people as scientists engaged in a pursuit of epistemic and practical goals as a socially coordinated activity. From the point of view of this analogy, Loasby discusses the institutions of science and the institutions of the economy, and the twin role of institutions and their evolution as both causes and effects of individual human behaviour. He suggests that both scientists and economic agents conjecture, use, test, revise and replace hypotheses, and that this process is guided by institutional frameworks which consist of rules or conventions. They are akin to Kuhnian paradigms or Lakatosian research programmes, institutionally conceived. These frameworks constrain and coordinate the formation of hypotheses and the interpretation of evidence within the relevant communities. This amounts to recognizing the socially or institutionally conditioned character of action, both within and outside science. Loasby also points out that the emergence and evolution of these institutional frameworks themselves are the unintended or at most partly intended consequences of boundedly rational actions by agents. He discusses the business organization as a cluster of routines or research programmes, analogous to a 'visible college', and the market network as constituting an interactive system or research programme which functions as a means of organizing the search for knowledge, analogous to the 'invisible college' of academic science. Since the research programmes of science, business organizations and the market are imperfectly specified, they function so as to combine coordination and flexibility, continuity and creativity, in varying combinations.

The evolutionary perspective on institutions, discussed already by Vanberg, is discussed more thoroughly in Chapter 9 by Geoffrey Hodgson. He examines critically the nature and implications of the evolutionary analogy as used in economics. His first major suggestion is concerned with the character of the outcomes of evolutionary processes. He argues that recent work in evolutionary biology shows that evolution is not identical with progress to higher forms of organization, that it does not represent some kind of optimizing procedure: natural selection does not necessarily lead to survival, and survival is not necessarily an indication of efficiency. Therefore, as against Oliver Williamson, Milton Friedman, and others, Hodgson suggests that the evolutionary analogy does not unambiguously serve as an argument for the notion that competition leads to efficient forms of organization. He concludes that sometimes there may be room for 'the judicious intervention of the invisible hand'. Hodgson's second major suggestion is about the appropriate unit of selection and the nature of the evolutionary process. Appealing to recent work in biology again, he argues against explanatory individualistic reductionism that treats the individual gene as the basic unit; instead, he maintains, selection may be considered to operate on various kinds of unit at different hierarchical levels (gene, organism, species), depending on the time scale and the kind of selection process. In economics, the relevant units comprise individuals, habits, groups, institutions, routines, and whole socio-economic systems. The selection process is multi-layered and comprises learning and imitation; hence, it has a Lamarckian character. Such multiplicity, Hodgson suggests, can be used as an argument against methodological individualism and for the viability of a mixed economy. Many of Hodgson's suggestions are in a sense compromises between some aspects of the 'old' and the 'new' lines of institutionalism, but they also indicate how easily these labels can be rendered more or less irrelevant.

In Chapter 10 Douglass North provides a concise account of his approach to the study of institutions. His focus is on how institutions affect the performance of economies. He outlines a framework for articulating the idea that institutions serve to structure the incentives of economic and political agents and that these incentives shape the evolution of economies. Institutions comprise formal rules, informal constraints and their enforcement properties. Together with the traditional constraints of standard theory, they define the opportunity set. They all affect the costs of transacting and have to be taken into account in the analysis (in contrast to the property rights approach which deals only with formal rules). Furthermore, North argues that the effectiveness of the enforcement of contracts is the most important determinant of economic performance. Also, unlike many other recent writers on transaction cost economics, he points out that not only do institutions affect transaction costs, they also affect production costs. In North's model the agents respond to the existing institutionally shaped incentive structure, and if this institutional structure is such that it rewards productive activity, the economy grows, but if it rewards redistributive and rent-seeking activities, the economy does not grow. North also outlines a model of institutional change in which the entrepreneurial agents of organizations, by pursuing profitable opportunities shaped by existing institutions, gradually alter the institutional constraints of their action. North emphasizes that inefficient economic institutions are the rule, not the exception, and that there is no process of evolutionary selection that would result in efficient institutions and weed out the inefficient ones. Here he agrees on one of Hodgson's claims. North's chapter is concluded by a brief, lucid account of the intellectual benefits of institutional analysis.

The contributions to this book and to the economics of institutions in general exemplify a number of at least partly rival or complementary approaches, which is why the reader may find it difficult to find his or her way through the intellectual landscape. The book is concluded by a chapter which should bring some help to the situation. Chapter 11 by Christian Knudsen classifies and discusses some of the alternative explanatory modes within the economic study of institutions.

NOTES

1 I wish to thank Christian Knudsen and Markku Ollikainen for comments on an earlier draft of this chapter.
2 There now exist fairly good general overviews of the recent developments in the economics of institutions, including methodological discussions. See, for example, Langlois 1986a, Hodgson 1988, Eggertson 1991, and the final chapter (Chapter 11) of this volume by Christian Knudsen.
3 One can also argue in more general terms that methodological research should enjoy a legitimate position in economics. This is what Bruce Caldwell does in Chapter 2 of this book.
4 For fresh accounts of the current situation in economic methodology, see Caldwell in the present volume (Chapter 2); Salanti 1989; Hands 1990; Mäki 1990a.
5 For examples of the Popperian dominance, see Latsis 1976a; Blaug 1980; Boland 1982, 1989; Klant 1984; Weintraub 1985; de Marchi 1988; de Marchi and Blaug 1991; for criticisms of Popperian views of science in the context of economics, see Caldwell 1982, 1984, 1991; Hands 1992; Hausman 1985, 1988; for criticisms of the Popperian dominance itself, see Mäki 1990a.
6 Popper, of course, is a realist himself, but his realism seems not sufficiently rich and powerful to be helpful for economic methodologists in detailed studies of the realist option in economics.
7 In Mäki (1989), I coined the term '(un)realisticness' in order to distinguish

it from '(non-)realism' and thereby to suggest a correction of an established but misleading practice among economists of talking about the 'realism' of their theories. While varieties of 'realisticness' and 'unrealisticness' designate attributes of representations such as the 'assumptions' of economic theories, varieties of 'realism' and 'non-realism' designate philosophical theses about the world, language, knowledge, etc.

8 Understandably perhaps, no established and unambiguous terminology for labelling schools or streams of institutionalist thought is available. The distinction between the 'new' and the 'old' strands represents one recent usage. (For a useful source of insights into what is formulated as the confrontation between the 'old' and the 'new' institutionalism, see a special issue of *Review of Political Economy*, November 1989, containing contributions by Geoffrey Hodgson, Richard Langlois, Malcolm Rutherford, Anne Mayhew, Viktor Vanberg, and Charles Leathers.) For another usage, see Eggertsson (1990: 6–9), who suggests the further distinction between what he calls *'neoinstitutionalist'* economics and the *'new institutionalist'* economics; while neoinstitutionalists subscribe to the neoclassical notion of rational optimization (and stable preferences and equilibria), the new institutionalists employ Simon's idea of satisficing or some other non-neoclassical behavioural assumption. One problem with this usage is that some of the present-day 'old' institutionalists also identify themselves as 'neoinstitutionalists' (e.g. Tool 1986). I suggest that what Eggertsson calls 'neoinstitutionalism' should more appropriately be called *neoclassical institutionalism*. In what follows, no emphasis is placed upon the distinction between neoclassical institutionalism and the new institutionalist economics.

9 Comparing the three themes to [MinI], we notice that Langlois's list is richer in that it comprises general statements on the nature of rationality and explanation. This does not yet imply that his list is also more specific; that is, it is possible that themes 1 and 2 are prerequisites for minimal institutionalism. If this were the case, [MinI] would be more parsimonious but contain roughly the same information as Langlois's list of themes. If this were not the case, his list would be more specific and thus more restrictive than [MinI].

10 Langlois rightly has a reservation on that part of Schotter's definition which says that the regularity 'is agreed to by all members of society'. Indeed, such a requirement would lead to an unnecessarily restricted notion of institution.

11 While Langlois's definition of the concept of institution in terms of a simple concept of a rule is very general, Douglass North formulates a definition which is specific and restrictive: 'Institutions are a set of rules, compliance procedures, and moral and ethical behavioral norms designed to constrain the behavior of individuals in the interests of maximizing the wealth or utility of principals' (North 1981: 201–2).

12 Note that if institutions consisted simply of rules of the form 'always react in manner X to event Y', then the standard formulations of Popper's and Lakatos's methodologies would immediately count as institutionalist philosophies of science. Popper is usually thought of as stating rules such as 'always regard the hypothesis under test as falsified if it faces negative evidence'. Lakatos has the notion of heuristics, sets of rules of some sort; negative heuristics, for instance, prescribes 'never reject the hard core statements in the face of negative evidence'. If it is suggested that such rules make up the institutions of science and that this is all there is to the institutional aspect of science, then at least two questions arise. First, the

empirical criticism levelled against the theories of Popper and Lakatos according to which the normative rules they have formulated are not obeyed by actual scientists implies that the Popperian and Lakatosian scientific institutions are fictions of some sort. Second, it may be suggested that there is more to the institutions of science than rules of the Popperian and Lakatosian sort. There are other kinds of powerful rules and there are social organizations. Third, while institutionalist economists are often preoccupied with how institutions emerge and develop, some of the most basic rules of science are fixed in Popper and Lakatos.

13 In note 14 of chapter 5 in the present volume, Langlois and Csontos appear to suggest that Simon's behaviouralist approach is concerned, not with human action, but with behaviour devoid of intentionality. This is inconsistent with Simon's own characterization of bounded rationality but more easily reconcilable with Langlois's and Csontos's special characterization of behaviouralism as an approach which assumes that economic agents are either 'hard-headed rule-followers' or 'preprogrammed satisficers *ab ovo*'.

14 Regarding the *explanandum* of economic explanations, it is interesting to recognize a latent tension in formulations even within the present volume. While Wade Hands (in his note 19) writes that 'according to Popper's situational analysis view of social science, the action of an individual agent is explained', Langlois and Csontos imply a criticism of this idea when they say that economics using situational analysis 'does not seek to explain individual behavior *per se* . . . Rather, economic theory most often *uses* assumptions about individual behavior' (115) in the attempt to explain market phenomena. Note, however, that in [SA] the *explanandum* [SA4] concerns individual behaviour. Indeed, it is evident that [SA] and its variations have to be supplemented by something else to attain invisible-hand explanations of the kind endorsed by some versions of the new institutionalist economics. The discussion of situational analysis by Langlois does not seem to be sufficiently clear about this. For a discussion of a parallel problem, see Mäki 1990c. There I point out that the so-called practical syllogism which comes close to situational analysis is insufficient for explaining both individual entrepreneurial action and its unintended consequences mediated by the invisible hand.

15 It is notable that in their discussion of the neoclassical mode of explanation in Chapter 5, Langlois and Csontos use Popper's term 'situational analysis' and avoid using Latsis's term 'situational determinism'. This may make it easier for them to argue that situational analysis respects the 'free will' of economic agents, whereas Latsis (1976b: 6–7, 16) found it somewhat paradoxical that the general ideology of the free will and a situationally determinist approach to rational action combine in neoclassical economics. To Latsis, neoclassical agents are just puppets which do not act – they merely react.

16 McCloskey continues: 'The applied economist can be viewed as a realistic novelist or a realistic playwright – a Thomas Hardy or a George Bernard Shaw. The theorist, too, may be viewed as a teller of stories, though a non-realist – whose plots and characters have the same relation to truth as those in *Gulliver's Travels* or *A Midsummer Night's Dream*. Most economics is saturated with narration' (McCloskey 1991: 64).

17 It is another question whether Williamson's theoretical work actually lives up to this meta-theoretical statement. This is related to the presumed functionalism of his approach.

18 Mark Blaug has suggested, albeit without documentation, that this characterization may apply, within the old institutionalist camp, to Veblen, Ayres and Myrdal, but not to Commons, Mitchell and Galbraith. He also suggests that 'a much better description of the working methodology of institutionalists is . . . storytelling' (Blaug 1980: 126–7). As we noticed, however, in Wilber and Harrison's characterization pattern modelling is *one variety of* storytelling.
19 Those wishing to take the task on should consult works such as Diesing (1971), Boland (1982, Ch. 2) and Hodgson (1988, Ch. 3) among those few that are available.
20 Note that Hejdra *et al.* here evoke Popper's falsificationism as providing a criterion of demarcation between science and non-science. In Chapter 3, Wade Hands suggests that this has not been the main role of Popper's metatheory in economics – instead, it has usually been used for prescribing canons of theory choice.

REFERENCES

Alchian, A. and Demsetz, H. (1972) 'Production, information costs, and economic organization', *American Economic Review* 62: 777–95.
Aoki, M., Gustafsson B. and Williamson, O.E. (eds) (1990) *The Firm as a Nexus of Treaties*, London: Sage.
Barry, N. (1979) *Hayek's Social and Economic Philosophy*, London: Macmillan.
Blaug, M. (1980) *The Methodology of Economics*, Cambridge: Cambridge University Press.
Boland, L. (1982) *The Foundations of Economic Method*, London: Allen & Unwin.
—— (1989) *The Methodology of Economic Model Building*, London: Routledge.
Brennan, G. and Buchanan, J. (1985) *The Reason of Rules: Constitutional Political Economy*, Cambridge: Cambridge University Press.
Bush, P. (1987) 'The theory of institutional change', *Journal of Economic Issues* 21: 1075–116.
Caldwell, B. (1982) *Beyond Positivism: Economic Methodology in the Twentieth Century*, London: Allen & Unwin.
—— (1984) 'Some problems with falsificationism in economics', *Philosophy of the Social Sciences* 14: 187–94.
—— (1991) 'Clarifying Popper', *Journal of Economic Literature* 29: 1–33.
Coase, R. (1984) 'The new institutional economics', *Journal of Law and Economics* 27: 229–31.
Commons, J. R. (1934) *Institutional Economics*, London: Macmillan.
Davis, L. and North, D. (1971) *Institutional Change and American Economic Growth*, Cambridge: Cambridge University Press.
Diesing, P. (1972) *Patterns of Discovery in the Social Sciences*, London: Routledge & Kegan Paul.
Dow, G. K. (1987) 'The function of authority in transaction cost economics', *Journal of Economic Behavior and Organization* 8: 13–38.
Dugger, W. (1990) 'The new institutionalism: new but not institutionalist', *Journal of Economic Issues* 24: 423–31.
Eggertsson, T. (1990) *Economic Behavior and Institutions*, Cambridge: Cambridge University Press.
Furubotn, E. and Pejovich, S. (eds) (1974) *The Economics of Property Rights*, Cambridge, Mass.: Ballinger.
Gray, J. (1984) *Hayek on Liberty*, Oxford: Blackwell.
Gruchy, A.G. (1972) *Contemporary Economic Thought: The Contribution of Neo-institutional Economics*, New York: Macmillan.

—— (1982) 'The current state of institutional economics', *American Journal of Economics and Sociology* 41: 225–42.

—— (1990) 'Three different approaches to institutional economics: an evaluation', *Journal of Economic Issues* 24: 361–9.

Hands, D. W. (1985a) 'Karl Popper and economic methodology: A new look', *Economics and Philosophy* 1: 83–99.

—— (1985b) 'The structuralist view of economic theories: the case of general equilibrium theory in particular', *Economics and Philosophy* 1: 303–35.

—— (1988) 'Ad hocness in economics and the Popperian tradition', in N. de Marchi (ed.) *The Popperian Legacy in Economics*, Cambridge: Cambridge University Press, pp. 121–37.

—— (1990) 'Thirteen theses on progress in economic methodology', *Finnish Economic Papers* 3: 72–6.

—— (1992) *Testing, Rationality and Progress: Essays on the Popperian Tradition in Economic Methodology*, Latham: Rowman and Littlefield.

Hausman, D.M. (1985) 'Is falsificationism unpractised or unpractisable?' *Philosophy of the Social Sciences* 15: 313–19.

—— (1988) 'An appraisal of Popperian methodology', in N. de Marchi (ed.) *The Popperian Legacy in Economics*, Cambridge: Cambridge University Press, pp. 65–85.

—— (1992) *The Inexact and Separate Science of Economics*, Cambridge: Cambridge University Press.

Hejdra, B.J., Lowenberg, A.D. and Mallick, R.J. (1988) 'Marxism, methodological individualism, and the new institutional economics', *Journal of Institutional and Theoretical Economics* 144: 296–317.

Henderson, W., Dudley-Evans, A. and Backhouse, R., (eds) (1992) *Economics and Language*, London: Routledge.

Hodgson, G. (1988) *Economics and Institutions: A Manifesto for a Modern Institutional Economics*, Cambridge: Polity Press.

—— (1989) 'Institutional economic theory: the old versus the new', *Review of Political Economy* 1: 249–69.

Jensen, M. and Meckling, W. (1976) 'Theory of the firm: managerial behavior, agency costs and ownership structure', *Journal of Financial Economics* 3: 305–60.

Kaplan, A. (1964) *The Conduct of Inquiry*, San Francisco: Chandler.

Klamer, A. (1983) *Conversations with Economists*, Totowa, New Jersey: Rowman & Allanheld.

—— A., McCloskey, D. and Solow, R. (eds) (1988) *The Consequences of Economic Rhetoric*, Cambridge: Cambridge University Press.

Klant, J. (1984) *The Rules of the Game*, Cambridge: Cambridge University Press.

Koertge, N. (1979) 'The methodological status of Popper's rationality principle', *Theory and Decision* 10: 83–95.

Lachmann, L. (1971) *The Legacy of Max Weber*, Berkeley, California: Glendessary Press.

Lakatos, I. (1970) 'Falsification and the methodology of scientific research programmes', in I. Lakatos and A. Musgrave (eds) *Criticism and the Growth of Knowledge*, Cambridge: Cambridge University Press, pp. 91–196.

Langlois, R., (ed.) (1986a) *Economics as a Process, Essays in the New Institutional Economics*, Cambridge: Cambridge University Press.

—— (1986b) 'The new institutional economics: an introductory essay', in R. Langlois, (ed.) *Economics as a Process, Essays in the New Institutional Economics*, Cambridge: Cambridge University Press, pp. 1–25.

—— (1986c) 'Rationality, institutions, and explanation', in R. Langlois (ed.)

Economics as a Process, Essays in the New Institutional Economics, Cambridge: Cambridge University Press, pp. 225–55.

—— (1989) 'What was wrong with the old institutionalism (and what is still wrong with the new)?' *Review of Political Economy* 1: 270–98.

Latsis, S. (1972) 'Situational determinism in economics', *British Journal for the Philosophy of Science* 23: 207–45.

—— (ed.) (1976a) *Method and Appraisal in Economics*, Cambridge: Cambridge University Press.

—— (1976b) 'A research programme in economics', in S. Latsis (ed.), *Method and Appraisal in Economics*, Cambridge: Cambridge University Press, pp. 1–41.

McCloskey, D. (1985) *The Rhetoric of Economics*. Madison, Wisconsin: Wisconsin University Press.

—— (1991) 'Storytelling in economics', in D. Lavoie (ed.) *Economics and Hermeneutics*, London: Routledge, pp. 61–75.

Mäki, U. (1987) Review of R. Langlois (ed.) *Economics as a Process, Economics and Philosophy* 3: 367–73.

—— (1989) 'On the problem of realism in economics', *Ricerche Economiche* 43: 176–98. (Reprinted in B. Caldwell (ed.) *The Philosophy and Methodology of Economics*, Aldershot: Edward Elgar.)

—— (1990a) 'Economic methodology: complaints and guidelines', *Finnish Economic Papers* 3: 77–84.

—— (1990b) 'Scientific realism and Austrian explanation', *Review of Political Economy* 2: 310–44.

—— (1990c) 'Practical syllogism, entrepreneurship, and the invisible hand', in D. Lavoie (ed.) *Economics and Hermeneutics*, London: Routledge, pp. 149–76.

—— (1992a) 'On the method of isolation in economics', *Poznan Studies in the Philosophy of Science and the Humanities* 26: 319–54.

—— (1992b) 'The market as an isolated causal process: A metaphysical ground for realism', in S. Boehm and B. Caldwell (eds) *Austrian Economics: Tensions and New Developments*, Boston: Kluwer Publishers.

—— (1992c) 'Issues of isolation in transaction cost economies', Mimeo.

de Marchi, N. (ed.) (1988) *The Popperian Legacy in Economics*, Cambridge: Cambridge University Press.

—— N. and Blaug, M. (eds) (1991) *Appraising Economic Theories, Studies in the Methodology of Research Programs*, Aldershot: Edward Elgar.

Mayhew, A. (1989) 'Contrasting origins of the two institutionalisms: the social science context', *Review of Political Economy* 1: 319–33.

Mirowski, P. (1987) 'The philosophical bases of institutionalist economics', *Journal of Economic Issues* 21: 1001–38.

Mitchell, W. (1913) *Business Cycles*, Berkeley, California: University of California Press.

Neale, W.C. (1987) 'Institutions', *Journal of Economic Issues* 21: 1177–206.

Nelson, R. and Winter, S. (1982) *An Evolutionary Theory of Economic Change*, Cambridge, Mass.: Harvard University Press.

North, D. (1981) *Structure and Change in Economic History*, New York: Norton.

—— (1990) *Institutions, Institutional Change and Economic Performance*, Cambridge: Cambridge University Press.

—— and Thomas, R.P. (1973) *The Rise of the Western World: A New Economic History*, Cambridge: Cambridge University Press.

Olson, M. (1965) *The Logic of Collective Action*, Cambridge, Mass.: Harvard University Press.

Popper, K. (1959) *The Logic of Scientific Discovery*, London: Hutchinson.

41

—— (1983) 'The rationality principle', in D. Miller (ed.) *A Pocket Popper*, Oxford: Fontana, pp. 357–65. (First published 1967.)

Posner, R. (1973) *Economic Analysis of Law*, Boston: Little, Brown.

Ramstad, Y. (1986) 'A pragmatist's quest for holistic knowledge: the scientific methodology of John R. Commons', *Journal of Economic Issues* 20: 1067–105.

Rowe, N. (1989) *Rules and Institutions*, New York: Philip Allan.

Rutherford, M. (1989) 'What is wrong with the new institutional economics (and what is still wrong with the old)?' *Review of Political Economy* 1: 299–318.

Salanti, A. (1989) 'Recent work in economic methodology: much ado about what?' *Ricerche Economiche* 43: 21–39.

Samuels, W. (ed.) (1990) *Economics as Discourse*, Boston: Kluwer.

Schotter, A. (1981) *The Economic Theory of Social Institutions*, Cambridge: Cambridge University Press.

—— (1986) 'The evolution of rules' in R. Langlois (ed.) *Economics as a Process* Cambridge: Cambridge University Press, pp. 117–33.

Simon, H.A. (1947) *Administrative Behavior*, New York: Macmillan.

—— (1976) 'From substantive to procedural rationality', in S. Latsis (ed.) *Method and Appraisal in Economics*, Cambridge: Cambridge University Press, pp. 129–48.

—— (1991) 'Organizations and markets', *Journal of Economic Perspectives* 5: 25–44.

Sugden, R. (1986) *The Economics of Rights, Co-operation and Welfare*, Oxford: Blackwell.

Tool, M. (1979) *The Discretionary Economy*, Santa Monica, California: Goodyear.

—— (1986) *Essays in Social Value Theory, A Neoinstitutionalist Contribution*, Armonk, California: M.E. Sharpe.

Vanberg, V. (1986) 'Spontaneous market order and social rules: a critical examination of F.A. Hayek's theory of cultural evolution', *Economics and Philosophy* 2: 75–100.

—— (1989) 'Carl Menger's evolutionary and John R. Commons' collective action approach to institutions: a comparison', *Review of Political Economy* 1: 334–60.

Veblen, T. (1924) *Absentee Ownership and Business Enterprise in Recent Times: The Case of America*, London: Allen & Unwin.

Ward, B. (1972) *What's Wrong with Economics?* New York: Basic Books.

Weintraub, R.E. (1985) *General Equilibrium Analysis: Studies in Appraisal*, Cambridge: Cambridge University Press.

Wilber, C.K. and Harrison, R.S. (1978) 'The methodological basis of institutional economics: pattern model, storytelling, and holism', *Journal of Economic Issues* 12: 61–89.

Williamson, O.E. (1975) *Markets and Hierarchies: Analysis and Antitrust Implications*, New York: Free Press.

—— (1985) *The Economic Institutions of Capitalism: Firms, Markets, Relational Contracting*, New York: Free Press.

—— (1986) 'The economics of governance: framework and implications', in R. Langlois (ed.) *Economics as a Process, Essays in the New Institutionalist Economics*, Cambridge: Cambridge University Press, pp. 171–202.

—— (1990a) 'A comparison of alternative approaches to economic organization', *Journal of Institutional and Theoretical Economics* 147: 61–71.

—— (1990b) 'The firm as a nexus of treaties: an introduction', in M. Aoki, B. Gustafsson and O.E. Williamson, (eds) *The Firm as a Nexus of Treaties*, London: Sage, pp. 1–25.

Part II

APPROACHES TO ECONOMIC METHODOLOGY

2

ECONOMIC METHODOLOGY
Rationale, Foundations, Prospects[1]
Bruce J. Caldwell

ABSTRACT

The chapter introduces the general reader to some important issues in the field of economic methodology. In the first section, methodological work is defended against some common criticisms. The relationship between methodology and such disciplines as philosophy, sociology of science, and rhetoric is explored in the second section. Three areas worthy of further study are highlighted in the third section.

DOES METHODOLOGY MATTER?

At the History of Economics Society meetings in Spring 1989 there was a session entitled, 'Should methodology matter to the economist or to the historian of economics?' Some of the participants answered in the negative. As an observer I was disappointed in the session, not because the study of methodology was attacked, but because the attack was such an anaemic one. The major worry seemed to be that many economists think that methodological study is a waste of time. One panelist even suggested that it would be acceptable to continue to pursue methodological investigations, but that we should call them by another name so as not to offend our fellow economists.

Lest there be any doubt, it should be stated at the outset that, at least in the US, many economists are indifferent towards methodology, and most of the rest are openly hostile to it. Indeed, *explaining* these attitudes is a topic worthy of further study. But their existence, at least for now, should be taken as a given.

In this first section I will survey some of the more common objections raised by economists against the study of methodology, then try to answer them. My goal is to show the fair-minded economist that methodological study need not necessarily be a misallocation of scarce intellectual resources.

Though others exist, five of the most commonly encountered objections to methodology are:

A. One does not learn how to 'do' economics by studying methodology, one learns it by doing economics

A knowledge of methodology is neither a necessary nor a sufficient condition for becoming a good economist. Given that time is a scarce resource, students would better spend theirs mastering economic theory, econometrics, and the sundry applied fields rather than confusing themselves debating the imponderable questions of methodology.

B. Methodologists pretentiously and arrogantly try to tell economists how to do economics

Most methodological prescriptions are based on philosophical notions about how best to do science. But what do philosophers know about economics? The models philosophers develop are not formulated with economics in mind and, indeed, often have little contact with the issues which most concern economists.

Sometimes this argument reduces to a simple questioning of the relevance of studying philosophy. But it can also be encountered in a more sophisticated form, in which the arguments of various philosophers and historians of science (e.g. Thomas Kuhn, P.K. Feyerabend, Richard Rorty) are used against 'positivism' or Popperian thought or the very idea of methodology itself.

C. Methodological debates between opposing research traditions in economics are sterile: they never reach any conclusive results

This argument is the obverse of the one above. Methodology is now found deficient because it *fails* to provide grounds for deciding among competing claims. This position was probably first articulated by Schumpeter in reference to the *Methodenstreit*.

D. Only 'fringe' groups in the profession are interested in methodology

Mainstream economists busy themselves with the practice of economics. The only ones who care about methodology are critics of the mainstream, be they Marxists or Austrians or Institutionalists or Post-Keynesians or what have you. Such groups care about methodology because they have an axe to grind. Real economists actually do economics while the malcontents mostly talk about how to do it.

E. I know what economics is, so methodology is superfluous

This argument is doubtless the most fundamental one. If one thinks that it is not difficult to know 'good economics' when one sees it, then the study of methodology must seem like an enormous waste of time.

The arguments above are presented in an exaggerated form, but they are not extreme caricatures. Each contains an element of truth, though each can also be answered.

A' – Rebutting the first objection

It is true that one does not learn how to do economics by studying methodology. If anything, the situation is the reverse: one must know economics thoroughly before one can hope to make a contribution to the methodological literature. If we grant the obvious point that the best way to learn how to do economics is by studying economics, there are still two problems with this argument against methodology.

Problem 1

For the argument to have much force, economics should be a monolithic, homogeneous discipline. If there is broad agreement about what the content of an economist's education should be, then methodology will appear to be an esoteric and unnecessary field of study. It becomes more interesting and relevant when there exists disagreement over what constitutes the proper content, scope and methods of economics.

Economists differ, of course, in their perceptions concerning the homogeneity of the discipline. One reason why many economists in the USA do not have much use for methodology is that they perceive the discipline as a settled one. How that view got to be so well-established there should be studied further.

Problem 2

More fundamentally, the above argument misunderstands the *goal* of methodological study. The goal is not to teach one how to do economics. Rather, it is to help one to think more clearly about what it means to do economics, to understand better what the practice of economics in all its diversity is all about. What sorts of questions do economists focus their attention on? Which do they ignore, or consider unimportant? What are the peculiarities of their approaches, and what accounts for them? What is the best way to characterize the structure of economic theories? How do the practices of theorists and empirical economists differ, and how are they alike? How does economics compare to other sciences, both social and physical? These are the sorts of questions which methodologists ask.

I have elsewhere described in greater detail some suggestions for how to do methodological work, a meta-methodological programme which I originally called methodological pluralism but which is probably better dubbed critical pluralism (e.g. Caldwell 1982, 1984, 1988, 1989). I will not repeat this account, except to make the following two points. First, critical pluralism broadens the definition of methodology to include the study of things like rhetoric, sociology, and history. Some may quibble with me over terminology, but the point of such obfuscation is simply this: these fields are best viewed as complements rather than substitutes in the quest to understand economics better. Second, to see that studying methodology is *not* the same thing as studying economics, one can compare the travails of a methodologist to those of, say, an academic theologian or a sociologist of religion. The analogy is a simple one. One does not study theology or the sociology of religion to become more religious. One does it to understand religious phenomena better.

B′ – Rebutting the second objection

The second argument, that methodologists pretentiously and arrogantly tell economists what to do, is probably best viewed as a backlash against a specific and concrete episode in the history of ideas. For the first half of the twentieth century, various narrowly empiricist and heavily pre-scriptivist visions of what constituted science dominated the philosophy of science. These ideas, often in perverse and idiosyncratic forms, percolated down into the methodological literature in economics. Some-times the borrowings were explicitly acknowledged by the economist (as in the case of Fritz Machlup), and sometimes the expropriation was an unconscious one (as in the case of Milton Friedman). Sometimes the economist was a theorist trying to show how scientific economics is (as in the case of Paul Samuelson), at other times the point was to show how economics could become more scientific by following the prescriptions of the philosophers (as in the cases of T.W. Hutchison or Mark Blaug).

There are a number of reasons why methodology took this path. Most fundamentally, economics like many of the other social sciences was very eager to establish its scientific credentials. As Philip Mirowski (1989) recently showed, one way of accomplishing this goal was to adapt the models of energy physics to the dismal science. Mouthing the rhetoric of positivism was another. Donald McCloskey (1985) is exactly right in his characterization of the result that this had on how economists communicate: we owe many of our stilted language games to this quest for scientific credibility. Our indignation may be tempered somewhat when it is recalled that the authors of the doctrines were men whose experiences with Fascism and totalitarianism were direct and personal. For these men the ability to demarcate science from dogma clearly and unambiguously was more than the solution to a technical problem of philosophy.

Most now agree that the positivist programme in its many variants has failed, and that the interpretations of the works of philosophers like Karl Popper and Imre Lakatos which have made their way into economics have little to offer us. (These are dominant themes in Caldwell 1982, as well as in much of the recent literature, e.g. Hands, 1985a,c; de Marchi, 1988.) If this account is correct, then it is no longer appropriate to accuse methodology of being arrogant and pretentious. The appropriate question is: what direction should methodology take given the collapse of positivism? That question is taken up in the next section.

C' – Rebutting the third objection

It is true that many methodological debates are sterile, and that progress in the field seems always to come very slowly.

But there *has* been progress, especially in the last ten years or so. There are now a number of scholars who are interested in methodology (broadly defined) not with the hope of attacking or defending a particular research programme, but because they wish to better comprehend the discipline. There are many problems which remain to be solved, and many solutions which are in the process of being proposed. Methodology currently is an exciting and vibrant area in which to work.

As to the sterility of certain debates, surely it is a topic of the first importance to discover *why* it is that communication between rival groups sometimes breaks down so badly. Is it because of incommensurable theoretical or conceptual paradigms? Or are there perhaps incommensurabilities at deeper levels, having to do with metaphysical, or epistemological, or ethical frameworks? Can the true differences separating such groups be discovered? Are they capable of articulation? Is it even reasonable to have faith in rational discourse about such matters?

D' – Rebutting the fourth objection

Heterodox groups usually *are* more interested in methodology than are members of the 'neoclassical orthodoxy' (whatever *that* is), and for the reason stated: methodology is another potential source for generating arguments about why the approach of the mainstream is wrong.

But methodology is not the exclusive province of the fringes of the profession. Mainstream economists make methodological decisions and arguments all the time, they just do not always recognize them as such.

When, say, a George Stigler or a Paul Samuelson dismisses a Marxist or Institutionalist critic as being unscientific, he is making a methodological claim. Less dramatically, decisions to employ specific modelling and testing strategies quite often are founded, at least in part, on methodological considerations. Methodology, like interpretations, is ubiquitous. To deny it is to engage in obscurantism.

E' – Rebutting the fifth objection

One might accept that methodology, though not something which helps one to become an economist, might help one to understand better what economists do. One might accept further that the practice of methodology need not commit one to giving arrogant advice or to engaging in sterile debates. One might even accept the ubiquity of methodological discourse. But even then, one might wonder about why it is necessary to ask methodological questions. For one could still argue that all of the important questions are settled in everyone's mind except the philosopher's; that, for example, any economist worth his salt can tell good economics from bad. If this is so, why do we need to study methodology?

Perhaps the most effective way to rebut this argument is to request that the speaker provide a description of 'good scientific practice'. The typical answer (which can also be found in the first chapter of many undergraduate economics textbooks) might look like this: science uses theory. Theories, because they are abstractions, are unrealistic. We decide which theory is best by testing them. The best theories are testable (or, more strongly, falsifiable), and have survived frequent attempts to refute them (or, more weakly, are confirmed). If the speaker is sociologically inclined, he might also make reference to the scientific community: good science is what a community of specialists who are perceived as experts say it is.

Having set the trap, there are two ways to attack this characterization. One is to demonstrate that certain fields generally regarded as scientific do not meet the criteria outlined above. For example, one can show that biology, though excellent at explaining how random variation and selection lead to the evolution of the species, is unable to predict the evolutionary path that any particular species will take. But it is more fun to show how areas of enquiry not generally considered to be scientific can be fitted into the model of 'good scientific practice'. Consider, then, the similarities between economics and astrology.

Both of them make predictions. Both can point to confirmations of their theories, though there are also instances in which the results of testing failed to confirm the theory. Indeed, it is possible to define the term 'prediction' in such a way that their predictive records are roughly comparable. And though both economics and astrology are in the

50

business of making predictions, it is usually difficult to get practitioners in either field to state what sorts of outcomes, if they occurred, should lead one to abandon the theory.

Neither field is '*ad hoc*': both base their predictions on a theory. In both cases the theory is 'unrealistic', something that critics of each frequently point out. In both cases the theory is sufficiently complex that it takes experts in the field to understand it.

In both cases just such a community of specialists has formed. These experts are usually willing to explain the theory to the uninitiated for a fee. In the non-specialist population, each group has its critics. But there is also a fairly substantial portion of the non-specialist population which 'believes in' the prognostications of each group. It might even be plausibly asserted that astrology has a larger and more faithful following than does economics. Ronald and Nancy Reagan are a nice example: he does not believe in the predictions of economists, whereas she does believe in those of astrologers.

What conclusions do we draw from this? Is there no difference between economics and astrology? Are we trying to draw the distinction in the wrong way? Is there no such a thing as science? If there is, how do we demarcate it? Or is demarcation less important than other questions? These are the sorts of questions with which methodology grapples. It is understandable that some economists choose not to spend their time investigating them. But it is wrong to think that all the questions have been answered. There is still plenty of work to be done.

PHILOSOPHICAL, NON-PHILOSOPHICAL, AND ANTI-PHILOSOPHICAL FOUNDATIONS FOR METHODOLOGY

The eclipse of positivism had a profound effect on the philosophy of science. It led some to propose that alternative philosophical frameworks be employed to investigate the sciences. Others argue that the philosophy of science should be complemented by another discipline if one wishes to better understand the nature of scientific enquiry. There are also more radical proposals whose primary goal is to extinguish epistemological discourse altogether. Sometimes there are sharp divisions among the various proposals, at other times the borderlines are fuzzy. Only a few of the more prominent positions will be mentioned here. Each has implications for how to pursue methodological work in economics.

Philosophical foundations

Among philosophical alternatives, three which have been discussed in the methodological literature in English are structuralism, hermeneutics, and realism. The first, which is perhaps best viewed as a philosophically neutral technique rather than as a comprehensive philosophical position, is surveyed by Hands (1985b). The second, most recently associated with the Austrian movement in economics, is introduced in works by Lachmann (1986) and Lavoie (1990). I will comment briefly on the third.

There are many varieties of realism: commonsense and scientific realisms; metaphysical, ontological, and semantic realisms; normative and descriptive realisms (Mäki 1989a). If one were to describe a 'representative realist', the (in many ways unrealistic!) representation of his most basic beliefs might look as follows. The world exists; it is structured, multi-layered and complex; the properties and mechanisms which govern the structures are in principle discoverable; and it is the goal of science to try to discover them. Scientific theories refer to really existing entities, properties, mechanisms and structures; theories attempt to represent them; theories may be judged as true or false according to how well they correspond, in some sense, to what exists in the world.

Realists provide enriched and at times novel analyses of the nature of categories like necessity, causal power, essence, and universals. There are alternative models of the nature of scientific explanation, of the interpretation of theories, of the nature of truth. Most realist philosophers of science have concentrated on the physical sciences: that much within philosophy has *not* changed. The best general introduction for social scientists is probably Christopher Lloyd's (1986) *Explanation in Social History*. Lloyd compares realism with other approaches within philosophy, then shows how it is able to resolve or avoid many of the problems which proved so lethal for its positivist predecessors. He then argues for a realist (he calls it a 'structurist') approach to the question of human action and institutional change within the social sciences. The book combines a superb critical survey with a finely-crafted substantive proposal for change, and carries a complete bibliography. He is not kind towards what he dubs 'economistic' explanations. But then, what social scientist who is not an economist is?

Realism will be difficult to apply in economics for two reasons. The first is that it will take a massive effort to introduce the large, complicated and unfamiliar realist literature to economists. Realism is not like Popperian thought: it is not easily accessible, it does not provide simple formulas for demarcation, it does not quickly translate into a set of methodological rules. The arduous task has been started by Uskali Mäki, who in a series of papers (Mäki 1989a,b, 1990, 1992) introduces a number of realist categories into economics. In my opinion, this is some of the most exciting work currently being done in the field. It is encouraging that others are now beginning to provide additional realist investigations (e.g. Lawson 1989, 1992).

The second obstacle is more troublesome. A variant of instrumentalism as an approach to the cognitive status and purpose of theories is well-entrenched in economics. Part of its influence is due to Friedman's famous essay, part is due to the type of theories which dominate standard neoclassical analysis, and part is due to the nature of some empirical work within economics. This poses a problem for realism because instrumentalism and realism are usually viewed as incompatible with one another. If one is to make the case for realism, this tension will have to be overcome.

I think that the tension can be overcome, and have suggested one possible line of attack in which the central theses of economics are given a realist interpretation, while the models are given an instrumentalist one (Caldwell 1992). Mäki (1989a) has taken another route by coining the awkward but precise terms 'realisticness' and 'unrealisticness', which are predicates attributable to representations. Economists can still be realists, even though they employ representations which are in various ways 'unrealistic'. Recently Mäki (1989b, 1992) has expanded on the ways in which a representation might be unrealistic: for example, besides hopeless falsity, there is simplification, exaggeration, isolation, approximation, and understatement.

Having said all this, the crucial tasks facing those who would reconstruct economics along realist lines are to establish just what kinds of economic entities, structures, and processes are said to exist, to explain convincingly how our unrealistic theories represent them, and to show how the empirical studies which so many economists undertake can be made consistent with realist prescriptions about the search for causal mechanisms. The success or failure of these endeavours will determine the success or failure of the realist programme within the dismal science.

Non-philosophical foundations

Disciplines other than philosophy are available to those who would understand better the practice of economics. Perhaps the most obvious of these is the sociology of science. It is difficult to understand why so little work has been done in this area. There are, of course, the oft-repeated departmental rankings, as well as the occasional humorous depiction of the norms of the profession (e.g. Leijonhufvud 1973). Of a more serious nature are the attitudinal surveys which have recently been undertaken (e.g. Frey, Pommerehne *et al.* 1984; Colander and Klamer 1987). There have been exhortations to do more sociology of economics, and frameworks for such study have been recommended (Coats 1985, 1986). But much awaits the sociologist of economics.

There has been more activity in other areas. The most prominent contribution is the path-breaking work of Donald McCloskey (1985) on the rhetoric of economic argumentation. The oral history projects executed by Arjo Klamer (1983, 1989), in which leading economists are interviewed on matters both disciplinary and personal, constitute another important advance.

Are such approaches best viewed as substitutes for or complements to more traditional philosophical investigations? I will assert without providing arguments that, at least for now, the latter scenario seems preferable. Surely there is enough work to be done within each of the traditions without spending time debating which one is the most insightful, especially at this early date. This conciliatory view has other advocates in the literature (e.g. Lloyd, 1986: 103 contains numerous references; see also Mäki 1988), and with luck it will become dominant.

Anti-philosophical foundations

There is, however, another view, one which denies that the traditional philosophical (and particularly epistemological) approaches have anything of value to offer to those who seek a better understanding of the scientific enterprise. This view has entered the methodological literature, taking the form of an argument against methodology itself.

Elements of the argument can be found in the early chapters of McCloskey (1985). Given that McCloskey's work was also mentioned in the last section, it would appear that there are at least two ways to read him. Let us posit a strong version and a weak version of McCloskey's position. The weak version is the pluralistic plea to pay more attention to the nuances of language and to the workings of language communities. This version is the one encountered in the last section, and is one which seems to make good sense. The strong version disparages capital-M Methodology as overbearing and attacks the pursuit of capital-T Truth as chimerical. It is the strong version which many methodologists find objectionable.

McCloskey's sometime antipathy towards methodology pales in comparison to recent work by Roy Weintraub (1989), for whom there is no weak version. For a long time Imre Lakatos was Weintraub's philosopher of choice, but recently he has fallen under the influence of the literary theorist Stanley Fish. Fish is an impressive debater but, more important, an honest scholar. He notes that his own position, if followed to its logical conclusion, is one which will forever change the way one perceives a discipline (it is a position which can be applied to any discipline). But he also states that it is a position which has no consequences for the discipline itself. I suspect that the latter point is Fish's way of acknowledging that his programme is essentially a sceptical one. In any case, it seems to me that Weintraub's position leads directly to scepticism.

Some may respond: so what? What is so bad about scepticism? And it must be admitted that scepticism is not altogether unattractive. It is very appealing to the iconoclast, it is notoriously difficult to refute, and it can even be made to appear modest.

This is not the place for a sustained analysis of the merits and faults of scepticism. But it does seem clear that the critical arguments of the anti-epistemologists have made it necessary for methodologists to put such an analysis on their agenda. It was because Karl Popper attempts to deal with the question of scepticism that I recently returned, with renewed interest, to the non-justificationist side of his philosophy (Caldwell 1991). But as for now, the arguments of the sceptics have yet to be adequately answered.

ASSUMPTIONS, PREDICTIONS AND ETHICS

Let us now examine three areas within economic methodology which appear ripe for further investigation. Other areas could have been chosen, and much more could be said about those which were selected.

The rationality assumption

More has been written on the role of assumptions in economics than on any other methodological topic. As a result, the literature is by now fairly well advanced. What is needed now is a synthesizer, someone to bring together all of the good work already done. The present discussion focuses on the rationality assumption.

Why is it that some economists consider the rationality assumption to be unrealistic, if not false, while others would include it among those propositions which, in Robbins' memorable phrase, are 'so much the stuff of our everyday experience that they have only to be stated to be recognized as obvious' (Robbins 1935: 79)? The problem is in supposing that there is a single rationality assumption. In fact, there are many. Three are identified here; note too that each has spawned a literature which criticizes it.

The first is consistency in choice. In the standard formulation, this involves consistency in choice over a well-defined preference function. Nothing is said about the rationality of the choices themselves: one might be maximizing over 'goods' which will lead to one's premature demise. Challengers offer experimental results in which consistency is systematically violated in risky choice settings. Alternative explanations of choice under risk have been offered, as well as amendments to the standard axioms (for reviews, see Schoemaker 1982; Machina 1987). Disconfirmation can be avoided completely by dropping the requirement of a *well-defined* preference function, thereby emptying the assumption of any empirical content. This is the route taken by Mises

(1949), who claimed that preferences are revealed in the act of choice. Apparent inconsistencies are always attributable to changes in subjective preferences; all human action is by definition rational.

The second defines rationality as self-interested behaviour, a form of egoism. One can also empty this definition of any content by defining all behaviour as self-interested, but typically it is taken to mean that such things as altruism or public-spiritedness are ruled out. It is possible to model the latter behaviour by positing interdependent utility or meta-preference functions (e.g. Sen 1974). But as North (1981) argues, economists have not been able to provide a model which adequately *explains* why agents sometimes fail to act as egoists. A possible (though deservedly controversial) explanatory candidate is sociobiology.

The third aspect of the rationality assumption which has been roundly criticized is that agents have perfect information, not only about their own preferences, but about the range of choices they face, about current and future states of the world, and about the intentions and actions of other agents. Hayek, for whom the problem of social coordination is 'the central question of all social sciences' (Hayek 1948: 54), argues that the assumption of perfect foresight rules out the possibility of discoordination of agents' plans. He proposes an alternative formulation in which the knowledge which agents are assumed to possess is subjectively-held and dispersed.

The idea that there is only one rationality assumption has been very helpful to workaday neoclassical economists who wish to justify their unrealistic assumptions to critics or in the classroom. When challenged, one can easily move around among the various definitions (for example, one can respond to complaints about egoism by redefining rationality as consistency), or even retreat to the empirically empty ones. Hopefully even so simple a classification system as the one above may help to clarify some of these issues.

The larger task is more formidable. What is needed is a general theory of rational desires, beliefs, and actions. In the best of all worlds, such a general theory would be able to incorporate both the existent various definitions of rationality and their challengers. A more likely first step is the provision of a complete typology of the multiple rationality assumptions and of their exceptions. Whenever possible, the exceptions would be developed into positive theories, as has been done, for example, by Kahneman and Tversky (1979). The next step would be an investigation of how each of the assumptions and exceptions fit in with various models of human behaviour. The final step would be to link up such models to theories of social and economic interaction.

Prediction

As with rationality, different economists seem to mean different things when they speak of prediction. This is why some agree with Milton

Friedman that the predictive record of neoclassical economics is its strongest virtue, while others agree with Tony Lawson (forthcoming) that prediction is impossible in economics. A wonderfully witty intermediate position is McCloskey's (1988) demonstration that neoclassical economics itself can explain (predict?) why economists cannot predict certain phenomena any better than anyone else.

As with rationality, a typology of prediction is probably the best place to start. On one end would be the sort of conditional, *ceteris paribus* predictions with which academic economists successfully win over generation upon generation of students in introductory courses, the effects of price controls being perhaps the most vivid and widely-used example. On the other would be the sort of open-ended and notoriously inaccurate forecasts which 'financial consultants' of various stripes are more than willing to sell to anyone silly enough to buy them. Surely a more thorough investigation would establish not only the varieties of predictions which economists make, but the conditions under which one might expect such predictions to hold.

There are many additional questions. What is the nature of the empirical work which is done in economics? How does it relate to the many models of empirical studies in the philosophy of science? What are the methodological implications of the various methods for handling uncertainty across models, as reported on in, for example, Sims (1988)? Of what import are alternative interpretations of the foundations of probability? Though a few econometricians, notably E.E. Leamer and David Hendry, exhibit familiarity with some of the philosophical and methodological literature, for the most part the links between these subject areas await investigation.

Ethics and economics

A final fertile field is the relationship between ethics and economics. Three research areas will be mentioned.

Though economists make reference to the field of ethics with increasing frequency, they are not always clear about what the subject of reference is. What is the current state of development of ethical and meta-ethical theory? Meta-ethics is mentioned because the problem of justifying moral claims is directly analogous to the problem of justifying knowledge claims, a point which must be unsettling for those who would reduce epistemology to ethics. What approaches to the problem of the justification of moral claims have been tried, and do any of them look promising? Given the recent interest among economists in realism, should the realist approach in ethics (as explicated in, for example, Brink 1989) be given more attention?

A second question worthy of investigation concerns the relationship between various ethical theories and economic theory. Which ethical theories underlie economics? What is their relationship to such doctrines as liberalism, Paretianism or contractarianism? A considerable amount of work has already been done in this area. Hamlin (1986) provides an accessible summary of the literature, and demonstrates the links between ethical theory and alternative theories of rationality, a theme which has also been important in the work of Sen (e.g. 1987).

Finally, what is the role of an ethical system in the workings of an economy? In a book review, Ernest Gellner wrote:

> The right question is not, Why is this or that civilization cruel? They all are. It is, rather, What are the conditions that make possible the occasional emergence of a gentler social order? These conditions evidently include affluence, political stability, and a certain moral climate.
>
> (Gellner 1989: 34)

It seems clear that the existence of 'a certain moral climate' is indeed a necessary condition for an economy to be able to function adequately. Douglass North (1981) provides one framework for analysing this topic. Within his framework, a system of ethics legitimizes existing institutions and, to the extent that this is done successfully, reduces enforcement costs and increases efficiency. On the other hand, the specialization which accompanies economic growth increases the opportunities for free riding as well as the costs of devising moral and ethical codes. Most important of all, there is still no theory to help explain why (and predict when) agents will act like free riders and when they will not. North concludes (1981, Ch. 5) that the development of such a theory is an essential task not just for economists, but for all social scientists. In addition, the origins and evolution of ethical systems might be discussed, as well as whether differing economic systems either engender or require different ethical norms.

NOTE

1 Parts of this chapter draw directly from 'Does methodology matter? How should it be practiced?' which has appeared in *Finnish Economic Papers*, Vol. 3, 1990. I thank the editors of the present volume for providing a number of valuable comments. Remaining errors are my own.

REFERENCES

Baxter, J.L. (1988) *Social and Psychological Foundations of Economic Analysis*, Hemel Hempstead: Harvester Wheatsheaf.

Brink, D. (1989) *Moral Realism and the Foundations of Ethics*, Cambridge: Cambridge University Press.

Caldwell, B. (1982) *Beyond Positivism: Economic Methodology in the Twentieth Century*, London: Allen & Unwin.

—— (1984) 'Economic methodology in the postpositivist era', *Research in the History of Economic Thought and Methodology* 2 (1984): 195–205.

—— (1988) 'The case for pluralism', in N. de Marchi (ed.) *The Popperian Legacy in Economics*, Cambridge: Cambridge University Press.

—— (1989) 'Post-Keynesian methodology: an assessment', *Review of Political Economy* 1 (1989): 43–64.

—— (1991) 'Clarifying Popper', *Journal of Economic Literature* 29 (March): 1–33.

—— (1992) 'Human molecules: a comment on Nelson', in N. de Marchi (ed.) *Post-Popperian Methodology of Economics*, Boston: Kluwer Academic.

Coats, A.W. (1985) 'The sociology of knowledge and the history of economics', unpublished manuscript.

—— (1986) 'Review of Richard Whitley, *The Intellectual and Social Organization of the Sciences*', *History of Political Economy* 18 (Winter): 683–6.

Colander, D. and Klamer, A. (1987) 'The making of an economist', *Journal of Economic Perspectives* 1 (Fall): 95–111.

de Marchi, N. (ed.) (1988) *The Popperian Legacy in Economics*, Cambridge: Cambridge University Press.

Frey, B., Pommerehne, W., et al. (1984) 'Consensus and dissension among economists: an empirical survey', *American Economic Review* 74 (December): 986–94.

Gellner, E. (1989) 'Up from imperialism: review of David Pryce-Jones, *The Closed Circle*', *New Republic* (May 22): 34–8.

Hamlin, A. (1986) *Ethics, Economics and the State*, New York: St Martin's Press.

Hands, D.W. (1985a) 'Karl Popper and economic methodology: a new look', *Economics and Philosophy* 1 (April): 83–99.

—— (1985b) 'The structuralist view of economic theories: the case of general equilibrium theory in particular', *Economics and Philosophy* 1 (October): 303–35.

—— (1985c) 'Second thoughts on Lakatos', *History of Political Economy* 17 (Spring): 1–16.

Hayek, F.A. (1948) 'Economics and knowledge', in F.A. Hayek *Individualism and Economic Order*, Chicago: University of Chicago Press, pp. 33–56. (First published in 1937.)

Kahneman, D. and Tversky, A. (1979) 'Prospect theory: an analysis of decision under risk', *Econometrica* 47: 263–91.

Klamer, A. (1983) *Conversations with Economists*, Totowa, New Jersey: Rowman & Allanheld.

—— (1989) 'A conversation with Amartya Sen', *Journal of Economic Perspectives* 3 (Winter): 135–50.

Lachmann, L. (1986) *The Market as an Economic Process*, Oxford: Basil Blackwell.

Lavoie, D. (ed.) (1990) *Economics and Hermeneutics*, London: Routledge.

Lawson, A. (1989) 'Realism and instrumentalism in the development of econometrics', *Oxford Economic Papers* 41: 236–58.

—— (1992) 'Realism, closed systems and Friedman', *Research in the History of Economic Thought and Methodology*, 10.

Leijonhufvud, A. (1973) 'Life among the econ', reprinted in A. Leijonhufvud (1981) *Information and Coordination*, Oxford: Oxford University Press, pp. 347–59.

Lloyd, C. (1986) *Explanation in Social History*, Oxford: Blackwell.

McCloskey, D. (1985) *The Rhetoric of Economics*, Madison, Wisconsin: University of Wisconsin Press.

—— (1988) 'The limits of expertise: if you're so smart, why ain't you rich?', *The American Scholar* (Summer): 303–406.

Machina, M. (1987) 'Choice under uncertainty: problems solved and unsolved', *Journal of Economic Perspectives* 1 (Summer): 121–54.

Mäki, U. (1988) 'How to combine rhetoric and realism in the methodology of economics', *Economics and Philosophy* 4: 89–109.

—— (1989a) 'On the problem of realism in economics', *Ricerche Economiche* 43, 1–2: 176–98. (Reprinted in B. Caldwell (ed.) *The Philosophy and Methodology of Economics*, Worcester: Edward Elgar.)

—— (1989b) 'Types of unrealisticness in economics: the case of J.H. von Thunen's isolated state', unpublished manuscript.

—— (1990) 'Scientific realism and Austrian explanation', *Review of Political Economy* 2: 310–44.

—— (1992) 'Friedman and realism', *Research in the History of Economic Thought and Methodology*, 10, 171–95.

Mirowski, P. (1989) *More Heat than Light: Economics as Social Physics, Physics as Nature's Economics*, Cambridge: Cambridge University Press.

Mises, L. von (1949) *Human Action: A Treatise on Economics*, New Haven, Connecticut: Yale University Press.

North, D. (1981) *Structure and Change in Economic History*, New York: W.W. Norton.

Robbins, L. (1935) *An Essay on the Nature and Signficance of Economic Science*, 2nd editions, London: Macmillan.

Schoemaker, P. (1982) 'The expected utility model: its variants, purposes, evidence and limitations', *Journal of Economic Literature* 20 (June): 529–63.

Sen, A. (1974) 'Rational fools: a critique of the behavioral foundations of economic theory', *Philosophy and Public Affairs*, 6: 317–44. (Reprinted in F. Hahn and M. Hollis (eds) (1979) *Philosophy and Economic Theory*, Oxford: Oxford University Press, pp. 87–109.)

—— (1987) *On Ethics and Economics*, Oxford: Blackwell.

Sims, C. (1988) 'Uncertainty across models', *American Economic Review Papers and Proceedings*, 78 (May): 163–7.

Weintraub, E.R. (1989) 'Methodology doesn't matter, but the history of thought might', in S. Honkapohja (ed.) *Whither Macroeconomics?*, Oxford: Basil Blackwell.

3

POPPER AND LAKATOS IN ECONOMIC METHODOLOGY[1]

D. Wade Hands

ABSTRACT

The purpose of this chapter is to critically reappraise the methodological advice offered to economists by Popperian philosophy, in particular Popperian falsificationism and Lakatos's 'methodology of scientific research programmes'. These two philosophical positions and the difficulties they raise for economic methodology are carefully considered in the chapter. It is argued that while economists have benefited from the influence of Popperian philosophy in a number of ways, neither falsificationism nor Lakatos's methodology provide an appropriate guide to the acceptance or rejection of economic theories. The implications and caveats surrounding this argument are considered in the conclusion.

INTRODUCTION

Popperian philosophy of science has been extremely influential in economic methodology. Popperian 'falsificationism', first introduced into economics by Hutchison (1938), remains one of the dominant approaches to economic methodology. In addition to this direct influence, Popperian philosophy has also affected economic methodology through the work of Imre Lakatos. A fairly extensive literature has developed around the question of the applicability of Lakatos's 'methodology of scientific research programmes' (MSRP) to economics.[2]

The purpose of this chapter is to critically reappraise the methodological advice given by Popperian philosophy. In this reappraisal both Popperian falsificationism and Lakatos's MSRP will be examined. Neo-institutionalist economics will not be explicitly discussed; instead the focus will be the general standards for economic theory choice which influence every economic theory (including neo-institutionalism). Throughout the discussion the philsophical positions will be appraised only with respect to *economic methodology*: 'economic' in that only economics and not other fields of enquiry will be discussed, and 'methodology' in that only questions of theory choice and theory appraisal (not more general philosophical considerations) will be examined. In particular, questions such as whether 'economic methodology' should be pursued at all (recently raised by McCloskey (1985)) will not be examined here.

FALSIFICATIONISM

No doubt Karl Popper is best known for his falsificationist approach to the philosophy of science: a theory first presented in *Logik der Forschung* in 1934 (English translation, Popper 1959). Falsificationism represents Popper's view of the growth of scientific knowledge as well as his solution to (or dissolution of) the problem of induction. It is for falsificationism that Popper claims responsibility for the death of logical positivism (Popper 1976b: 88).

Popperian falsificationism is actually composed of two separate theses: one on demarcation (demarcating science from non-science) and one on methodology (how science should be practised). The demarcation thesis is that for a theory to be 'scientific' it must be at least potentially falsifiable by empirical observation, that is, there must exist at least one empirical basic statement which is in conflict with the theory.[3] This potential falsifiability is a logical relationship between the theory and a basic statement; in particular, the demarcation criterion only requires that it be logically possible to falsify the theory, not that such a falsification has ever been attempted.[4] While Popper's demarcation criterion has been the subject of an extensive debate in the philosophical literature, demarcation is seldom the issue in economics. For economists the more important issue is methodology (choosing between/among theories not merely labelling them scientific or unscientific) and Popperian *methodology* requires the practical (not just logical) falsifiability of scientific theories.

In a nutshell, falsificationist scientific practice proceeds as follows. The scientist starts with a scientific problem situation (something requiring a scientific explanation) and proposes a bold conjecture which might offer a solution to the problem. Next the conjecture is severely tested by comparing its least likely consequences with the relevant empirical data. Popper's argument for severe testing is that a test will be *more severe* the more prima facie *unlikely* the consequence that is being tested; the theory should be forced to 'stick its neck out', to 'offer the enemy, namely nature, the most exposed and extended surface' (Gellner 1974: 171). The final step in the falsificationist game depends on how the theory has performed during the testing stage. If the implications of the theory are not consistent with the evidence, then the conjecture is falsified and it should be replaced by a new conjecture which is *not ad hoc* relative to the original, that is, the new conjecture should not be contrived solely to avoid this empirical anomaly.[5] If the theory is not falsified by the evidence then it is considered corroborated and it is accepted provisionally. Given Popper's fallibilism this acceptance is provisional forever; the method does not necessarily result in true theories, only ones that have faced a tough empirical opponent and won.

Now while there are a number of reasons why economists have felt that Popperian falsificationism would be a desirable methodology, the fact is that *falsificationism is seldom if ever practised in economics*. This seems to be the one point generally agreed upon by recent methodological commentators. In fact, this (empirical) claim is supported at length by the case studies in Blaug (1980), a book which consistently advocates falsificationism as a normative ideal. The disagreement between critics and defenders of falsificationism is *not whether it has been practised*, basically it has not, but rather *whether it should be practised*. The real questions are whether the profession should 'try harder' to practise falsificationism though it has failed to do so in the past, and the related question of whether the discipline of economics would be substantially improved by a conscientious falsificationist practice.

One approach to the question of the appropriateness of falsificationism in economics would be to directly address the question of the adequacy of Popper's falsificationist methodology as a *general* approach to the growth of scientific knowledge; this is not the approach that will be followed here. Rather than delving into this general question, the following discussion will simply survey some of the criticisms which falsificationism has received explicitly as an economic methodology. This list of criticisms is not exhaustive, but it does capture the major concerns which have been raised regarding the falsificationism in economics. The list is not necessarily in order of importance.[6]

1 For a number of reasons, the so-called Duhemian problem (or Duhem–Quine problem) presents a great difficulty in economics.[7] First, the complexity of human behaviour requires the use of numerous initial conditions and strong simplifying assumptions. Some of these restrictions may actually be false (such as the infinite divisibility of commodities), some of these assumptions may be logically unfalsifiable (such as the assumptions of eventually diminishing returns), while still others may be logically falsifiable but practically unfalsifiable (such as the completeness assumption in consumer choice theory). Even where assumptions and restrictions can be tested, such testing is very difficult because of the absence of a suitably controlled laboratory environment.[8] In the presence of such a variety of restrictions it is virtually impossible to 'aim the arrow of *modus tollens*' at one particular problematic element of the set auxiliary hypotheses when contrary evidence is found. Second, there are many questions and

disagreements about the empirical basis in economics. It is always possible to argue that what was observed was 'not really' involuntary unemployment or 'not really' economic profit, etc. Although it is fundamental to Popperian philosophy that the empirical basis need not be incorrigible, it is necessary that there be a generally accepted convention regarding the empirical basis,[9] and in economics even such conventions are often not available. Third, even if these first two problems have somehow been eliminated it is still possible for the social sciences to have feedback effects that do not exist in the physical sciences. The test of an economic theory may itself alter the initial conditions for the test. Conducting a test of the relationship between the money supply and the price level may alter expectations in such a way that the initial conditions (which were true 'initially') are not true after the test (or if the 'same' test were conducted again).

2 Related to, but actually separate from the Duhemian problem, is the problem that the qualitative comparative statics technique used in economics makes severe testing very difficult and cheap corroborational success 'too easy'. In economics it is very often the case that the strongest available prediction is a qualitative comparative statics result which only specifies that the variable in question increases, decreases, or remains the same. Since having the correct sign is much easier than having both the correct sign and magnitude, an emphasis on such qualitative prediction generates theories which are low in empirical content, have few potential falsifiers, and are difficult if not impossible to test severely. The result is often economic theories which are confirmed by the evidence but provide very little information.[10]

3 Popper's 'admitted failure' (1983: xxxv) to develop an adequate theory of verisimilitude[11] presents a fundamental difficulty for a falsificationist methodology in economics. Popper's theory of verisimilitude developed as an attempt to reconcile his falsificationist methodology with scientific realism. For a realist science aims at 'true' theories; according to falsificationism, scientific theories should be chosen if they have been corroborated by passing severe tests. If the falsificationist method is to fulfil the realist aims of science it should be demonstrated that more corroborated theories are closer to the truth. Such a demonstration was precisely the goal of Popper's theory of verisimilitude. Actually a satisfactory theory of verisimilitude would serve Popperian philosophy in at least two different ways. One way, as already mentioned, would be to provide an epistemic justification for playing the game of science by falsificationist rules. Such a justification is very important for Popperian philosophy since without a theory of verisimilitude it can be argued that there are philosophically 'no good reasons' (Popper 1972: 22) for choosing theories as Popper recommends. The second function of a theory of verisimilitude is

more practical. Verisimilitude would provide rules for choosing the 'best' theory in troublesome cases: like the situation where both available theories have been falsified. A theory of verisimilitude would help in such cases because it would provide a rule for determining which of the two theories in question actually has more verisimilitude: which is closer to the truth. A similar argument could be made for cases involving a choice between a falsified but bold theory and a corroborated but modest theory; having a way to determine which has more verisimilitude would allow us to choose a theory which is more consistent with the aims of science, which is closer to the truth. This second, more practical, function of the theory of verisimilitude is very important in economic methodology. The reason is that economists are almost always faced with choosing between two falsified theories, or choosing between a bold falsified theory and a more modest corroborated one. If Popper's theory of verisimilitude had been a success and it could be added to the norms of simple falsificationism (both to justify the norms and to help in making the practical decisions of theory choice) then falsificationism might have an important role to play in economic theory choice. Without such a link between severe testing and truth-likeness, the method is of limited value in pursuing the realist aim of science.

4 Popper's rules for progressive theory development (non *ad hocness*) are seldom appropriate in economics. Popper argues that if one theory is to constitute 'progress' over a predecessor the new theory must be 'independently testable'; it must have 'excess empirical content', predict 'novel facts'.[12] This issue will be examined more carefully in the Lakatos section which follows, but for now it should be noted that while Popperian progress may sometimes be of interest to economists, often progress in economics is (and should be) very different to what Popper prescribes. Economists are often concerned with finding new explanations for well-known (non novel) facts, or alternatively, with explaining known phenomena by means of fewer theoretical restrictions. What constitutes 'progress' in economic theory (or what should constitute progress) is a complex and ongoing question, but it is apparent that any suitable answer will require a different, and possibly much more liberal, set of standards than those offered by strict Popperian falsificationism.

All of these criticisms add up to a negative appraisal of falsificationist economic methodology. Despite the fact that preaching falsificationist methodology has been very popular among economists, the method fails to provide a reasonably adequate set of rules for doing economics. Strict adherence to falsificationist norms would virtually *destroy all existing economic theory* and leave economists with a rule book for a game unlike anything the profession has played in the past. This high cost would be paid without any guarantee that obeying the new rules would result in theories any closer to the truth about economic behaviour than those currently available. How this result should be interpreted will be discussed in the conclusion, for now let us turn to Lakatos's MSRP.

LAKATOS'S METHODOLOGY OF SCIENTIFIC RESEARCH PROGRAMMES

Lakatos's work in the philosophy of science first appeared in the early 1970s (Lakatos 1970, 1971) and it was endorsed almost immediately by a number of economists. Numerous papers on Lakatos have appeared in the economics literature, many as a result of the Nafplion Colloquium on Research Programmes in Physics and Economics in 1974 (Latsis 1976a). This literature on 'Lakatos and economics' has basically been of two types. The first type is historical, it attempts to 'reconstruct' some particular episode in the history of economic thought along Lakatosian lines. The second type is more philosophical, it attempts to appraise Lakatos's methodology of scientific research programmes as an economic methodology and/or compare it to other philosophies such as Kuhn or Popperian falsificationism.

Lakatos's MSRP is clearly part of the Popperian tradition in the philosophy of science but it was also motivated by philosophically minded historians of science such as Kuhn (1970). For Lakatos the primary unit of appraisal in science is the 'research programme' rather than the scientific theory. A research programme is an ensemble consisting of a hard core, the positive and negative heuristics, and a protective belt.[13] The hard core is composed of the fundamental metaphysical presuppositions of the programme; it defines the programme, and its elements are treated as irrefutable by the programme's practitioners. To participate in the programme is to accept and be guided by the programme's hard core. For example, in Weintraub's Lakatosian reconstruction of the Neo-Walrasian research programme in economics, the hard core consists of propositions such as: agents have preferences over outcomes and agents act independently and optimize subject to constraints. The positive and negative heuristics provide instructions about what should and should not be pursued in the development of the programme. The positive heuristic guides the researcher toward the right questions and the best tools to use in answering those questions; the negative heuristic indicates what questions should not be pursued and what tools are inappropriate. Again using Weintraub's analysis of the Neo-Walrasian programme as an example, the positive heuristic contains injunctions such as: construct theories where the agents optimize, while the negative heuristic implores researchers to avoid theories involving disequilibrium. Finally, the protective belt consists of the programme's actual theories, auxiliary hypotheses, empirical conventions and the (evolving) 'body' of the research programme. The major activity of the programme occurs in the protective belt, it occurs as a result of the interaction of the hard core, the heuristics, and the programme's empirical record. For Weintraub's Neo-Walrasian programme the protective belt includes almost all of applied microeconomics.

A research programme is appraised on the basis of the theoretical and empirical activity in the protective belt. There is *theoretical progress* if each change in the protective belt is empirical content increasing; that is if it predicts *novel facts*.[14] The research programme exhibits *empirical progress* if this excess empirical content actually gets corroborated (Lakatos 1970: 118). Lakatos also requires a third type of progress, heuristic progress (non-ad hoc$_3$ness), which specifies that the changes be consistent with the hard core of the programme. Lakatos's definitions of theoretical and empirical progress presuppose that the changes in question are consistent with heuristic progress.

One obvious example of the link between Lakatos and Popper is the way in which Lakatos characterizes empirical content and novel facts. Lakatos, like Popper, defines the empirical content of a theory to be 'the set of its potential falsifiers: the set of those observational propositions which may disprove it' (Lakatos 1970: 98, n. 2). Thus, even though Lakatos considers empirical progress to come through empirical corroboration rather than falsification, his characterization of the relationship between theory and fact is still basically falsificationist. There are many other signs of Lakatos's Popperian lineage but his definition of empirical content and novel facts are the most important in the appraisal of Lakatosian economic methodology.

On the other hand, there are many aspects of the MSRP which are fundamentally at odds with Popperian falsificationism. The most significant of these is the immunity of the hard core to empirical criticism; immunizing any part of scientific theory would be in conflict with Popper's falsificationist method of bold conjecture and severe test. Popper clearly recognized that science has experienced periods of Kuhnian 'normal science' where the critical spirit seems to be temporarily arrested, but for Popper these episodes are something to lament not praise (Popper 1970). Another point of disagreement is the question of corroboration versus falsification. While Lakatos defines empirical content in a thoroughly Popperian way, he has no respect for the role of falsification in science. For Lakatos all theories are 'born refuted' (1970: 120–1) and the task of philosophy of science should be to develop a methodology which *starts* from this fact. For Lakatos progress comes from the corroboration not falsification of novel facts. Finally, Lakatos clearly embraces a historical meta-methodology whereby the actual history of science is used to appraise various methodological proposals.[15] This is very different from Popper where methodology is purely a normative affair and where there is no pathway open for the actual history of science to help evaluate methodologies.

These places where Lakatos differs from Popper are exactly the places where Lakatos is likely to win the favour of economists since these happen to be areas where there is substantial tension between falsificationism and the actual practice of economics. Certainly economics is replete with metaphysical 'hard cores'; there is not much consensus on what these hard core propositions should be, but there seems to be a consensus that such hard core presuppositions exist and that they often define alternative research programmes in economics. A philosophical programme such as Popperian falsificationism which requires practitioners to be willing to give up almost any part of their research programme at any time will not provide as adequate a guide for economists as Lakatos's methodology which allows for such pervasive hard cores. This economic preference for Lakatos over Popper also extends to the issue of corroboration versus falsification. It is clear that falsificationism has not been practised in economics and there is good reason to believe that enforcement of such strict standards would all but eliminate the discipline as it currently exists. On the other hand, there *is* a great amount of empirical activity in economics, the facts do matter, but they matter in a much more subtle and complex way than falsificationism allows.

Finally, economists would prefer Lakatos to Popper on the question of the role of the history of science in supporting particular methodological proposals. The general question of the relationship between the history of science and the philosophy of science is an unsettled question which continues to be debated in the literature, but economists have recently been very sympathetic to methodological proposals that are sensitive to the actual history of their discipline. Economists have produced an extensive literature using the Lakatosian categories to reconstruct various parts of the history of economic thought. Most of this literature focuses on a particular research programme in economic theory (past or present) and tries to isolate the hard core, the positive and negative heuristics, and the type of theoretical activity occurring in the protective belt. Such work usually results in a positive or negative Lakatosian appraisal of the 'progressivity' of the particular economic research programme. Examples of these reconstructions range widely over various topics in the history of economic thought.

An overall assessment of this Lakatosian historical literature is very difficult because many of the economists writing in the field have taken very little care in the way they use the Lakatosian terminology. This lack of fidelity to Lakatosian terminology has resulted in 'hard cores', 'heuristics' and (particularly) 'novel facts' which bear little resemblance to their Lakatosian analogues or how these terms have been used in reconstructions in the physical sciences. Much of this literature has provided valuable and independently interesting history of economic thought, but it sheds little light on the methodological adequacy of the MSRP. The only general conclusion that can be reached from this historical literature is that *in the case studies where the relevant language is consistent with Lakatos, 'progress', and the prediction of novel facts it necessarily implies, has been a rare occurrence.* There have been some well-researched cases where novel facts actually seem to have been uncovered;[16] but these cases correspond to only a very small portion of what the economics profession would consider its major theoretical 'advances'. Lakatos's criterion for 'theoretical progress', the prediction of novel facts, may have been sufficient for what economists have considered to be theoretical progress in certain special cases, but it does not seem to be generally necessary. Just as 'the development of economic analysis would look a dismal affair through falsificationist spectacles' (Latsis 1976b: 8), it seems that economics would look almost as dismal on a strictly Lakatosian view.

The argument that empirical and theoretical advances in economics occur (and should occur) in ways other than Lakatos specified in the MSRP, reflects very poorly (again) on Popper. The reason is that *where economics is most likely to part ways with Lakatos is precisely where Lakatos borrowed most heavily from Popper.* In certain respects, Lakatos's work is much better suited to economics than Popper's; it seems that looking for the types of things which Lakatos suggests one should look for in the history of economics has helped guide a number of important historical studies. Certainly this historical research has drawn attention to the metaphysical hard core of certain economic research programmes and it has motivated enquiry into the important methodological question of the relationship between empirical and theoretical work in economics, that is, between econometrics and economic theory. What the MSRP does not provide is an appropriate model for the acceptance or rejection of economic theories. Lakatos's MSRP may constitute methodological progress over falsificationism, but it still fails to provide economists with an acceptable criterion for theory choice (or progressive problem shifts). This is particularly telling for Popper since the Lakatosian fit seems to be poorest where older Popperian parts were used with the least modification.

CONCLUSION

In the final evaluation it seems that 'Popperian' economic methodology must be given low marks. Falsificationism, Popper's fundamental programme for the growth of scientific knowledge, is particularly ill-suited to economics and while the interest in Lakatos has produced some valuable historical studies,[17] the overall fit between economics and the MSRP is not good: and not good precisely where Lakatos is the most Popperian.

This evaluation should not be too harshly interpreted though. It has been argued that Popperian methodology, both in its falsificationist and MSRP forms, does not provide a very good standard for judging the adequacy of economic theories; this does not mean that Popperian philosophy has not provided any insight at all into economic theorizing. In particular, the above argument does *not* say that testing should be unimportant in economics, that Lakatosian reconstructions in the history of economic thought have not provided valuable contributions to the historical literature, or that economists would have gained more by listening to some other particular school of philosophy.

In addition to the above disclaimers it should also be noted that the discussion has entirely neglected Popper's writings on the philosophy of *social science*: his so-called 'situational analysis' approach to social science.[18] This method, the method of explaining the behaviour of a social agent on the basis of the logic of the agent's situation and the 'rationality principle', was proposed by Popper as a result of 'the logical investigation of economics' and it provides a method 'which can be applied to all social science' (Popper 1976a: 102). It is often argued that the rationality principle is in conflict with Popper's falsificationist standards,[19] but regardless of how one views this controversy, the point here is simply to note that none of the above criticisms automatically transfer to Popper's work on situational analysis.

The task of this chapter was narrowly defined: to evaluate falsificationism and the MSRP as a methodology – as a tool for choosing between/among economic theories/research programmes. It has been argued that Popperian philosophy should be negatively appraised in this respect, it does not say that economists have nothing to learn from the Popperian tradition.

NOTES

1 Helpful comments on an earlier draft were received from a number of people; in particular I would like to mention Bruce Caldwell, Christian Knudsen, Uskali Mäki, and Jorma Sappinen. Partial support for the research was provided by University of Puget Sound Martin Nelson Award MNSA-4489 and portions of the argument also appear in Hands (1992). The recent article by Caldwell (1991) also provides an excellent discussion of these issues.

2 Blaug (1976, 1991), Cross (1982), de Marchi (1976), Diamond (1988), Fisher

(1986), Fulton (1984), Glass and Johnson (1988), Hands (1985b), Latsis (1972, 1976b), Maddock (1984), and Weintraub (1985a,b, 1988), is a partial list of the work on Lakatosian economics. A more complete list is contained in Hands (1985b) and (1992).

3 The expression 'basic statement' has a rather narrow interpretation in Popperian philosophy. The concept was introduced in chapter V of Popper (1959) and it is nicely summarized in Watkins (1984: 247–54).

4 Actually, as will be discussed below, scientific theories are not *by themselves* logically falsifiable. Rather, scientific theories along with (usually numerous) auxiliary hypotheses may form logically falsifiable *test systems* (see Hausman 1988: 68–9).

5 There are a number of different types of *ad hocness* in Popperian philosophy; these are discussed in detail in Hands (1988). The type of *ad hocness* considered here, modification solely to avoid falsification, is called $ad\ hoc_1$. Popper developed his notion of independent testability to avoid this type of *ad hocness* ($ad\ hoc_1ness$). Another notion of *ad hocness* is $ad\ hoc_2ness$; a theoretical modification is non $ad\ hoc_2$ if some of the independently testable implications actually get corroborated. A third type of *ad hocness* ($ad\ hoc_3ness$) was developed more fully by Lakatos. *Non-ad hoc_3ness* is equivalent to Lakatosian heuristic progress.

6 The main sources for this list of criticisms are Caldwell (1984), Hausman (1985, 1988), Latsis (1976b), and Salanti (1987).

7 The Duhemian problem (Duhem 1954) arises because theories are never tested alone, rather they are tested in conjunction with certain auxiliary hypotheses (including those about the data). Thus if T is the theory, the prediction of evidence e is given by $T \cdot A => e$, where A is the set of auxiliary hypotheses. The conjunction $T \cdot A$ forms a test system and the observation of 'not e' implies 'not $(T \cdot A)$' rather than simply 'not T'; the test system is falsified, not necessarily the theory. The Duhemian problem is a standard issue in the philosophy of theory testing but it has only recently been recognized as an issue for economic methodology (see Cross 1982, for instance).

8 Experimental economics is still too young to tell whether it can substantially improve this situation. For a general discussion of the methodological implications of the literature on experimental economics see Roth (1986), and Smith (1982, 1985).

9 Popper (1965: 42, 267, 387–8; 1959: 43–4, 93–5, 97–111; 1983: 185–6).

10 This is one source of the 'innocuous falsification' mentioned by Blaug (1980: 128, 259) and Coddington (1975: 542–45). The problem of such qualitative (or generic) predictions is discussed in detail in Rosenberg (1989).

11 Popper's most important writings on verisimilitude are contained in Popper (1965) and (1972). Useful discussions of the topic are presented in Koertge (1979), Radnitzky (1982), and Watkins (1984). The question of the relationship between Popperian verisimilitude and economic methodology is examined in more detail in Hands (1991).

12 These concepts are discussed in detail with appropriate references to Popper's writings in Hands (1988). Other general discussions of these Popperian concepts include Dilworth (1986), Koertge (1979), Watkins (1978, 1984), and Worrall (1978).

13 Many summaries of the MSRP are available in the economics literature (Blaug (1980), Hands (1985a), Pheby (1988), and Weintraub

(1985a, 1985b, 1988) for example) but the single best presentation of the argument remains Lakatos (1970). As with Popper's falsificationism, only a sketch of the main argument is provided here.

14 The definition of 'novel fact' has been much discussed in the Lakatosian (and Popperian) literature. See Carrier (1988), Gardner (1982), Hands (1985b) and Worrall (1978) on the different notions of novelty.

15 'A general definition of science thus must reconstruct the acknowledgedly best gambits as "scientific:" if it fails to do so, it has to be rejected' (Lakatos 1971: 111).

16 Particularly Blaug (1991), Maddock (1984), and Weintraub (1988), though even here it depends on the exact definition of novelty one uses.

17 In addition to those mentioned in note 16, Cross (1982), de Marchi (1976) and Latsis (1972, 1976b) should be added to this list.

18 Popper's clearest writings on situational analysis are (1976a) and (1985); also see Hands (1985a, 1992) and Langlois and Csontos (this volume).

19 According to Popper's situational analysis view of social science, the action of an individual agent is explained by describing the 'situation' the agent is in (their preferences, beliefs, constraints, etc.) and the 'rationality principle' that all agents act appropriately (rationally) given their situation. The potential problem arises because the rationality principle serves as the universal law in such scientific 'explanations' and yet it is not clear that the rationality principle is (even potentially) falsifiable as Popper the falsificationist would require for the laws used in any valid scientific explanation. This is one of the reasons that Popper$_n$ (Popper the falsificationist) was distinguished from Popper$_s$ (Popper the philosopher of situational analysis) in Hands (1985a).

REFERENCES

Blaug, M. (1976) 'Kuhn versus Lakatos, or paradigms versus research programmes in the history of economics', in S.J. Latsis (ed.) *Method and Appraisal in Economics*, Cambridge: Cambridge University Press, pp. 149–80.

—— (1980) *The Methodology of Economics*, Cambridge: Cambridge University Press.

—— (1987) 'Ripensamenti sulla rivduzione Keynesiana', *Rassegna Economica*, 51: 605–34.

—— (1991) 'Second thoughts on the Keynesian revolution', *History of Political Economy* 23: 171–92 (English translation of Blaug 1987).

Caldwell, B.J. (1982) *Beyond Positivism: Economic Methodology in the Twentieth Century*, London: Allen & Unwin.

—— (1984) 'Some problems with falsificationism in economics', *Philosophy of the Social Sciences* 14: 489–95.

—— (1991) 'Clarifying Popper', *Journal of Economic Literature* 29: 1–33.

Carrier, M. (1988) 'On novel facts: a discussion of criteria for non-ad-hocness in the methodology of scientific research programmes', *Zeitschrift für Allgemeine Wissenschaftstheorie* 19: 205–31.

Coddington, A. (1975) 'The rationale of general equilibrium theory', *Economic Inquiry* 13: 539–58.

Cross, R. (1982) 'The Duhem–Quine thesis, Lakatos, and the appraisal of theories in macroeconomics', *Economic Journal* 92: 320–40.

de Marchi, N. (1976) 'Anomaly and the development of economics: the case of the Leontief paradox', in S.J. Latsis (ed.) *Method and Appraisal in Economics*, Cambridge: Cambridge University Press, pp. 109–27.

—— (ed.) (1988) *The Popperian Legacy in Economics*, Cambridge: Cambridge University Press.

Diamond, A.M., Jr. (1988) 'The empirical progressiveness of the general equilibrium research program', *History of Political Economy* 20: 119–35.

Dilworth, C. (1986) *Scientific Progress: A Study Concerning the Nature of the Relations Between Successive Scientific Theories*, second edition, Dordrecht, Netherlands: D. Reidel.

Duhem, P. (1954) *The Aim and Structure of Physical Theory*, (translated by P.P. Wiener), Princeton, New Jersey: Princeton University Press.

Fisher, F.M. (1986) *The Logic of Economic Discovery*, Washington Square, New York: New York University Press.

Fulton, G. (1984) 'Research programmes in economics', *History of Political Economy* 16: 187–205.

Gardner, M.R. (1982) 'Predicting novel facts', *British Journal for the Philosophy of Science* 33: 1–15.

Gellner, E. (1974) *Legitimation of Belief*, Cambridge: Cambridge University Press.

Glass, J.C. and Johnson, W. (1988) 'Metaphysics, MSRP and economics', *British Journal for the Philosophy of Science* 39: 313–29.

Hands, D.W. (1985a) 'Karl Popper and economic methodology: *A New Look*', *Economics and Philosophy* 1: 83–99.

—— (1985b) 'Second thoughts on Lakatos', *History of Political Economy* 17: 1–16.

—— (1988) 'Ad hocness in economics and the Popperian tradition', in de Marchi, N. (ed.) *The Popperian Legacy in Economics and Beyond*, Cambridge: Cambridge University Press, pp. 121–37.

—— (1991) 'The problem of excess content: economics, novelty and a long Popperian Tale', in N. de Marchi and M. Blaug (eds) *Appraising Economic Theories*, Aldershot: Edward Elgar 58–75.

—— (1992) 'Falsification, situational analysis and scientific research programs: the Popperian tradition in economic methodology', in N. de Marchi (ed.) *Post-Popperian Methodology of Economics*, Boston: Kluwer.

Hausman, D.M. (1985) 'Is falsificationism unpracticed or unpracticable?', *Philosophy of the Social Sciences* 15: 313–19.

—— (1988) 'An appraisal of Popperian economic methodology', in de Marchi, N. (ed.) *The Popperian Legacy in Economics and Beyond*, Cambridge: Cambridge University Press, 65–85.

Hutchison, T.W. (1938) *The Significance and Basic Postulates of Economic Theory*, London: Macmillan (reprinted, 1960, New York: Augustus M. Kelley).

—— (1988) 'The case for falsificationism', in de Marchi, N. (ed.) *The Popperian Legacy in Economics and Beyond*, Cambridge: Cambridge University Press, pp. 169–81.

Koertge, N. (1979) 'The problems of appraising scientific theories', in P.D. Asquith and H.E. Kyburg, Jr. (eds) *Current Research in Philosophy of Science*, East Lansing, Michigan: Philosophy of Science Association, pp. 228–251.

Kuhn, T.S. (1970) *The Structure of Scientific Revolutions*, second edition, Chicago: University of Chicago Press. (First edition 1962, Chicago: University of Chicago Press.)

Lakatos, I. (1970) 'Falsification and the methodology of scientific research programmes', in I. Lakatos and A. Musgrave (eds) *Criticism and the Growth of Knowledge*, Cambridge: Cambridge University Press, pp. 91–196.

—— (1971) 'History of science and its rational reconstructions', in R.C. Buck and R.S. Cohen (eds) *Boston Studies in the Philosophy of Science*, Vol. 8, Dordrecht, Netherlands: D. Reidel, pp. 91–136.

Latsis, S.J. (1972) 'Situational determinism in economics', *British Journal for the Philosophy of Science* 23: 207–45.

—— (ed.) (1976a) *Method and Appraisal in Economics*, Cambridge: Cambridge University Press.

—— (1976b) 'A research programme in economics', in S.J. Latsis (ed.) *Method of Appraisal in Economics*, Cambridge: Cambridge University Press, pp. 1–41.

McCloskey, D. (1985) *The Rhetoric of Economics*, Madison Wisconsin: University of Wisconsin Press.

Maddock, R. (1984) 'Rational expectations macrotheory: A Lakatosian case study in program adjustment', *History of Political Economy* 16: 291–309.

Pheby, J. (1988) *Methodology and Economics: A Critical Introduction*, London: Macmillan.

Popper, K.R. (1959) *The Logic of Scientific Discovery*, London: Hutchinson.

—— (1965) *Conjectures and Refutations*, second edition, New York: Harper & Row.

—— (1970) 'Normal science and its Dangers', in I. Lakatos and A. Musgrave (eds) *Criticism and the Growth of Knowledge*, Cambridge: Cambridge University Press, pp. 51–8.

—— (1972) *Objective Knowledge: An Evolutionary Approach*, Oxford: Oxford University Press.

—— (1976a) 'The logic of the social sciences', in T.W. Adorno et al. (eds) *The Positivist Dispute in German Sociology*, (translated by G. Adey and D. Frisby), New York: Harper & Row, pp. 87–104.

—— (1976b) *Unended Quest*, La Salle, Illinois: Open Court.

—— (1983) *Realism and the Aim of Science*, (edited by W.W. Bartley III) Totowa, New Jersey: Rowman & Littlefield.

—— (1985) 'The rationality principle', in D. Miller (ed.) *Popper Selections*, Princeton: Princeton Universtiy Press, pp. 357–65.

Radnitzky, G. (1982) 'Knowing and guessing: if all knowledge is conjectural, can we then speak of cognitive progress? on persistent misreading of Popper's work', *Zeitschrift für Allgemeine Wissenschafstheorie* 8: 110–21.

Rosenberg, A. (1989) 'Are generic predictions enough?', *Erkenntnis* 30: 43–68.

Roth, A.E. (1986) 'Laboratory experimentation in economics', *Economics and Philosophy* 2: 245–73.

Salanti, A. (1987) 'Falsificationism and fallibilism as epistemic foundations of economics: a critical view', *Kyklos* 40: 368–92.

Smith, V.L. (1982) 'Microeconomic systems as an experimental science', *American Economic Review* 72: 923–55.

—— (1985) 'Experimental economics: reply', *American Economic Review* 75: 265–72.

Watkins, J. (1978) 'The Popperian approach to scientific knowledge', in G. Radnitzky and G. Anderson (eds) *Progress and Rationality in Science*, Dordrecht, Netherlands: D. Reidel, pp. 23–43.

—— (1984) *Science and Skepticism*, Princeton, New Jersey: Princeton University Press.

Weintraub, E.R. (1985a) 'Appraising general equilibrium analysis', *Economics and Philosophy* 1: 23–37.

—— (1985b) *General Equilibrium Analysis: Studies in Appraisal*, Cambridge: Cambridge University Press.

—— (1988) 'The NeoWalrasian program is empirically progressive', in de Marchi, N. (ed.) *The Popperian Legacy in Economics and Beyond*, Cambridge: Cambridge University Press.

Worrall, J. (1978) 'The ways in which the methodology of scientific research programmes improves on Popper's methodology', in G. Radnitzky and G. Anderson (eds) *Progress and Rationality in Science*, Dordrecht, Netherlands: D. Reidel, pp. 45–70.

4

SOCIAL THEORIES OF SCIENCE AND THE FATE OF INSTITUTIONALISM IN ECONOMICS[1]

Uskali Mäki

INTRODUCTION

In this chapter I discuss, in a tentative and partly speculative fashion, a perspective on science which should be found appealing by institutionalist economists. The simple idea is to view science as a social institution. I will discuss a few rudimentary theoretical accounts of science as an irreducibly social or institutional entity and point out some possible implications of this insight for understanding the fate of institutionalist thought in economics.

I imagine there are institutionalist economists who would be prepared to argue that (1) their theoretical constructions are more adequate than those of neoclassical orthodoxy if measured in terms of their relative scientific merits, especially those related to how theories fit the empirical realities of contemporary economies. Despite this, they would be forced to admit that (2) neoclassical theory is more popular, being more widely accepted and practised. As an explanation of this some institutionalists might feel tempted to maintain that (3) there are irrational or immoral factors in play such as intellectual dogmatism or ideological distortion or false images of science which lend support to the reign of the neoclassical orthodoxy. Of these three imagined claims, (2) is the least problematic. Claims (1) and (3) are both unclear and controversial. A committed neoclassical economist would deny them both and argue that, unlike traditional forms of institutionalism, (3′) neoclassical theory is an exemplification of scientific rigour and rationality (or at least the best available approximation thereof) and therefore deserves the mainstream status that it actually enjoys.

Both claims (3) and (3′) might be false. The correct explanation might be much more complicated. In what follows I discuss some conceptual tools and theoretical ideas which might be usefully employed in a project for constructing a more adequate meta-theoretical account of the

76

situation in economics. Such an account would involve a systematic social theory of economics as a scientific discipline, citing various social factors and processes as conditioning whatever it is that takes place in economics. The approach gives an idea of how economists' beliefs might be formed without being either entirely constrained by empirical evidence or determined by irrationality or immorality. There might be a third way between narrow empiricist rationality and vicious irrationality. This approach is not devoid of problems, however. The main problem that motivates the considerations to follow is that we do not yet have an analysis of explanations having (aspects of) economics as the *explananda* and social factors as the *explanantia*.

The literature on the sociology or social theory of science is both vast and conceptually hazy. The literature on the sociology of economics is very scarce and also often conceptually obscure.[2] Both build upon often radical philosophical presuppositions but leave them more or less unscrutinized. Keeping these facts in mind I propose to do the following in this chapter: first, to provide a partial analytical survey of some aspects of a selected set of recent social theories of science with an eye on their implied views of precisely what the social conditioning of science amounts to. Second, as an illustration of these theories or some of their aspects, I mention some attempted accounts and provide a few unelaborated hunches concerning the fate of institutionalism in economics with a focus on how and why economic theories are suggested, accepted, rejected, generated, revised, taken seriously, neglected, etc. Third, related to these aspects of the scientific endeavour, I point out some of the critical implications of the social theories of science regarding traditional methodologies of economics, particularly the Popperian versions.

To reveal a fragment of my own meta-theoretical preferences, I subscribe to two limiting perspectives on an acceptable account of science: on the one hand, asocial or weakly social theories of science constitute the Scylla, whereas antirealist relativisms will be taken as the Charybdis, both to be avoided in making admissions about the social conditioning of science. The standard readings of the Popperian tradition exemplify the former, while some social theories of science dealt with in the present essay incorporate the latter. As I point out towards the end of the essay, in most cases this incorporation is not necessary.

THE RATIONAL AND THE SOCIAL

There is a realm of pure scientific rationality postulated in the philosophies of science such as those of Karl Popper, Imre Lakatos, and Larry Laudan. The idea gets expression in some traditional dichotomies. Hans Reichenbach's distinction between the context of discovery and the context of justification is one of these. For Popper, only the latter is characterized by systematic rationality, while the discovery process is open to various non-rational and contingent influences the workings of which cannot be systematized philosophically, but should be studied by sociology, psychology, even political science. Lakatos draws the distinction between internal and external history of science, where the former is an autonomous realm governed by the rules of rationality, suitable for philosophical generalization, while the latter is a sort of irrational residue caused by contingent factors amenable to psychological and sociological description.

For Popper, Lakatos, and Laudan, rational acceptances, rejections and transitions are phenomena in need of no explanation by recourse to social factors. The task of the sociology of scientific knowledge is restricted to explaining deviations from the rational course of events. From such a 'rationalist' point of view, Laudan puts the scope of the sociological approach succinctly:

> When a thinker does what it is rational to do, we need inquire no further into the causes of his action; whereas, when he does what is in fact irrational – even if he believes it to be rational – we require some further sociological explanation. . . . Whenever, for instance, a scientist *accepts* a research tradition which is less adequate than a rival, whenever a scientist *pursues* a theory which is non-progressive, whenever a scientist gives greater or lesser *weight* to a problem or an anomaly than it cognitively deserves, whenever a scientist chooses between two equally adequate or equally progressive research traditions; in all these cases, we must look to the sociologist (or the psychologist) for understanding, since there is no possibility of a rational account of the action in question.
>
> (Laudan 1977: 188–9, 222)

As can be seen, the diagnosis of the situation in economics given by our imaginary institutionalist economist at the beginning of this chapter comes very close to this idea: given the rules of scientific rationality, economists should prefer institutionalist theories to those of the neoclassical orthodoxy; but since most economists do not have this preference ordering, their beliefs and behaviour are irrational and as such amenable to sociological explanation.

On the opposing side in the issue about the proper relationship between the rational and the social, there are those contemporary social theorists of science who think that science is irreducibly social all down the line and that the rational and the social are not mutually exclusive attributes. They argue that there is no dividing line between the social and the asocial that would overlap with that between the rational and the irrational. All beliefs are socially caused or constituted. As Barnes and Bloor argue:

All beliefs are on a par with one another with respect to the [social] causes of their credibility. . . . The incidence of all beliefs without exception calls for empirical investigation and must be accounted for by finding the specific, local causes of this credibility. This means that regardless of whether the sociologist evaluates a belief as true or rational, or as false and irrational, he must search for the causes of its credibility.

(Barnes and Bloor 1982: 23)

This also calls the Reichenbachian distinction into question. From the point of view of the social theories of science, a sharp distinction between the non-rational context of discovery and the rational context of justification is itself not justified drawing. As Knorr-Cetina points out:

Whether a proposed knowledge claim is judged plausible or implausible, interesting, unbelievable or nonsensical, may depend upon *who* proposed the result, *where* the work was done, and *how* it was accomplished. . . . Thus, the scientific community itself lends crucial weight to the context of discovery in response to a knowledge claim.

(Knorr-Cetina 1981: 7)

It would not be surprising to find ample evidence for this statement applied to economics.

FROM UNDER-DETERMINATION BY DATA TO SOCIAL CONDITIONING

The standard textbook view of the methodology of economics (encompassing several possible specified versions) depicts the acceptance and rejection of economic theories as ruled by deductive and/or inductive logic, incontrovertible empirical evidence, and strict methodological rules. On a simple version of this view, the rational acceptance and rejection of economic theories is determined by empirical data. As many commentators have pointed out, economists do not behave in the way prescribed by the standard view. Mark Blaug (1980), for instance, makes this observation, and also insists that economists should behave according to the falsificationist prescriptions, to which, after all, they themselves subscribe in their own methodological declarations.

Neither Blaug nor many others have shown what in fact takes place in economics and why. They have shown that economists do not behave in certain ways and that the theories they espouse do not satisfy certain requirements. However, this is not yet *to explain why economists do not behave in the prescribed way, or to describe how economists do in fact behave, or to explain why they behave in the way they do and why their theories have the characteristics they do.* Social theories of science may have some contribution to make in trying to answer these questions. On the other hand the Popperian tradition has to a large extent lost its momentum since it is regarded as descriptively too inadequate and therefore unable to provide answers to the above questions.

A minimal ground for a descriptive approach based on social theories of science is the following. Critical work in the philosophy of science and on the textbook view of economic methodology has pointed out the possibility of logically incompatible but empirically equivalent theories, that is, there is an infinitely large number of logically possible theories which are compatible with given empirical data. In other words, economic and any other theories are *under-determined by empirical evidence*. The choice of a theory from among the set of logical possibilities is not determined by available evidence. This implies that there is room for other determinants, or, rather, constraints or conditioners. This last claim can be formulated more strongly. The under-determination thesis says that data and logic fail to constrain the scientist to a unique decision as to the acceptance or rejection of a given theory. Since we know that such decisions are in fact being made, we have to admit that other constraints *must* creep in, if we do not want to think of the process as a random one. Various social factors are among the possible additional (or sole) constraints or conditioners. It is the purpose of this chapter to enquire what some of these factors may be and how they may influence economics.

The same conclusion can be supported by evoking the Duhem–Quine thesis. It says that every hypothesis under test involves a whole range of other assumptions and that therefore empirical tests cannot be conclusive. In the case of a negative test result, the hypothesis under test can be saved from falsification by revising some of those auxiliary assumptions. For instance, tests of the hypothesis of the stability of the demand for money failed to settle the issue between the monetarists and the Keynesians since the tests involved a large number of manipulable auxiliary assumptions (see Cross 1982). What the Duhem–Quine thesis shows us is that there is no logical necessitation of theory by statements of empirical evidence. Neither strict verification nor strict falsification of theory by empirical tests is forthcoming. While this is not yet to prove that theoretical beliefs are necessarily socially determined, it nevertheless indicates the logical possibility of social determination or conditioning. Whether this possibility is actualized in the world of science is a question to be settled in an empirical way. First we have to clarify the substantive nature of the possibility itself.

'SCIENCE IS SOCIALLY CONDITIONED'

To hold the view that science is a social institution does not yet fix one's ideas in a clear and unique fashion. I approach the clarification of the possible contents of the view by rephrasing it as the statement that *science is socially conditioned*. This encompasses the notions of science being socially shaped and constituted, socially constrained and enabled, socially determined and organized, and so on. The statement, 'science is socially conditioned', is, as such, multiply ambiguous. For the sake of clarification, three questions have to be answered. First, what is the object of conditioning? That is, how should we characterize the notion of science, including economics and its aspects? Second, what is the subject of conditioning? In other words, what is the character and forms of the social? Third, what is the relationship between the subject and the object like? Precisely how is science conditioned by the social?

In regard to the term *'science'*, a major distinction can be made between viewing science as *a body of knowledge* and science as *a process of action*, ending up with something that may be regarded as knowledge. Further divisions can then be drawn within these two categories. This endeavour results in a set of concepts each of which characterizes what may be called an *aspect of science*.

In clarification of the attribute *'social'*, we may say that entities (things, states, events, processes, systems, etc.) are minimally social if they 'invariably involve more than one individual, and . . . normally involve individuals at variance with one another in relevant respects' (Knorr-Cetina 1983: 117). This gives a possible minimal specification for the intension of the term 'social'.

As to the extension of the term, I condense the range of its application into three realms. First, we may refer to the social as an attribute of the contents of elements *within individual scientists' actions*; that is, their goals and beliefs about means, and so on. For instance, scientists may have social states or processes as their goals, manifesting itself in things such as careerism, pursuit of power, moral responsibility for the underdog, or concern for the efficient workings of the economy. Second, the property of being social may be attributed to elements *within scientific communities*. The set of such social elements comprises research traditions and paradigms, norms of action and networks of communication, structure of authority and power, etc. (I do not want to subscribe to strong presumptions about the existence and nature of such communities; it is sufficient to assume that scientists communicate with each other, have power over one another, etc.) Third, the term 'social' is very often taken as denoting social, political, and economic structures and interests, cultural meanings and norms, and other similar matters *within society at large*.

These three categories should not be taken as excluding each other; rather, they are often interdependent. For example, social factors in the second and third senses can have an influence on economics only by somehow affecting or entering into individual economists' actions, and processes such as the institutionalization and professionalization of economics belong to more than one of these realms of the social.

The remaining element in the phrase, 'social conditioning of science' is *'conditioning'*. I have chosen the term deliberately so as to suggest a degree of generality and neutrality of the concept. It depicts the ways in which social factors determine, enable, constrain, enter, or influence aspects of science. Here I am going to be content with distinguishing between two broad categories of conditioning: causation and constitution. In the case of *causation*, the conditioning entity brings about an aspect or feature in the conditioned entity. In the case of *constitution*, the conditioning entity 'enters' the conditioned entity as its constituent or aspect. When considering some of the existing social theories of science, it might seem that the list should be left open so as to include analogy, correlation, functional dependence, and other such relations. I refrain from doing so because they, analogy and correlation in particular, are problematic as forms of conditioning.[3]

A framework within which various views of the social conditioning of science in general and economics in particular could be discussed could be constructed along these lines. The question to be answered within such a framework concerns *the numerous ways in which several kinds of social factors can condition different aspects of science.*

Among others, these three conceptions of social conditioning of science can be formulated within the framework:

1 The goals of scientists' actions are social states or processes (such as credibility or reputation and their growth). Here the social constitutes an aspect of science.
2 The justification of scientific theories is a social process of negotiation and rhetorical persuasion within scientific communities. Again, the social constitutes an aspect of science.
3 The contents of accepted theory (or of its metaphysical presuppositions) is caused (in an unspecified way) by social factors (such as social interests external to science). Here the social causally generates an aspect of science, namely the propositional contents of knowledge claims.

These three conceptions can be revealed as underlying some recent sociologies or social theories of science. Statements (1) and (2) can be found in the so-called ethnographic and constructivist approaches and elsewhere, amongst people like Bruno Latour, Steven Woolgar, Karin Knorr-Cetina and others. Together with other considerations, statement (3) is characteristic of the so-called strong programme of the Edinburgh School, comprising Barry Barnes, David Bloor, Steven Shapin and others. I will discuss each of the three conceptions as a hypothetical explanatory scheme, using a presumed fact about economics as an illustrative *explanandum*.[4]

THE *EXPLANANDUM*

To illustrate some of the insights of the social theories of science, I now formulate an unashamedly simplified idea of a complex phenomenon in need of explanation. The *explanandum* is a simple ranking order between three streams of economic thought, namely 'narrow neoclassical economics', the 'new institutionalist economics' and the 'old institutionalist economics'. To give very rough characterizations, neoclassical economics in the narrow sense consists of formal modelling with constrained optimization, given preferences and a focus on equilibrium states instead of processes and institutions. People like Paul Samuelson and Gerard Debreu have contributed to this stream. The new institutionalist theories variously share some of the traditional neo-classical concepts and commitments but reject or modify some others and, in particular, are emphatically focused on aspects of institutions. Ronald Coase, Harold Demsetz, Oliver Williamson, Douglass North, Richard Nelson, Sidney Winter, James Buchanan and Friedrich Hayek can be mentioned as some of the well-known representatives of this heterogenous stream. We may say that combined with narrow neoclassicism, some of the contributions from this stream constitute neoclassical economics in a broad sense. (For short, I will often use 'neoclassicism' for narrow neoclassicism.) Finally, the old institutionalist economics rejects the major neoclassical convictions and pursues an account of the institutional structure and evolution of the economy on a non-neoclassical basis. The works of people like Thorstein Veblen, John Commons, Wesley Mitchell, and Clarence Ayres belong to this stream.[5]

The relative positions of the three streams in the ranking are intuitively measured in such social terms as popularity, prestige, and academic power. The suggested ranking order is this: narrow neoclassicism ranks highest, the new institutionalist economics comes next, whereas the old institutionalist economics ranks lowest. Let us formulate the *explanandum* in this way:

[E] There is a social ranking order in economics between three streams of thought which tends to persist: narrow neo-classical economics – the new institutionalist economics – the old institutionalist economics.

Of course, [E] states a radically stylized fact. It abstracts and aggregates. It ignores internal heterogeneity and fluid boundaries. It suggests depicting a state of affairs which may be temporary and short-lived. Yet, I suppose [E] is or at least some time ago used to be familiar and acceptable as a factual statement to most economists. It is also found puzzling by many of them, but good, theoretically systematic explanations do not abound.

Thus formulated, it is clear that an aspect of the *explanandum* is the existence and power of narrow neoclassicism itself. In other words, in order to be able to explain the relative position in the ranking order of the two or more institutionalisms we have to understand why a certain stream of economic thought enjoys a mainstream position. (The usage of economists is nowadays often to refer to broad neoclassicism as the mainstream.)

Our task is to see how [E] might be explained on the basis of the three specifications of the statement that science is socially conditioned. We get three types of attempted explanations. One cites economists' pursuit of social facts in a market of ideas as a constituent of economics. Among other things, we will discuss the implications of taking academic credibility as the goal of economists. The second explanation cites rhetorical processes of persuasion as constituting justification within economics. This involves rhetorical and methodological conventions incorporating the advisable vocabulary and argumentative structure, the dominant image of scientific theory and modelling strategy; these serve as entry conditions to the market. The third explanation cites social facts external to economics as causes of economists' beliefs. Here we may try to refer to the search for social legitimacy by the economics profession and to the cosmological commitments involved in economic theories, in particular individualism and holism as visions of the constitution of society. In regard to such presumed facts, the three streams of economic thought are both similar and dissimilar in ways that may be helpful for explanatory purposes, that is, for the three *schemata* of social explanation to do their work.

It is important to understand that the hypothetical explanations to be suggested for [E] are bound to be incomplete. There is the formal shortcoming that the explanatory arguments formulated are enthymemes: they are logically incomplete reasonings in that not all necessary premises and steps in the arguments will be spelled out. A substantive incompleteness is due to the fact that the set of suggested explanatory factors is severely limited in each argument, a situation familiar to economists. Each of the hypothetical explanatory schemes is radically partial; they might, at best, throw some light on a restricted aspect of the fact stated in [E]. First, we can hope to explain a social order only, not an epistemic ranking order. Second, we have to be content with attempted explanations of the persistence of the ranking order, not of how it came into being in the first place. Third, the hypothetical explanations can claim to imply statements of tendencies at most. The explanatory question is this: *Why is it that the social ranking order tends to persist?*

In the course of the following speculations, I will make remarks about some of the problems and limitations of the three schemes. It will be shown how some of these limitations might be overcome by making the three schemes complement one another, but gaps remain to be filled and obscurities clarified in future research.

PURSUIT OF SOCIAL GOALS IN A MARKET

One conception of science that has recently gained some popularity is based on empirical investigations and on an economic analogy. The empirical orientation is exemplified in the so-called ethnographic approach. Like anthropologists studying alien tribes, some social theorists of science have approached scientific work as participant observers, interpreting their findings, for instance, of the life of biochemists in a laboratory. On the other hand, some of the resulting conceptions of science are built upon loose analogies drawn from economic visions of the market. The institution of science is viewed as analogous to a capitalist market economy in which the agents are competitive producers who pursue their self-interest by endeavouring to produce and sell whatever they believe there is demand for among the community of scientists or in the society at large. The goal is to maximize an asset, such as what Latour and Woolgar in their *Laboratory Life* (1986 [1979]) call *credibility*. This specific notion of credibility is indebted to Bourdieu's (1975) notion of scientific *credit* which denotes a kind of symbolic capital, a combination of scientific competence and social authority. It is symbolic because it is immaterial in nature, and is exemplified in the use of language and the creation of ideas. It has the character of capital because it can be converted into new resources (research positions, financial resources, technical facilities, etc.).

Credibility is a resource that can be cashed in. Scientists are viewed as maximizers who invest their energies in the research fields, topics, and techniques which they anticipate will yield the best return. The credibility they acquire by doing so leads to new rewards such as research grants, titles, honours, publications accepted, and so on. These, in turn, generate more credibility. The ensuing process of what Latour and Woolgar (1986, Ch. 5) call the *cycle of credibility* constitutes the ultimate dynamic of science. The action of scientists so characterized does not constitute a Popperian process of bold conjectures and critical refutations nor a Lakatosian process of progressive research pro- grammes, guided by the acknowledgement of corroborated novelty.

The focus of the credibility model is on scientists' actions. There are two important senses in which scientists' action is here understood as being socially conditioned. First, the goal that scientists pursue, namely credibility, is a social property. One scientists's credibility is dependent for its existence and utility-yielding properties on other scientists in a social context. Second, action oriented towards achieving this goal is a process of social interaction among scientists. Participants in the market choose their strategies and tactics constrained by the anticipated and actual reactions of other scientists.

Here is a tentative suggestion of how the credibility model of scientists' action could be used for explaining the persistence of the ranking order stated in [E]:

[Cred] (1) All economists pursue maximum credibility *qua* economists.

(2) The acquisition and use of neoclassical qualifications yields the greatest amount of credibility to an economist, while action based on the old institutionalist economics yields the smallest amount of credibility; action based on the new institutionalist economics yields an outcome in between the two.

(3) Therefore, [E].

Given the way in which we characterized the ranking order in [E], it might seem that [Cred] is nothing but a tautology; [E] would appear to be implied in premise (2). However, this is not quite the case, since [Cred] provides a link between economists' actions and the ranking order, while this link is missing in [E]. Premise (2) is indeed particularly noteworthy, since it contains the idea that the ranking order already exists. This means that by linking the order to economists' actions [Cred] provides a hypothetical explanation of the persistence of the order. It also suggests an explanation of the persistence of one type of action, consisting of the acquisition of neoclassical qualifications and producing neoclassical research. The situation looks like one of mutual reinforcement. What counts as credible as the goal of economists' action is based on the ranking order, while the persistence of the ranking order is based on the reproductive activities of credibility-seeking economists. [Cred] thus suggests a mutually reinforcing relationship between economists' action and the ranking of streams of economic thought.

Several limitations of [Cred] can be pointed out. First, as already noted, it suggests an explanation of the persistence of the ranking order, but keeps silent about its origins. Second, it also says nothing about the potential for change in the ranking order. Third, it does not seem easily to accommodate the fact that the old institutionalist economics, or even the new institutionalist economics, survive at all. It is not [E] but an exclusive reign of narrow neoclassicism that seems to be implied by the premises. [Cred] faces these limitations because it excludes explanatory factors that would be needed for accounting for these other aspects of economics. Let us look at this more closely, beginning with the last-mentioned problem.

If the devotion to the neoclassical approach yields an economist the greatest amount of credibility, and if credibility is all that matters, why should anybody care to take institutionalist ideas seriously as part of a research agenda? A very partial answer to this would be to recall the capital-character of credibility and of the temporality and roundabout-ness of capital-using production. Keeping this in mind, the credibility model might be made quite forceful in explaining why an Arrow, equipped with a lot of credibility gathered though his generally acknow-ledged earlier contributions to highly-ranked neoclassical themes, immediately gets a wide hearing without a depreciation in his credibility when he writes about institutions, whereas a graduate student from a peripheral institute, with a novel (and what later may turn out to be an excellent) theory of institutions, has difficulties. Two problems remain. First, why is it that the credibility of an Arrow does not necessarily depreciate as a result of his excursions into the study of institutions? Second, why is it that a number of non-Arrows manage to survive as institutionalist economists, in particular as old institutionalists?

This puzzle is related to general problems about the notion of credibility. Latour and Woolgar do not have much to say about the nature of credibility as the entity to be maximized, nor about why scientists would be motivated in maximizing it, nor about how the sole concentration on credibility could be justified.

It has been suggested by Williams and Law (1980: 313) that: 'to view science as the disinterested search for credibility is, in its own way, as misleading as to view it as the disinterested search for truth'. They argue that science is more broadly social than suggested by the credibility model: calculations about credibility usually are moderated by the social context in which they take place, and these contexts are characterized by the presence of various non-credibility considerations. That is, considerations of credibility are shaped by a broader interactional order with contingent entanglements and commitments. 'Actors come to value their colleagues as friends, confidants or opponents. Time and effort are invested in these other involvements, public positions are adopted, and the network of side-bets grows and becomes constraining' (ibid., p. 313). While the market analogy of the credibility model depicts scientists' actions in terms of one social goal, these remarks characterize science in broader and more detailed socio-psychological terms.

It seems that some of these non-credibility factors can be used for explaining the survival of institutionalist thought in economics, in particular of the old variety. For one thing, the role of institutionalists as the opponents of standard neoclassical economics may not, after all, serve merely a negative function in regard to their survival. If opponents are valued as opponents, this role may sometimes serve a positive function in promoting survival. Secondly, the fellow-feelings among various groupings of institutionalists may contribute to the formation of viable traditions. The establishment of informal and formal networks, including scholarly organizations and publication outlets, helps strengthen the identity of non-neoclassical streams of economic thought.

A suggestion related to [Cred] is Peter Earl's (1983) 'behavioural model of economists' behaviour', specifically tailored to give an account of the situation in economics. It specifies the goal component of scientists' actions in terms of several sub-components, consisting of several kinds of psychic and monetary cost and return. The picture becomes richer than that given by Latour and Woolgar. Furthermore, unlike the latter, Earl is interested in the motivations underlying scientists' actions. Earl considers the academic economist's position as analogous to that of managers in business firms as conceptualized in a behavioural framework.

Earl's model represents scientists as having lexicographic preferences so that there choices are based on certain priorities rather than trade-offs among their goals. The set of goals that he thinks 'an academic economist will rank highly' includes predictive power, fame and prestige, high income and a certain lifestyle, a pleasant social, natural and academic environment, minimum effort and avoidance of anxiety (Earl 1983: 94). Most of these goals are social in character or are dependent on social matters.

The fate of ideas in economics is dependent on those goals. Earl argues that 'ideas find academic acceptance not necessarily because of their intrinsic scientific worth . . . but rather because they are saleable as tools which enable their users more easily to reach their goals' (ibid., p. 90). But the goals of economists presumably do not reside in a social vacuum. Earl takes a further step by making the point that the 'choice between theories ultimately rests on personal preferences and percep-tions, shaped as they are by predispositions, by upbringing in a social/ academic/economic context, and by the selectivity of cognitive processes' (ibid., p. 118). This statement contains not only the notion that some of the ends of economists' actions are social states and processes, but in addition the notion that the ends and means of economists' actions are influenced by social matters. This means that such action is doubly socially conditioned.

Earl argues that his model can be used to explain facts such as the reign of neoclassical equilibrium theorizing by referring to the alleged fact that economists 'will tend to be attracted by the leisure or promotion advantages that come from practising as a technically competent equili-brium theorist rather than attempting to swim agaist the tide as, say, a behavioural economist' (ibid., p. 101).

This insight applies directly to our case. Economists committing themselves to the old institutionalist economics are forced to swim against a higher tide than advocates of the new institutionalist economics.

They are often not generously rewarded for their efforts, and promotion advantages tend to be poor. They easily suffer from anxiety, and have to invest a lot of energy into justifying themselves as economists with minimum credibility. Advocates of the new institutionalist economics also swim against the tide but in their cases the tide is lower. Increasingly, they do not have to justify themselves as economists or suffer from anxiety. *Ceteris paribus*, they are promoted more easily than their fellow old institutionalists. Yet the problem remains of why there is institutionalist economics at all. Why would any economist wish to swim against the tide, higher or lower?

We can find some hints towards an answer in Earl's essay. When discussing the chances of economists of getting papers accepted for publication, he writes that 'anyone considering devoting effort to writing unorthodox papers must have high tolerance of anxiety and be willing to risk a failure to obtain professional approval' (ibid., p. 96). This suggests that economists are not equally insistent on avoiding anxiety and risking their careers. Those who are less so, are among the potential institutionalists. More generally, the reason why not all economists are attracted by neoclassical theory is that they are not all alike. Some economists find their aspirations satisfied within the institutionalist streams. Preferences simply are not identical across the economics profession. Therefore the following argument might be of some help in accounting for the existence of institutionalist economics: 'It will be rare for a body of thought to be perceived as dominating over its rivals in all of its characteristics. Because of this, the academic's own priority ranking, rather than any unanimously agreed logic of appraisal, has the final say in determining which theories she will accept' (p. 120).

This dissimilarity factor is supported by a market-level factor making room for non-orthodox economics, namely 'the presence of imperfections or a segmented market for academic contributions. Just as . . . slack allows financial and product markets to function in a relatively orderly manner conducive to risk taking, so slack in the academic "market" permits the survival, at least for a time, of maverick thinkers fascinated by particular ideas from which ultimately progress may come' (ibid., p. 99). The presence of slack is what a behavioural theory makes us expect. We may conclude that slack in the academic market also contributes to the survival of institutionalist streams of economic thought.

I pointed out that [Cred] is not suitable as such for explaining possible change in economists' beliefs. There is, of course, the familiar fact that change in economists' or any other scientists' fundamental opinions and orientations does not occur easily. Earl's framework can be used for accounting for this fact. Economists are not critical Popperians:

If an anomaly is discovered, information overloads are avoided by not asking difficult questions. A limited rule-guided search will

89

usually provide a way of coping with a difficulty without challenging fundamental questions . . . As long as [the rules] seem to be working and the scientist is able to meet her aspirations she will have no obvious reason to question them.

(Earl 1983: 101)

Economists are also too conservative and too much guided by their personal aspirations to be real Lakatosians.

If a switch to a new [scientific research programme] would have no positive career payoff, yet would involve an admission that she believes she has hitherto been foolishly wasting her time [thus hurting her self-image], the economist may carry on as before.

(Earl 1983: 103)

On the other hand, change in economists' beliefs is not entirely absent. This is evidenced, for example, by the increasing popularity of new institutionalist ideas within economics. How can scientific change be explained? The major point in Latour and Woolgar's credibility model and Earl's behavioural model is the alleged dependence of the acceptance and rejection of ideas on the social goals of scientists. Scientists make investments and expect returns in terms of credibility and other outcomes. Scientists tend to be committed to particular theories and techniques to the extent that they have made prior investments of time, effort, and money in the acquisition of the mastery of those theories and techniques. In the early stages of those prior investments it is relatively easier for a scientist to change beliefs and orientation, but once they become established in the form of institutions and traditions, a change will be more difficult.

However, change of beliefs should not be impossible. The credibility of scientists and the reseach groups they form is dependent on their continued ability to produce new marketable results. This ability depends on both the investments made and the demand in the market. This demand is not, of course, fixed and given. It is not independent of the marketing efforts of the producers of those results, but it is not completely determined by them either. There is fluctuation in the market value of research results.

Taking into account the fluctuation of this market, scientists invest their credibility where it is likely to be most rewarding. Their assessment of these fluctuations both explains scientists' reference to "interesting problems", "rewarding subjects", "good methods", and "reliable colleagues" and explains why scientists constantly move between problem areas, entering into new collaborative projects, grasping and dropping hypotheses as the circumstances demand, shifting between one method and another and submitting everything to the goal of extending the credibility cycle.

(Latour and Woolgar 1986: 206–7)

This suggests that scientists act as entrepreneurs, constantly in search of profitable opportunities (cf. Bellinger and Bergsten 1990). This picture implies that if the demand for or the marketability of a particular kind of scientific work decreases considerably, the only option available to a scientist wanting to stay in the business may be to change beliefs. Beliefs are or are not rejected depending on the cost of such rejection to the standing of the scientist or the research group.

The above statement by Latour and Woolgar depicting scientists as being constantly on the move, ready to shift to new problems and hypotheses almost frictionlessly, is problematic, and must be qualified. First, there is an element of friction in that the entrepreneurial activity of scientists is shaped by what we may call *credibility institutions*, that is the established rules and conventions, norms and arrangements that enable and constrain the production and reproduction of credibility. In economics, the credibility institutions comprise the tradition of powerful theoretical frameworks, an established hierarchy of sub-fields, journals and universities, standardized textbooks and curricula, and so on. The entrepreneurial pursuit of credibility takes place most of the time within the limits set by such institutions. Kuhn called such research 'normal science'. *Ceteris paribus*, a piece of research yields more credibility if it conforms to the credibility institutions than if it does not. More credibility is forthcoming from an article published in a journal closer to the top of the hierarchy of prestige. Credibility comes more easily if problems are switched within the established framework than if the problem of switching to a new framework is suggested. Research based on the integration of a new idea to the ruling theory with little or no revision in the latter is better for one's credibility than research based on or pursuing an entirely different theory. These are some of the other reasons for the higher ranking of the new institutionalist economics compared to the old one.

The second qualification is that Latour and Woolgar's statement may apply more accurately to biochemistry and management studies than to theoretical economics and more accurately to applied economics than to theoretical economics. It is, indeed, important to bear in mind that scientific disciplines are not alike in relevant respects (cf. Whitley 1984). In economics, the major element of institutional friction to intellectual movements comes from the powerful role of basic neoclassical theory, but it is clear that there is some room for reacting to changing circumstances by revising research questions and suggested answers in economics as well. One factor supporting this feature is the dependence

91

of economics on a wider social context. The credibility model represents science as a game that scientists play with their disciplinary colleagues in pursuit of credibility, while in fact the game is played with others as well, such as with journalists, with those who are interested in practical applications and with those who control important resources of research. The market of scientific work encompasses *trans-scientific arenas*, to use Knorr-Cetina's phrase (1981, 1982). Credibility is not merely created in the 'internal' market of science but also in the 'external' market of society in large. Disciplines differ here, too. Some scientific fields are more and some others are less dependent on success in the trans-scientific arena. Again, economics is less dependent than management research. Yet, it is not entirely independent. Some demand for new ideas comes from outside the discipline, in forms such as policy issues, and some of this demand is responded to.

Not all segments of economics are equally responsive to the movements of demand in the external market, the trans-scientific arena. Theoretical research is less so than applied or empirical research. Since external demand is relatively more varied, applied economics tends to be also more varied, thus often having room for and inspiring institutionalist ideas among others. At the same time, the applied sub-fields of economic research are relatively less prestigious than the sub-fields in economic theory, thus yielding less credibility to the practitioners (see Whitley 1984; 1986).

THE ROLE OF RHETORICAL CONVENTIONS IN JUSTIFICATION

The study of the use of language by scientists has been one of the preoccupations of the recent sociology of science. The underlying suggestion is that a major part or the whole of the linguistic behaviour of scientists consists of the use of language for the purpose of persuading audiences. This suggestion continues the old tradition of the study of rhetoric, with its domain today extended to cover science in addition to politics, the law courts and commercial marketing. In this usage, the term 'rhetoric' does not have its popular pejorative meaning, designating the ideas of deception or pretension, semantic depletion, or merely symbolic use of language or the like; in any case something that has to be avoided by serious scholars. Nor is rhetoric here understood in the narrow sense related to eloquence. Rhetoric is rather a matter of effectiveness, of bringing about changes in states of affairs; eloquence is often ineffective.

In the general sense relevant here, rhetoric is a matter of the exercise and study of how people use language and argument in order to persuade their audiences, the persuadees. Persuasion is a matter of influencing the intensity of the beliefs of a persuadee concerning an idea. The rhetorical perspective on science suggests that scientists construe and use arguments formulated in language in order to raise or lower the plausibility of statements as perceived by relevant audiences. To use an apt metaphor, scientists persuade each other to *buy* ideas. Arguing is marketing. The idea of scientific rhetoric is now well-established in the study of economics (see McCloskey 1985; Klamer *et al.* 1988; Samuels 1990; Henderson *et al.* 1992).

The credibility model also depicts scientists as marketing their skills and research products in the intellectual market. In the previous section we did not discuss the rhetorical means used for such marketing efforts. The present section goes some way to supplement the picture in this respect.

The means of persuasion are varied. They range from mathematical proofs to appeals to authority, from statistical tests to jokes, from the conformity to the commitments of a powerful tradition to the use of the latest fashionable jargon, from emotionally evocative metaphors to facial expressions. Usually only linguistic means are analysed by the students of rhetoric, but it should be clear that non-linguistic means play a role, too. Most importantly, the rhetorical insight implies that justification in science is not a matter of empirical evidence speaking for or against hypotheses through the channels of deductive or inductive logic. It is *scientists* who use evidence and logic and other means to speak for or against hypotheses. Evidence is mute; scientists speak. Justification is a matter of scientists exercising rhetorical persuasion.

Latour and Woolgar's study is an early example of this orientation. To them, scientific work is a form of writing; it is the production of what they call 'literary inscriptions'. Among the literary inscriptions are computer printout data sheets and tables of figures, curves and diagrams, working papers and published articles. Science builds upon the rhetorical use of language in social contexts, it is 'the organization of persuasion through literary inscription' (Latour and Woolgar 1986: 88). The recognition of this fact is not an established part of the self-image of science, hence the popularity among scientists of the pejorative usage of the term 'rhetoric'.

An interesting suggestion is that one of the purposes of rhetoric is to hide its own existence.

> The function of literary inscription is the successful persuasion of readers, but the readers are only fully convinced when all sources of persuasion seem to have disappeared. In other words, the various operations of writing and reading which sustain an argument are seen by participants to be largely irrelevant to 'facts', which emerge solely by virtue of these same operations.
>
> (Latour and Woolgar 1986: 76)

Justification in science is a rhetorical process whereby statements are gradually transformed from hotly contested conjectures to self-evident assertions of fact. In the process of increasing 'facticity' or of the establishment of statements as self-evident, all traces of authorship and the rhetorical background disappear. This is why the outcome is dependent on 'hiding' its process of origin. Scientificity is attained through what we might call *the rhetoric of decontextualization*. This is a major reason why the self-image of science tends to abhor the idea of science having a rhetorical dimension.

The rhetoric of decontextualization is what Latour and Woolgar have in mind when they suggest that the 'construction of facts' in science is a rhetorical process of gradual transformation of statements from speculative conjectures to uncontroversial facts. They separate five stages and the corresponding types of statements in this process (ibid., pp. 76–9). Each type of statement depicts a relation between some A and B, denoted by A•B. It is depicted with or without what Latour and Woolgar call 'modalities', that is, statements about statements about A•B. These modalities tend to disappear as the process evolves.

Type 1 statements are 'conjectures or speculations [about A•B] which appear most commonly at the end of papers, or in private discussions'. They are heavily modalized in that they accompany admissions of highly tentative character and subjective origin.

Type 2 statements are contentious claims which involve 'modalities which draw attention to the generality of available evidence (or the lack of it)' and which 'sometimes take the form of tentative suggestions usually oriented to further investigations'.

Type 3 statements depict established facts and often occur in review articles. They are modalized by references to literature, the merit of the author or dates and priority of discovery.

Type 4 statements are uncontroversial assertions of A•B without modalities. They typically appear in teaching texts.

Type 5 'statements' are part of the tacit system of shared beliefs of the members of a discipline or a laboratory. They denote taken-for-granted facts, but do it implicitly; relation A•B is not mentioned explicitly as in type 4 statements. No modalities appear either.

Latour and Woolgar then point out some of the operations related to the modification of the target statements and their modalities that are performed in the attempted transformation of statements from speculations to self-evident facts (ibid., pp. 81–6, 174–83). In this light, laboratory activity and scientific discourse in general appear as 'the organisation of persuasion through literary inscription' (ibid., p. 88; see also Latour 1987: 22–9).

This suggestion gives us an idea of one aspect of justification in science conceived as a rhetorical process. However, the above transformation model may mislead us to adopt a picture of scientific persuasion which would be less useful for our purposes since it lacks certain conceptual means. In this picture the alleged process of justification takes place in what might be called an *institutionally homogeneous rhetorical space*. Justification appears as a matter of credible scientists playing a rhetorical game according to shared rules in an accessible market. The game starts when all players have entered the field, and the transformation model can be used to follow the fate of each statement suggested by a participant. The fate of statements is determined by the rhetorical skills of their supporters and opponents. This picture of institutionally homogeneous rhetorical space omits various institutional constraints which may shape all stages of the process, including the entry to the market, also omitted in the above picture.

The postulation of institutionally homogeneous rhetorical space seems to be a feature of Donald McCloskey's approach to the rhetoric of economics. Most of the time he appears to posit a sort of perfect market of economic ideas, an idea of unrestricted conversation with free entry, shared rules of the game, and evenly distributed power. The idea of institutionalized entry conditions, to be emphasized in what follows, does not fit this image neatly. For this reason, his work does not seem to be particularly useful for understanding the fate of dissenting ideas in economics, one of the aims of our explanatory endeavours. (For criticisms of this aspect of McCloskey's work, see, for example Coats 1988, Mirowski 1987, Mäki 1992b.)

Let us see more closely how science might look through institutionally enriched rhetorical spectacles. It would seem fruitful to think of persuasion or rhetorical justification in science taking place on at least three interrelated *levels*.

1 On level 1, scientists attempt to persuade each other to buy this or that scientific idea about their domain of study: 'so and so is the case in this region of reality' (the level of selling empirical or theoretical claims).

2 On level 2, scientists attempt to sell the idea of this or that approach or method of studying the domain better than its rivals: 'this region of reality should be studied in such and such a way' (the level of selling methodological claims).

3 On level 3, scientists attempt to market themselves as competent and credible scholars in their field, worth being listened to and receiving resources for further research: 'I am a credible researcher in this field' (the level of selling sociological claims).

These three levels are usually closely interrelated or, more strongly, sometimes totally intermingled, in that an argument on level 1 implicitly constitutes other arguments on levels 2 and 3, and vice versa. In selling an empirical claim you at the same time come to sell (a) a theoretical claim which is believed to be supported by the empirical claim; (b) a methodological claim which is believed to be exemplified by the empirical and theoretical claims (as 'applications' of the method or approach in question); (c) a sociological claim to the effect that you are a credible researcher competent to produce permissible and advisable kinds of results (level 1) using permissible and advisable methods (level 2).

The rhetorical process of persuasion has several *stages*. The temporally first stage may be called the *entry stage*. This involves crucial social mechanisms regarding the fate of institutionalist economics. At this stage it is the vital task of the persuader to alert the audience, to make it pay attention. 'It is not enough for a man to speak or write; he must also be listened to or read' (Perelman and Olbrechts-Tyteca 1969: 17). The idea is that successful persuasion presupposes adaptation of the persuader to the persuadee, 'a meeting of minds between speaker and audience' (Perelman 1982: 9–10). It presupposes that the attention of the audience be guaranteed, otherwise rhetorical argumentation does not get off the ground. In order to be taken seriously by the scientific audience the idea or claim being marketed has to satisfy what we may variously call *entry conditions* or *recognizability conditions* or *relevance conditions*. 'For a scientific claim to be seriously advanced it must fit into a framework within which the claim is to be validated and argumentation advanced and assessed' (Weinstein 1990: 272). Anybody willing to enter the business (and to stay there) has to conform to a set of established *rhetorical conventions*. Rhetorical conventions are among what were called the credibility institutions in the previous section.

From the rhetorical point of view, science is socially conditioned in an interesting way. The concept of rhetoric itself implies a minimal degree of social conditionality: justification is a matter of rhetorical communication between people. The idea of rhetorical conventions as entry conditions makes the social conditioning of science stronger and more complex. The question of whether the entry or recognizability conditions are satisfied by a given idea is a highly socially impregnated question, or, if you like, a political issue. Here we meet with various 'gate-keeping' conditions and procedures tacitly or explicitly accepted by a disciplinary profession that delimit the protagonists and the contents and styles of claims and arguments to those that are recognized by the profession as worthy of further consideration.

First of all, the protagonist has to be a bona fide member of the disciplinary profession in order to be heard at all. People gain this status by going through a process of scientific education whereby they learn how to speak and write in a way that is recognized by the profession as the scientific way (see Overington 1977: 155). Furthermore, they have to establish themselves as legitimate and credible members of the profession, capable of producing valuable results. This is the feature captured by the notion of credibility discussed in the previous section. It is the task of rhetoric on level 3 to ascertain the fulfilment of this condition. Secondly, the idea suggested has to satisfy certain constraints, both formal and substantive. It has to be formulated within an established framework and be based on certain unquestioned axioms. It has to suggest a solution to a recognized problem in the field. It has to employ recognized methods to find the solution. It has to satisfy expectations concerning argumentative form, and so on. Rhetoric on levels 1 and 2 is relevant for taking care of this condition.

The dependence of recognition by a relevant external audience on such rhetorical conventions suggests the existence of a sort of *private rhetoric*, rhetoric directed to an *internal audience*. The idea is that a person socialized into the 'culture' of his or her scientific field rhetorically tests the ideas and arguments first privately, in his or her mind, before they are presented to an external audience. Such private rhetoric is based on anticipations of the forthcoming receptions of this or that idea or argument. The idea or argument is then adjusted accordingly to meet the anticipated requirements of the external audience. Private rhetoric functions as a censor or filter between the creation of an idea and its public submission. There is no doubt that private rhetoric directed to an 'internal audience' is a ubiquitous aspect of human communication.

It should be obvious that there is an in-built conservative tendency in such 'internal' and 'external' tests of disciplinary appropriateness. Such tests favour ideas from established members of the discipline in conformity with the prevailing rhetorical conventions. In general, 'a scientific argument is relevant, in the sense of worthy of consideration, based on a reasoned judgement made in respect of the protagonist's position in the field and the appropriateness of arguments presented, given accepted standards of professional practice' (Weinstein 1990: 273).

Judgements of relevance and recognizability are made at various stages and by various agents. In the early stages there are, for instance, confrontations between students and their teachers in lecture and seminar rooms. A student raises a question or suggests an idea to which the professor responds by commenting on its appropriateness and relevance. Another situation is the one where a paper submitted to a journal for publication is scrutinized by the editor and the referees. The crucial criteria in their judgement have to do with the problem stated, the theories and methods employed, the style used, and in general with whether the paper submitted fits the generally accepted framework and problem situation of the field. Even the institutional affiliation of the author may play a role, the idea being that 'institutions have standing as initial arbiters of scientific adequacy. That is, prima facie, a scientist writing on the stationery of a major research university will have shown competence in the basic protocols of scientific practice in order to have achieved a position that entitles him to present his views under the aegis of his institution' (Weinstein 1990: 274). *Ceteris paribus*, a submission to the *Journal of Political Economy* by a scholar affiliated to the University of Chicago may have an easier life than a submission from Northern Illinois University. The authority and reputation of institutions tend to be transmitted to individual scientists.

The rhetorical conventions belong to the institutions of the discipline of economics, thus constraining and enabling economists' belief formation. Like any institutions, the rhetorical institutions are more or less stable relative to individual research efforts on a short-term basis. Even though the conventions are revisable, they are taken as given constraints most of the time. It may be conjectured that the more powerful of those institutions consist of the rhetorical conventions of the mainstream, therefore functioning as barriers to entry to non-orthodox endeavours. We may cite Robert Solow's hypothesis:

> In any period the dominant school of thought is likely, consciously or unconsciously, to impose on professional discussion rhetorical conventions that favor the case it has to make. The dominant school then has the advantage of being able to rule some of its opponents' ideas out of court on methodological [and linguistic] grounds.
>
> (Solow 1988: 35)

It is easy to see that Solow's hypothesis might have some explanatory power in regard to our *explanandum* [E]. Much of new institutionalism conforms more closely to the rhetorical conventions of the neoclassical mainstream than does the old institutionalism, therefore having fewer difficulties in finding receptive audiences. The versions that employ formal game theory are an obvious case.

Let us consider the case of Thorstein Veblen, examined by Waller and Robertson (1990). They try to solve the following problem. 'Except for ['old'] institutional economists, Veblen is understood by economists as offering an ironic social commentary rather than a unified and coherent economic theory' (Waller and Robertson 1990: 1028). In brief, their suggested solution is this: 'We think it is because the prior assumptions of economists, including McCloskey, about the nature and purpose of economic inquiry, make them very bad readers. It is difficult if not impossible for neoclassical economists to understand and respond to the way Veblen writes' (ibid.). In other words, Veblen and the neoclassicals do not share the ruling rhetorical conventions of economics. Veblen's writing did not and does not satisfy the entry conditions of the mainstream of economics.

The rhetoric of Veblen's writing is similar to that of Marx. He

> wraps himself in the tradition of disinterested objective scholarship, while systematically substituting terms that either suggest moral disrepute or that systematically devalue the behavior under examination. . . . Everyone notes the implicit moral content in the substitution of 'predation' and 'force and fraud' for the traditional descriptions of business activity.
>
> (Waller and Robertson 1990: 1031)

Veblen was not one who practised what we called the rhetoric of decontextualization, the rhetorical hiding of the rhetorical context of theory and research claims; the social context of theory and the persuasive aims of argumentation are more obvious in Veblen than in standard orthodox economists. 'They naturally look with bewilderment upon anyone – such as Veblen – who tries to make the point that their ideas have arisen from a particular historical moment and serve particular social and economic interests' (ibid., p. 1037).

Gaps in communication due to discrepancies in rhetorical conventions are different from genuine disagreements.

> It is one thing to disagree with someone who thinks differently from you. It is quite another to have such a limited capacity for comprehending discourse that you simply cannot grasp that someone else has challenged your fundamental way of conceptualizing the world. It is this latter case that we think explains the problems Veblen presents to mainstream economists.
>
> (Waller and Robertson 1990: 1028)

This then suggests itself as an explanation, from one perspective, for the relatively poor social performance of the old institutionalist economics, measured in terms of its ranking. On the other hand, much of the new institutionalist economics does share some of the important rhetorical conventions with the mainstream, and therefore gets a hearing more easily. The obstacles that the new institutionalist economics encounters are less often problems of comprehension than those of disagreement, respectability, etc. In other words, while the old institutionalist economics fails to satisfy the necessary entry conditions in economics, some versions of the new institutionalist economics succeed in doing so. They manage to find more or less attentive audiences by getting papers accepted for delivery at mainstream conferences and for publication in top journals. The new institutionalist economics, then, manages to enter the subsequent stages of the rhetorical process more easily.

We may now try to formulate parts of a hypothetical explanation of the ranking order with reference to the rhetorical process of persuasion.

[Rhe] (1) In order to enter the rhetorical process of persuasion within a scientific discipline, a theory, a piece of research work or a stream of thought has to satisfy certain established rhetorical conventions which serve as entry conditions.

(2) In economics, the ruling rhetorical entry conditions are best satisfied by narrow neoclassical economics, and better by the new institutionalist economics than by the old institutionalism.

(3) Therefore, [E].

The recognizability conditions are very different in the case of rhetorical argumentation in ordinary life situations. They are usually more permissive than in scientific contexts. No professional boundaries, for instance, are strictly guarded, nor is the style of expressing one's ideas strictly regulated in ordinary life. Again, however, it has to be remembered that science is not uniform in this regard either. Scientific disciplines are not all alike regarding the strictness of required obedience to the prevailing rhetorical conventions. A given discipline is not uniform in this respect either spatially or temporally. Economics in many times and places seems to be much less permissive than business studies and other social sciences, and it might be even less permissive than some natural sciences. In some other times or places, the situation may be different.

No rhetorical conventions are entirely fixed. Some are more stable than others within a discipline. There is room for rhetorical variation and novelty, but at any given moment and situation, there are limits beyond which one loses the audience. The recognition that rhetorical conventions have their histories and are sometimes more flexible than at other times, is relevant for our case. [Rhe] has been outlined to give an account of a fixed ranking order, not for changes in it. I said that the new institutionalist economics has been able, to a large extent, to enter the later stages of the rhetorical process within economics. This means that silence and ignorance is being replaced by communication, incomprehension is being replaced by disagreement and sometimes agreement. The message sent is being received. Minds are being converted. It is not unimaginable that, in ten years, the ranking order (and also the contents and boundaries of the streams ranked) may be different to that suggested in [E]. Since [Rhe] talks about the rhetorical entry conditons, it keeps silent about the rhetorical process of such a possible conversion within the discipline.

100

SOCIAL CAUSATION OF THE CONTENTS OF BELIEFS

Thus far, we have had nothing to say about the specific contents of economic theories as *explananda* of social theories of science. Furthermore, our main focus has been on the reproductive aspects of the social conditioning of economics; we have had little to say about the production or genesis of economic theories. In this section, the focus is changed to cover these two aspects; we will be preoccupied with the genesis of the contents of economics. Here we meet some of the most controversial suggestions of recent sociology of science, namely the so-called strong programme of the Edinburgh School. This school is far from uniform, but I am not going to pay attention to its heterogeneity. I use a simplified version to illuminate another perspective on our explanatory problem.

The primary aim of the 'strong programme' is to attempt to provide sociological explanations of *the contents of beliefs or theories held by scientists*. Three tenets formulated by Bloor (1976: 4–5) for the sociology of scientific knowledge are relevant for us:

(1) The principle of causality: 'It would be causal, that is, concerned with the conditions which bring about beliefs or states of knowledge'.
(2) The principle of impartiality: 'It would be impartial with respect to truth and falsity, rationality or irrationality, success or failure. Both sides of these dichotomies will require explanation'.
(3) The principle of symmetry: 'It would be symmetrical in its style of explanation. The same types of cause would explain, say, true and false beliefs'.

First, these tenets imply that the main focus of the strong programme is not on scientists' actions but instead on the beliefs they hold, not so much on science as a process of social action but rather as the epistemic outcome of that process. The primary *explananda* of the endeavour are the forms and contents of what passes as scientific knowledge. Second, the explanation of the contents of beliefs cites social facts as their *explanantia*, having the character of causes (albeit not necessarily their only causes). Thus the social conditioning of science acquires the form of causation instead of constitution. In the background there is the belief that the principle of causality, together with a 'moral' neutrality about truth and falsity, rationality and irrationality, turns the sociology of scientific knowledge into a scientific discipline itself. The sociology of scientific knowledge is a matter of applying science to itself. Third, the set of the explanatory social facts encompasses social facts external to the scientific disciplines themselves. Much of the strong sociology of science is externalist in this sense. However,

Where broad social factors are not involved, narrow ones take over.
. . . As well as an external sociology of knowledge, there is also an

internal sociology of knowledge. By this I mean that the social factors concerned may be ones which derive from the narrowly conceived interests or traditions or routines of the professional community.

(Bloor 1981: 203)

Here are some examples of the kinds of questions that the sociologist has to ask in his or her explanatory endeavour: She will ask

if a belief is part of the routine cognitive and technical competences handed down from generation to generation. Is it enjoyed by the authorities of the society? Is it transmitted by established institutions of socialization or supported by accepted agencies of social control? Is it bound up with patterns of vested interest? Does it have a role in furthering shared goals, whether political, technical, or both? What are the practical and immediate consequences of particular judgements that are made with respect to the belief?

(Barnes and Bloor 1982: 23)

The suggested explanatory factors vary from case to case. A sociologist may cite features of systems of social relations or of dominant cultural values and intellectual atmosphere as causes of scientific beliefs. For instance, in explaining the ideal of axiomatizability in science, the hierarchical order of the major social relations within relevant social systems as the cause of the intellectual ideal may be invoked. He or she may also try to identify the cognitive and social interests of a disciplinary profession and relate them to wider ideological and political interests and cite them as the causes of whatever theories are held by the profession. The idea might be that those theories will be accepted which are better in rationalizing the interests of the dominant groups in society.

There are many suggestions in the study of economics that share some of the intimations of the strong programme. Attempts to explain the contents of economic theories by relating them to contemporary policy issues is one example (e.g. Stigler 1960). Attempts to account for economists' beliefs by maintaining that they serve certain class or group interests in society is another example (e.g. Bucharin 1926). Attempts to explain economic theories by referring to the model provided by physical theories and to the professionally functional 'physics envy' is yet another (e.g. Mirowski 1989).

Let us briefly discuss one recent example of a sociological explanation along roughly Edinburgh lines. There is an evident spirit of the strong programme in the following attempted explanation of the reign of the neoclassical orthodoxy in economics. It argues that 'in some way, and for some as yet unexplained reason, the neoclassical ideology is a part

102

of – or, indeed, the best representative of – Anglo-American ideology' (Burkhardt and Canterbery 1986: 245). One possible way of elaborating this idea is to employ the concepts of profession and legitimation and to argue that, in general:

> Professional experts transform, in the very process of practising their craft, a heterogeneous set of societal values into a coherent, logical, and ultimately self-serving system of beliefs. In other words, the professions shape for a society a world view in the very process of acting under the rubric and disguise of a narrower professional ideology.
>
> (Burkhardt and Canterbery 1986: 236)

To apply this line of reasoning to the case of orthodox economics would presuppose that, first, economics is a profession; second, in order to survive, the economics profession has to gain social legitimacy; and third, in order to legitimate themselves as a profession, economists have to legitimate the prevailing social ideology (by giving it a theoretical formulation that is put beyond doubt). Assuming that 'individualism is perhaps the dominant feature of Western society' (ibid., p. 239), it is the idea of individualism that plays the key role in this exercise. The presumed commitment to methodological individualism in the dominant economic theory would be accounted for as a reflection of general ideological individualism in contemporary Western or American society (ibid., p. 244). Or, as an institutionalist economist puts it, 'orthodox economic theory is wedded to the classic liberal ideology where the individual is regarded as an autonomous and elemental unit' (Hodgson 1988: 16).

Those who find these ideas persuasive may then try to use them to give an explanation for [E].

[LI] (1) The economics profession can legitimate its own existence only by conforming to or legitimating the prevailing social ideology.

(2) Individualism is the prevailing social ideology in the Western world.

(3) Standard neoclassicism and the new institutionalist economics subscribe to (methodological) individualism, while the old institutionalist economics is holistic.

(4) Therefore, [E].

Argument [LI] ('L' for 'legitimation', 'I' for 'individualism') cites social facts external to academic economics to explain a feature of academic economics. The contents of economists' beliefs are not the only ultimate *explananda* but constitute an essential phase of the *explanandum*.

[LI] is in many respects incomplete. First, it fails to explain why

103

standard neoclassical economics ranks higher than the new institution-alism; it only suggests an explanation of why those two rank higher than the old institutionalist economics. Second, it fails to explain why old institutionalism is able to survive at all. Third, it does not show the required intimate connection between the ideological or political in-dividualism presumably prevailing on a societal level and the method-ological individualism of economic science. Fourth, it neglects the fact that some new institutionalist theories are not clear exemplifications of individualism, and that not all of old institutionalism is clearly in contradiction with individualism (see Chapter 1, this volume). Since a non-individualist version of new institutionalist theory may rank higher than all of old individualism and even much of narrow neoclassicism, there have to be other factors in work not included in [LI].

[LI] has the character of a functionalist explanation. In effect, it says that it is functional for the economics profession to subscribe to individualism. It does not say that economists intentionally use their commitment to individualism in order to promote the legitimacy of the profession. To be precise, [LI] does not cite individual economists and their action at all; thus [LI] itself violates the principle of methodological individualism. As with functionalist explanations in general, one problem with [LI] is that the mechanisms of mediation are left untheorized. It may be plausible to argue that 'the neoclassical economic system is and remains the dominant paradigm in Western academic professional economics precisely because of its having come to reflect and define behaviors and attitudes as legitimate ones, for individuals, for corporate bodies, and for society', but an important admission then follows: 'How this occurred is anybody's guess' (Burkhardt and Canterbery 1986: 248). This is a widely recognized problem. As a major architect of the strong programme admits, 'we lack a precise and detailed account of the relationship between goals and interests on the one hand, and concepts and beliefs on the other' (Barnes 1982: 103).

The strong programme advocates causal explanation of beliefs. A complete causal argument would have to indicate the existence and functioning of one or more mediating mechanisms that would make it possible for the social cause to produce the epistemic effect. Such mediating mechanisms no doubt contain the aims and beliefs, delibera-tions and routines by individual economists, in addition to details of the institutional structure of academic economics and its relations to the surrounding society. Therefore, arguments [Cred] and [Rhe] most naturally suggest themselves as partially complementing [LI].

LESSONS AND FURTHER ISSUES

The minimum suggestion of this chapter is that the methodologists of economics would do wisely to recognize and analyse and tentatively apply the varieties of social theories of science suggesting a number of ways in which science may be socially conditioned. This should be a special concern for those of institutionalist persuasions. The various statements of the social conditioning of science all imply the idea that scientific practice and belief involve a number of powerful social institutions.

Departing from these premises, an explanation of the ranking of the three streams of economic thought would not refer to their relative degree of corroboration, their differential tenacity in surviving severe attempts at falsification, nor to their relative success in formulating theories in a falsifiable form, nor to their relative progressiveness as research programmes in the Lakatosian sense. Rather, an explanation would cite institutions of various sorts, such as credibility institutions and rhetorical conventions, and point out that the more closely an economic theory or research practice comes to neoclassical theory or practice, the more easily it manages to conform to these institutions. These are some of the ingredients that could be used for constructing an institutionalist theory of economics. No such theory exists. All the explanatory arguments formulated above are imprecise and incomplete sketches, at most steps on the way towards a well-developed theory. Each of them sheds light on a limited aspect of science at most. They cite the institutions of science as the explaining entities but leave them unexplained. Their final assessment is not possible until they are given more refined formulations.

An interesting dilemma for an institutionalist suggests itself even with what we have now. To hold an institutionalist theory of science may enable one to provide an explanation of the low ranking of an institutionalist theory of the economy. What would be the grounds then for holding either theory? An explanatory theory of science is not easily usable as a tool for criticizing the ranking order among economic theories, whereas an institutionalist economist is most likely inclined to challenge the order in normative terms. The elements of social theories of science discussed in the foregoing are candidates for explainers, but their normative power is suspect. The institutionalist theorist of science may therefore feel the need for pursuing a normative theory of science as well. The Popperian methodologist may take this as providing some consolation. His theory of science is perhaps not to be denounced just because it is normative in character. Indeed, I am inclined to think that the fundamental issue is concerned not with descriptive versus normative theory of science but rather with the substance and way of justification of whatever norms of rationality are suggested.

It might be useful to make clear what else is not implied by taking the social theories of science seriously. Even though much of the recent sociology of science is radically relativist and anti-realist, no anti-realist relativism need be accepted along with admitting that science is socially

105

conditioned. First, take the case of economists pursuing credibility or other social goals. Admitting that this might be the case does not preclude the possibility that along with such social goals, economists might pursue epistemic goals, such as theories that help us approach truths about the economy. Even if veracity played no explicit role in economists' practical deliberations, they might, as a collective, at least end up with epistemic outcomes with veristic virtues. It might even be that the successful pursuit of certain social goals is a prerequisite for attaining ambitious epistemic outcomes.

Second, even though McCloskey and some others tend to think that rhetoric and realism are mutually inconsistent, there is no compelling reason to agree on this idea. I do not think that the admission that economics and science in general is rhetorical somehow implies that the concept of truth in a realist sense becomes a useless notion. The presence of rhetorical persuasion does not in any way preclude the possibility of an economics along realist lines. Rhetoric is not intrinsically anti-realist. Rhetorical persuasion can be used to pursue and support theories with both high and low veristic virtues. Rhetoric is a matter of justification, while truth is a matter of how theories relate to reality irrespective of who speaks for or against them and how (see Mäki 1988, 1992b).

Third, even if it were the case that scientific beliefs were indexical or relative in the sense that their genesis and persistence were causally dependent on certain social conditions, there is no necessity to think that those beliefs therefore lose their semantic properties, such as being true or false. Also, the admission of the existence of such causal influences from social conditions to the contents of beliefs does not imply that there are no other causal influences deriving from the objects of those beliefs. This is not precluded by the protagonists of the strong programme either; they admit that even 'the segment of unverbalized reality' may influence beliefs (Barnes and Bloor 1982: 33).

Take the example of individualism as part of both economic theory and Western culture in general. It is not the case that if someone suggests [LI] as an explanation for the relative popularity of the new institutionalist economics, they thereby commit themselves to some strong form of relativism. Namely, it may be argued that the general individualist ideology is a more or less accurate reflection of the social and mental realities dominant in Western societies, and that therefore an economic theory based on individualist premises can be presumed to capture these realities better than theories with non-individualist foundations. The representational accuracy of the theory would not be undermined by the possible fact that the popularity of the theory is based on its being instrumental in sustaining the social legitimacy of the economics profession. Of course, the acceptance of this argument may depend on making a distinction between representational accuracy and explanatory completeness.

Finally, let me address the difficult issue of the relationship between the social and the epistemic, between considerations of social conditioning and considerations of veracity, in the context of [E]. What I have said in the foregoing is perfectly compatible with claiming that the social ranking of the three streams of economic thought may or may not coincide with their epistemic ranking in terms of their veristic virtues. I have suggested nothing that would by itself exclude the possibility of any one of them being true or leading us closest to the truth about the economy. In other words, this chapter cannot be read as an epistemological defence of either neoclassical or institutionalist economics in any of their forms. It is just a reminder that the discipline of economics might be somewhat more complex than suggested by standard traditional methodologies.

NOTES

1 I wish to thank Bruce Caldwell, Neil de Marchi, Donald McCloskey and Oliver Williamson for comments on early versions of this chapter.
2 For contributions to the underdeveloped field of the sociology of economics, see, for example, Katouzian 1980, chap. 5; Earl 1983; Coats 1984; Maloney 1985; Burkhardt and Canterbery 1986; Loasby 1986; Whitley 1986; Bellinger and Bergsten 1990; Klamer and Colander 1990; Mäki 1992a.
3 Much more refined distinctions should be drawn between forms and aspects of conditioning. We could distinguish between causal production and pre-conditioning, and between causal production and causal transmission. We might also distinguish between the causes of the existence of a possibility, potentiality, liability, or tendency, on the one hand, and the causes of the actualization thereof on the other hand. Furthermore, we may also distinguish between necessary and sufficient conditions and their combinations; that is, we may ask whether a social 'factor' or several such 'factors' are necessary or sufficient or both in generating or constituting facts about economics. Unfortunately, the literature on the social theory of science is not of much help in clarifying these various forms and aspects of the social conditioning of science.
4 In Mäki (1992a), I have suggested this threefold division and discussed the relevant sociological literature in more detail.
5 For discussions of the contents, relative merits and problematic characterizations of the 'old' and 'new' institutionalisms, see Langlois 1986, papers in the November 1989 issue of *Review of Political Economy*, and the introductory chapter to the present volume.

REFERENCES

Barnes, B. (1982) *T.S. Kuhn and Social Science*, New York: Columbia University Press.
Barnes, B. and Bloor, D. (1982) 'Relativism, rationalism and the sociology of knowledge', in M. Hollis and S. Lukes (eds) *Rationality and Relativism*. Oxford: Basil Blackwell, pp. 21–47.

107

Bellinger, W.K. and Bergsten, G.S. (1990) 'The market for economic thought: an Austrian view of neoclassical dominance', *History of Political Economy* 22: 697–720.

Blaug, M. (1980) *The Methodology of Economics*, Cambridge: Cambridge University Press.

Bloor, D. (1976) *Science and Social Imagery*, London: Routledge & Kegan Paul.

—— (1981) 'The strengths of the strong programme', *Philosophy of the Social Sciences* 11: 199–213.

Bourdieu, P. (1975) 'The specificity of the scientific field and the social conditions of the progress of reason', *Social Science Information* 14: 19–47.

Bucharin, N. (1926) *Die politische Ökonomie des Rentners* 2nd edition, Berlin: Verlag für Literatur und Politik.

Burkhardt, J. and Canterbery, E.R. (1986) 'The orthodoxy and professional legitimacy: toward a critical sociology of economics', *Research in the History of Economic Thought and Methodology* 4: 229–50.

Coats, A.W. (1984) 'The sociology of knowledge and the history of economics', *Research in the History of Economic Thought and Methodology* 2: 211–34.

—— (1988) 'Economic rhetoric: the social and historical context' in A. Klamer, D. McCloskey and R. Solow (eds) *The Consequences of Economic Rhetoric*, Cambridge: Cambridge University Press, pp. 64–84.

Cross, R. (1982) 'The Duhem–Quine thesis, Lakatos and the appraisal of theories in macroeconomics', *Economic Journal* 92: 320–40.

Earl, P.E. (1983) 'A behavioral theory of economists' behavior', in A.S. Eichner (ed.) *Why Economics is not yet a Science* London: Macmillan, pp. 90–125.

Henderson, W., Dudley-Evans, A. and Backhouse, R. (eds) *Economics and Language*, London: Routledge.

Hodgson, G. (1988) *Economics and Institutions: A Manifesto for a Modern Institutionalist Economics*, Cambridge: Polity Press/Philadelphia: University of Pennsylvania Press.

Katouzian, H. (1980) *Ideology and Method in Economics*, London: Macmillan.

Klamer, A. and Colander, D. (1990) *The Making of an Economist*, Boulder, Colorado: Westview.

——, McCloskey, D. and Solow, R. (eds) (1988) *The Consequences of Economic Rhetoric*, Cambridge: Cambridge University Press.

Knorr-Cetina, K. (1981) *The Manufacture of Knowledge*, New York: Pergamon.

—— (1982) 'Scientific communities or transepistemic arenas of research? A critique of quasi-economic models of science', *Social Studies of Science* 12: 101–30.

—— (1983) 'The ethnographic study of scientific work: towards a constructivist interpretation of science', in K. Knorr-Cetina and M. Mulkay (eds) *Science Observed: Perspectives on the Social Study of Science*, London: Sage.

Langlois, R. (ed.) (1986) *Economics as a Process: Essays in the New Institutional Economics*, Cambridge: Cambridge University Press.

Latour B. (1987) *Science in Action*, Cambridge, Mass.: Harvard University Press.

—— and Woolgar, S. (1986) *Laboratory Life: The Construction of Scientific Facts*, Second edition, Princeton, New Jersey: Princeton University Press. (First published 1979).

Laudan, L. (1977) *Progress and its Problems* London: Routledge & Kegan Paul.

Loasby, B.J. (1986) 'Public science and public knowledge', *Research in the History of Economic Thought and Methodology* 4, 211–28.

McCloskey, D. (1985) *The Rhetoric of Economics*, Madison, Wisconsin: University of Wisconsin Press.

Mäki, U. (1988) 'How to combine rhetoric and realism in the methodology of economics', *Economics and Philosophy* 4: 89–109.

—— (1992a) 'Social conditioning of economics', in N. de Marchi (ed.) *Post Popperian Economic Methodology*, Boston: Kluwer, pp. 65–104.

—— (1992b) 'Two philosophies of the rhetoric of economics', in W. Henderson, A. Dudley-Evans and R. Backhouse (eds) *Economics and Language*, London: Routledge, pp. 23–50.

Maloney, J. (1985) *Marshall, Orthodoxy and the Professionalization of Economics*, Cambridge: Cambridge University Press.

Mirowski, P. (1987) 'Shall I compare thee to a Minkowski–Ricardo–Leontief– Metzler matrix of the Mosak–Hicks type? or, rhetoric, mathematics, and the nature of neoclassical economic theory', *Economics and Philosophy* 3: 67–95.

—— (1989) *More Heat than Light: Economics as Social Physics, Physics as Nature's Economics*, Cambridge: Cambridge University Press.

Overington M.A. (1977) 'The scientific community as audience: toward a rhetorical analysis of science', *Philosophy and Rhetoric* 10: 143–64.

Perelman, C. (1982) *The Realm of Rhetoric*, Notre Dame, Indiana: University of Notre Dame Press.

—— and Olbrechts-Tyteca, L. (1969) *The New Rhetoric: A Treatise on Argumentation*, Notre Dame, Indiana: University of Notre Dame Press.

Samuels, W. (ed.) (1990) *Economics as Discourse*, Boston: Kluwer.

Solow, R. (1988) 'Comments from inside economics', in A. Klamer, D. McCloskey and R. Solow (eds) *The Consequences of Economic Rhetoric*, Cambridge: Cambridge University Press, pp. 31–7

Stigler, G.J. (1960) 'The influence of events and policies on economic theory', *American Economic Review* 50: 36–54.

Waller, W. and Robertson, L.R. (1990) 'Why Johnny (Ph.D., Economics) can't read: a rhetorical analysis of Thorstein Veblen and a response to Donald McCloskey's *Rhetoric of Economics*', *Journal of Economic Issues* 24: 1027–44.

Weinstein, M. (1990) 'Towards an account of argumentation in science', *Argumentation* 4: 269–98.

Whitley, R. (1984) *The Intellectual and Social Organization of the Sciences*, Oxford: Oxford University Press.

—— (1986) 'The structure and context of economics as a scientific field', *Research in the History of Economic Thought and Methodology* 4: 179–209.

Williams, R. and Law, J. (1980) 'Beyond the bounds of credibility', *Fundamenta Scientiae* 1: 295–315.

Part III

BROADENING THE NOTION OF RATIONALITY

5

OPTIMIZATION, RULE-FOLLOWING, AND THE METHODOLOGY OF SITUATIONAL ANALYSIS

Richard N. Langlois and László Csontos

ABSTRACT

Much of modern economics is concerned with broadening the basic conception of economic action to include such factors as imperfect information and social institutions. But there are two rather divergent approaches to accomplishing this goal. One group, by far the largest, begins with the neoclassical model of rational optimization and then attempts modifications of various sorts in an effort to model social institutions, capture their effects on behaviour, or treat problems of less-than-perfect knowledge. Another group, influenced by the work of Herbert Simon and a few others, argues that the basic neoclassical model is ill-adapted to the problems of imperfect knowledge and that we need instead a wholly different model of behaviour.

This chapter argues that the apparent gulf between the two approaches can in fact be bridged. Rather than seeing the optimizer and the rule-follower as mutually exclusive ideal types, we propose to understand them as the same ideal type viewed at two different levels of generality and realisticness. This implies a change not so much in our conception of the bounded-rationality approach as in our understanding of the neoclassical approach. The methodology of situational analysis is not coextensive with the modern neoclassical positive heuristic. And rule-following or satisficing models often fit the situational-analysis paradigm better than do neoclassical models. The approach from situational analysis may thus prove a common methodological ground on which neoclassical and alternative approaches to the 'new institutional economics' may unite.

INTRODUCTION

Much of modern economics is concerned with broadening the basic conception of economic action to include such factors as imperfect information and social institutions. The theoretical and empirical investigation of factors like these makes economic theory, in some vague sense of the word, 'more realistic'. But there are two rather divergent approaches to accomplishing this goal. One group, by far the largest, begins with the neoclassical model of rational optimization and then attempts modifications of various sorts in an effort to model social institutions, capture their effects on behaviour, or treat problems of less-than-perfect knowledge. Another group, influenced by the work of Herbert Simon and a few others, argues that the basic neoclassical model is ill-adapted to the problems of imperfect knowledge and that we need instead a wholly different model of behaviour. Although proponents of the neoclassical approach have tried to portray such 'boundedly rational' action or 'satisficing' behaviour as merely a special case of the neoclassical model, adherents to the alternative approach continue to argue for their fundamental dissimilarity. This chapter is an attempt to sort through the claims of the two approaches and to place their relationship in a methodological context.

In particular, this chapter is an essay in clarification. Our central argument is that the debate between neoclassical optimizers and boundedly rational satisficers is usually miscast because of a confusion of explanatory categories. It is a mistake, we argue, to identify optimizing behaviour exclusively with the method of situational analysis and to identify satisficing (or, more broadly, rule-following) behaviour exclusively with the method of behaviouralism.[1] Seen in this light, the method of situational analysis emerges as a way of clarifying and uniting the optimizing and satisficing strands of 'the new institutional economics'.[2]

Before making this case, however, we need to address a few preliminary matters having to do with the scope and role of behavioural assumptions in economic theory.

BEHAVIOURAL ASSUMPTIONS IN ECONOMIC THEORY

One of the most widespread, and most naive, complaints about neoclassical economic models is that the behavioural assumptions they incorporate are 'unrealistic'. As is often the case with naive opinions, especially widely held ones, this complaint is a large grey oyster of misunderstanding carrying an important pearl of truth.

The principal problem with this standard complaint is that it opens itself to easy rebuttal. It takes little reflection to recognize that complete 'realisticness' of theoretical terms is an illusory and perhaps undesirable goal. In theory as in art, perfect trueness to life is seldom if ever the point, and some level of abstraction is essential to the enterprise. It does not follow from these obvious truths, however, that we must embrace abstract minimalism[3] and view 'realistic' assumptions as completely undesirable. One can assert the proposition that abstraction is necessary and simultaneously believe that representational realisticness[4] (all other things equal) is a desirable goal of theory.

The key to sorting out the issues here is to think clearly about the role of behavioural assumptions. On the one hand, defenders of the neo-classical model have been quite correct in pointing out their opponents' confusion (or at best ambiguity) about the proper *explanandum* of economic theory. Economics does not seek to explain individual behaviour *per se*, an undertaking that would no doubt require a picture of the agent that is quite complex and hence 'realistic' in any number of senses. Rather, economic theory most often *uses* assumptions about individual behaviour as an intermediate element in the explanation of various economic phenomena (changes in price and quantity, for example).[5] If we want realistic assumptions in such theories, it must be either (a) because a less concrete and detailed set of assumptions would not properly fulfil the methodological functions as an intermediate theoretical element or (b) because realisticness itself serves some ancillary explanatory function.

The first of these reasons has, implicitly or explicitly, animated much of the debate about the realisticness of assumptions, from the famous 'marginalist controversy'[6] to the present time. The methodological role of behavioural assumptions will also be our primary concern in what follows. For the moment, however, let us consider the second reason for wanting realistic assumptions: the possibility that realistic theories may have explanatory functions quite apart from the instrumental usefulness of a concrete and detailed set of assumptions.

The most powerful and important tradition to assert a possibility of this kind is that emanating from Max Weber. In the words of Fritz Machlup, an heir to this tradition, the fundamental assumptions of economic theory are subject to 'a requirement of understandability in the sense in which man can understand the actions of fellowmen' (Machlup 1955: 17 [1978: 153]). This is essentially Weber's notion of *Verstehen* or understanding. If one takes this requirement seriously, then behavioural postulates must be 'realistic' in one important sense. Those assumptions must be true enough to life that we could imagine ourselves, or some other human, behaving in the manner postulated. This requirement pins down another sense of 'realisticness' in economic theory. Assumptions are 'realistic' in this sense only if they provide for understandability.

Much of the discussion of the realisticness of assumptions has been clouded by confusion, and an ensuing side-argument, over the empirical character of economic assumptions. Influenced no doubt by positivism, a number of critics have associated realisticness with verifiability and therefore insisted on direct empirical verification of the assumptions of economic theory.[7] Indeed, in the hands of Herbert Simon, the demand for realisticness of assumptions sometimes comes across as a demand for an inductive method of research.[8] Now, it is certainly the case that any conception of representational realisticness must be empirical in some sense. But this certainly does not imply a commitment to a positivist (or even falsificationist) theory of science, much less a call for inductivism. In fact, realisticness-as-empirical-verifiability is a much-impoverished notion of realisticness when compared to the Weberian standard of *Verstehen*. For it is precisely the extent to which behavioural assumptions resonate with something like 'understanding' that their realisticness serves any ancillary explanatory function. Only when behavioural postulates make the world more intelligible to us do they go beyond their role as purely instrumental elements in the explanatory process; only then do they 'explain' in a sense richer than that in which simple empirical generalizations explain.

Nonetheless, the requirement of *Verstehen*, or something like it, speaks to what is still only an ancillary explanatory function of well-chosen behavioural postulates. The function is ancillary in that it is subservient to the role of the behavioural postulates in the larger explanation of economic phenomena. All other things equal, we want assumptions that are 'more realistic' in the sense of understandability, i.e. in the sense of meeting the Weberian requirement of *Verstehen*. But all other things are not always equal. In general, there is a trade off between the realisticness of the behavioural postulates in a theory (assuming direct understandability) and the general applicability of that theory to a wide range of economic phenomena. In an early essay, Machlup (1936 [1978: 64]) provides us with a set of three propositions that nicely illustrate the point.

> Proposition (1) 'If, because of an abundant crop, the output of wheat is much increased, the price of wheat will fall'.
>
> Proposition (2) 'If, because of increased wage-rates and decreased interest rates, capital becomes relatively cheaper than labour, new labour-saving devices will be invented'.
>
> Proposition (3) 'If, because of heavy withdrawals of foreign deposits, the banks are in danger of insolvency, the central bank authorities will extend the necessary credit'.

All three of these propositions seek to explain not the behaviour of individuals *per se* but such economic phenomena as changes in the price of wheat, the introduction of labour-saving devices, or the extension of bank credit. But all three propositions do make use of economic agents, and behavioural postulates about those agents, as links in the explanation. The behaviour of the 'theoretical' (ideal-typical) wheat farmer, innovator, or central banker is part in each case of what determines the economic outcome.

Consider, in particular, the difference between propositions (1) and (3). (Proposition (2) is an intermediate case.) Proposition (1) is more generally applicable than proposition (3). Most economists would consider this proposition applicable to almost all (if not indeed all) wheat markets at all times and places.[9] By contrast, proposition (3) may or may not be applicable to all central banks at all times and places. Its applicability will depend crucially on the behaviour of particular central bankers, whereas proposition (1) does not depend on the characteristics of particular wheat farmers. Some central bankers may be inflationists, others may hold to tight-money principles. We need to know more about the bankers than we need to know about the farmers. In the language of the Weberian tradition, the wheat farmer is a highly anonymous ideal type, while the central banker is a less anonymous type.

Suppose, first of all, that we had chosen a complex and non-anonymous ideal type to represent the wheat farmer. Ockham's razor would very quickly have shorn off much of that detail. Whatever the behavioural assumption involved, the wheat farmer is tightly constrained by the press of external circumstances in the wheat market. More precisely, he or she is constrained by the interactions among the large numbers of wheat farmers. This is one form of what we might call a 'system constraint', on which more below. The behavioural assumption thus carries little of the explanatory weight, and too much complexity in that assumption is just excess baggage, even from the point of view of understandability. This is the essence of Machlup's defence of marginalism.[10]

Suppose next that we had chosen an anonymous and abstract ideal type to represent the central banker. Perhaps we could assign the agent some specific maximand (e.g. maximizing support for the political party to which he or she happens to belong)[11] and pretend that the banker is a character like the wheat farmer in all essential respects. But this would be thin gruel at best. At worst, the anonymous ideal type would provide not only an unsatisfactory and implausible representation but also a causally inadequate behavioural assumption. We can see this most clearly by moving from the example of the central banker to the case of the oligopolist – the case that figures most prominently in the behaviouralist indictment of neoclassical assumptions.[12] In the case of perfect competition, the wheat-farmer example, there is no problem. In the case of monopoly, we can perform the trick just suggested: we can provide the monopolist with a maximand, simple profit, and suggest that he or she merely maximizes on that basis. This may or may not be plausible. But the rub comes in the case of oligopoly. Here there is no single obvious solution to the maximization problem. The behaviour of each player depends on the behaviour of all others in an often complicated way, and one has now to specify not merely the maximand (that is easy) but also the rules of interaction among the agents. The result is an edifice built on double layers of the *ad hoc*. This is the essence of the behaviouralist critique of marginalism.

SITUATIONAL LOGIC AND BEHAVIOURALISM

In his important work in the 1970s, Spiro Latsis recast the methodological debate in terms of a conflict between two distinct research programmes: the programme of situational analysis or situational logic (SL) and the programme of behaviouralism. This work helped to clarify a number of issues. But it also helped, we argue, to obscure some important distinctions.

Situational logic, as we understand it, is based on the following propositions: (1) the agent acts reasonably under the circumstances, that is, he or she is able to give reasons for actions; and (2) the logic of those circumstances dictates or allows for only one particular course of action. The behaviouralist approach, by contrast, rests on the idea of constraining the agent by the introduction of a set of behavioural assumptions fixed *ex ante*. More specifically, behaviouralists tend to assume that agents are (1) hard-headed rule-followers or (2) pre-programmed satisficers *ab ovo*.[13]

If we compare the 'programmes' of situational logic and behaviouralism, we find close family resemblances as well as important differences. What unites the two programmes is a similar explanatory objective: to generate determinate conclusions from models that employ assumptions about human behaviour.[14] The principal difference between the two approaches lies in the way in which they achieve determinateness.

As developed out of the Weberian tradition by Mises, Hayek, Popper, Watkins, Albert and others, the method of situational analysis attempts to achieve determinate results without overtly compromising the free will of the economic agent. If an agent has genuine free will, how can we be sure what he or she will do? The SL approach answers this question by placing the hypothetical (and free) agent in a situation that guides behaviour along determinate lines, and by assuming that the agent is able and willing to evaluate the situation and to choose, from among the set of perceived alternatives, the most desirable course of action. Latsis gives the example of a spectator at a football game. The spectator is technically free to leave the stadium from any exit; but a reasonable, we might even say rational, spectator would leave by the nearest exit. An SL model of this sort is thus a 'single exit' model.

This part of the story is well known. Few have seemed to notice, however, that the agent may be 'coerced' in two differnt ways or, we might say, at two different levels. The *source* of coercion is the same at both levels, namely the postulated one-to-one relationship between the structure of the situation and the expected course of action. The *nature* of 'coercion' can be different, however, and this difference may have explanatory import. We want to distinguish two, partly overlapping, cases here. In the first case the agent is coerced by exogenous physical and institutional features of the situation only, that is, by *situational* constraints *strictu senso*. In the second case, the feasible set is reduced not only by situational constraints, but also by the repercussions of the agent's own actions as he or she interacts with other agents. The coercive force of this feedback upon the agent is what we mean by the system constraint.[15]

To illustrate the eventual explanatory import of the system constraint, let us return to the example of the spectator in the football stadium. Our initial assumption is (a) that a spectator would seek to leave the stadium as comfortably and expeditiously as possible and (b) that, in view of this goal, egress through a nearby (rather than a distant) exit is the most reasonable course of action. This assumption is determinate, it coerces the agent, quite apart from any added pressure that a large jostling crowd might bring to bear. That there is also a crowd in the stadium pressuring the spectator toward the nearest exit is in the nature of a system constraint. Even if it is part of the agent's perceived situation, it does not have any explanatory import.

The theory of pure monopoly is an SL model of the empty-stadium variety. The monopolist faces a situation implying a single exit: he or she will maximize profit in the same way that the spectator will choose the nearest exit in an empty stadium. Either of them *could* have chosen otherwise; but such a choice would have been arguably less reasonable. By contrast, the theory of perfect competition is an SL model of the crowded-stadium type. The wheat farmer faces a situation analogous to that of the monopolist: a resource-allocation problem in which he or she must set price. The rational wheat farmer will of course set price equal to the prevailing market price, since that will maximize profit (minimize loss). Unlike the monopolist, however, the wheat farmer is also pressured by the system constraint, the large numbers in the wheat market, in a way that overwhelms the exogenously given situational constraints. In one sense, then, Latsis (1976b: 27) is right when he remarks that pure monopoly and perfect competition are not opposites but 'heuristic twins'. The situational logic – *at the level of the initial assumptions* – is the same in both models. But the system constraint is quite different in the two cases: absent in one and overpowering in the other.

From a methodological point of view, the upshot of this argument is the following. The system constraint has explanatory import only if, and to the extent that, the agent's awareness of the constraint would affect the model's predicted outcome. In the case of monopoly, there is no such interaction to worry about; in the case of perfect competition, the wheat farmer may well know about the effect of large numbers on price, but it matters not a jot. In intermediate cases like oligopoly, however, the system constraint may well play an important role. This is the world of strategy, of game theory, of Schelling.

It is characteristic of these textbook models of the firm, and perhaps of much of neoclassical modelling generally, to rely on what we might call a rather 'thin' conception of rationality. At a minimum, this has meant calculative behaviour along fairly narrow lines; at a more typical maximum, it has involved perfect information; reflexive, transitive, and complete preference orderings; and the constrained optimization of an objective function. A major theoretical innovation and a distinctive characteristic of the behaviouralist programme is the dismissal or relaxation of some of these rigid assumptions. Behaviouralists are in general advocates of a 'thicker' conception of rationality. When theorists argue that economic actors are looking for alternatives that are 'good enough' rather than optimal, they are trying to bring back real people, to replace the shallow concept of the ideal maximizer with assumptions about what 'real' people do. Information is not perfect, and finding better alternatives is a costly procedure. 'According to this emergent [behaviouralist] programme', writes Latsis:

> Instead of attempting to explain the behavior of economic agents as best decisions in a constraining situation we should attempt to explain them as more or less good (or possibly disastrously bad) solutions in fluid and partially known or even completely misunderstood situations.
>
> (Latsis 1972: 229)

But this way of framing the distinction between SL models and behaviouralist models misses the crucial issue. In fact, Latsis is really confusing matters here by focusing on knowledge assumptions. There is nothing inherent in the SL approach that requires perfect information or a 'thin' conception of rationality. We can place the agent in any kind of situation we choose, with one proviso: the logic of the situation must be such that it leaves the agent with only a single exit. Latsis seems determined to equate SL models with a thin conception of rationality. 'The neoclassical view', he says at one point (1972: 233–4), 'stresses the *situation* and turns the decision-making agent into a cipher; the behavioural view focuses on the nature and characteristics of the *decision making agent*'. But it is not a focus on the situation rather than on the agent that necessarily turns the agent into a zero. The cipherness of the agent, as we saw above, is a matter of the appropriate level of anonymity of the ideal type contained in the model's behavioural assumptions. And the appropriate level of anonymity is dictated, or at least ought to be dictated, not by the form of the behavioural assumption but by the nature of the model's *explanandum*.

It is true, however, that the SL approach focuses on the situation, whereas the behaviouralist approach focuses on the agent. And herein lies the real difference between the two: they are two different ways of constructing determinate assumptions about action or behaviour out of indeterminate and unpredictable humanity. As we saw, the SL method uses the coercive logic of a situation in order not to encroach on the agent's free will. The behaviouralist approach is far less troubled by the problem of free will and chooses to construct a determinate behavioural assumption in the most direct fashion possible: by programming the agent to behave as instructed.[16] We can see this clearly in the behaviouralist's emphasis on rule-following behaviour in general and satisficing behaviour in particular. An agent who is programmed acts in a determinate way even in the most open and unconstrained situations, whereas the agent with free will does not. A strict satisficer stops seeking income when he or she has reached an aspiration level – even if a $50 bill suddenly appears on the sidewalk. The SL agent might pick up the bill.

OPTIMIZATION, RULE-FOLLOWING, AND SITUATIONAL LOGIC

In this section we want to discuss briefly the relationships between optimization, rule-following, and situational logic. More specifically, we are going to argue: (1) that the SL approach cannot be identified with models of constrained optimization employing a 'thin' conception of rationality, and, consequently, (2) the method of situational analysis is not equivalent to the programme of neoclassical economics (broadly understood) to which the method(s) of behaviouralism would represent a distinct alternative.

The first of these propositions is perhaps the less controversial. It is also the more clearly wrong. It is certainly true that all SL models are 'constrained optimization' in that the agent is constrained and is trying to do the best possible under the circumstances. But this does not demand that we view the agent as having a formal maximization problem – let alone perfect knowledge; a complete, transitive, etc., preference ordering; a well-defined objective function; and so on. It simply means that the agent does the best that he or she can under the circumstances. It is thus quite possible to have SL models employing as 'thick' a conception of rationality as one might need in view of the *explanandum* in question. By the same token, it is just as possible to have behaviouralist models (i.e. models using programmed puppets) tied to a 'thin' conception of rationality.[17]

The second issue, which is closely related to the first, is perhaps more controversial. There is a strand of literature that has long argued that some types of models advocated by behaviouralists, notably rule-following or satisficing models, actually *reduce* to optimization models in a certain sense (Baumol and Quandt 1964; Day 1967). This is an important issue, on which we hope to cast some light below. But few would disagree that an optimization model must be an SL model and a satisficing or rule-following assumption implies a behaviouralist model. We argue, to the contrary, that this is not the case if we adhere to the distinction we suggested earlier: that the real methodological difference between situational analysis and behaviouralism is the difference between an SL behavioural assumption and an assumption of programmed behaviour. Using this criterion, it is not at all far-fetched to make an attempt at reinterpreting part of the neoclassical programme as behaviouralism and a good deal of bounded-rationality modelling as situational analysis. What follows, however, cannot be more than a first step in this direction.

1   Optimization as situational logic

It is clearly the case that *some* optimization models are examples of the method of situational analysis. That class of models has in common with the SL approach the ideas of constraint and optimization. In particular, most of the basic and simple models of textbook marginalism probably do qualify as situational analysis.

1′   Optimization as behaviouralism

It does not follow from this that *all* neoclassical models fit best into the SL category. In Karl Popper's (1966, 1967) well-known formulation of the method of situational logic, the 'rationality principle' insists that the agent act not *optimally* but merely *reasonably* under the circumstances. We consider an action reasonable if the agent is (or would be) able to justify it in terms of his or her desires, beliefs and preferences. It is clear enough that acting optimally would sometimes be equivalent to acting quite *unreasonably*. Behaviouralists and other critics have pointed out relentlessly the narrow-mindedness or even straightforward irrationality of an agent actually trying to solve a foot-long Lagrangian as a guide to action. As a consequence, and more to the present point, it is not at all clear that we should classify such optimization models as situational analysis. Solving a complex optimization problem is an easy task for a computer: it is a matter of following an algorithm, programmed in much the same way one could programme satisficing behaviour or rule-following. Why not call these behaviouralist, that is, programmed-agent, models? Solving a huge optimization problem may be a lousy decision procedure; but it *is* a decision procedure.

2 Rule-following as behaviouralism

It is also the case that some models of rule-following behaviour fit quite naturally under the rubric of behaviouralism. Although following rules and habits does not necessarily imply completely preprogrammed behaviour, it is certainly true that rule-following is closer to the 'behaviour' end of the action–behaviour spectrum.[18] Moreover, just as people do not choose their habits, they do not choose some of the rules they follow either. Rather, these latter form a background of institutions against which the agent chooses. Models of behaviour following such 'ground-rules' seem to be consistent even with a very narrow conception of behaviouralism.

2′ Rule-following as situational logic

On the other hand, one might also easily construe the following of a rule as a reasonable response to particular decision situations. If, as behaviouralists like to imagine, the situation is uncertain and complex, following a rule may well be the agent's most reasonable course of action. Here perhaps is the import of those models, mentioned earlier, that show the convergence of satisficing to optimizing. But the point is even clearer if we examine not the early approaches to bounded rationality but their modern successors. Following the advice of Simon and others, a number of writers have looked to psychology to understand better the nature and sources of the rules agents follow. What turns out to be crucial in this work is, in effect, the importance of the *situation* in which the agent operates. Heiner (1983, 1986), for example, derives rule-following from the complexity of the environment: it is literally the agent's only choice when competence is low relative to the complexity of the situation. Similarly, for psychologists (Tversky and Kahneman 1974; Kahneman and Tversky 1981), the heuristics people use under uncertainty depend critically on the particular facts of their situations: how they frame the problem is the clue to their biases and their decision-rules.

METHODOLOGICAL ARGUMENTS FOR AND AGAINST SITUATIONAL LOGIC

If one accepts the argument that we can represent 'thickly' rational agents and interpret rule-following behaviour along *either* situation-analytic or behaviouralist lines, the question remains: *which* approach should one choose? There is probably no definitive answer to this question, at least apart from a consideration of the specifics of the *explanandum* at hand. But we will attempt in the remainder of this chapter to present the case for the SL approach. Before turning to an affirmative defence of that approach, let us first consider the behaviouralist critique.

In essence, as we saw earlier, the hard core of neoclassical theory implies (1) perfect or hardly-less-than-perfect information; (2) reflexive, symmetric and complete preference ordering; and (3) the constrained optimization of an objective function. Behaviouralists, however, accuse neoclassical economics not only of a too-thin conception of rationality but also, relatedly, of *adhocery* in defence of the programme's hard core. The neoclassical theory of the firm is the usual case in point. Whereas perfect competition and (arguably) monopoly work well enough within the usual profit-maximizing framework, oligopoly is an anomaly. The hard-core assumptions of neoclassical economics do not, in their very logic, provide a determinate solution to the oligopolist's problem. In order to close the oligopoly model, neoclassical theorists thus must import from the outside notions – of which the Sylos Postulate[19] is but one tiny example – that do not arise from within the logic of the programme's hard core. Neoclassical oligopoly theorists thus experience a close encounter with what Wade Hands (1988), following Lakatos, calls *adhocery* of the third kind.

This is certainly a damaging criticism of the neoclassical theory of oligopoly. Pushed a bit further, in fact, it is a critique of all of neoclassical theory. For if we take the hard core seriously to mean that the agent always behaves 'rationally' in the sense of choosing optimally within a given means/ends framework, then we can begin to wonder how the agent rationally chooses the *framework itself*. If we say that the framework is the result of an optimal choice within a higher-level framework, then we can ask about the rationality of the higher-level framework. And so on. The whole system thus spirals in to infinite regress or *adhocery*.[20]

This argument fails as a criticism of the methodology of situational analysis, however, to the extent that it misidentifies that methodology with the programme of neoclassical economics. At the heart of the SL approach are the propositions that (1) the agent acts reasonably under the circumstances and that (2) the logic of those circumstances allows for only one exit. Nothing here requires the rarefied assumptions of the neoclassical core.

None the less, a behaviouralist might argue along the following lines. Even though SL is not identical with neoclassicism, does not the SL approach also fall down in regard to oligopoly and similar cases? It is really difficult to see a single 'exit' for the oligopolist under *any* assumptions. Oligopoly is inherently a multi-exit situation. As a consequence, we need to import from the outside certain decision procedures that make the agent's choices determinate. 'Programming' the agent is necessary to some extent, rendering *ad hoc* any determinate SL model.

In the end, however, this argument fails as well. It is certainly true that we can portray many situations, like oligopoly, as implying many exits, especially if the agent facing the situation is an anonymous and thinly rational one. But we can get determinate results in such situations not only by programming the agent but also by closing down the exits. We can do this in two complementary ways. First of all, we can thicken up the agent's rationality. That is, we can give the agent not a standard neoclassical logic but a more complicated decision-making apparatus. As Lawrence Boland (1982) suggests, we need not even see this 'thickening' as a matter of psychology: it is as much a matter of giving the agent a more sophisticated philosophy of knowledge.[21] And selecting a unique 'exit' to a problem-situation is as much a matter of the philosophy of knowledge the agent brings to the situation as it is of the structure of the situation itself. The two, indeed, are interdependent.

The second way to close up the exits is to alter the structure of the situation. This may indeed involve importing such artefacts as rules, habits, and customs. But these artefacts are not necessarily algorithms programmed into the agent; instead, they might form a background of institutions against which the agent chooses. Is such importation outside the logic of the SL approach? – not at all. It may well be part of the programme of neoclassical institutional economics to reduce all choice to preferences and ultimate givens;[22] but such a reduction need not be the programme of a more general SL approach. It is by no means inconsistent with situational analysis to follow the programme Joseph Agassi (1975) calls institutional individualism, in which various rules, habits, and conventions form part of the 'givens' of the agent's problem-situation. These background 'givens' break the chain of infinite regress, and do so in a way that, while perhaps *ad hoc* from the point of view of the hard core assumptions of neoclassical theory, is not at all *ad hoc* from the point of view of situational analysis.

Moreover, what is seldom noticed about the behaviouralist critique from adhocery is that behaviouralism, assuming programmed rule-following *ab ovo*, is no less guilty of being *ad hoc*, that is, of making rather arbitrary behavioural assumptions. Where do the postulated rules come from? How do we know the agent is following a habit, is satisficing, or is employing some decision-making heuristic? Close reading of behaviouralist manifestos, from early Simon (1955) through, say, Winter (1985), suggests that empirical observation is supposed to be the source of behavioural assumptions. But this will not do. Understood as part of the positive heuristic of the behaviouralist programme, the injunction to go forth and observe is so broad as to be compatible with virtually any kind of behavioural assumption. This may not be bad. It may even be unavoidable. But it is weak grounds from which to criticize even neoclassical economics for adhocery.

THE EXPLANATORY IMPORT OF SITUATIONAL LOGIC

We have so far argued that situational analysis can answer the objections of anti-neoclassical critics quite as well as can behaviouralism. Is there any argument for preferring the SL approach? The answer, we argue, is yes. And the reason is somewhat ironic: situational analysis provides a richer *explanation* of economic behaviour than does behaviouralism (understood as the assumption of programmed behaviour *ab ovo*).

We suggested earlier that explanation in economics involves showing how individual behaviour (appropriately specified) leads, through some compositional principle, to social outcomes. But, according to an honourable tradition in the philosophy of social science, explanation also involves the understanding or intentionalistic interpretation of a recurrent behavioural pattern *as* human action. This latter is a complicated analytical process that aims at answering two different types of questions.

At a minimum, we must first ask a '*What* did the agent do?' type of question. We get a definite anwer to this sort of question by identifying the behavioural pattern under discussion with a particular type of action, that is, by subsuming it under an appropriate intentionalistic description. Although the assumption of programmed behaviour is clearly deficient in this respect, there are no a priori reasons why both behaviouralism and situational analysis could not do this. Thus, despite possible substantive differences, there is no *logical* difference between the two approaches on this score.

As good and curious theorists, however, we want to know more than *what* the agent did. Having specified (directly or, in Max Weber's words, 'actually' understood) the action or action-type under discussion,[23] we also want to answer the more fundamental question: 'Why did the agent do what he or she did?' When we answer this question, we usually refer to the beliefs and desires – in one word: motives – of the agent under discussion. Consequently, understanding is a two-stage process. While in the first stage understanding of the observed behavioural pattern implies an interpretation in terms of imputed goals or intentions, in the second stage, we argue, understanding basically involves an interpretation in terms of the motives underlying the action or action-type under discussion.

SL models answer such 'why?' questions not directly but in what we might call an oblique manner. But this may be a virtue rather than a vice. Consider a fairly standard neoclassical version of an SL model in which, let us say, the actor wants to maximize the objective function $y = f(x)$. If it turns out that the observed outcome and action were y' and x' instead of y^* and x^* (that is, if both the actual outcome, y', and the actual behaviour, x', deviate in certain respects from the 'ideal' outcome and the 'ideal' action), we can begin to wonder: why did the actor do x'? Notice, however, that this is equivalent to the query: how can we explain the difference between x^* and x'? Now, it seems to go without saying that without the help of appropriate standards of comparison, set by an underlying analytic model, we either cannot raise this problem or, when answering the original 'Why did the agent do x'?' question, we must, *faute de mieux*, rely on completely *ad hoc* assumptions.[24]

If we have a well-formulated and well-specified SL model at our disposal, we can proceed with the explanation roughly in the following way.

1 We first ascertain whether an empirical situation under discussion really matches the situation-type specified in our model. Let us suppose that they are in fact structurally isomorphic.

2 Let us suppose further that our model rests on, say, five basic assumptions. (a) The actor tried to maximize $y = f(x)$, the objective function, under certain constraints. (b) The agent knew all the relevant means-ends relationships. (c) The agent was perfectly rational in the sense that his or her preferences satisfied the usual conditions imposed on 'rational' preference orderings. (d) There were no costs associated with the search for the best available alternative. And (e) the alternatives the agent took into account were all economically and technologically feasible ones.

3 Now, if we want an explanation of the deviation $x^* - x'$, that is, if we want a motivational understanding of x', we can simply scan the well-specified presuppositions of our SL model to find some hints to the possible source of the observed deviation. It may well turn out that, rather than being a maximizer in our sense, the agent had simply set an aspiration level, y'. The reasons for doing so might have had to do with the fact that the agent had to take certain costs of search into account. Or, alternatively, the agent may have acted value-rationally, that is, on the basis of a lexicographical ordering of the alternatives, and so forth, not *ad infinitum*, but until we find the conditions specified in the chosen SL model that were violated in the empirical situation under investigation and thus might be held responsible for the observed deviation of the actual from the ideal outcome.

The upshot of the foregoing argument is simply this. Although SL models do not always have direct empirical import, they help us explain recurrent action-types or actions in an essentially *oblique* manner. SL models have this instrumental value not because they are 'realistic' but because they specify very general single-exit means-ends frame-works. We would maintain, moreover, that this kind of obliqueness is unavoidable.

To see why this is so, consider the alternative of programmed (e.g. satisficing) behaviour assumed *ab ovo*. Just as it is hard to maintain that people 'in reality' *are* ideal maximizers in some sense, we cannot say either that in the ultimate analysis people *are* ideal satisficers in some other sense. In our opinion (but this is a substantive assumption, we readily admit), people *are* neither maximizers, nor satisficers, but optimizers (in a weak sense) out of necessity. That is, most of the time they do what their material and ideal interests dictate. The scarcity of resources and the omnipresence of a wide variety of situational con-straints make people constantly compare and weigh the costs and benefits of possible courses of action. This suggests a little-noticed problem with the satisficing assumption.[25] People cannot know, even if they are supposed to be satisficers *ab ovo*, what is enough for them if they do not know at the same time what would be more than enough. And if they know what would be more than enough, and if they could achieve it without incurring further psychological or economic costs, why would they not try to achieve it?

The answer seems obvious, and it applies equally to other types of rule-following behaviour. The satisficers; those who follow habits, tradition, and fashion; those who act under diverse, for us sometimes hardly understandable institutional constraints – all of these calculate differently from the hypothetical maximizer of our standard models. It seems an indisputable fact, however, that they try to act reasonably, sometimes even calculatively, under the circumstances they face. In the end, this is what satisficing frequently boils down to: the assumption of reasonable behaviour, which, for its own part, is arguably a method-ologically sound and theoretically indispensable working hypothesis for the social sciences.

NOTES

1 We make these terms more precise below.
2 It is, of course, somewhat controversial to say that there are two strands to the 'new institutional economics'. But see Langlois (1986a, 1989) for a defence of this view. Some writers, for example Richard Posner or Andrew Schotter, would represent different versions of the optimizing approach. Others, notably Oliver Williamson, pay great heed to the notion of bounded rationality, even if the resulting approach does not stray far from neoclassical optimization. And Nelson and Winter, to the extent they can be included under this rubric, use satisficing models explicitly.
3 In the manner of Milton Friedman (1953), author of the famous 'F-twist'.
4 For a definition of this term, and a general discussion of the many meanings of the term 'realistic', see Mäki (1989, 1992).

5 We have in mind here a model of explanation along the lines of Machlup's 'analytical apparatus', in which fundamental assumptions like behavioural postulates are elements in a logically consistent deductive system (Machlup 1955: 12–16). Although we use the language of causality, we do not mean to endorse strictly causal explanation in Elster's sense but rather the mixed case of 'intentional explanation of individual actions together with causal explanation of the interaction between individuals' (Elster 1983: 84, emphasis deleted). For a defence of this model of explanation see below and also Langlois (1986b, 1989).

6 For a discussion of this controversy, as well as an amplification of some of the themes of this section, see Langlois and Koppl (1991).

7 See, for example, the debate between Terence Hutchison (1938, 1956) and Machlup (1955, 1956).

8 On this point see Latsis (1972: 229). Much of the rhetoric of the behaviouralist approach is concerned with insisting that theory be informed by observation of what economic actors actually do. (See, for example, Winter (1985).) This is valuable advice when not interpreted as a demand for inductivism. For a classic critique of inductivism, see Popper (1974).

9 Absent, of course, the intervention of governments or, say, a large wheat cooperative. The presence of such actors would give proposition (1) more of the character of proposition (3).

10 That this argument puts marginalism into an extremely small (albeit important and highly defensible) corner has not often been noticed (Langlois and Koppl 1991). One exception is Latsis (1976b: 55), who notes in passing that 'when Machlup extols the virtues of the neoclassical theory of sellers' behaviour, he is really talking about Marshallian demand and supply and in particular about long-run price adjustments'. See also Loasby (1976: 45–6).

11 For an analysis along these lines of the application of economic models to political decisions, see Langlois (1988).

12 See expecially Latsis (1972, 1976a,b).

13 Although this is a rather narrow and highly stylized characterization of behaviouralism, we still believe that our criticism is not directed against straw men.

14 To the extent, however, that we distinguish between human *action* and human *behaviour*, then only the SL approach appears consistent with what D.C. Dennett (1987) calls 'the intentional stance'. Action and behaviour may be conceived as occupying two extreme positions on a conceptual spectrum. Fully conscious, intentional conduct fades into involuntary reflex behaviour as we move along this spectrum.

15 Cf. Langlois (1986b: 235–41).

16 This pre-programming approach to determinateness in behavioural assumptions is not new, of course. It was, in fact, a possibility entertained within the Weberian tradition. To the Austrian sociologist and philospher Alfred Schutz, for example, the 'puppet called "personal ideal type" is . . . never a subject of or a centre of spontaneous activity. . . . His destiny is regulated and determined beforehand by his creator, the social scientist, and in such a perfect pre-established harmony as Leibniz imagined the world created by God' (Schutz: 1943: 144–5).

17 Indeed, the psychological content of the agents in Nelson-and-Winter's evolutionary model (especially Nelson and Winter 1982, ch. 7) is not all that much greater than that of Machlup's wheat farmer – and appropriately so. In both cases, a rather anonymous ideal type is in order given the nature of the common *explanandum* of these models and the severe pressure of the

system constraint. Although the aggregate predictions of the two analyses are in the end almost identical, there are explanatory differences worthy of discussion. This is not the place for such a discussion, however.

18 See note 14, *above*.

19 On which see Latsis (1976b).

20 For an analysis of this problem, see Knudsen (Chap. 6, this volume). In addition to the references he cites, however, see also Kirzner (1982: 143–5) and Langlois (1986b, *passim*).

21 On this point compare Loasby (1986).

22 For the classic critique of this reduction, see Field (1979, 1981, 1984).

23 In economics, in contrast to other social sciences, this sort of understanding is assumed to be self-evident. Although it has far-reaching methodological consequences, this is not the place to go into the reasons for this difference.

24 The economic theory of the business cycle might be an obvious case in point. Consider this distinction offered by Hayek (1939), cited in Boland (1982):

> Every explanation of economic crises must include the assumption that entrepreneurs have committed errors. But the mere fact that entrepreneurs do make errors can hardly be regarded as a sufficient explanation of crises. Erroneous dispositions which lead to losses all round will appear probable only if we can show why entrepreneurs should all simultaneously make mistakes in the same direction. The explanation that this is just due to a kind of psychological infection . . . does not carry much conviction. It seems, however, more likely that they may all be equally misled by following guides or symptoms which as a rule prove reliable. Or, speaking more concretely, it may be that the prices existing when they make their decisions and on which they had to base their views about the future have created expectations which must necessarily be disappointed. In this case we might have to distinguish between what we may call justified errors, caused by the price system, and sheer errors about the course of external events.
>
> (Boland 1982: 47)

Clearly, we cannot make such a distinction without having a clear-cut SL model of entrepreneurial behaviour to begin with.

25 Sidney Winter has made a similar point. 'At some level of analysis, all goal seeking behavior is satisficing behavior. There must be limits to the range of possibilities explored, and these limits must be arbitrary in the sense that the decision maker *cannot know* that they are optimal' (Winter 1964: 264, emphasis original).

REFERENCES

Agassi, J. (1975) 'Institutional individualism', *British Journal of Sociology* 26: 144–55.

Baumol, W.J., and Quandt, R.E. (1964) 'Rules of thumb and optimally imperfect decisions', *American Economic Review* 54: 23–46.

Boland, L.A. (1982) *The Foundations of Economic Method*, London: Allen & Unwin.

Day, R.H. (1967) 'Profits, learning, and the convergence of satisficing to marginalism', *Quarterly Journal of Economics* 81(2): 302–11.

Dennett, D.C. (1987) *The Intentional Stance*, Cambridge, Mass.: MIT Press.

Elster, J. (1983) *Explaining Technical Change: A Case Study in the Philosophy of Science*, Cambridge: Cambridge University Press.

Field, A.J. (1979) 'On the explanation of rules using rational choice models', *Journal of Economic Issues* 13(1): 49–72.

—— (1981) 'The problem with neoclassical institutional economics: a critique with special reference to the North/Thomas model of pre-1500 Europe', *Explorations in Economic History* 18: 174–98.

—— (1984) 'Microeconomics, norms, and rationality', *Economic Development and Cultural Change* 32: 683–711.

Friedman, M. (1953) 'The methodology of positive economics', in M. Friedman *Essays in Positive Economics*, Chicago: University of Chicago Press.

Hands, D.W. (1988) 'Ad hocness in economics and the Popperian tradition', in N. de Marchi (ed.) *The Popperian Legacy in Economics*, Cambridge: Cambridge University Press.

Hayek, F.A. (1939) 'Price expectations, monetary disturbances and malinvestments', in F.A. Hayek *Profits, Interest and Investment*, London: Routledge.

Heiner, R.A. (1983) 'The origin of predictable behavior', *American Economic Review* 73: 560–95.

—— (1986) 'Uncertainty, signal-detection experiments, and modeling behavior', in R.N. Langlois (ed.) *Economics as a Process: Essays in the New Institutional Economics*, Cambridge: Cambridge University Press, pp. 59–115.

Hutchison, T. (1938) *The Significance and Basic Postulates of Economic Theory*, New York: Augustus M. Kelley.

—— (1956) 'Professor Machlup on verification in economics', *Southern Economic Journal* 22: 476–83.

Kahneman, D. and Tversky, A. (1981) 'The framing of decisions and the psychology of choice', *Science* 211: 453–8.

Kirzner, I.M. (1982) 'Uncertainty, discovery, and human action: a study of the entrepreneurial profile in the Misesian system', in I.M. Kirzner (ed.) *Method, Process, and Austrian Economics: Essays in Honor of Ludwig von Mises*, Lexington, Mass.: D.C. Heath, pp 139–59.

Langlois, R.N. (1986a) 'The new institutional economics: an introductory essay', in R. Langlois (ed.) *Economics as a Process: Essays in the New Institutional Economics*, Cambridge: Cambridge University Press, pp. 1–25.

—— (1986b) 'Rationality, institutions, and explanation', in R. Langlois (ed.) *Economics as a Process: Essays in the New Institutional Economics*, Cambridge: Cambridge University Press, pp. 225–55.

—— (1988) 'Are economic models applicable to politics?' *Economia delle Scelta Pubbliche/Journal of Public Finance and Public Choice* 1988 (2): 83–93.

—— (1989) 'What was wrong with the "Old" Institutional Economics? (and what is still wrong with the "New"?)' *Review of Political Economy* 1(3): 272–300.

—— and Koppl, R. (1991) 'Fritz Machlup and marginalism: a reevaluation', *Methodus*, December, 3(2): 86–102.

Latsis, S.J. (1972) 'Situational determinism in economics', *British Journal for the Philosophy of Science* 23: 207–45.

—— (1976a) 'The limitations of single-exit models: reply to Machlup', *British Journal for the Philosophy of Science* 27: 51–60.

—— (1976b) 'A research programme in economics', in S.J. Latsis (ed.) *Method and Appraisal in Economics*, Cambridge: Cambridge University Press.

Loasby, B.J. (1976) *Choice, Complexity, and Ignorance*, Cambridge: Cambridge University Press.

—— (1986) 'Organization, competition, and the growth of knowledge', in R.N. Langlois (ed.) *Economics as a Process: Essays in the New Institutional Economics*, Cambridge: Cambridge Unversity Press, 41–57.

Machlup, F. (1936) 'Why bother with methodology?' *Economica* N.S., 3: 39–45.

—— (1955) 'The problem of verification in economics', *Southern Economic Journal* 22: 1–21.

—— (1956) 'Rejoinder to a reluctant ultra-empiricist', *Southern Economic Journal* 22: 483–93.

—— (1978) *Methodology of Economics and Other Social Sciences*, New York: Academic Press.

Mäki, U. (1989) 'On the problem of realism in economics', *Ricerche Economiche* 43(1–2): 176–98. (Reprinted in B. Caldwell (ed.) *The Philosophy and Methodology of Economics*, Worcester: Edward Elgar.)

—— (1992) 'Friedman and realism', *Research in the History of Economic Thought and Methodology* 10: 171–95.

Nelson, R.R. and Winter, S.G. (1982) *An Evolutionary Theory of Economic Change*, Cambridge, Mass.: Harvard University Press.

Popper, K.R. (1966) *The Open Society and Its Enemies*, (Vol. II), 2nd edition, Princeton, New Jersey: Princeton University Press.

—— (1967) 'La rationalité et le statut du principe de rationalité, in E.M. Claassen (ed.) *Les Fondements Philosophiques des Systèmes Economiques*, Paris: Payot.

—— (1974) 'Replies to my critics', in P.A. Schillp (ed.) *The Philosophy of Karl Popper*, La Salle, Illinois: Open Court, pp. 1013–30.

Schutz, A. (1943) 'The problem of rationality in the social world', *Economica*, N.S. 10: 130–49.

Simon, H.A. (1955) 'A behavioral model of rational choice', *Quarterly Journal of Economics* 69: 99–118.

Tversky, A. and Kahneman, D. (1974) 'Judgments under uncertainty: heuristics and biases', *Science* 185: 1124–31.

Winter, S.G. (1964) 'Economic "natural selection" and the theory of the firm', *Yale Economic Essays* 4: 225–72.

—— (1985) 'The research program of the behavioral theory of the firm: orthodox critique and evolutionary perspective', in B. Gilad and S. Kaish (eds) *Handbook of Behavioral Economics*, Greenwich, Connecticut: JAI Press.

6

EQUILIBRIUM, PERFECT RATIONALITY AND THE PROBLEM OF SELF-REFERENCE IN ECONOMICS[1]

Christian Knudsen

ABSTRACT

Over the last two decades a number of attempts have been made to broaden the behavioural foundation of economics. This chapter looks especially at Herbert Simon's attempt to replace the 'substantive' concept of rationality with a 'procedural' one. Starting with the 'growth of knowledge' literature it is attempted to clarify what theoretical problems, anomalies, antinomies, etc. within the optimization paradigm, are the reasons behind this development. First the so-called 'general argument' in favour of the procedural concept of rationality is discussed, which maintains that we encounter a self-reference problem when we attempt to incorporate optimization costs into the optimization calculus. While this anomaly is found in an analysis of a single economic agent, the chapter argues that a far greater problem of self-reference is posed in analyses of the interaction between economic agents. This anomaly was first pointed out in the 1930s by, respectively, F.A. Hayek (1937) and Oskar Morgenstern (1935). The chapter attempts to demonstrate how this problem emerges in different areas of the optimization paradigm such as the theory of perfect competition, oligopoly theory, the theory of rational expectation and finally non-cooperative game theory.

INTRODUCTION

In an article from 1976, entitled 'From substantive to procedural rationality', Herbert Simon argued that in the future economists would increasingly build their theories on a procedural concept of rationality at the expense of the more traditional concept of substantive rationality.[2] In order to support his thesis empirically, Simon pointed out a number of concrete economic theories and theoretical fields characterized by this trend. By this, he tried to justify empirically a thesis that economic theory underwent a form of a quiet and prolonged scientific revolution during which the neoclassical research programme slowly was being transformed.

In this chapter, I shall try to sustain Simon's thesis, but at the same time offer a more comprehensive explanation than just referring to some empirical material. My point of departure is that a research programme, based on a substantive concept of rationality, encounters a series of fundamental conceptual problems in modelling the interaction between individual agents and explaining how equilibria outcomes emerge as the result of the rational deliberations of the agents. In his article from 1976, Simon briefly touches upon a similar explanation in relation to his discussion of imperfect competition:

> More than a century ago, Cournot identified a problem that has become the permanent and ineradicable scandal of economic theory. He observed that where a market is supplied by only a few producers, the notion of profit-maximization is ill-defined. The choice that would be substantively rational for each actor depends on the choices made by other actors; none can choose without making assumptions about how others will choose. ... I have referred to the theory of imperfect competition as a 'scandal' because it has been treated as such in economics, and because it is generally conceded that no defensible formulation of the theory stays within the framework of profit-maximization and substantively rationality. ... *There remains, however, a lingering reluctance to acknowledge the impossibility of discovering at last 'The Rule' of substantively rational behaviour for the oligopolist. Only when the hope of that discovery has been finally extinguished will it be admitted that understanding imperfect competition means understanding procedural rationality.*
>
> (Simon 1976: 140–1, emphasis added)

Explaining how equilibrium emerges in an oligopolistic market as the outcome of the interaction between 'profit-maximizing' firms will then, according to Simon, not just be an anomaly but indeed an antinomy within the paradigm of substantive rationality. By insisting on working within an orthodox framework, economists have only succeeded in solving this problem by introducing *ad hoc* hypotheses of a more and more elaborate kind. However, finding a genuine or *non-ad hoc* solution to this problem seems to require a broadening of the behavioural foundation of economics insofar as one has to emphasize not only the substantive, but also the procedural and epistemic aspects of rationality.

Taking for my point of departure in the second section, the growth of knowledge literature, I start by reconstructing Simon's thesis that economics is undergoing a quiet and prolonged scientific revolution. In

134

general, most of this historiographic literature seems to have under-estimated the importance of conceptual problems such as paradoxes, antinomies and other kinds of theoretical anomalies in the evolution of economic theory. In fact, conceptual problems seem to be of utmost importance in understanding the 'hidden mechanism' behind the dynamics of theoretical economics in general, as well as in the specific development referred to in Simon (1976). I sketch a model of scientific progress in economics, which portrays the dynamics of the discipline as analogous to what Schumpeter in another context called: *creative destruction*.

The following, third, section is then a first step towards disclosing the character of the conceptual problems, which according to the above presentation, exist within the paradigm of substantive rationality. In this section the so-called *general argument* for a concept of procedural rationality is analysed more thoroughly. According to this argument, the paradigm of substantive rationality runs into a serious anomaly when trying to incorporate optimization costs into the calculus of optimization itself. Behind this problem one can detect what philosophers refer to as a self-reference problem making it impossible to define an optimal solution.

However, this type of problem is not only confined to models of individual decision makers, but seems even more common in analysis of systems of interacting decision makers. In the fourth section it is then argued that one can detect some similarities behind the numerous paradoxes, anomalies, and *ad hoc* hypotheses, that economists have identified in this paradigm explaining or justifying how the different equilibria emerge. In fact, it is postulated that all attempts to solve this problem within the paradigm of substantive rationality have been *ad hoc*, since they have suppressed the procedural and epistemic aspect of rationality by not being able to explain how the economic agents acquire the necessary knowledge to be substantive rational. This problem was already carefully analysed in the 1930s by Friedrich Hayek (1937) and Oskar Morgenstern (1935). Their argument was something like this: in any system of interaction the agents will base their decision partly on expectations or predictions on what other agents will do. However, to make substantive rational decisions the agents have to justify their expectations/predictions as sensible or rational. But this seems, however, to be an impossible task due to the self-referential problem involved: to justify one's expectations as well founded, one must have some know-ledge about all the other agents' knowledge, because the future depends partly on their predictions and the action based on these. But a part of these agents' knowledge will depend on what they know about the first agent's knowledge. And so on. The general structure of this problem is an example of what is known as a self-reference problem.

However, problems of self-reference also lead to another conceptual difficulty, which the German philosopher and sociologist Hans Albert denotes as the 'trilemma of Münchhausen'.[3] Demanding a complete justification of any claim of knowledge leads, inevitably, to one of the following three consequences: an *infinite regress*, a *vicious circle*, or a *dogmatic interruption*. Since each of these three consequences is inconsistent with the demand for a complete justification, the demand is self-contradictory. If we try to comply with it, we will automatically violate it.

This trilemma is encountered in economics whenever we try to justify the use of the equilibrium concept by telling a story of how this state emerges as the result of the agents' substantive rational deliberation. The main thesis of this chapter is that it will be impossible to construct such a story that stays within the orthodox paradigm and is consistent/ non-contradictory/*non-ad hoc*. For as in the general case of the Münchhausen trilemma, we end up either in an infinite regress, a vicious circle or making a dogmatic interruption.

The discussion of how this problem manifests itself in different parts of economics, is then structured on the basis of how economists within the paradigm of substantive rationality have been modelling different kinds of interaction. Taking our point of departure in indirect, unconscious and parametric interaction as in the theory of perfect competition, we go on to analysis of indirect and functional interaction known from studies of oligopolistic interaction, to rational expectation theory and we finally come to non-cooperative game theory. In all these cases, it will be impossible to find genuine *non-ad hoc* solutions to how such systems adjust to a state of equilibrium which remains within a research programme based on substantive rationality.

After having studied this anomalous problem of self-reference within the 'paradigm of substantive rationality' I discuss in the final section how this problem gradually seems to 'create' the seeds of a new evolutionary theory of institutions.

THE ROLE OF CONCEPTUAL PROBLEMS IN THE DEVELOPMENT OF ECONOMICS

Thomas Kuhn's theory of 'scientific revolutions' may be summarized as an attempt to describe the research process in terms of what Schumpeter in another context called processes of 'creative destruction'. By this I mean that every paradigm creates the seeds of its own destruction by bringing forth the anomalous problems that eventually will be the reason why a new paradigm replaces an old one. In fact, by stressing the importance of conceptual problems, economics seems to have followed a pattern of development which seems much closer to one we usually associate with the mathematical and logical disciplines rather than with the empirical sciences.

In this section an attempt is made to outline the main component of such a process of creative destruction by describing it in terms of and comparing it with some growth of knowledge models that has been applied to economics. As Kuhn's theory of scientific revolution leaves much to be desired as regards clarity and definition of the basic concepts, I have chosen to take my point of departure in Lakatos' 'methodology of scientific research programmes' (MSRP).[4] As I shall stress below, his usage of the '*ad hoc*' concept as a counterpart of Kuhn's concept of an anomaly, is essential in this connection.

A research programme can, according to Lakatos (1970), be characterized by the following three concepts: a set of irrefutable propositions called the hard core (H), a protective belt of successive auxiliary and refutable hypotheses ($B_1, B_2, \ldots B_n$) and a set of suggestions on how to develop the programme called the positive and negative heuristic. By the help of these three concepts, the theoretical development: $T_1, T_2, \ldots T_n$ within a research programme (i.e. normal science) may be described as follows: $T_1 = H + B_1$, $T_2 = H + B_2$, $\ldots T_n = H + B_n$, where the hard core by decision is made irrefutable. According to Lakatos such a decision will only be rational as long as the programme is both theoretical and empirical progressive. That is, every new theory within the programme *predicts* some novel, hitherto unexpected facts (theoretically progressive) and some of this excess content is sooner or later *corroborated* (empirically progressive). A theory that fails to meet these two criteria is called an *ad hoc*$_1$ or an *ad hoc*$_2$ modification, indicating that the research programme is degenerating theoretically and empirically.

But will a theoretical and empirical degeneration of the neoclassical research programme in this specific sense be seen as a sign of crises by the economic profession? I think not. And my reason for not doing so is that Lakatos' MSRP seems to give us a far too restricted conception of theoretical research in economics. In a case study analysing how economists actually used the *ad hoc* concept in their scientific discourse, Wade Hands came to a similar conclusion: 'Thus, for economic theorists, the sin of *adhocness* seems infidelity to the metaphysical presuppositions of the neoclassical program rather than face-saving adjustment in response to recalcitrant data' (Hands 1988: 128). This conclusion ought, in my opinion, to seriously affect our understanding of the character of economic research and what 'mechanism' drives the theoretical development of our subject.

It seems to be the underlying Popperian hypothetico-deductive understanding of research in Lakatos' MSRP which is at stake here. By focusing on the role of 'empirical falsifications' in generating new

problems of research, the Popperian as well as the Lakatosian methodology gives us a far too restrictive conception of what constitutes an
anomaly or an *ad hoc* hypothesis within economics. This is true not only
in the sense that the methodologies in question underestimate the role
of conceptual problems, but also in the sense that it would be incorrect
to equate 'empirical problems' with 'empirical falsifications'.

Most of the empirical problems economic theorists try to solve
seem not to originate from falsification of predictions, but emerge
because the prevalent research programmes impede or make the
occurrence of certain empirical phenomena impossible. One prominent
example of this was the coexistence of stagnation and inflation during
the 1970s. This so-called phenomenon of stagflation constituted an
empirical problem in macroeconomics not because it falsified any
theories, but because the very existence of the phenomenon was
impeded by the prevalent macroeconomic theories at that time.
Another analogous example of this is the emergence of Kelvin
Lancaster's new theory of consumer behaviour. The historical background of this theory is not to be found in any successful attempts of
falsifying the predictions of the Hicks–Allen theory. The problem was
rather that this theory, according to Lancaster, was 'completely incapable of handling the most important aspect of demand in an advanced
consumer society – the effects of product variations and differentiates,
model changes, and new variants of existing goods' (Lancaster 1971: 8).
This 'empirical problem' was solved through generalizing the utility
function of the orthodox theory by replacing a vector of goods with a
vector of characteristics. By doing so, Lancaster was able to deal
with some of the empirical phenomena that earlier were impossible to
even formulate within the orthodox research programme of consumer
behaviour.

However, Lakatos (1970) seems to have been aware of some of the
problems which his underlying Popperian philosophy created for him
in constructing an adequate and sufficiently broad characterization of
scientific research. By arguing for a third type of *ad hoc* hypotheses,
anomalies or non-acceptable modifications of a research programme
called *ad hoc₃* hypotheses, he tried to accommodate other types of
anomalies into his methodological framework.

Ad hoc₃ hypotheses are defined as extensions of the protective belt of
a research programme, which is not in accordance with the spirit of its
positive heuristic.[5] In fact, the rationale for avoiding such *ad hoc₃*
modifications seems to be to secure a high degree of continuity and
organic unity in the programme by protecting it against threats of
fragmentation and disintegration.[6] Lakatos even goes as far as to claim
that the absence of such *ad hoc₃* hypotheses is the distinguishing mark
between 'mature science' consisting of problem solving within one or

more research programmes and 'immature science' consisting of a mere patched-up pattern of 'trial and error' (Lakatos 1970: 175).

The importance of ad hoc₃ hypotheses and the associated stress on heuristic compared to theoretical and empirical progress in economics, must, however, make us reconsider the appropriateness of the whole Lakatosian conception of our field of enquiry. Wade Hands (1988) makes the following suggestion:

> Although heuristic progress (*non-ad hoc₃ness*) seems to be precisely what concerns economic theorists the most, it is almost never mentioned in the extensive literature that applies the MSRP to economics. ... On the negative side, it seems that theorists' revealed preference for heuristic over theoretical/empirical progress (as Lakatos defines these terms) will make it hard to reconcile the history of economic thought with Lakatos' requirement that novel facts be predicted (though they need not be confirmed) at each stage in the program's development. ... In any case, it appears that philosophers and economists taking a Lakatosian approach to economics seriously reconsider the question of heuristic progress (*non-ad hoc₃ness*) and its role in the evaluation of economic theory.
>
> (Hands 1988: 134–5)

I would even go further and argue that Lakatos's introduction of heuristic progress (*non-ad hoc₃ness*) into the Popperian methodological research programme by itself constitutes such an *ad hoc₃* hypothesis. In fact, the introduction of the idea of heuristic progress or degeneration (*ad hoc₃ness*) does not live up to Lakatos' own requirement that 'the additional assertion [in this case: heuristic progress/degeneration] must be connected with the original assertions [in this case: the Popperian MSRP] *more intimately* than by mere conjunction' (Lakatos 1970: 136). Instead of having one single and precise criterion of scientific progress, Lakatos gets a situation of having conflicting yardsticks for methodological appraisal, where he has to make trade-offs between theoretical and empirical progress on the one hand and heuristic progress on the other hand.[7] Another and more fruitful way of approaching this problem from the point of view of economics would be to make a more dramatic break with or generalization of the underlying falsificationist framework. One such alternative perspective is to look upon science as a problem solving activity as suggested by Larry Laudan (1977), Thomas Nickles (1981), and many others (even including Karl Popper (1972)).

From the point of view of such a methodological framework, the evolution of, for example, the paradigm of 'substantive rationality' should be regarded as an attempt to solve successively emerging theoretical and empirical problems. According to this point of view there is no basic

139

difference between theoretical and empirical problems, as theoretical problems are only perceived as belonging to a higher order than the empirical ones, because they question the solidness of the conceptual structures that has been constructed in order to solve problems of the first order. Compared to a Popperian–Lakatosian understanding of economic research, a number of advantages are obtained from not operating with a trichotomy between theoretical, empirical, and heuristic problems, but rather with a continuum or hierarchy of problem types.

By subordinating the importance of empirical tests of predictions in relation to the theoretical development, the *problem-solving perspective* makes it possible to give a more balanced and adequate picture of the theoretical development of economics. An example of this is, for instance, that one is not forced, as in the case of the Hands' quotation above, to characterize the majority of advances within economic research as heuristic rather than theoretical or empirical. However, the best argument in favour of a problem solving methodology will be to prove how, in practice, it can provide us with a deeper understanding of the nature of economic research and the underlying mechanisms constituting the basis for the scientific development of the field.

According to Larry Laudan (1977), empiricist as well as falsificationist's methodologies have underestimated the role of theoretical or conceptual problems within scientific research as a whole. This especially applies to economics. In what follows I will try to remedy this by analysing in detail what he calls *internal conceptual problems* as applied to economics.[8] Such problems occur when real or apparently 'insoluble' problems are encountered in a research programme during periods of normal science – often taking the shape of paradoxes that cannot be resolved within the same paradigm. Such conceptual problems have often proved to be caused by the fact that the concepts of the hitherto problem solutions are too 'narrow' or too 'special' to conceptualize that or those phenomena encountered. In the course of the development of a research programme such a conceptual problem will occur when it proves impossible to construct a solution or theory that *both* applies the hard core of the programme (e.g. the concept of substantive rationality) *and* comply with the maxims that constitute the positive heuristic of the programme. In reality this implies a confrontation with the following dilemma: *either* the hard core of the programme must be refuted, which in practice is equivalent to abandoning the whole programme, *or* an inadequate solution must be constructed – in the shape of what Lakatos described as an *ad hoc₃-modification* of the paradigm – by violating the maxims of the positive heuristic.

Historically, a majority of the conceptual problems have proven resolvable. By, for example, generalizing the concepts of the theory, it has proven possible to get rid of inconsistencies of the old theory and thus solving a number of apparently insoluble problems. However, it may, to some extent, be appropriate to doubt whether all the internal conceptual problems of a research programme can be solved in this way within the frames of the same paradigm. Kant, for example, asserts the existence of a number of so-called *antinomies* which can be characterized as deeply rooted conceptual problems to which no adequate and final solution seems to exist.

It is my thesis that the so-called 'adjustment problem' represents such an antinomy within the 'substantive rationality' paradigm. In their attempt to solve this problem economic theorists have just replaced one *ad hoc*$_3$ modification with another – although at a higher level – without ever escaping the original dilemma. This was probably what made Simon claim that this problem must ultimately lead, because of its character of an antinomy, to a break with the programme of substantive rationality in favour of a research programme based upon a procedural concept of rationality.

However, I shall first present the traditional, or what Jon Elster (1983) calls the *general argument*, for preferring a procedural over a substantive concept of rationality. This argument shows that the introduction of calculation costs in the optimization paradigm leads to some very deep-seated conceptual problems at the same time as it creates a clearer basis for what the outlines for a new research programme based on a procedural concept of rationality will look like. In fact, this summarizes the content of what was called a *process of creative destruction* in economics: the old paradigm produces itself the anomalies that lead to its own destruction and create the basis of a new paradigm.

INDIVIDUAL RATIONALITY, CALCULATION COSTS, AND THE PROBLEM OF SELF-REFERENCE

All human behaviour may *ex post* be regarded as optimizing behaviour, if a sufficient number of objective and subjective situational constraints are included as secondary conditions in the decision making problem of the agent and the observed behaviour thus becomes the 'only feasible behaviour'. This is one of the main conclusions of the so-called strong version of the *Duhem–Quine thesis*, which Quine has formulated in the following way: 'any statement can be held true come what may, if we make drastic enough adjustments elsewhere in the system' (Quine 1961: 43). It is exactly such a strategy that a group of researchers pursues when they 'decide' to work within a certain paradigm, research programme, or tradition by not questioning the fundamental assumptions of the paradigm or what Lakatos calls its 'hard core'.[9] By not subjecting this core to any kind of attempts of falsification but rather solving problems by modifying or revising the hypothesis of what Lakatos calls the protective belt of the research programme, all possible issues may be brought within the scope of this programme. Or as stated by Sidney Winter:

> Given evidence that some particular observed behavior is not optimal in some specific sense, the traditional response in economic theory is to reconsider the 'sense'. One asks what costs or objectives may be present in the real situation that have not been properly accounted for in the optimization calculus. This heuristic principle [my interpretation: the strong version of the Duhem–Quine thesis] is admirably effective at bringing all possible empirical issues within the scope of the theory, so that the question posed is not *whether* the theory is consistent with the facts, but *how* it is consistent with them. Given this principle, the sort of empirical challenge sketched above is doomed to failure from the start: The findings of Aharoni or Elliason, even the apparently gross blundering of General Dynamics, can only serve to suggest an intriguing range of puzzles concerning optimization in the face of information costs, uncertainty, and perhaps managerial objectives that diverge from stockholder interest.
>
> (Winter 1975: 81–2)

But it is one thing to bring all possible issues within the scope of the paradigm. It is a quite different thing to claim that such a heuristic inevitably leads to scientific progress in a theoretical, empirical, or heuristic sense, or in relation to the programme's overall capacity of solving problems. The problem of the strong version of the Duhem–Quine thesis is, as the Winter quotation above indicates, that this thesis makes it possible to immunize the hard core, that is the optimization principle, from any imaginable attempt of falsification. In this way we are thus able to defend any research programme and its hard core, something which makes the defence both tautological and quite trivial.[10] It was exactly this problem which sophisticated falsificationists such as Lakatos opposed, demanding a more aggressive methodological framework. By demanding that a research programme is to produce new theories of an increasing theoretical and empirical content, certain methodological demands were expected to be fulfilled by the programme and its hard core, the redemption of which were to justify a continual acceptance of its hard core and its heuristic.[11] The theoretical modification to be dealt with below concerns the way in which theorists working within the 'paradigm of substantive rationality' have tried to provide for the fact that calculations are costly and that optimization involves a certain positive amount of calculations.[12] This problem was introduced and discussed systematically for the first time by Marschak (1954) and Stigler (1961);[13] they were both searching for a solution to

this problem that was intended to be within the frames of the optimization paradigm. They claimed that it would often be rational to refrain
from an optimal choice, because the costs (including the consumption
of time) of obtaining the necessary information would make this
economically rational. Until then, researchers working within the paradigm of optimization had taken it for granted that all resources, with
the exception of the decision making capacity of the agents, were scarce
resources. When Marschak and Stigler now claimed that the costs of
information and calculus also ought to be economized on, by making a
marginal calculus of second order, the aim was to construct a solution
to the problem which met the demand for perfection. But then we run
up against the so-called problem of self-reference. Sidney Winter has
formulated it elegantly in the following passage:

> Consider the costs of a particular optimization in relation to the
> scope of the optimization itself. Either they are neglected – in
> which case we label this particular example a 'suboptimization' –
> or they are not – in which case we may label this a 'true'
> optimization or 'superoptimization' provided no other costs or
> considerations have been neglected. The latter alternative – the
> optimization whose scope covers all consideration including its own
> costs – sounds like it may involve the logical difficulties of self-
> reference. To demonstrate this – to prove logically that there is no
> superoptimization – would require the development of a formal
> framework within which the statement could be interpreted. That
> would be an interesting project.
>
> (Winter 1975: 83)

Sidney Winter then concludes:

> Given these premises [positive costs of calculus, etc.], the conclu-
> sion that there is no superoptimization follows, as a matter of logic,
> for the real world just as for the hypothetical one. In this sense,
> the image of firm optimising behaviour that, in the discussion
> above, was granted the status of a 'reasonable guess' appears not
> so reasonable, so far as the demand for 'globalness' is concerned.
>
> (Winter 1975: 85)

The problem of self-reference may also be represented as a Münchhausen
trilemma, where we end up in one of the following three situations: an
infinite regress, a dogmatic interruption or a vicious circle. This shows
that the 'solution of superoptimization' is contradictory and thus un-
attainable.[14] If we try to take all costs into consideration within the
calculus of optimization, including the costs of the calculus itself, the
result is that it is impossible in these situations to define an optimal
choice: to make a decision is cost consuming; therefore it must be

decided whether it is worth making a decision. But to make a decision implies costs; therefore we must decide, whether it is worth making a decision on whether it is worth making a decision, etc. Sooner or later, however, this infinite regress must be interrupted which leads to the second of Münchhausen's trilemmas: a dogmatic interruption. In this case one accepts what Sidney Winter called a suboptimizing result because not all the costs of calculation related to achieving the optimal solution have been taken into consideration. On the basis of the paradigm of optimization this is unacceptable for two reasons. Firstly, because optimal behaviour is never defined when such a calculation involves costs. Secondly, because the result shows that the assumption or principle of bounded or procedural rationality cannot be arranged according to or reduced to the principle of optimization, but must be regarded as an autonomous principle of explanation on which alternative economic research programmes may be founded.[15] The third possibility: a vicious circle, would exist if a marginal calculation was used to justify a marginal calculation of a higher order that already at an earlier stage had formed part of the attempt of justification.

PERFECT RATIONALITY, EQUILIBRIUM, AND SELF-REFERENCE

The argument presented above is the one that traditionally has been advocated in favour of a concept of procedural rationality and against a concept of substantive rationality. However, I will assert that a far stronger argument in favour of the concept of procedural rationality may be obtained by not focusing on the level of the individual decision maker. This will be the case if we instead take our point of departure in the internal conceptual problems which the paradigm of optimization has encountered in studying systems of interdependent decision makers. These problems are all connected with attempts to explain the emergence of various states of equilibria as the result of the interaction between perfect rational agents.

The discussion in the following subsection on how these problems emerge within different areas of economic theory will be structured on the basis of the character of interaction discussed by the theory in question. According to Leif Johansen (1981) it is possible to distinguish between three different types of interaction. The first type – which among other things is known from the theory of perfect competition – is labelled: *unconscious*, *indirect*, and *parametric*. It analyses the interaction between *parametrical* rational agents, that is, agents which make a choice *without consciously* considering which actions the other agents may take and the effect of their own decision on that of the others. Hence the term: unconscious and parametric. Finally, it is characterized as *indirect* because there is no direct exchange of information between the agents and they are not allowed to make any binding commitments. This also applies to the other type of interaction, which Leif Johansen (ibid.) labels: *indirect* and *functional*. Here, the individual agent's awareness of the other agents is more pronounced and more advanced than in the first type. It is assumed that they are acquainted with the other agents' reactional patterns in the shape of functional relations (hence the name 'functional'). This type of interaction is, for instance, known from various theories of imperfect competition such as models of oligopolistic interaction. Finally, Leif Johansen (ibid.) points out a third type of interaction which he calls *direct* interaction in which agents are allowed to exchange information, make commitments and form coalitions. An example of this is cooperative game theory.

When studying different systems of interaction, economics has used almost all its intellectual resources on solving the problem of whether an equilibrium exists and if so, what characterizes it. The conditions for the emergence of such a state of equilibrium has, however, not attracted an equal amount of attention. This is probably the single most important reason for economists almost exclusively having applied a concept of substantive rationality, which historically has been closely linked with the static type of analysis and not a procedural concept of rationality intended for more process-oriented types of analysis.

At the methodological level attempts have been made to legitimize this priority by referring to an instrumentalist philosophy of science, represented by for example Milton Friedman's 'Methodology of positive economics' (1953). According to such a point of view, there is no reason for specifying the process generating equilibrium, all energy should be concentrated on characterizing it and deducing comparative static theorems/predictions. Regardless of which motives the agents may have for acting during the process of attaining equilibrium, a mechanism of market selection would guarantee that the agents' behaviour in the end state/equilibrium would be substantive rational.

The criticism directed towards this research strategy and its methodological legitimation has primarily been raised by adherents to a realist philosophy of science. They have claimed that it is difficult to justify the vast amount of research invested in studying different states of equilibria as long as the process whereby it is attained has not been specified, including the reasoning of the individual agents. Such an argument was already introduced by Friedrich Hayek in the 1930s:

> The statement that, if people know everything, they are in equilibrium is true simply because that is how we define equilibrium. The assumption of a perfect market in that sense is just another way of saying that equilibrium exist, but does not get us any nearer

an explanation of when and how such a state will come about. It is clear that if we want to make the assertion that under certain conditions people will approach the state *we must explain by what process they will acquire the necessary knowledge.*

(Hayek 1937: 45, emphasis added)

Thus, viewed in the light of a realist philosophy of science, it will only make sense to study a specific state of equilibrium and deduce comparative static theorems from it if, at the same time, one *explains* what brings about equilibrium by explicitly modelling the underlying process or mechanism. To Hayek this implies, among other things, that we explicitly model the learning process which the agents go through in order to have acquired sufficient information to act substantively rational in equilibrium. Without such a story the theory will appear as a predictive instrument devoid of any explanatory content.

According to the game theorist Ken Binmore (1987: 184) there are two possible types of mechanism which could be used to explain how a state of equilibrium emerges. The first one he refers to as '*eductive*' by which he understands 'a dynamic process by means of which equilibrium is achieved through careful reasoning of the players'. Opposite to this is a mechanism described by the adjective '*evolutive*' which is defined as 'a dynamic process by means of which equilibrium is achieved through evolutionary mechanisms'. The most important difference between these two mechanisms is whether or not they assume the existence of human intentions. The most significant characteristic of 'natural' selection and reinforcement mechanism, as examples of evolutionary processes, will be the absence of any kind of human intentions. Opposite to this are pure 'eductive' processes based on the assumption that nothing will occur behind the back of the individual agents as they are able to anticipate any imaginable situation in rational terms. *In this chapter I shall argue in favour of a thesis that it is impossible within the paradigm of substantive rationality to find a non-ad hoc solution to the problem of adjustment. A non-ad hoc solution is to be understood as an explanation of how an equilibrium is brought about exclusively based on an eductive type of process and thus not including any evolutionary elements.* It is thus postulated that no history can be constructed permitting the agents in a situation of social interaction to make the substantively rational decisions 'for the right reason', but that they, as claimed by William Fellner 'turn out to be right for the wrong reason' (Fellner 1949: 63).

In a situation of social interaction each single agent will form some expectations regarding what decisions the other agents in the system will make. In order to characterize this process as an eductive process a *deliberate* rational procedure for how the individual agent has reached, or successively converges to the state of equilibrium and thus the substantive rational behaviour, must be specified.

146

Individually, each agent may be able to base his decision on such rational beliefs. However, in a social system it will be impossible for all the agents at the same time to justify their beliefs as rational, since it is illegitimate to generalize from the premiss 'that it is possible for each agent to form rational beliefs separately' to the conclusion 'that it is possible for all agents to form such beliefs at the same time'. A very similar argument was brought forward by Oskar Morgenstern in his 1935 paper 'Vollkommene voraussicht und wirtschaftliches gleichgewicht'.[16] In this paper he was occupied by the paradoxes arising in equilibrium theories based on the assumption of perfect foresight. Similar problems seem to emerge in theories based on assumptions of rational expectations and common knowledge. Applied to a single agent, these assumptions might seem reasonable enough. However, were the objective to justify how several agents simultaneously might come to possess such knowledge in terms of an eductive story, a number of conceptual problems arise: how can several agents in an interactive environment simultaneously form beliefs about each other's decisions in a rational and conscious way? Due to the self-reference problem involved it seems impossible to specify such a procedure by which the agents can justify their beliefs as fully or perfectly rational. In the simple case of only two agents this implies that the first agent must be acquainted with the knowledge of the other agent, since the future partly depends on his actions. But part of this second agent's knowledge will consist of what he knows about the first agent's knowledge. And so on *ad infinitum*. This self-reference problem leads to an infinite regress which according to Oskar Morgenstern makes it impossible for the agents involved to justify their beliefs as perfectly rational:[17]

> There is exhibited an endless chain of reciprocally conjectural reactions and counter-reactions. This chain can never be broken by an act of knowledge but always only through an arbitrary act — a resolution. This resolution, again, would have to be foreseen by the two or more persons concerned. The paradox still remains no matter how one attempts to twist or turn things around. *Perfect foresight and economic equilibrium are thus irreconcilable with one another*.
> (Morgenstern 1935: 174, emphasis added)

The demand for consistency proves to be irreconcilable with the demand for perfection. In order to explain the emergence of equilibrium, the concept of perfect rationality must be abandoned (the realist alternative) or the theoretical possibility of disequilibrium and the relevance of the adjustment problem must be completely refuted at the expense of the explanatory content of the model (the instrumentalist alternative). In terms of Münchhausen's trilemma this means: either, we end up in an infinite regress, which is either never interrupted or which is interrupted at an arbitrary level, or we end up in a vicious circle taking for granted what we were to prove. In neither of these cases will the agents be able to justify their beliefs as perfectly rational.

The problem of self-reference and unconscious, indirect and parametric interaction

The most prominent example that economics is strong on equilibrium outcomes but weak on the process whereby equilibrium is attained is the Walrasian tradition of general equilibrium codified in the so-called Arrow–Debreu–McKenzie model. This model has aimed at proving the existence of a set of prices that coordinates the plans of the individual agents and thus ensure full coordination in a decentralized economy consisting of parametric rational agents. How this state of equilibrium may emerge and what demands it has lead to concerning the individual agents' knowledge about each other's plans has not been very well explored. This is the so-called *problem of stability* about which Franklin Fisher has said:

> As I go on to consider what we know [about stability] and as you are tempted to grow impatient with the sorry state of that knowledge, please bear in mind that every economist continually behaves as though the unsolved question I am addressing had long ago been satisfactory resolved.
>
> (Fisher: 1976: 5)

An important example of this is the widespread use of the analysis of comparative statics in which it is implicitly taken for granted that the underlying dynamic process, leading the system from one state of equilibrium to another, is stable.

But how have the economists actually tried to handle the problem of stability? Almost all modern theory of stability takes its point of departure in Paul Samuelson's (1941, 1947) attempt to formalize Walras's construction with an auctioneer and a 'process of tâtonnement' by the help of the following equation of price adjustment:

$$dp/dt = f (Dt - St), \text{ where f}' > 0 \text{ and f } (0) = 0$$

This apparently quite innocent account of how the prices move in time towards a state of equilibrium as a function of the excess demand has, however, been subjected to intense criticism by a number of prominent neoclassical economists, as it is claimed to constitute an unacceptable *ad hoc* hypothesis. On the face of it one finds this characterization strange, because according to Paul Samuelson (1947) it is one of the most important sources of, or conditions for, deriving 'operationally meaningful theorems' or assertations which in principle are falsifiable. That is, it meets Popper's requirements for being a *non-ad hoc* hypothesis as its 'introduction does not diminish the degree of falsifiability or testability of the system in question, but on the contrary increases it' (Popper 1959: 82–3). This means that we can exclude the notion that the formula of adjustment constitute an *ad hoc$_1$*- or an *ad hoc$_2$* hypothesis.

However, the explanation is to be found in T.C. Koopmans:

> The various assumptions that have been used to describe the adjustment of price or quantity in a commodity market clearly show their parentage in the laws of the physical sciences. If, for instance, the net rate of increase in price is assumed to be proportional to the excess of demand over supply, *whose behavior is thereby expressed? And how is that behavior motivated?* And is the alternative hypothesis, . . . *any more plausible, or any better traceable to the behavior motivation.*
>
> (Koopmans 1957: 179, emphasis added)

The formula of adjustment is perceived as suspect because it is not constructed according to the central maxims of the positive heuristic of the paradigm of substantive rationality: *methodological individualism*. This objection is even more explicitly formulated by Arrow: If we assume that all the agents are parametric rational and the interaction hence can be described as indirect, unconscious, and parametric, it will, according to Arrow, be impossible within the same frame of reference to justify any changes in prices. If everybody considers the prices as externally given '*there is no one left over whose job it is to make a decision on price*' (Arrow 1959: 382). The problem of this explanation of how equilibrium emerges as the result of decisions taken by the individual rational agents, is that no attempts have been made to try to integrate it into the analysis of the behavioural pattern of firms and consumers. Gordon Hynes expresses it this way: 'This methodology is anomalous, and may not yield powerful operational theorems, *precisely because the adjustment mechanisms are not linked to the analysis of utility or profit-maximizing behaviour of the relevant economic units in the disequilibrium positions*' (Gordon and Hynes 1970: 371, note).

The formula of adjustment – and the solution it represents as to how equilibrium is established – is in other words a clear example of what Lakatos labels as an *ad hoc$_3$* hypothesis. That is, a hypothesis which is just added to the original theory of consumers and firms without becoming an integrated part of it.

It is the same problem that has made a number of modern Austrians to question whether the theory of general equilibrium actually constitutes a reasonable formalization of Adam Smith's 'invisible hand'.[18] General Equilibrium Theory is a purely static theory, whereas Adam Smith tried to communicate a more procedural view on competition.

Seen in this perspective, the attempt to solve the so-called problem of coordination by dividing it into a problem of existence and a problem of stability, respectively, must therefore be considered as extremely problematic. On the contrary it seems to be a necessary precondition that these two problems are solved simultaneously. According to Franklin Fisher this will affect economic theory as a whole extensively:

> The theory of value is not satisfactory without a description of the adjustment processes that are applicable to the economy and the way in which individual agents adjust to the disequilibrium. In this sense, stability analysis is of far more than merely technical interest. *It is the first step in a reformulation of the theory of value.*
>
> (Fisher 1983: 16, emphasis added)

The chief point of view in this section has been the impossibility of explaining the emergence of equilibrium on the basis of a purely intentional (rational) analysis, that is, by way of dynamic processes generating the emergence of equilibrium as a result of the explicit reasoning implemented by perfect rational agents. This is because perfect rationality is exclusively a quality that characterizes the agents who are in the state of equilibrium whereas the procedures the agents had to apply in order to achieve this state, are not specified. The main thesis of this chapter is that such a specification is not possible within the frames of a purely intentional or eductive analysis. This must inevitably lead to an abandoning of the concept of perfect rationality at the expense of a more procedural concept of rationality.

The problem of self-reference and indirect functional interaction: from Cournot to the theory of rational expectations

An obvious way of circumventing Arrow's problem is to introduce agents that are able to both fix and change prices as in E.S. Phelps and S.G. Winters (1970). In this way we introduce an element of imperfect competition, the result of which is that we are dealing with a new type of interaction where the individually achievable results must be assumed to depend on what decisions the other agents make and vice versa. This is the type of interaction that earlier was labelled *indirect and functional*.

This type of interaction was introduced by Cournot more than 150 years ago in connection with his duopoly model. It is characteristic of this that each duopolist wants to achieve a maximum yield. But as the interaction is indirect and functional, the yield achieved by the individual duopolist depends on the decisions they both make. Therefore, each duopolist must make his own decision in the light of the expectations he holds to be the behavioural pattern of the other duopolist. Assume, for example, that the first duopolist expects the other one to comply with a decision making rule of the type: 'Keep production at its present level'. This expectation must lead to duopolist 1 applying the decision making rule: 'Maximize the yield according to the secondary condition that duopolist 2's production is unchanged'. It was in an attempt to deduce the implications of both duopolists complying with such a decision making rule that Cournot advanced his theory of duopoly.

On the basis of the paradigm of substantive rationality, Cournot's solution to the problem of duopoly must be regarded as an unsatisfactory *ad hoc* solution. The reason is that the emergence of a Cournot-equilibrium cannot be regarded as the final result which the two rational duopolists end up with and later on do not feel any incentive to diverge from after having analysed their respective situations rationally. Cournot's model, however, does not anticipate that the agents are epistemically rational as they base their decisions on 'irrational expectations'.[19] The following argument is due to Alan Coddington (1968).

The situation analysed by Cournot is characterized by duopolist 1 expecting duopolist 2 to apply the decision making rule A ('maintain production at the present level') resulting in 1 applying the decision making rule B ('maximize the yield according to the condition that 1 keeps his production at the present level') at a higher level. The problem of this way of reasoning is that each duopolist does not ascribe the same rational qualities to his counterpart as he does to himself. If 1 had done so, and anticipated that 2 was in exactly the same position as himself, nothing would have kept 2 from reaching the same decision making rule B. However, this would result in that 1 would have to apply a new decision making rule C of an even higher level.[20] This, however, opens up for an infinite regress. If 1 is capable of reaching the conclusion that he ought to use decision making rule C, 2 must, according to the arguments above, be capable of reaching the same conclusion. If 1 takes this into consideration, he is forced to apply a new decision making rule D to an even higher level, and so on *ad infinitum*. The reason is that the theory is based upon what Alan Coddington (1973) has called *self-replacing decision making rules*, that is, if an agent expects the other one to follow rule B, he will always apply another decision making rule of a higher level himself.

But what are the problems, which such self-replacing decision making rules and the consequential infinite regression pose to the paradigm of maximization? The answer is that in principle it would be impossible to give an adequate, *non-ad hoc*, eductive explanation of how equilibrium emerges as a result of the agents' perfectly rational deliberations. Such a condition would be characterized by the individual agent's expectations to the other agents' decisions being confirmed by their actual actions implemented. However, it can be demonstrated that – because of the self-replacing decision making rule – it is impossible to construct an eductive story of how an equilibrium emerges, because at least one agent must act on the basis of incorrect expectations that are not confirmed by the actual decisions of the other(s).

Assume, for example, that we are in the situation where duopolist 1 applies a rule of the nth degree, then his expectations will only be correct if 2 applies a decision making rule of level $n - 1$. On the other hand, 2's expectations would only be correct if 1 applies a decision-rule of level $n - 2$, which conflicts with the original assumption. *Therefore, we reach the conclusion that a conceptual system based upon self-replacing decision making rules at the most will contain one agent who bases his decisions on correct expectations regarding the decision making rules of the other agents.* The question of how equilibrium emerges, that is, a state where everybody's expectations are fulfilled, cannot be answered in this specific context within an eductive story and therefore cannot be solved within the paradigm of substantive rationality. Equilibrium is, thus, in this case irreconcilable with ascribing perfect (epistemic) rationality to all agents.

The conceptual problem resulting from applying the rules of self-replacing decisions, may also be characterized as a Münchhausen trilemma. If we are to follow the rules of the paradigm of substantive rationality we are committed to ascribe perfect epistemic rationality to all economic agents. However, the self-replacing decision rules lead us into an infinite regress which proves that the concept of perfect rationality is not well-defined when we are studying systems of two or more interacting decision makers.

However, a way of evading the above mentioned infinite regress would be to abandon the concept of perfect or substantive rationality: that each agent operates with an inconsistency between the decisions he makes himself and those he expects others to make, should be regarded as an *empirical* and not as a formal or conceptual problem. The infinite regress which agents applying self-replacing decision rules are let into by being forced to apply still more complex decision making rules, will sooner or later be interrupted, when the decision making rules of the agents become so complex and the calculational problems so vast that they, because of internal limitations, must abandon the endless pursuit of substantively rational solutions. Such a *dogmatic interruption* of the infinite regression is exactly the main argument for Herbert Simon's concept of bounded rationality.[21]

The theory of rational expectations is another theory studying an indirect and functional type of interaction. This theory was originally proposed by John Muth in 1961 as a radical solution to how to model expectations in a Cobweb-model. Muth was very careful in stating that he interpreted the 'rational expectation hypotheses' (REH) as concerned not with the expectation of single economic agents, but with the '*average of expectations of individual agents*' (Muth 1961, emphasis added).

When the REH hypothesis was reintroduced in 1972 by Robert Lucas it was, however, put forward as a solution to the difficult problem of how to model the expectations of individual agents. That is, the REH was now interpreted as an extension of the maximizing assumption to the use of information. Previous solutions to the problem of how expectations were formed, such as the hypothesis of 'adaptive expectations', were all at odds with individual rationality and the positive heuristic of the neoclassical research programme. Against this background the REH was regarded by economists within the neoclassical research programme as a 'heuristic progress', because it was able to dispense with earlier theories' use of *ad hoc₃* hypotheses about non-maximizing or non-rational expectations. This is stated very clearly by M.H. Pesaran:

> Most economists who work within the neoclassical paradigm are attracted to the idea of REH not necessarily because they think that it represents an 'adequate' description of reality but because the REH can be easily integrated within the basic postulates of neoclassical economics.

> (Pesaran 1988)

The theory of rational expectations is essentially an equilibrium theory, since equilibrium is assumed, not explained. Like other equilibrium theories, however, the theory of rational expectations can be subjected to either an instrumentalist's or a realist's interpretation.

From an instrumentalist's point of view the theory of rational expectations with its equilibrium analysis is not intended as being descriptive of the process by which expectations are formed and decisions are reached. This has been stated very explicitly by Robert Lucas, Jr: 'Technically, I think of economics as studying decision rules that are steady states of some adaptive process, decision rules that are found to work over a range of situations and hence are no longer revised appreciably as more experience accumulates' (Lucas 1987: 218). So even if the term 'rational' is used to refer to the expectation of an agent, instrumentalists do not feel obliged to specify any eductive process by which the equilibrium beliefs are consciously formed. Instead, Lucas refers to a trial-and-error process or a reinforcement mechanism that works perfectly well without any kind of intentions or consciousness.

From a realist point of view, however, the study of rational expectation equilibria cannot be legitimized, unless we are able to specify an eductive mechanism that shows how the individual agents can acquire sufficient knowledge to converge to the parameters of the equilibrium probability distribution. That is, in constructing such a story the realist demands that the only information available to the agent is the information he can acquire according to the model in the process of making decisions and operating in the market. It seems, however, as in the general case to be impossible to find a *non-ad hoc* solution to this problem within the paradigm of substantive rationality.[22]

So, when it comes to explaining how individual agents converge toward an equilibrium in such a context, rational expectation theorists appear to introduce a new *ad hoc$_3$* hypothesis although on a higher level than the adaptive expectation hypothesis. The reason why any forecast rule must be an *ad hoc* hypothesis is, according to Roman Frydman, due to the self-replacing character of such rules:

> If all other agents use specific least square forecast functions, an individual agent has an incentive to use different forecast functions. Thus, even if convergence to the rational expectations equilibrium could be established in cases of specific forecast functions, agents would have to be assumed to use non-optimal forecast rules and to adhere to them collectively.
>
> (Frydman 1982: 653)

The impossibility of a purely eductive story is therefore due to the fact that individual agents cannot correctly estimate the 'average opinion', that is, the average of forecasts of next period's price level. Since everyone knows that everyone else is trying to guess what the average opinion is, each agent will try to form expectations about the average opinion about the average opinion, and so on *ad infinitum*. According to Michael Bacharach (1989) this 'Orpheus effect' due to the self-replacing decision rules opens up to an infinite regress, which makes it impossible even to define a substantive rational decision and shows that the agents' subjective beliefs will not converge to the objective beliefs.

What we are confronted with here is in fact the famous 'beauty contest' example of John Maynard Keynes. The aim of this contest is not to find the most beautiful one of the contesting young ladies, but to predict the result of the voting. According to Keynes:

> Each competitor has to pick, not those faces which he himself finds prettiest, but those which he thinks likeliest to catch the fancy of the other competitors, all of whom are looking at the problem from the same point of view. It's not a case of choosing those which, to the best of one's judgement, really are the prettiest, nor even those which average opinion genuinely thinks prettiest. We have reached the third degree where we devote our intelligence to anticipating what average opinion expects average opinion to be.
>
> (Keynes 1936: 154)

So, it turns out that the theorists, trying to explain how rational expectations are formed, have just replaced one *ad hoc* hypothesis with another. By assuming that the agent's expectations are rational they circumvent the basic problem of adjustment: How can several interacting agents simultaneously form rational expectations about each other's behaviour and expectations without being caught in a self-reference problem.

The problem of self-reference within non-cooperative game theory: can rationality be common knowledge?

It is generally acknowledged that there exists an unsolved problem in Walrasian general equilibrium theory in explaining how the system adjust to a state of equilibrium. That a similar shortcoming exists within non-cooperative game theory is probably less well known.

Non-cooperative game theory studies the possible outcomes of strategically rational agents in an indirect and functional type of interaction. As in other types of interaction the notion of the player's rationality is here crucial. As I shall try to show in this section, non-cooperative theory has almost exclusively emphasized the substantive aspects of rationality. As in other parts of economic theory this is due to its strong equilibrium orientation with its suppression of the epistemic conditions under which a game is played. In not explicitly taking account of the players reasoning procedures and capabilities, that is the procedural aspects of rationality, the proposed solution of how a state of equilibrium emerges leads to contradictions. These often take the form of *ad hoc*[3] solutions, since in order to explain how an equilibrium emerges game theorists introduce more or less arbitrary imperfections in the agent's reasoning procedures as for instance in Selten's 'trembling hand model' or impose some kind of incomplete information at the beginning of the game as in Kreps *et al.* (1982). In this and similar models based on a backward induction argument, it is not the perfect foresight assumption, but the important, but often implicit, assumption that it is common knowledge that all players are 'perfectly rational' which is troublesome.

Since the Nash equilibrium concept is exceptional within non-cooperative game theory, let us start by defining and explaining this concept. An interesting introduction and interpretation of this concept is to be found in Leif Johansen (1982).

Assume that we study a social system comprising n players $i = 1, 2, \ldots n$, where player i may choose a strategy a_i within the set A_i of possible actions. Let the pay-off or utility of player i be represented by the function: $R_i = F(a_1, \ldots a_i, \ldots a_n)$, so that player i aims at achieving a value R_i which is as high as possible.

This decision situation is not, however, an ordinary maximization problem, since the players are in a situation, where the pay off for each player will depend on actions taken by the others as well as on his or her own action and vice versa. That is, player i will not be able to predict the other's action: $a_1, \ldots a_{i-1}, a_{i+1}, \ldots a_n$ and then use this prediction to maximize R_i. The reasons for this is, of course, that the other players are in the same situation as player i. Therefore they have to give some thought as to what player i is going to do before they can decide about their own action and vice versa. This problem has been appropriately termed by Thomas Schelling (1961) as one of 'coordination of expectations' and by J. Harsanyi (1965) as one of mutual rational beliefs'.

When a player i is to decide on his action a_i it is therefore assumed that he has not received any information from other players about their action. Instead game theorists assume that player i must consider all the decisions $a_1, \ldots a_n$ simultaneously when deciding about his own action a_i. That is, since a player does not know the decisions to be taken by the others, each of them is assumed to solve the full analytical problem of finding a configuration of decisions: $a_1{}^*, \ldots a_n{}^*$ for each $i = 1, 2, \ldots n$ such that these are the best responses to the other agents optimal strategies.

$$R_i (a_i{}^*, \ldots a_i{}^*, \ldots a_n{}^*) = \text{Max } R_i (a_1{}^*, \ldots a_i{}^*, \ldots a_n{}^*)$$
$$a_i{}^* \, EA_i$$

In the derivation of the Nash solution to non-cooperative games two types of assumptions are normally used. The first assumption states that the players act so as to maximize expected utility. According to this assumption each player is equipped with subjective probability distributions over the other player's choices. These distributions are exogenous variables since the theory does not explain how the players obtain them as the result of some rational procedure. The second and more revolutionary assumption is the so-called common or mutual knowledge assumption according to which both the structure of the game and the rationality of the players are said to be common knowledge among them.

That the structure of the game is *common knowledge* among the players implies that they are not only assumed to know the action possibilities $A_1, \ldots A_n$ and the preference functions: $R_1, \ldots R_n$ of all the players, but also that this is known to be known, known to be known to be known, . . . *ad infinitum*.[23] Similarly the assumption that it is common knowledge that players are rational implies that each player believes each other to be rational, believes that all the other players believe each other to be rational, and so on *ad infinitum*. This assumption is necessary, because the Nash strategy is not a necessary consequence of rationality and could not even be anticipated if the opponent were irrational. Or as stated by Luce and Raiffa: 'Even if we were tempted at first to call a (Nash) non-conformist "irrational", we would have to admit that (his opponent) might be "irrational" in which case it would be "rational" for (him) to be "irrational"' (Luce and Raiffa 1957: 63).

As in other parts of economics and the paradigm of substantive rationality the study of Nash equilibria has mainly been limited to defining what an equilibrium is and what set of mutual rational beliefs support such a state. What seems to be missing is an explicit story of how the players come to hold these beliefs or how they come to attain the common knowledge of rationality so that they in fact choose their equilibrium strategies.

The problem of how players can attain common knowledge is common both to games in normal and extensive form representation. However, since only the extensive form shows the sequential nature of the game and therefore makes it possible to analyse the belief-formation process, I shall restrict my discussion to such games and then only to games of finite length. The main thesis of this section is that an assumption of 'common knowledge of beliefs' is paradoxical in that it leads to an inconsistency. And this problem seems further to correspond exactly to the one identified by Morgenstern in 1935 and from which he draws the conclusion 'that perfect foresight and economic equilibrium are thus irreconcilable with one another'. That is, we cannot construct an eductive story of how an equilibrium emerges if we start out with an assumption of perfect foresight or an assumption of common knowledge of rationality. But what is so paradoxical about this problem? At an intuitive level one might expect that the more the players know about each other, the easier it will be for them to replicate each others' reasoning and to predict each other's choice of strategy. To show that this intuition is false is the aim of the argument below.

I take my point of departure in the extensive form of finite games. Examples of such games are the finitely repeated prisoner's dilemma game, Selten's chain store paradox and Rosenthal's centipede example. All these games are solved by using a backward induction argument (Kuhn 1953), and this procedure gives a unique solution. Take as an example the following modification of Rosenthal's centipede game shown in Figure 6.1:[24] Each player has two strategies: Either to play 'across' or to play 'down' and thus end the game. The game is performed sequentially and at each node the previous choices are known. At the first node I can either play down and end the game, whereby he gets 4 and his opponent 1, or he can decide to leave the next move to II. Correspondingly II can play down and have 4 (while I gets 3) or play across and leave the next move to I. At the very last node II can end the game in one of two ways: By playing down II can achieve 100 for

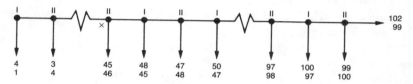

Figure 6.1 Rosenthal's centipede game.

himself while I only gets 99. If II decides to play across he gets 99, while I receives 102.

But what will the result of this game be? The classical equilibrium solution to such games is obtained by backward induction. If the last node were to be reached, player II has the choice between 100 by playing down and 99 by playing across. In this situation rationality dictates that II plays down. At the penultimate node, player I needs only consider what he thinks will happen at the last node, since only that is strategically relevant. If he expects II to be rational and play down at the last node, I's rational choice at the penultimate node will be to play down, which gives him 100 rather than playing across. Going all the way back to the first node and successively delete all non-optimal choices, we come to the conclusion that I should play down at his very first node.

Such a 'backward induction argument' seems, however, by closer inspection to be rather shaky.[25] Let us imagine that player I finds himself called upon at node 80 to decide whether he should play down or across. According to the backward induction argument the rational choice in this situation would be to play down. But does this make sense? Finding himself at node 80 player I would have to explain in the first place why he is called upon to make a decision at this node, if the rational choice of both players would have been to play down at one of their former 40 decision nodes. So, why should I imagine that the game will continue if a perfect rational player would have brought it to an end at his very first move? The hypothetical or counterfactual reasoning that the game has lasted till the eightieth round must imply that one of the players does not possess perfect rationality; or the belief that the other one is not perfectly rational; or the belief that the other one thinks that he or she is not rational *himself*, and so on *ad infinitum. However, this is at variance with the assumption that rationality is common knowledge in the backward induction argument*, that is, this assumption proves to be *contradictory*.

So, reaching the eightieth node is at variance with the assumption that rationality is common knowledge. That is, this node will only be reached if both of the players deviate from their equilibrium strategies. In fact, this conclusion seems identical to the one reached by Morgenstern that in explaining how an equilibrium is reached: 'Perfect foresight and economic equilibrium are thus irreconcilable with one another' (Morgenstern 1935: 174). In our case it is the assumption that 'rationality is common knowledge' which makes the theory 'overdetermined' and thus 'paradoxical'.[26]

But what kind of stories or explanations can be constructed to explain deviations from the equilibrium strategies? One of the motivations behind the so-called programme for perfecting the notion of a Nash equilibrium was, in fact, to answer this question. That is, to construct 'out-of-equilibrium' stories that restrict what players might do following such deviations.

The programme of refining Nash equilibria was launched by Richard Selten (1965, 1975), who proposed a refinement called 'subgame perfection' or 'perfect equilibrium'. Deviations from the equilibrium strategy were in his model explained as a result of *mistakes*. That is, when a player had decided on a specific strategy it was assumed that there existed a small probability of him picking another action by mistake or because his hand trembled. However, such mistakes were assumed to be completely at random and uncorrelated to make the notion of rationality compatible with the existence of mistakes. That is, if player I observed player II choosing a disequilibrium strategy, he would never expect him to make further mistakes. Instead the game would proceed within this subgame and the history of the game up to this point would be regarded as irrelevant by both players in their choice of future strategies.

However, in repeated games solved by backward induction a story based on mistakes does not seem very convincing: does I really have to interpret II's previous departures from his equilibrium strategy as uncorrelated 'mistakes', even in cases where he has to explain his arrival at the eightieth node as the result of no less than forty uncorrelated random errors on the part of his opponent?

The trembling hand model is not only inadequate in answering this question. It may also be criticized on a more general level as an unsatisfactory *ad hoc*₃ solution within the substantive rationality paradigm: assuming that player I interprets II's departure from his equilibrium strategy as a mistake will according to Nicholas Rowe: 'not [be] to interpret, but to *fail to interpret* II's departure. It amounts to assuming that I simply ignores a logical contradiction in his belief system between his knowledge of how II will rationally move and his observation of II's actual moves' (Rowe 1989: 54).

Let us now assume that player I and II are playing a finitely repeated game of prisoner's dilemma. According to the orthodox backward induction solution of this game it would be rational for player I to defect in his very first move. However, according to Petit and Sugden (1989) the assumption that players will uphold a common belief in their rationality, regardless of how the game unfolds, seems to be a highly questionable assumption in this model. Another way of stating this objection is to argue that agents in finitely repeated games will not only base their strategies on backward induction, but will also use forward induction taking into account how the game historically unfolds.

This will, of course, make it impossible to deduce a priori the outcome of the game. This implies, however, that player II's moves could just as well be deliberately chosen as a result of a trembling hand. But if we do not know, a priori, how I should react to II's departure, we would not know either, if it would be rational for II to depart from his conjectured equilibrium strategy. If I were to interpret II's play of the cooperative strategy as a mistake it would of course be rational for him to continue to defect. But I could just as well interpret II's cooperative play as rational *given* some belief on II's part as to how I would react. In this case II's play of the cooperative strategy should be seen as an attempt to *communicate* to I II's beliefs about I's reaction to II's initial cooperative move. If the communication succeeds II can get I to believe that II believes that it is rational to cooperate, then I will expect II to cooperate in the future and will reply with the cooperative strategy, as II wants him to do.

According to Ken Binmore the above anomalous problems in the trembling hand model must be faced directly by game theorists. That is, they must go beyond the *ad hoc* solutions of the substantive rationality paradigm:

> To seek to tackle procedural questions seriously is to commit oneself to an attempt to model the thinking processes of the players *explicitly*. Traditional game theory lacks such a model and hence is helpless in the face of counterfactual: suppose a perfect rational player made the following sequence of irrational moves then. . . . But an equilibrium analysis cannot evade such counterfactuals. What keeps players on the equilibrium path is their expectation of what *would* happen if they *were* to deviate from equilibrium play. However, the traditional straitjacket makes it very hard to confront such issues squarely. The result is the construction of magnificent mathematical edifices of which a medieval scholastic might justly be proud, but little in the way of genuine progress.
>
> (Binmore 1988: 10)

To these problems of self-reference a 'normal scientist' within the paradigm of substantive rationality would perhaps raise the objection that a game including common knowledge, just like perfect knowledge, may be seen as a limit to a game of 'almost common knowledge'. Ariel Rubinstein has, however, demonstrated that this is *not* the case and concludes:

> It may mean that common knowledge is an 'isolated' state of mind which is not approximated by the state where a large finite number of the 'I know that you know' statements are true. This observation may be relevant to the question of whether it is useful to formalise common knowledge from more basic primitives or whether we do better to regard it to be itself a primitive.
>
> (Rubinstein 1989: 9)

CONCLUDING REMARKS

In almost any subject we start out with premises which intuitively appear self-evident and apply forms of thought which at first appear valid. Nevertheless, such ways of thinking often leads to paradoxes, contradictions, or antinomies. When that happens, we experience periods forcing us to throughly scrutinize our way of thinking and the frames of reference we normally base our work on. Contradictions, paradoxes, and antinomies thus often become the background for new theories. However, as experienced in the case studied here, it is important to emphasize the duration of such periods of 'creative destruction'. Our modern numerical system is just one example of an idea that was created by a number of successive transgressions or destructions of more particular numerical systems with its origin in the Ancient Greek.

This chapter has tried to identify and study such a conceptual problem in 'the paradigm of substantive rationality'. In this concluding section some suggestions for how the problem of self-reference can 'create' or become the background for a new paradigm within economics are presented. In fact, it is argued that economics in general will follow a course, which to some degree is similar to the one that Hayek followed in his own personal career. After having identified an anomalous problem in the orthodox paradigm in 1937 in 'Economics and knowledge', Hayek has been struggling to develop an evolutionary theory of institutions, which he himself regards as a rough solution to exactly this problem (cf. Hayek 1967b).

As stated in the third section admitting that economic information and decision making capacity also can be a scarce and henceforth costly resource, leads to a self-reference problem: to make a decision is cost consuming, therefore it must be decided whether it is worth making a decision. But to make a decision implies costs; therefore we must decide, whether it is worth making a decision on whether it is worth making a decision, etc. Since this infinite regress can only be stopped at an arbitrary point, it will be impossible to find an optimal solution to this decision problem. However, several interesting implications of how to model individual decision makers can be drawn from this problem. Firstly, in a regime of costly calculations it will be impossible for economic agents to obtain perfect and articulated information about themselves. Instead they have to base their decisions partly on competencies, which are tacit and therefore cannot be fully articulated by themselves. Secondly, due to the infinite regress and the impossibility to define a super-optimizing choice we have to characterize these as what Ron Heiner (1983) refers to as 'imperfect decisions' using decision rules in situations with a 'competence-difficulty-gap'. And thirdly, to explain the decision making rules actually used we have to understand the underlying evolutionary process by which these and the economic competencies on which they are based have emerged.

As argued in the fourth section the problem of self-reference makes it impossible to formulate theories of social interaction of a purely eductive type. That is, we cannot explain how equilibria or coordinated social patterns emerges as the result of the agents rational deliberations only, but have to introduce some kind of evolutionary mechanism working behind the back of the agents. According to Hayek this implies:

> To those familiar with the celebrated theorem due to Kurt Gödel it will probably be obvious that these conclusions are closely related to those Gödel has shown to prevail in formalized arithmetical systems. It would thus appear that Gödel's theorem is but a special case of a more general principle, namely the principle that among their determinants there must always be some rules which cannot be stated or even be conscious. At least all we can talk about and probably all we can consciously think about presupposes the existence of a framework which determines its meaning, i.e. a system of rules which operate us but which we can neither state nor form an image of and which we can merely evoke in others in so far as they already possess them.
>
> Hayek 1967a: 62)

NOTES

1 I am indebted to Nicolai Juul Foss, Wade Hands, Thomas Lindh, Manfred Holler, Uskali Mäki, and Sidney Winter for comments on an earlier draft of this chapter. My special thanks to Thomas Schelling for his written comments.

2 According to Herbert Simon's definition behaviour is 'substantively rational when it is appropriate to the achievement of given goals within the limits imposed by given conditions and constraints' (Simon 1976: 130). The concept is closely connected to a static frame of analysis in which the existence of equilibrium is assumed. The process whereby equilibrium is obtained, is not modelled explicitly. The result is that the information, which must be available to the agents in order for them to act rationally, is only assumed to be present. Hence, the problem of explaining what procedures the agents apply in order to achieve the necessary knowledge to act rationally is suppressed. However, it is exactly this problem that the concept of procedural rationality gives first priority.

3 Cf. Hans Albert (1985).

4 Another reason for this is that the discontinuity caused by a shift of paradigm is over-dramatized both in Kuhn's own theory and in most of its many applications within the social sciences. In line with the views of Herbert Simon referred to in the introduction, the specific 'shift of paradigm', which this article deals with, may be characterized as a quiet and prolonged scientific revolution.

5 According to Zahar a 'theory is said to be *ad hoc₃* if it is obtained from its predecessor through a modification of the auxiliary hypotheses which does

not accord with the spirit of the heuristic of the programme' (Zahar 1973: 101).

6 The demand that a new theory should be, not just theoretically and empirically progressive, but heuristically progressive also, can be traced back to Popper (1963, p. 42). After introducing the criteria of theoretical and empirical progress, Popper faced the so-called tacking-paradox. The problem was that it was too simple to construct a new theory T_2 that was theoretically (and possible also empirically) progressive, just by adding an auxiliary hypothesis h to an original theory T_1. In order to avoid this extremely trivial method of obtaining 'scientific growth', Popper formulated the demand that a new theory must 'proceed from some simple, new and powerful unifying idea' and, correspondingly Lakatos demanded that 'the additional assertion must be connected with the original assertions *more intimately* than by mere conjunction'. The fact that Lakatos and Popper have hit upon a conception that is also widespread within the actual discourse of economics, appears from the following example. Let T_1 be Hick–Allen's theory of consumer behaviour from which it will not be possible to deduce the so-called 'law of demand' since the utility functions have not been subjected to such restrictions that make it possible to determine the relative size of the income effect and substitutional effect. That is, the possibility of an increasing demand curve is not excluded a priori. In order to avoid this, an auxiliary hypothesis may be formulated which states that the numerical value of the income effect is less than the numerical value of the substitution effect. If the auxiliary hypothesis h is added to the Hick-Allen theory T_1 it may be asserted that a new theory T_2 has emerged, from which one can deduce the law of demand. Paul Samuelson comments on this way of achieving scientific progress: 'It is only by making *additional*, and *demonstrably arbitrary* assumptions that various writers have been able to derive the so-called law of diminishing demand' (Samuelson 1947; 115, emphasis added). That is, the auxiliary hypothesis h is condemned as being an ad hoc_3-hypothesis.

7 According to Martin Carrierer the disadvantages of this strategy should be seen against the following background:

> One of the primary merits of Lakatos' methodology is his replacement of the traditional multitude of contrasting or even, conflicting methodological demands with a single, precise, and sophisticated criterion of fertility, supplemented by empirical demands. This avoids Kuhn's problem. Reintroducing a number of possibly conflicting yard-sticks for methodological appraisal means that none of the competing theories can be unambiguously assessed methodologically, not even in retrospect. Methodology can do nothing but shrug its shoulders and suspend judgement.

(Carrierer 1988: 212)

8 Larry Laudan's (1977) contrast to this is: *external conceptual problems* which emerge as a consequence of a series of 'tensions' or 'inconsistencies' between competing research programmes.

9 According to Sidney Winter such a decision may also be subjected to the perspective of economizing knowledge:

> In making this judgment, it is appropriate to take into account the much larger costs associated with a shift in fundamental assumptions as opposed to revision of minor assumptions and semantical rules. There is inevitably a large sunk investment in training, education, and the

development of theoretical and empirical results that would have to be repeated to a large extent if fundamental assumptions were discarded.

(Winter 1982: 280)

Conversely, the costs of maintaining the 'hard core' of the programme and its 'heuristic' may also, in certain cases, prove to be too comprehensive. This may be the case, for example, if it is not possible to find 'solutions that are sufficiently economical' within the programme, but one must fall back on constructing *ad hoc₃* modifications. Or as expressed by Sidney Winter:

> Of course, if repeated attempts to assimilate recalcitrant facts by marginal theoretical revisions meet with no success, the possibility that some fundamental assumption is the barrier to progress must eventually be considered. Essentially, the various costs of creating an elaborate and unappealing structure of auxiliary hypotheses to explain away particular facts are finally considered to outweigh the costs of fundamental revision.

(Winter 1982: 280)

Viewed in this light, the abandoning of *ad hoc₃* hypotheses may be seen as a rule for economizing knowledge that, for example, proved damning to Ptolemy's geocentric theory with its increasingly complicated *ad hoc* explanations of epicycles.

10 It is in connection with such a methodology that Spiro Latsis (1976) has introduced the term a 'too liberal' methodology.

11 According to Lakatos:

> The sophisticated falsificationist allows *any* part of the body of science to be replaced *but* only on the condition that it is replaced in a 'progressive' way, so that the replacement successfully anticipates novel facts. He sees nothing wrong with a group of brilliant scientists conspiring to pack everything they can into their favourite research programme ('conceptual framework', if you wish) with a sacred hard core. As long as their genius – and luck – enables them to expand their programme 'progressively', while sticking to its hard core, they are allowed to do it.

(Lakatos 1970: 187)

12 It is interesting here to notice how the optimization paradigm and the behavioural paradigm respectively diverge as to their respective positive heuristics, i.e. the way the problem of information cost is sought solved. According to James G. March:

> Awareness of limitations on attentions has led to concern for making the costs of obtaining information an explicit part of the structure of decision problems, and to the development of various forms of information and transaction cost economics that comprise a large part of contemporary microeconomic theory.

This he contrasts with the behavioural theorists, who:

> Have been less interested in treating observed anomalies in organizational behaviour in terms of information cost than in developing behavioral theory of attention allocation. That interest leads them to see organization of attention as a central process out of which decisions arise, rather than simply one aspect of the cost structure.

(March 1988: 3)

13 The problem was, however, already touched upon by Lionel Robbins (1932: 92) who asserted that 'the marginal utility of not bothering about marginal utility' always could be used as a way of explaining inconsistent behaviour.

14 Apart from Sidney Winter (1975) this anomaly has been discussed by John Conlisk (1988), R.H. Day (1987), R.A. Heiner (1983), and Roy Radner (1968, section 12). In his book from 1954 L.J. Savage already stressed that attempts to take all the costs of optimization into consideration would possibly lead to infinite regression:

> It might be . . . stimulating, and it is certainly more realistic, to think of consideration or calculation as itself an act on which the person must decide. Though I have not explored that latter possibility carefully, I suspect that any attempt to do so leads to fruitless and endless regression.
>
> (Savage 1954: 30)

15 Some have disagreed with the idea that the procedural concept of rationality should constitute such an autonomous and independent principle of explanation. By introducing the concept of 'optimal imperfect decisions' Baumol and Quandt (1964) argued that it would be possible to reduce this principle to the orthodox paradigm of optimization. This problem has, however, on the other hand also been seen as one of the main reasons for preferring a procedural concept of rationality. Jon Elster (1983) refers to this problem as the *general argument* for procedural rationality.

16 According to Oskar Morgenstern (1977) this article was the direct cause for his subsequent cooperation with John von Neumann. After having presented his article to the 'Wiener Kreis', invited by Moritz Schlick, Morgenstern was later asked to present his article at the Karl Menger Colloquium. Following this presentation, the mathematician Eduard Cech pointed out to Morgenstern that several of the issues he had raised were identical with those discussed by Neumann in an article entitled: *Zur Theorie de Gesellschaftsspiele* from 1928. However, Morgenstern and von Neumann did not meet until several years later in 1938 after Morgenstern had emigrated to the USA as a result of Germany's occupation of Austria.

17 As an example, Morgenstern, in his article from 1935, had not only partly anticipated the theory of rational expectations, but also much of the criticism that it could be subjected to.

18 The point of objection is, among other things, the attitude expressed in the following quotation by F. Hahn:

> Adam Smith . . . first realized the need to explain why this kind of social arrangement does not lead to chaos. . . . Smith not only posed an obviously important question, but also started us off on the road to answering it. General Equilibrium Theory was classically stated by Arrow and Debreu . . . is near the end of that road.
>
> (Hahn 1980: 123)

To the Austrian School, General Equilibrium Theory is an extremely imperfect formalization of Adam Smith's invisible hand explanation. They especially emphasize that Adam Smith's explanations were of a procedural and evolutionary character, that the Arrow–Debreu tradition has not been able to maintain. F. von Hayek, F. Knight, and Schumpeter have tried to develop this tradition. More recent contributions have been offered by Nelson and Winter (1982), Brian Loasby (1976), and B. Klein (1977).

19 William Fellner formulates this weakness of Cournot's concept of equilibrium as follows:

It is essential to realize that, as long as the firms make the Cournot assumptions concerning their rivals' behavior, the analysis cannot be adjusted in such a way as to make the firms be right for the right reasons, instead of describing a situation in which *they turn out to be right for the wrong reasons*.

(Fellner 1949: 63, emphasis added)

This will, of course, only be a problem for an eductive theory.

20 Such a situation in which both duopolists expect the other one to follow rule *B* and thus apply rule *C* themselves, is labelled a *Stackelberg-disequilibrium*.

21 See the quotation in the section 'Introduction'.

22 In his very last article, the late Professor Fritz Machlup passes almost similar strictures on the theory of rational expectations:

The 'strong' assumption of the formation of 'rational' expectations is far more complex and, in fact, self-contradictory. . . . Members of this school or movement and their still unconvinced fellow-analysts speculate about the 'existence', the 'uniqueness', and the 'stability' of this equilibrium, about the path towards it. . . . Among the most serious and most questionable issues, in my opinion, are the 'infinite regress' in taking account of other decisionmakers' and policymakers' reactions to any moves made as a result of the successive revisions of expectations.

(Machlup 1983: 180–1)

This view on the theory of rational expectations is interesting because it clearly marks Fritz Machlup's methodological point of view in relation to Friedman's instrumentalism. After the methodological debates within economics during the 1940s and 1950s there has been a tendency to regard the methodological point of view of these two economists as almost identical. However, on one point they diverge considerably. Where Friedman in his 'as if' defence of the assumption of optimization within economics bases his arguments on a relatively modified version of empiricism, Fritz Machlup asserts that ideal types ought to be 'understandable' by which he means 'that we could conceive of sensible men acting (sometimes at least) in the way postulated by the ideal type in question' (Machlup 1955: 17). Contrary to the position of instrumentalism the demand that ideal types should be understandable leads to the following criticism of the theory of rational expectations:

Even those of us who allow the theorist to construct his ideal types any way he likes, may object: economic man ought not to be endowed with superhuman abilities, at least not if we want him to serve in applied economics, as a heuristic instrument for explaining observable reality.

(Machlup 1983: 175)

23 Although common knowledge assumptions is now very central to game theory, it was the two philosophers David Lewis (1969) and Schiffer (1972) who were the first ones to clarify and explicate its content. Today their assumption is vividly discussed within modern game theory as a result of Aumann's (1976) attempt to formalize it in his article: 'Agreeing to disagree', see for example, Binmore (1987).

24 This game has been scrutinized by Cristina Bicchieri (1989) and Jon Elster (1989), but is also discussed in, among others, Binmore (1987: 194–200).

25 That arguments based on 'backward induction' can lead to paradoxes is well known in philosophy from the so-called 'surprise text paradox', also known as the 'class A blackout', the 'hangman paradox', the 'prediction paradox',

etc. The story behind this paradox goes as follows: 'A teacher announced to his pupils that on exactly one of the days of the following school week (Monday to Friday) he would give them a test. But it would be a surprise test; on the evening before the test they would not know that the test would take place the next day. One of the brighter students in the class then argued that the teacher could never give them the test. "It can't be Friday", she said, "since in that case we'll expect it on Thursday evening. But then it can't be Thursday, since having already eliminated Friday we'll know Wednesday evening that it has to be Thursday. And by similar reasoning we can also eliminate Wednesday, Tuesday and Monday. So there can't be a test!" The students were somewhat baffled by the situation. The teacher was well-known to be truthful, so if he said there would be a test, then it was safe to assume that there would be one. On the other hand, he also said that the test would be a surprise. But it seemed that whenever he gave the test, it wouldn't be a surprise. Well, the teacher gave the test, on Tuesday, and, sure enough, the students were surprised.' (cf. Halpern and Moses 1986: 281). As in the famous 'liar paradox' the teacher's statement in this story has some self-referential features making it paradoxical in the sense that it is consistent if and only if it is inconsistent.

26 As shown by Cristina Bicchieri (1989) this inconsistency or over-determination problem is produced by assuming levels of beliefs (in the assumption of common knowledge of rationality) higher than those which are sufficient for the backward induction argument to work. If we let R_1 stand for 'player I is rational', R_2 for 'player II is rational', and B_1R_2 'that player I believes that player II is rational', etc. the necessary assumptions of the backward induction argument can be stated as follows. At the very last node it will be sufficient to assume R_2 to predict II's choice. At the penultimate node one must assume that I believes II to be rational B_1R_2. And at the nth level of the game player would have a $n - 1$ level belief that II believes him to be rational.

REFERENCES

Albert, H. (1985) *Treatise on Critical Reason*, Princeton, New Jersey: Princeton University Press.

Arrow, K.J. (1959) 'Toward a theory of price adjustment' in I.M. Abramouwitz (ed.) *The Allocation of Economic Resources*, Stanford, California: Stanford University Press.

Aumann, R.J. (1976) 'Agreeing to disagree', *Annals of Statistics* 4: 1236–39.

Bacharach, M. (1989) 'Expecting and affecting', *Oxford Economic Papers* 41: 339–55.

Baumol, W.J. and Quandt, R.E. (1964) 'Rules of thumb and optimally imperfect decisions', *American Economic Review* 54: 23–46.

Bicchieri, C. (1989) 'Self-refuting theories of strategic interaction: a paradox of common knowledge', *Erkenntnis* 30(1–2): 69–85.

Binmore, K. (1987) 'Modelling rational players: Part I', *Economics and Philosophy* 3: 179–214.

—— (1988) 'Modelling rational players: Part II', *Economics and Philosophy* 4: 9–55.

Caldwell, B. (1982) *Beyond Positivism: Economic Methodology in the Twentieth Century*, London: Allen & Unwin.

Carrier, M. (1988) 'On novel facts: A discussion of criteria for non-ad-hoc-ness in the methodology of scientific research programmes', *Zeitschrift für Allgemeine Wissenschaftstheorie* 19: 205–31.

Coddington, A. (1968) *Theories of the Bargaining Process*, London: Allen & Unwin.
—— (1973) 'Bargaining as a decision process', *Swedish Journal of Economics* pp. 397–405.
Conlisk, J. (1988) 'Optimization cost', *Journal of Economic Behavior and Organization* 9: 213–28.
Day, R.H. (1987) 'The general theory of disequilibrium economics and of economic evolution' in Batten, Casti, and Johansson (eds) *Economic Evolution and Structural Change*, Berlin: Springer Verlag.
Elster, J. (1983) *Explaining Technical Change*, Cambridge: Cambridge University Press.
—— (1989) *The Cement of Society*, Cambridge: Cambridge University Press.
Fellner, W. (1949) *Competition Among the Few*, New York: Augustus, Kelley.
Fisher, F. (1976) 'The stability of general equilibrium: Results and problems' in M. Artis and R. Nobay (eds) *Essays in Economic Analysis*, Cambridge: Cambridge University Press, pp. 3–29.
—— (1983) *Disequilibrium Foundations of Equilibrium Economics*, Cambridge: Cambridge University Press.
Friedman, M. (1953) 'The methodology of positive economics' in M. Friedman (ed.) *Essays in Positive Economics*, Chicago: Chicago University Press.
Frydman, R. (1982) 'Towards an understanding of market processes: Individual expectations, learning, and convergences to rational expectation equilibrium', *American Economic Review* 72: 652–68.
Gordon, R.A. and Hynes, A. (1970) 'On the theory of price dynamics' in E.S. Phelps (ed.) *Microeconomic Foundation of Employment and Inflation Theory*, London: W.W. Norton.
Hahn, F. (1980): 'General equilibrium theory', *The Public Interest* special issue.
Halpern, J.Y. and Moses, Y. (1986) 'Taken by surprise: the paradox of the surprise test revisited', *Journal of Philosophical Logic* 15: 281–304.
Hands, D.W. (1988) '*Adhocness* in economics and the Popperian tradition' in N. de Marchi (ed.) *The Popperian Legacy in Economics*, Cambridge: Cambridge University Press, pp. 121–37.
Harsanyi, J. (1965) 'Bargaining and conflict situations in the light of a new approach to game theory', *American Economic Review* 55: 447–57.
Hayek, F.A. (1948) 'Economics and knowledge' in F.A. Hayek (ed.) *Individual and Economic Order*, London: Routledge. (First published 1937.)
—— (1967a) 'Rules, perception and intelligibility', *Studies in Philosophy, Politics and Economics*, London: Routledge & Kegan Paul.
—— (1967b) 'Kinds of rationality', *Studies in Philosophy, Politics and Economics*, London: Routledge & Kegan Paul.
Heiner, R.A. (1983) 'The origin of predictable behavior' *American Economic Review*, 73: 560–95.
Johansen, L. (1981) 'Interaction in economic theory', *Economie Appliquée* 3: 229–67.
—— (1982) 'On the status of the Nash type of noncooperative equilibrium in economic theory', *Scandinavian Journal of Economics* 84: 421–41.
Keynes, J.M. (1936) *The General Theory of Employment, Interest, and Money*.
Klein, B.H. (1977) *Dynamic Economics*, Cambridge, Mass. Harvard University Press.
Koopmans, T.C. (1957) *Three Essays on the State of Economic Science*, New York: McGraw Hill.
Kreps, D., Milgrom, P., Roberts, J. and Wilson, R. (1982) 'Rational cooperation in the repeated prisoner's dilemma', *Journal of Economic Theory* 27: 245–52.
Kuhn, H.W. (1953) 'Extensive games and the problem of information', in H.W.

Kuhn and A.W. Tucker (eds) *Contribution to the Theory of Games*, Princeton, New Jersey: Princeton University Press.

Lakatos, I. (1970) 'Falsification and the methodology of scientific research programmes' in I. Lakatos and A. Musgrave (eds) *Criticism and t e Growth of Knowledge*, Cambridge: Cambridge University Press, pp. 91–196.

Lancaster, K. (1971) *Consumer Demand: A New Approach*, New York: Columbia University Press.

Latsis, S.J. (1976) 'A research programme in economics' in S.J. Latis (ed.) *Method and Appraisal in Economics*, Cambridge: Cambridge University Press, pp. 1–41.

Laudan, L. (1977) *Progress and Its Problems*, Berkeley, California: University of California Press.

Lewis, D.K. (1969) *Conventions: A Philosophical Study*, Cambridge, Mass.: Harvard University Press.

Loasby, B.J. (1976) *Choice, Complexity, and Ignorance*, Cambridge: Cambridge University Press.

Lucas, R., Jr. (1987) 'Adaptive behavior and economic theory' in R.M. Hogarth and M.W. Reder (eds) *Rational Choice: The Contrast between Economics and Psychology*, Chicago and London: University of Chicago Press.

Luce, R. and Raiffa, H. (1957) *Games and Decision*, New York: Wiley.

Machlup, F. (1955) 'The problem of verification in economics' *Southern Economic Journal* 22: pp. 1–21.

—— (1983) 'The rationality of rational expectations', *Kredit und Kapital*, 2: 172–83.

March, J. (1988) 'Introduction: a chronicle of speculations about decision-making in organizations' in J. March *Decisions and Organizations*, Oxford: Oxford University Press.

Marschak, J. (1954) 'Toward an economic theory of organization and information' in R.M. Thrall, C.H. Coombs and R.L. Davis (eds) *Decision Processes*, New York: Wiley.

Morgenstern, O. (1935/1976) 'Vollkommene voraussicht und wirtschaftliches gleichgewicht', *Zeitschrift für Nationalökonomie* Vol. 6. (Translated by F. Knight to: 'Perfect foresight and economic equilibrium' and published in A. Schotter (ed.) *Selected Economic Writings of Oskar Morgenstern*, New York: New York University Press, pp. 169–83.)

—— (1977) 'The collaboration between Oskar Morgenstern and John von Neumann on the theory of games', *Journal of Economic Literature* 15: 805–16.

—— and von Neumann, J. (1947) *The Theory of Games and Economic Behavior*, Princeton, New Jersey: Princeton University Press.

Muth, J. (1961) 'Rational expectations equilibrium and the theory of price movements', *Econometrica* 29: 315–35.

Nelson, R. & Winter S.G. (1982) *An Evolutionary Theory of Economic Change*, Cambridge, Mass.: Harvard University Press.

Nickles, T. (1981) 'What is a problem that we may solve it?' *Synthèse* 47: 85–118.

Pesaran, M.H. (1988) *Limits to Rational Expectations*, Oxford: Basil Blackwell.

Petit, P. and Sugden, R. (1989) 'The backward induction paradox', *Journal of Philosophy* 86: 169–82.

Phelphs, E.S. and Winter, S.G. (1970) 'Optimal price policy under atomistic competition' in E.S. Phelphs (ed.) *Microeconomic Foundation of Employment and Inflation Theory*, London: W.W. Norton.

Popper, K. (1959) *The Logic of Scientific Discovery*, London: Hutchinson.

—— (1963) *Conjectures and Refutations*, London: Routledge & Kegan Paul.

—— (1972) *Objective Knowledge: An Evolutionary Approach*, Oxford: Oxford University Press.

Quine, W.V.O. (1961) *From a Logical Point of View*, Cambridge, Mass.: Harvard University Press.

Radner, R. (1968) 'Competitive equilibrium under uncertainty', *Econometrica* 36: 31–58.

Robbins, L. (1932) *An Essay on the Nature and Significance of Economic Science*, London: Macmillan.

Rowe, N. (1989) *Rules and Institutions*, New York: Philip Allan.

Rubinstein, A. (1989) 'The electronic mail game: strategic behavior under "almost common knowledge"', *American Economic Review* 79(3): 385–91.

Samuelson, P.A. (1941) 'The stability of equilibrium', *Econometrica* 9: 97–120.

—— (1947) *Foundations of Economic Analysis*, Cambridge, Mass.: Harvard University Press.

Savage, L.J. (1954) *Foundations of Statistics*, New York: Wiley.

Schelling, T. (1961): *The Strategy of Conflict*, New York: Oxford University Press.

Schiffer, G. (1972) *Meaning*, Oxford: Clarendon Press.

Selten, R. (1965) 'Spieltheoretische behandlung eines oligopolmodells mit nachfrageträgheit', *Zeitschrift für die Gesamte Staatswissenschaft* 121: 301–24.

—— (1975) 'Reexamination of the perfectness concept for equilibrium points in extensive games', *International Journal of Game Theory* 4: 25–35.

Simon, H. (1976) 'From substantive to procedural rationality' in S. Latsis *Method and Appraisal in Economics*, Cambridge: Cambridge University Press.

Stigler, G.J. (1961) 'The economics of information', *The Journal of Political Economy* 69: 213–25.

Winter, S. (1975) 'Optimization and evolution in the theory of the firm' in R.H. Day and T. Groves (eds) *Adaptive Economic Models*, New York: Academic Press, pp. 73–118.

—— (1982) 'Binary choice and the supply of memory', *Journal of Economic Behavior and Organization* 3: 277–321.

Zahar, E. (1973) 'Why did Einstein's programme supersede Lorentz's programme?, *British Journal for the Philosophy of Science* 24: 95–123, 223–62.

7

RATIONAL CHOICE, RULE-FOLLOWING AND INSTITUTIONS

An evolutionary perspective[1]

Viktor Vanberg

ABSTRACT

The concept of *rational choice* and the notion of *rule-following* have often been contrasted as conflicting and incompatible perspectives on human behaviour. A review of relevant contributions on this issue is used to suggest an interpretation of the two perspectives which allows for their consistent integration into a common theoretical framework. Implications of such integration for the study of social institutions are briefly discussed.

INTRODUCTION

Rational choice theory or, more specifically, the assumption of maximizing behaviour is generally viewed as the paradigmatic core of classical and neoclassical economics. It has also been the principal target of many criticisms that have been levelled over time against mainstream economics. Yet, as even a most cursory review of the relevant literature reveals, the extensive and continuing controversy surrounding this theory has by no means generated a commonly shared understanding of what, exactly, its methodological status and its explanatory substance are (Sen 1979: 94; Leibenstein 1980: 100). Any attempt to enter, as I plan to do in this chapter, the debate on the scope and the limits of rational choice theory has, therefore, to start with the recognition that, among its advocates as well as its critics, there may exist quite different interpretations of what it is they want to defend or object to.

Though meant as a contribution to the debate on rational choice theory, this chapter makes no claim to a general and systematic assessment of this debate. It has the much more limited purpose of drawing attention to a particular aspect of this debate, a recurrent theme which, more than any other, seems to be a common concern of critics who may, otherwise, hold quite different theoretical views. It is the notion that rational choice theory fails to account for what is seen as an important element of social reality, namely the role of *habits* and *routines* or, more generally, of *rule-following* in human behaviour. This is the issue which I want to discuss.

The chapter is organized as follows: section 1 reviews a sample of criticisms of mainstream economics, all of which thematize the issue of rule-following behaviour, despite their otherwise quite different theoretical orientations. In section 2 the concept of *rule-following behaviour* is specified in more detail and it is contrasted to an interpretation of *rational choice* as *situational, case-by-case maximization.* In sections 3, 4 and 5 arguments are discussed on why, and under what conditions, rule-following behaviour can be expected to be a more successful behavioural strategy than case-by-case maximization. Section 3 refers, in particular, to R.A. Heiner's theory of imperfect choice; sections 4 and 5 review H.A. Simon and F.A. Hayek's respective arguments on 'adaptive rationality' and the 'limits of reason'. Section 6 briefly looks at the orthodoxy's response to the criticisms of the maximization paradigm. Sections 7, 8 and 9 contrast the standard *teleological* interpretation of rationality (section 7) with a generalized evolutionary (section 8) and behavioural (section 9) perspective which provides an explanatory account for *rule-following* behaviour while, at the same time, accommodating the apparent functionality and adaptiveness of human action, typically considered the domain of rational choice theory. The discussion in this chapter is essentially about the 'individual' as opposed to the 'social' significance of rule-following, that is, it looks at rule-following as an attribute of individual human behaviour rather than at the role of rules in co-ordinating human social interaction. The latter issue is only briefly addressed in section 10 which comments on the relevance of the suggested evolutionary–behavioural perspective for the study of social institutions. Section 11 concludes the chapter.

1 ECONOMIC ORTHODOXY AND THE ISSUE OF RULE-FOLLOWING BEHAVIOUR

The 'rational choice vs. rule-following' dispute has found its most visible expression in the rivalry between economics and sociology as separate academic disciplines. Whilst most sociologists consider it a fundamental axiom that human behaviour is governed by social rules or norms, invoking a norm to explain behaviour is viewed by orthodox economists as an approach almost diametrically opposed to rational choice analysis (Coleman 1987: 133). As I have discussed in more detail elsewhere (Vanberg 1988b), the Durkheim–Parsons tradition in sociology defined this discipline's research programme in explicit contrast to the 'utilitarian individualism' of economic theory, which it criticizes for ignoring the significance of normative rules as an indispensable foundation for any cooperative social order.[2]

While it may have been most visible in the contrast between the sociological and the economic models of man – *Homo sociologicus* and *Homo oeconomicus* – the 'rational choice vs. rule-following' issue has also been raised within the economics profession, by 'unorthodox' critics, such as the American institutionalists Thorstein Veblen and John R. Commons. It is an issue which is clearly behind Veblen's famous satiric description of the 'hedonistic conception of man' in orthodox economics, a conception which, according to Veblen (1919: 73), depicts man as 'a lightning calculator of pleasures and pains'. As an alternative to the 'hedonistic conception' Veblen advocates an *evolutionary* approach which views man as 'a coherent structure of propensities and habits' (1919: 74) and apprehends the development of human nature 'in terms of a cumulative growth of habits of life' (1919: 78). Man is seen, Veblen (1919: 78) explains, as 'a creature of habits and propensities given through the antecedents, hereditary and cultural, of which he is an outcome; and the habits of thought formed in any one line of experience' (1919: 79). Whatever else might have been on Veblen's agenda, his plea for an *evolutionary economics* can, at least in part, be read as a plea for a research programme that focuses attention on the process in which man, guided by experience and trial and error, learns to adopt routines and habits which are continuously adapted to his problem-environment, and which are readapted as the environment changes (1919: 74f.). Evolutionary economics, in this interpretation, is the study of the cumulative process in which the set of routines and habits on which the social and economic order is based emerge, develop and change over time.

In John R. Common's reservations about orthodox economics the issue of habitual or routinized behaviour also plays a major role, a fact that has been emphasized in earlier as well as more recent comments on his work (Mitchell 1935; Rutherford 1989; Biddle 1990).

In his summary of what he refers to as 'the basic ideas of institutional economics according to Professor Commons', W.C. Mitchell describes one of these ideas as follows:

> Repetition of similar experiences makes it possible to test different modes of action by trial and error, to select those modes that seem most satisfactory, and to test ideas about physical phenomena or human behavior. From repetition arise habits and customs which conserve the lessons of past experience and provide a basis for future expectations.
>
> (Mitchell 1935: 640)

Rutherford (1989: 13) argues that Commons viewed human action as being both based on custom and habit as well as rationally deliberated, where habit 'looks after the routine' and, thus, frees the mind for dealing with the unexpected, while rational deliberation 'is concerning itself with the limiting factors of strategic transactions'. And J.E. Biddle (1990: 36) says about Commons that he held a 'relativistic' concept of rationality in the sense of emphasizing the crucial role of a person's *past experience* in shaping their *current beliefs* about what are useful and appropriate kinds of behaviour. As Biddle indicates, Commons does not consider habitual practices to be simply immune from changes in circumstances. He assumes, however, that adjustments to such changes come with some delay, that habitual practices tend to allow only 'for a slow infiltration of reason provoked by uncomfortable experience' (Biddle 1990: 37).[3]

Besides the critique from other social sciences, like sociology, and from unorthodox schools, like American institutionalism, the neo-classical mainstream tradition in economics has continuously attracted criticism from a wide range of authors who, in one way or another, also take issue with the rational maximization paradigm for not accommodating the reality of habitual and routinized behaviour. To name only a few: the most prominent among these critics is probably Herbert A. Simon whose argument will be discussed in more detail in section 4. Another tenacious critic is Amartya K. Sen who also seems to be concerned about the issue of habits and routines when he emphasizes that the 'main issue' in his criticism of the 'behavioural foundations of economic theory ... is the acceptability of the assumption of the invariable pursuit of self-interest in each act' (Sen 1979: 108f.), or when he objects to a concept of rational maximization that assumes 'act-by-act pursuit of each person's own goal in every isolated act of choice' (Klamer 1989: 144). Though, to be sure, such statements remain somewhat ambiguous as to what, in Sen's view, the 'main issue' really is. Whether it is the issue of 'self-interest' versus some other kind of *motivational* assumption, or the issue of case-by-case choice vs. some kind of rule-following behaviour, or both.

With his concept of *x-efficiency* Harvey Leibenstein also wants to explicitly account for habitual and routine behaviour, in contrast to the 'standard assumption of maximization behavior' (1980: 99). Human behaviour is viewed as shifting, dependent on context, between more or less calculating modes, ranging from pure routine to complete calculation (1980: 103, 1982: 92). And, to mention only one more example here, the notion of *routines* – as opposed to maximizing behaviour – also plays a central role in R.R. Nelson and S.G. Winter's *An Evolutionary Theory of Economic Change* (1982), which looks at the process in which, through trial and error, routines are developed and adapted to changing circumstances.

2 CASE-BY-CASE MAXIMIZATION, RULE-FOLLOWING AND RECURRENT PROBLEMS

The various criticisms of the orthodox maximization model, even those which concur in emphasizing the role of habitual and routinized behaviour, are by no means in agreement on the reasons of and remedies for the orthodoxy's shortcomings. In contrast to what some of the above quoted, as well as other, critics of the standard maximization paradigm seem to suggest, this chapter is based on the presumption that the orthodoxy's deficiency in accounting for rule-following behaviour is neither a matter of its underlying *methodological individualism*, nor a matter of its assumption of *self-interest motivation*. Instead, it is presumed here that this deficiency has its cause in an unnecessarily narrow interpretation of *rational behaviour* as *situational, case-by-case maximization*, an interpretation which is, even if only implicitly, quite common in orthodox applications of the *economic model of man*. Stated differently, I want to argue that a theoretical alternative to the 'case-by-case maximization' version of the rational choice notion can be specified which provides a systematic account for habitual and rule-following behaviour while retaining the two fundamental principles of the 'economic approach': its methodological individualism and the self-interest assumption.

The difference between the two interpretations of 'rational choice' which I want to contrast can probably be best explained in reference to the notions of *recurring situations* and *behavioural regularities*. Strictly speaking, every situation that one encounters is *unique* in the sense that there will always be *some* respect in which it is different from any situation one has encountered before or will encounter in the future. We can, nevertheless, meaningfully speak of *recurring situations* in the sense that any given situation is, *in certain respects*, similar to other situations, past and future. The term *behavioural regularity* can then be understood as describing the fact that in recurring situations, S_1 to S_n, a person is regularly exhibiting a particular behaviour A_i out of a set of potential alternatives A_1 to A_m. The difference between the two perspectives contrasted here can be expressed in terms of the different explanatory accounts they could offer for *behavioural regularities* so defined.

The logic of the *case-by-case maximization* model would require one to explain such a regularity by the assumption that, in every single-choice situation S_j, the incentive structure is such that, among the available alternatives A_1 to A_m, A_i happens always to be the alternative which the choosing person expects to carry the highest pay-off. That is, it is assumed that the person, assessing each situation separately, happens to find A_i to be the most attractive alternative in each and every case. If, to an observer, things appear differently, this can only mean that he or she fails to account for all the incentives and constraints that actually affect the person's behaviour. The possibility of a 'non-maximizing choice' is excluded by assumption.

By contrast, the logic of a *rule-following* perspective implies that observed behavioural regularities *can* be, and typically *are*, due to a general *disposition*, on the part of the acting person, to exhibit a particular kind of behaviour A_i in certain types of situations S_j, that is, in situations which the person identifies as belonging into the same class. In other words, it is assumed that behaviour A_i is regularly shown, not because the actor, upon separate assessment of each particular case, happens to always identify A_i as the most promising alternative, but because he identifies the respective situations as belonging into the same class of situations S_j in which A_i has been found to be a useful strategy. This does not exclude the possibility of behavioural regularities which are, *de facto*, due to A_1 being regularly the most attractive alternative. It allows, however, for the possibility that, in particular instances, A_i may be exhibited *even though* it would not be the actor's maximizing choice if the respective situations *were* to be separately assessed. Such a possibility is excluded by the case-by-case maximization model.

Central to the concept of rule-following behaviour is the assumption that actors do not respond to particular situations as unique events but, instead, tend to form categories of situations which they perceive as similar, in some behaviourally relevant sense. This is in fact an assumption which seems to be necessarily implied in the very notion that a person's behaviour is influenced by past experience. Because, it is difficult to see how past experience can be utilized in any other way than by classifying particular instances along generalized categories of 'types of situations' and 'types of behaviour'. If, however, behaviour is based on such generalizations, it would seem that the case-by-case maximization model cannot literally be meant to be concerned with unique choices in unique situations. Its advocates will probably not only be willing to admit that past experiences do affect current choices, they may also want to claim that their concept of rational choice accounts for such effects. Yet it is not only questionable whether such an account has been provided so far. More importantly, it seems questionable whether such an account *can* be consistently and systematically developed from within the orthodox maximization paradigm. Indeed, the argument in this chapter is based on the presumption that this is not possible without introducing, in one way or another, the notion of *rule-following*, that is, without divorcing the concept of rationality from the notion of case-by-case maximization.

3   THE RATIONALITY OF RULE-FOLLOWING

In a sequence of articles, starting with his 1983 essay on 'The origin of predictable behavior', Ronald A. Heiner has made an effort to develop a *theory of imperfect choice* which is meant to be an 'alternative to traditional optimization theory' (Heiner 1983: 560). The theory provides an argument for why rational, but *imperfect* agents may profit from following rules instead of attempting to maximize advantage on a case-by-case basis.

Heiner's argument has as its benchmark the notion of a *perfect* agent, that is, an agent who is able to determine with perfect reliability what, in particular situations, is the maximizing choice. For such an agent, Heiner argues, case-by-case maximization would obviously be the best policy. To the extent, however, that an agent is *not perfect*, in the sense defined, he may possibly fare better overall by adopting a rule for how to behave in recurring problem-situations, even though rule-following will inevitably result in less than optimal outcomes in those instances in which maximizing choice and rule-dictated behaviour do not coincide. The relevant comparison here is, of course, between, on the one side, the risk of, and the expected damage from, choosing a 'wrong' alternative while attempting to maximize case-by-case, and, on the other side, the risk of, and the expected damage from, missing out on 'preferred exceptions' when following a rule. The first risk is correlated with what Heiner calls the 'competence' of the agent, where competence is defined relative to the difficulty or complexity of the decision problem. The second risk is dependent on the nature of the rule in question. Hence, the question of whether rule-following may in fact be superior to attempted case-by-case maximization cannot be answered in general, but only by comparing (1) the complexity of the problem situation, (2) the competence of the agent and, (3) the nature, or 'quality', of the behavioural rule.

An imperfect agent apparently faces a problem of finding a proper balance between two 'imperfections': the imperfectness of his own choice, and the imperfectness of the decision-rule which he applies. The rule (if it can be called a 'rule') 'always choose the best alternative' would obviously generate optimal outcomes, if reliably administered. But it need not be the best strategy for an imperfect agent who is unable to optimally choose with perfect reliability. He may fare better with an imperfect rule, but one which he can apply more reliably (for example, the rule 'go on green, stop on red' as opposed to the rule 'cross an intersection when it is safe to do so'). A 'perfect rule' can be defined as one which, if applied with perfect reliability, results in optimal choices *in all instances*. Correspondingly, the degree of 'imperfectness' of a rule can be defined in terms of the relative share of non-optimal choices which result if it is reliably applied, or, stated differently, in terms of the rate of *preferred exceptions*, that is, the frequency of cases in which deviating from the rule would be preferable to the agent. It will in general be the case that *simpler* rules are more *imperfect*, have a higher

177

rate of 'preferred exceptions' than more sophisticated rules. But for the same reason, namely their simplicity, they can be applied more reliably. And what matters to imperfect agents is the combined product of the two aspects.[4]

Standard neoclassical choice theory, Heiner (1990: 24) argues, implicitly assumes that no gap exists 'between agents' decision making "competence" and "difficulty" of their decision problems'. It assumes that 'agents use information perfectly by always selecting actions that maximize expected utility based on observed information' (Heiner 1987). He presents his own approach as an attempt to generalize orthodox rational choice theory so to encompass 'both perfect and imperfect decisions' (1987). His analysis is intended 'to broaden the meaning of rationality' and to provide 'a theoretical characterization of rational behavior for imperfect agents' (1990: 31), the focus of which is on *rule-following* as a behavioural implication of imperfect choice.

Heiner takes pains to emphasize that the problem of *imperfect choice*, the principal subject of his own approach, is *different* from the problem of *imperfect information*, and that it ought to be treated as an issue 'separate from whether there are any costs of observing information in the first place' (1988a: 29). The 'imperfect information' argument is typically viewed by advocates of the orthodox maximization model as something that can be dealt with by simply incorporating appropriate additional cost terms into the function which is to be maximized, so that the 'cost-adjusted decisions can thereby still be regarded as optimal' (ibid.). Whether this can truly be regarded as a solution consistent with the maximization framework or not, and there are forcible arguments which suggest it may not be,[5] the 'imperfect choice' argument certainly cannot be integrated in the same manner without adjustments in the framework itself (Heiner 1987). As for such adjustments, Heiner suggests that an *evolutionary* theoretical framework be adopted which he views as being 'intrinsically connected to analyzing imperfect choice' (1988b: 155). The principles of imperfect choice, he argues, imply a 'need for explicit evolutionary modeling rather than postulating "as if" optimization' (1988b: 148).

Heiner's argument on *imperfect choice and rule-following* has much in common with the arguments on *adaptive rationality* and the *limits of reason* which have been advanced by H.A. Simon and F.A. Hayek respectively, arguments which are the subject of the two following sections.

4 ADAPTIVE RATIONALITY AND PROGRAMMED BEHAVIOUR

For more than three decades, Herbert Simon has been arguing that the orthodox neoclassical concept of *rationality as maximizing* implies an unrealistic view of man's cognitive abilities,[6] of his access to information and his computational capacities (1957: 241). The alternative concept of rationality which Simon proposes, namely that of *bounded, procedural* or *adaptive rationality* (1965: 88ff.; 1979a, 66f., 84), is in essence a theory of behavioural learning, a theory which seeks to understand a person's current behaviour in terms of his or her past experience.

The classical rationality concept, Simon (1984: 47) notes, 'require implicitly that the economic actor attend to all of the important variables about which he has to make decisions or that can inform him in his decisions,' a requirement which, in a world where the number of potentially relevant variables is virtually innumerable, can only be met by, what Simon refers to as 'Olympian rationality' (Simon 1984: 48). His alternative concept of 'bounded' rationality[7] assumes instead 'that human beings handle this difficulty by attending to only a small part of the complexity about them,' by making their decision on the basis of 'a highly simplified model of the world, and . . . the subset of variables that enter into it' (ibid.).

Obviously implied in the notion of an actor's 'model of the world' is the idea that there is a distinction to be made between the actor's *objective* and *subjective* environments, a distinction which, as Simon asserts, marks indeed a critical difference between his own view and the orthodox concept of rationality. The latter, he argues, implies that there is no need 'to distinguish between the real world and the decision maker's perception of it' (Simon 1987: 27). It is assumed that the decision maker 'perceives the world as it really is', and that we can predict his choices 'entirely from our knowledge of the real world' (ibid.), an assumption which, Simon notes, we can no longer make once we recognize 'that both the knowledge and the computational power of the decision maker are severely limited' (ibid.).[8] Recognition of these limitations, he insists, requires us to include in our analysis the perceptual and cognitive. processes which determine the *subjective environment* to which an actor responds.

A principal source of discrepancies between 'objective' and 'subjective' environment are, in Simon's account, the before-mentioned *simplifications* which help to bring the decision maker's 'model of the world' within the range of his 'computing capacity' (1957: 242, 256). The need for such simplification is, as Simon (1982a: 740) reasons, apparent from the fact that the 'bottleneck' of man's perceptual apparatus admits only a tiny fraction of available information and that 'equally important omissions characterize the processing that takes place when information reaches the brain'. The *selective mechanisms* which govern these perceptual and calculative processes, are viewed by Simon as the product of an actor's past experience. It is, he suggests, through 'experimenting and learning on the basis of his experience and his mistakes' (1965: 87), and

179

not through an optimization calculus, that a person is able to select, in a decision situation, a particular problem-solving path 'from the myriad that might have been followed' (1982a: 740). Actors use, he argues, *experience-based* 'selective heuristics ... to explore a small number of promising alternatives. They draw heavily upon past experience to detect the important features of the situation before them, features which are associated in memory with possibly relevant action' (1979a: 73).

Even though the issue of case-by-case optimization versus rule-following behaviour is not explicitly addressed in these terms, it is clearly the underlying theme of Simon's account for how past experience translates into current behavioural choices. The process of experience-guided learning is viewed as a process of behavioural programming, a process in which an actor adapts a repertoire of behavioural patterns, problem-solving skills and habits (1979a: 81). Simon notes that it is useful conceptually to distinguish between 'programmed' and 'non-programmed' behaviour (1982b: 1a) or, rather, to view choices as varying along a continuum with 'nonprogrammed' and 'programmed' choices at its respective ends (1982b: 2a). But it is apparent that, in his view, the truly 'nonprogrammed' end is more of conceptual relevance as a benchmark than an empirically relevant case. As Simon puts it, 'even searching through a haystack for a needle is programmed choice' (1982b: 2a). It is programmed choice in the sense that it will typically rely, to some extent, on behavioural patterns which have been found successful in comparable situations in the past.

Behavioural innovation − in Simon's terms, the 'construction of new programs' (1982b: 9a) − is initiated when previously practised programmes fail to work satisfactorily, where 'satisfactorily' is again a matter of previous experience, of learned aspirations.[9] And the 'search for a new program' is not a problem of finding an optimal programme, but one of finding a programme that works 'better' (1982b: 9b).[10]

The assumptions in Simon's theory that are of particular relevance in the present context, can be summarized as follows. As alternative to the orthodox maximization assumption Simon suggests a theory of human decision making which views an actor's choice−behaviour as based on a repertoire of behavioural patterns, routines or programmes. The repertoire reflects, at any point in time, the actor's past experience, and it is, through trial and error, continuously adjusted as new experiences are undergone. Routines that are found to 'work well' tend to be retained, while experience of failure encourages search for better programmes. It is this emphasis on behavioural routines or programmes which, I suppose, makes Simon's theory a genuine *alternative* to the optimization model, rather than a generalized version of the latter, as is suggested by those who find in his argument no more than a plea for incorporating additional cost-variables into the maximization calculus.

5 RULE-FOLLOWING AND THE LIMITS OF REASON

In his essay on 'Economics and knowledge' (1937), as well as in several of his later writings, F.A. Hayek has criticized mainstream economics for not dealing seriously with the *knowledge problem*, the problem of how knowledge of the 'data', which economic theory assumes as 'given', is actually acquired and communicated. By blurring the difference between *objective* and *subjective* 'data',[11] and by depicting *homo oeconomicus* as 'a quasi-omniscient individual' (ibid., p. 46) economics loses sight, so Hayek's argument goes, of what should be one of its main concerns: to explain how knowledge about 'objective data' is acquired, 'how experience creates knowledge' (ibid., p. 47). Directly related to his emphasis on the 'knowledge problem' is his argument on the systematic interconnection between the *limits of our reason* and the *reason of rules*, an argument that is central to Hayek's critique of what he calls 'constructivist rationalism'.

The 'constructivist' variant of rationalism, as depicted by Hayek, claims 'that conscious reason ought to determine every particular action' (Hayek 1973: 29), that 'man is capable of coordinating his activities successfully through a full explicit evaluation of the consequences of all possible alternatives of action, and in full knowledge of all possible circumstances' (Hayek 1967: 90). Such a claim implies, Hayek argues, 'not only a colossal presumption concerning our intellectual powers, but also a complete misconception of the kind of world in which we live' (ibid.). The constructivist approach, he censures, fails to recognize that the limited power of our reason implies the necessity for us to be guided by *rules* (Hayek 1973: 33).[12]

The notion that the limits of our reason require us to follow rules is one of the central themes of Hayek's work (Vanberg 1989a). The 'whole rationale of the phenomenon of rule-guided action' is, he submits, to be found in our 'inescapable ignorance of most of the particular circumstances which determine the effects of our actions' (Hayek 1976: 20). The reliance on rules 'is a device we have learned to use because our reason is insufficient to master the full detail of complex reality' (Hayek 1960: 66), rules are 'a device for coping with our constitutional ignorance' (Hayek 1976: 8).

Rules facilitate, Hayek explains, the making of decisions in complex situations. They 'limit our range of choice' (Hayek 1967: 90) by abbreviating 'the list of circumstances which we need to take into account in the particular instances, singling out certain classes of facts as alone determining the general kind of action which we should take' (Hayek 1964: 11). The fact that rules *abbreviate* what we need to take into account and *limit* our range of choice means, of course, nothing else than that they require us to *disregard* facts which we may well know and to leave potential courses of action *unconsidered*. How such disregarding of facts and limiting of choice should be to our advantage, should help us to make better decisions, is, as Hayek acknowledges, far from being intuitively obvious. But this seeming paradox can be explained, he states, by the very 'necessity of coming to terms with our unalterable ignorance of much that would be relevant if we knew it' (Hayek 1964: 12).[13]

We can impossibly act, he reasons, 'in full consideration of all the facts of a particular situation' (1973: 30) and, consequently, we inevitably have to act on the basis of *selective knowledge* that is, considering only a fraction of the innumerable, potentially relevant facts. The basic issue is, therefore, which *mode of selection* promises to render overall more preferable outcomes: the selectivity inherent in situational, case-by-case choices, or the selectivity of rules? And, as Hayek argues (1964: 12), it may well be that with the latter we fare better overall than with the former, that is, rule-following, on balance, is more successful than the attempt to identify the best course of action in a case-by-case manner.[14] Whether or not this is the case critically depends, of course, on the nature of the rules that are followed. Rules will differ in their 'quality' in the sense that the rates at which they generate non-preferred outcomes will differ. One can easily imagine rules which, measured in these terms, would be clearly inferior to case-by-case choice. And among the rules which 'work better' some will be more advantageous than others, an observation which raises the question of how actors come to adopt rules at all, and how they come to adopt certain kinds of rules rather than others.

Hayek approaches these questions from an evolutionary perspective. He suggests that we view the rules that govern human behaviour as the outcome of evolutionary processes operating on various levels. There are, on the one side, the *innate*, genetically transmitted, hard-wired behavioural rules that have been shaped in the *biological evolution* of *Homo sapiens*. On the other side, there are the learned rules which, on the individual level, reflect a person's learning history while, on the social-aggregate level, they are subject to a process of *cultural revolution* (Vanberg 1986).

6 THE MAXIMIZATION PARADIGM AND THE 'REALISM' ISSUE

The kind of critique of the orthodox rationality concept which has been reviewed in the previous sections is often advanced together with the argument that economics needs a more 'realistic' behavioural foundation, an argument which, to all appearances, has had little i on mainstream economics. The orthodoxy's remarkable obstinacy numerous and repeated attacks on the realism lacking in its beha assumptions can probably be attributed, in part, to the widespread acceptance, explicit or implicit, of M. Friedman's 'classical' argument that it is not the 'realism' of our theoretical assumptions which matters but whether they allow for good predictions.[15] This argument seemingly allows advocates of the orthodox rational maximization model to concede the descriptive inadequacies of the model and yet to claim that it is analytically fruitful.

Whatever the intrinsic methodological merits of the Friedman argument may be (I fail to recognize them), it is not at all evident that the orthodox maximization assumption does indeed fare so well when measured against the self-chosen criterion of *predictive power*. Critics have repeatedly argued that the alleged explanatory success claimed for the orthodox rationality concept can, in actual fact, not be credited to the maximization assumption as such, but to various kinds of surreptitiously added auxiliary assumptions which its advocates use very generously to achieve predictive fit. As J.G. Cross (1983: 3) puts it: 'When we defend the maximization paradigm by pointing to the similarity between its predictions and observed behavior, we often overlook the fact that the empirical "success" of many economic models is principally derived from accommodating adjustments in complementary hypotheses'.[16]

Another reason, other than Friedman's argument, for the orthodoxy's missing response to its critics may be seen in the latter's failure to go beyond exposing the inadequacies of the maximization paradigm and to offer an attractive alternative theoretical framework (Simon 1979b: 509; 1984: 52).[17] The classical rational choice paradigm seems to owe its appeal primarily to two facts: it provides a *unified theory* which applies to all human behaviour, independent of the particularities of time and place. And, second, its general thrust conforms to our common, everyday experience of *functionality* and *adaptiveness* in human behaviour. In order to be a viable competitor, an alternative approach should be an attractive substitute in both respects: it should, likewise, provide a *unified theory* of human behaviour, and it too should conform to our common experience of functionality and purposefulness in human behaviour. In the remainder of this chapter, an attempt is made to outline the basic structure of a theoretical conception that may provide, in the terms stated, a systematic and coherent alternative to the orthodox rational maximization model. It is a theoretical perspective towards which several approaches in modern economics, including some of the ones discussed above, appear to be converging, a perspective which can be labelled *evolutionary* as well as *behavioural*.

7 RATIONAL CHOICE THEORY AND TELEOLOGICAL EXPLANATION

There are basically two competing accounts for how functionality and adaptiveness in nature, human and non-human, can be explained, accounts which can be distinguished as *explanation by design* and *explanation by process*. The first explains functionality as the product of somebody's design, somebody's deliberate intervention. It provides, in other terms, a *teleological* account of functionality. The second provides an account in terms of some specified process which can be shown to systematically generate adaptiveness *without* design. It provides a 'non-teleological,' causal account of functionality.[18]

The essential contribution of Darwin's theory of evolution, and of the generalized evolutionary perspective that emerged from it, has been to demonstrate how adaptive phenomena which seem to require a teleological design explanation can be explained in non-teleological process terms. Rational choice explanations clearly do have a teleological structure. Adaptiveness in human action is explained as the result of rational foresight, of purposeful design. And it may appear as if there can hardly be a meaningful alternative to explaining action in terms of intention, purpose and design. Rational choice theory seems to be the natural, unchallengeable stronghold of teleological reasoning. And any effort to extend non-teleological reasoning into this area may seem futile. Yet, the idea that the adaptiveness of human action may, nevertheless, be fruitfully analysed from a generalized evolutionary perspective should appear less peculiar once one considers the simple, but fundamental fact that actions cannot literally be 'motivated' by their factual consequences, but only by the actor's *expectation* of consequences. As soon as one raises the question of how these expectations are formed, one's attention is automatically drawn to the *learning process* in which past experiences translate into current expectations and current experiences shape future expectations. It is exactly for such learning-processes, processes in which 'knowledge about the world' is acquired, that an evolutionary–behavioural perspective promises to be fruitful. It can, indeed, provide what H. Simon has called for: a theory about 'the ways in which expectations are formed about uncertain future events' (1984: 51).

I should add, as a note of caution, that advocating a non-teleological, evolutionary–behavioural approach to human behaviour is not the same as denying that purpose, planning and design play a fundamental role in human action. Such a denial would be absurd. The very fact that I write this chapter is the carrying out of a plan. The relevant issue is not whether men act on purpose. We all know that we do. The issue is how we can best understand why, in pursuit of their purposes, men employ certain practices and strategies rather than others. And it is with regard to this issue that an evolutionary–behavioural account emphasizes the role of past experience.

The emphasis on purpose and the emphasis on past experience are not mutually exclusive outlooks at human behaviour. The choice between the two may ultimately be a matter of how we define the explanatory problem that we want to address. If we ask for an explanation of *particular actions* ('Why did person *P* show behaviour *B* in situation *S*?'), we invite accounts in terms of intentions, purposes, etc. This is, however, not the explanatory focus of an evolutionary–behavioural approach. As I will argue in more detail later, the latter is not concerned with the explanation of particular actions. Rather, its concern is with the explanation of how the behavioural repertoires of persons are shaped and change over time, that is, the set of practices, strategies and routines that persons employ in coping with various kinds of problems.

In this sense, the issue of a 'teleological' versus a 'non-teleological' account of purposeful human action can be viewed as a matter of analytical fruitfulness: which of the two ways of specifying the explanatory problem generates the more interesting research agenda? In what follows, I shall try to show why I find that the evolutionary–behavioural perspective provides for a more promising agenda.

8   A THEORY OF ADAPTIVE RATIONALITY: EVOLUTIONARY EPISTEMOLOGY

The idea that a generalized Darwinian evolutionary perspective can be applied to all processes in which 'knowledge about the world' is acquired, is at the core of the research programme of *evolutionary epistemology*, major contributions to which have been made by authors like K.R. Popper, F.A. Hayek and D.T. Campbell. Evolutionary epistemology is based on the assumption that from natural selection to the growth of scientific knowledge the same basic principle of *trial and error-elimination* can be found operating. All organisms are, as Popper (1972: 255) puts it, constantly engaged in *problem-solving* which 'always proceeds by the method of trial and error: new reactions, new forms, new organs, new modes of behavior, new hypotheses, are tentatively put forward and controlled by error-elimination'.

The same general scheme applies, as Popper (1972: 288) argues, 'not only to the emergence of . . . new scientific theories, but to the emergence of new forms of behavior, and even to forms of living organisms.' It described a general pattern of 'learning' which, though its particular manifestations may be quite different, is ultimately the same 'from the amoeba to Einstein'.[19]

At whatever level a generalized evolutionary perspective may be applied, it always presumes the operation of three processes: first, a process by which constantly variation and novelty – in Popper's terms, new tentative solutions – are introduced; second, a process of systematic selection among the variants or, again in Popper's terms, a process of error-elimination; and, third, a process by which variants or tentative solutions are preserved, reproduced or propagated. Whatever particular form these processes or mechanisms may take, their interaction will always produce an increase in *adaptive fit* of some system relative to its environment (Campbell 1983: 34).

A Darwinian evolutionary perspective is characterized by what E. Mayr (1982: 46f) calls *population thinking*. It looks at the distribution of certain properties within a population of (unique) individuals who live in an environment in which they are confronted with various kinds of problems. And it studies the changes, over time, in the distribution of these properties within the population. To the extent that the capacity to cope with the problem-environment correlates with transmittable properties which vary within a population, and to the extent that the population's problem-environment remains unchanged in relevant respects, the distribution will gradually shift in favour of the 'more successful' properties, or, in other terms, it will shift in the direction of increased adaptive fit or improved problem-solving capacity.

Both, the generalized evolutionary paradigm and the rational maximization paradigm, aim at an explanation of how adaptiveness or 'efficiency' come about (Ursprung 1988). Yet, their explanatory logic is fundamentally different. Evolutionary adaptiveness is not a matter of calculation in advance, of forward-looking optimization. It is 'driven from behind,' it reflects what in the past has proven to be relatively more successful than other tried out alternatives (Axelrod 1986: 1097). While 'errors' and 'mistakes' do not have a systematic place within a rational maximization framework, they play an essential and critical role from an evolutionary perspective.[20]

Mistakes are not only an inherent part of evolutionary experimenting with new and different potential problem-solutions. They also reflect the 'backward-looking' nature of evolutionary adaptiveness. The 'knowledge' which evolutionary learning produces is always, and inevitably, wisdom about past environments (Campbell 1975: 1106). If a population's environment changes in relevant aspects, what used to be 'adaptive' may become useless or even dysfunctional. Therefore, what appears to be 'inefficient' in today's environment may only be the carrying forth of traits or strategies which were functional in yesterday's environment.

In order for trial-and-error learning to work, the behaving organism must somehow, explicitly or tacitly, *classify* problem-situations into categories of situations which are, in some relevant sense, 'similar'. Such classification embodies, in essence, a *conjecture* about what makes situations, in a behaviourally relevant sense, similar or different. And, as discussed above (section 2), such classifications are at the roots of all rule-following behaviour, whether we are dealing with instincts, unreflected habits or deliberately adopted rules. They determine what are, to the classifying agent, *recurring situations*, that is, situations which are responded to in certain ways. Behavioural rules are, in this sense, standard recipes for how to deal with certain types of situations. They are conjectural solutions for certain types of recurring problems.

The generalized model of 'evolutionary learning' provides a unifying theoretical framework for the study of the various kinds of processes in which experimenting with rules and selection among rules takes place: the process of *biological evolution* in which genetically transmitted behavioural dispositions are formed; the process of *individual learning* by which a person's behavioural repertoire is shaped;[21] and *cultural evolutions* in which the culturally transmitted rules which prevail within a social group or society are formed. In biological evolution the 'learning' takes place at the level of the species. It is the distribution of behavioural dispositions within a species which gradually shifts towards increased adaptive fit. In individual learning it is the composition of a person's behavioural repertoire which becomes more adapted to the relevant environment. And in cultural evolution it is a social group or society which 'learns' in the sense that its inter-generationally transmitted stock of rules changes over time.[22]

To the extent that the 'economic model of man', the behavioural foundation of economics, is supposed to capture the 'genetic make-up', the hard-wired behavioural repertoire of man, the question of its appropriate content can hardly be meaningfully discussed without reference to what can be plausibly assumed to have arisen in the process of biological evolution. Evolutionary biology provides, in this sense, a theoretical reference base against which different assumptions about 'human nature' can be critically discussed and compared. And, as D.T. Campbell (1987: 174) puts it, there is little reason to assume that an evolutionary perspective will automatically produce 'a "Panglossian" picture of perfect rationality or adaptiveness'.[23] Instead, it may help to systematically account for observed behavioural tendencies which appear to defy explanation in standard rationality terms, like the 'choice-anomalies' studied by A. Tversky and D. Kahneman (1987) or by R. Herrnstein (1988), and the role of emotions as discussed by R. Frank (1988).[24]

9 ADAPTIVE RATIONALITY AND BEHAVIOURAL LEARNING

One of the distinguishing characteristics of *Homo sapiens*, in comparison to other animals, is the much more limited role of *genetically hard-wired* behavioural programmes and the much greater significance of *learned* behavioural programmes. Man's behavioural repertoire is much more a matter of *individual* learning as opposed to *species*-learning. In other terms, it is to a much lesser degree genetically *pre*-programmed and much more programmable and re-programmable through individual learning and, therefore, much more adaptable, to different kinds of environment.

A theory of adaptive learning, for instance B.F. Skinner's theory of behavioural conditioning, seeks to explain how individual's behavioural repertoires change over time in response to experiences undergone. The repertoire of behavioural dispositions, routines, habits etc., which determine a person's behaviour at any point in time, is viewed as the (provisional) outcome of a process of trial-and-error. Individuals are not assumed to be capable reliably to determine which course of action will serve them best in any given situation. They are, however, assumed to be able to systematically learn from experience – from their own trials-and-errors as well as from observing others – what kind of behaviour is more likely to be successful in certain kinds of situations. And they are assumed to be able to develop over time a repertoire of behavioural routines which are functionally adapted to the kind of environment in which they live. In short, human behaviour is explained not in terms of a reliably forward-looking maximizing calculus, but in terms of a 'backward-looking' reliance on what in the past has been experienced as useful strategies.

George C. Homans, who endeavoured for years (with limited success though) to convince his colleagues in sociology that a Skinner-type theory of behavioural learning may provide a fruitful behavioural foundation for social science in general, has pointed to the fundamental similarity between the *behaviourist* and the *economic* model of man (1961: 12–14; 1974: 67–9).[25] In recent years this similarity has found some attention in economics and has led to several contributions which suggest that the adoption of a theory of adaptive learning in economics may help to remedy some of the notorious shortcomings of the rational maximization paradigm, without implying a break with the general thrust of the economic perspective. In his 1986 presidential address to the Public Choice Society, Dennis Mueller has made a case for replacing, what he calls, the 'rational egoism postulate' of economics by the 'adaptive egoism postulate' of behaviorist psychology (Mueller 1986: 19). As an 'advantage of starting with behaviorist psychology' Mueller (ibid., p. 15) notes that 'it allows us to begin with a unified view of human behavior' and that it 'is less of a methodological leap for a social scientist who works with rational egoist models than going to some competing sociological–psychological theories'. Efforts to begin carrying out what Mueller calls for have been made by D.A. Alhadeff (1982) and J.G. Cross

(1983), who show in some detail how standard explanatory problems of economics can be dealt with in terms of a theory of adaptive learning.[26]

What has been said above about the role of an evolutionary framework applies to a theory of adaptive learning as well. It provides a theoretical reference base against which different assumptions about individuals' learned behavioural programmes, their preferences and expectations, can be critically examined as to what can be plausibly assumed, given the learning-environment in which these preferences and expectations have supposedly been shaped. And it may also supplement the evolutionary perspective in providing a potentially unifying framework within which the before mentioned kinds of 'choice-anomalies' may be systematically accounted for.[27]

As mentioned earlier, a generalized evolutionary model can be applied to biological evolution as well as to individual learning and to *cultural evolution*. It would go beyond the scope of this chapter to discuss the latter,[28] but I would like, at least, to mention R.R. Nelson's and S.G. Winter's (1982) evolutionary approach as an example of this third category. The subject of their study are the changes, over time, in the composition or distribution of learned behavioural rules in a social setting. They look at the 'population' of firms in an industry or economy, and at the *routines* which these firms employ in coping with various kinds of problems. These routines vary, more or less, from firm to firm, and what Nelson and Winter seek to explain are the changes that occur, over time, in the distribution of routines across the entire population, changes that result from a process in which firms experiment with new strategies and tend to adopt routines which they experience or perceive as more successful than potential alternative strategies (Nelson and Winter 1982: 4, 14ff.).[29]

10 INDIVIDUAL ROUTINES AND SOCIAL INSTITUTIONS

Nelson and Winter essentially view firms as interconnected sets of behavioural routines, an interpretation which seems to me to provide a useful perspective for the study of social institutions in general, institutions in the sense of corporate entities, like firms, clubs, governments, etc., as well as institutions in the sense of general rules of conduct, like the rules of the road or criminal law (Vanberg 1983; 1989a: 173f.).

The interpretation of institutions as systems or networks of interrelated and mutually stabilizing routines is by no means uncommon in the social science literature, though it may have been stated in different terms and placed in theoretical frameworks different from the one advocated here.[30] It is an interpretation which is clearly implied in H.A. Simon's view of 'the role of institutions in creating for the individual a "simple" world within which his programmed decision-making can take place' (Simon 1982b: 3a). The programmed decision-making of one person is, as he argues, typically embedded in an environment of 'other programs' (ibid., p. 6a), and it is in such a sense, he notes, that the rationality of *Homo oeconomicus* must be interpreted: 'He does not stand on a mountain-top and, viewing the whole world at his feet, make a global, omniscient, rational choice. He is rational within the bounds set by his social role of economic man' (ibid.).

Simon deliberately chooses the sociological concept 'role' because the notion of *Homo sociologicus* as a role-player, and the sociological inter-pretation of institutions as networks of interrelated roles, are clearly intended to capture the phenomena of programmed behaviour and of mutually stabilizing routines (Simon 1982b: 6a). Yet, while borrowing the term, Simon does not want to subscribe to the theoretical connota-tion that goes with it in standard sociology, a connotation which, in his view, falls into the extreme of totally ignoring the part played by rational choice. The sociological role concept does, Simon notes, provide a 'label for phenomenon but not a useful tool for its analysis' (1982a: 742). What needs to be added to the emphasis on *programmed behaviour* is a theory which explains how individuals, in pursuit of their interests, come to adopt, modify and abandon the very kinds of behavioural routines which the 'role' concept is supposed to capture.

As far as the 'interests and rule-following' issue is concerned, the discussion in this chapter has in principal been focused on the question of why it can be beneficial *to an individual agent* to follow rules rather than to choose in a case-by-case manner. The discussion in this section on institutions as systems of interdependent and mutually stabilizing routines requires that the 'interests and rule-following' issue be addressed in a broadened perspective. We can, conceptually, distinguish between two kinds of interests in rules or, in different terms, between two kinds of 'reasons of rules', namely: first, reasons why a rational, self-interested agent may benefit from having *his own* behaviour governed by certain rules; and, second, reasons why a rational self-interested agent may want the behaviour *of others* to be governed by certain rules.

While reasons of the first kind have been emphasized in previous sections of this chapter, social institutions are clearly much more concerned with reasons of the second kind. They typically serve to provide standard solutions to recurring social interaction problems of various sorts. Where 'reasons of rule' of the first kind are present self-interested agents can be expected to learn to adopt such rules. By contrast, reasons of the second kind will not make the respective rules by themselves effective, even if these reasons are generally shared in a social community, that is, even if all its members wish that these rules be generally followed. In order for such rules to be effective, conditions must exist, or be created somehow, which provide reasons of the first kind, i.e. which make following these rules a prudent strategy for the individual members of the respective community.

The problem of creating and maintaining such conditions, either through informal mechanisms of mutual social control or through deliberately organized enforcement efforts, is a problem that all social groups face. It is a problem which in its most fundamental form is often referred to as the 'Hobbesian problem of social order'. As mentioned at the beginning of this chapter, it has been a central claim of the Durkheim–Parsons tradition in sociology that the individualistic–utilitarian tradition in social science (and this means, in particular, economics) has failed to provide a satisfactory solution to the Hobbesian problem. Though this claim rests, in my view (Vanberg 1975), essentially on erroneous assumptions, it is in one respect justified. If the individualistic–utilitarian approach is narrowly interpreted in the sense of a case-by-case maximization model, it may, indeed, be incapable of solving the Hobbesian problem. It is difficult to see how a viable moral order could ever be achieved if it were dependent on securing rule-compliance of situationally, case-by-case maximizing agents. If, however, the individualist–utilitarian tradition is interpreted in terms of a theory of *adaptive rationality*, as advocated in this chapter, the Hobbesian problem translates into a question which can well be answered, namely the question of how a moral order can emerge among individuals who are genetically programmed and behaviourally conditioned to adopt rules and routines which, though not optimal in every instance, generate an overall advantageous pattern of outcomes (Vanberg 1988a, b; Vanberg and Buchanan 1988).

In an ongoing social order the interconnection of individual routines creates mutually stabilizing forces, and the pattern of routines which exist at any point in time in a given social context constitutes effective constraints to which a new entrant has to adapt. In this sense any ongoing social order has, by necessity, a 'conservative bias'.[31] This does not mean however that such a system of mutually stabilizing routines works as a *perpetuum mobile*. Adaptively rational agents are not oblivious to changing opportunities and they are always, in varying degrees, looking for and exploring new ways of doing things. As the 'balance of advantage' shifts away from traditional routines established institutional structures may change or even collapse.[32]

11 CONCLUSION: EQUILIBRIUM ANALYSIS OR PROCESS THEORY

At a conference, held at the University of Chicago in 1985, on 'Rational Choice – The Contrast between Economics and Psychology' an exchange between Robert Lucas, as one of the paper authors (see Lucas 1987) and Sidney Winter, as his discussant, illuminated very instructively an important dimension of the issues discussed in this chapter. Lucas, in his contribution, made the following statement:

> In general terms, we view or model an individual as a collection of decision rules (rules that dictate the action to be taken in given situations) and a set of preferences used to evaluate the outcomes arising from particular situation–action combinations. These decision rules are continuously under review and revision; new decision rules are tried and tested against experience, and rules that produce desirable outcomes supplant those that do not. I use the term 'adaptive' to refer to this trial-and-error process through which our modes of behavior are determined.
>
> (Lucas 1987: 217)

The reader of such statement could be led to believe that Lucas wants to endorse a research agenda that focuses on the very trial-and-error processes in which decision rules are continuously reviewed. Yet, in actual fact, Lucas arrives at a quite different conclusion. Economics, he argues,

> had tended to focus on situations in which the agent can be expected to 'know' or to have learned the consequences of different actions so that his observed choices reveal stable features of his underlying preferences. . . . Technically, I think of economics as studying decision rules that are steady states of some adaptive process, decision rules that are found to work over a range of situations and hence are no longer revised appreciably as more experience accumulates.
>
> (Lucas 1987: 218).

As Winter pointed out in his comment, Lucas's definition of the economic perspective turns the issue essentially into a question of what can be considered more interesting and more fruitful: the study of steady states of adaptive processes, or the study of these adaptive processes themselves. It is, as Winter puts it, a question of whether one is 'willing to limit the aspirations of economic science to the study of steady states' (Winter 1987: 245), based on a theory which has no criteria of its own to determine when such steady states prevail and, thus, cannot theoretically identify its own range of applicability (ibid., p. 248). Not surprisingly, Winter judges Lucas's definition as 'far too small to be acceptable as a definition of the limits and ambitions of the discipline,' and he adds: 'There is an important role for inquiry into the learning and adaptive processes of boundedly rational economic actors who are forced to act in a changing world that they do not understand' (ibid., p. 249).

192

At any point in time we will find a more or less broad mix of strategies used by individuals to cope with the various types of problems that they face, where some of these strategies will be better adapted to the currently prevailing problem-environment than others. It is certainly true that, if the relevant characteristics of the problem-environment remain sufficiently stable long enough, competition will tend to induce convergence of adopted strategies towards some 'equilibrium'. This is the true kernel in Lucas's argument and in the earlier arguments by A. Alchian (1950) and M. Friedman (1953: 22) on 'rational maximization' as the product of 'natural selection' through market competition. However, this insight is of little help in understanding the dynamic *process* in which the set or mix of strategies is constantly, through the endogenous forces of human experimentation and innovation, changed over time and adjusted to new and unforeseeable circumstances. In a world in which humans, through their own inventiveness, constantly change the environment to which they have to adapt, there seems to be little else worthy to be studied, other than the process of adaptation itself.

It is interesting, though not necessarily encouraging, to note that the issue discussed here has been addressed by F.A. Hayek more than fifty years ago in his 1937 article mentioned earlier, on 'Economics and knowledge'. Hayek (1948: 45) argued there about the use of the equilibrium concept in economics that it 'does not get us any nearer an explanation of when and how such a state will come about,' and that, what is needed, is a theory of the underlying *process*.[33] Half a century later, there is still ample reason for confronting the economics profession with essentially the same argument. Yet, the prospects for an alternative theoretical perspective to take shape, an *evolutionary–behavioural* perspective, may be more promising today, due to theoretical developments in economics, such as those discussed in this chapter, and also due to such theoretical developments in the 'hard' sciences as the work of Ilya Prigogine and others on non-equilibrium systems, theoretical developments which may help to make departures from the Newtonian equilibrium framework in economics more reputable.[34]

NOTES

1 Chapter prepared for conference on 'Methodological Problems of New Institutional Economics,' August 17–19, 1989, Uppsala, Sweden.

2 Durkheim oriented his analysis directly to the system of economic individualism. He issued a fundamental challenge to the utilitarian analysis of it, couching his argument explicitly in terms of the problem of social order. The crucial factor, ignored in the utilitarian scheme, was that of an institutionalized normative order, of which the *institution* of contract was the key element in the economic context. This institution could not be derived from the interests of the contracting parties, but

presupposed an independent source in what Durkheim called the *conscience collective*.

(T. Parsons 1968: 233)

A.J. Fields echoes the sociological critique when – with a footnote reference to Emile Durkheim and Talcott Parsons – he argues:

> If the behavioral principle of social science models is to be self-interest maximization, and one wishes to model stable social orders, one must posit logically anterior rules or norms that help define the constraints and, thus, the arena within which such maximization takes place.

(Field 1984: 685)

3 That the issue of habitual and rule-following behaviour continues to be a major concern of writers who place themselves into the American institutionalist tradition is visible in G.M. Hodgson's (1988) 'Manifesto for a modern institutional economics'. Hodgson rejects what he calls 'the continuously calculating, marginally adjusting agent of neoclassical theory' (p. 138), because such a concept, he argues, is 'unable to appreciate the function of habit and routine in enabling individuals to learn and carry out complex action' in an uncertain and complicated world' (p. 118).

4 Heiner (1990: 24) puts this problem in terms of finding a balance between two types of errors: 'failing to make such preferred exception represents a *"Type 1 error"*, meaning failing to deviate from rules when there exist preferred exceptions to them. On the other hand, a *"Type 2 error"* means to mistakenly violate rules when there exists no preferred exception'.

5 Such arguments concern, in particular, the 'infinite regression', 'circularity' or 'self-reference' problem (J. Conlisk 1988; C. Knudsen Ch. 6, this volume). The claim to 'super-optimization' – to include decision making costs in the optimizing calculus – is, as Knudsen argues, contradictory: 'If we in the calculus of optimization try to take all costs into consideration, inclusive the costs of the calculus itself, the result is that it is impossible in these situations to define optimal choice: To make a decision is cost consuming; therefore it must be decided whether it is worth making a decision. But to make a decision implies costs; therefore we must decide, whether it is worth making a decision on whether it is worth making a decision, etc.'

6 Simon (1982a: 718) notes that his critique of the economic model of man does not focus – as much of the traditional critique does – on the motivational but on 'the cognitive aspects of economic behavior'.

7 Simon refers to the American institutionalists, in particular to Commons, as forerunners of a theory of bounded rationality (1979b: 499; 1982a: 718).

8 Simon (1982a: 738) Economics got along almost without psychological hypotheses about economic man's intellectual qualities by assuming him to be "objectively" rational, that is, rational in dealing with a given external environment as viewed by an omniscient being gifted with unlimited powers of computation.'

9 Aspirations are expectations – adjusted in the long run to realities – of the result that can reasonably be attained. They are not formed on the basis of detailed evaluation of alternative courses of action. Indeed, their principal usefulness lies in the fact that they remove the necessity for such evaluations until the failures of existing programs indicate the need for innovation. The innovation process then requires the discovery and elaboration of new programs that can be regarded as satisfactory – that is, as compatible with aspirations.

(Simon 1982b: 10b)

10 One of the core assumptions in Simon's theory is that rational man 'does not have the wits' to be an *optimizing* animal' (Simon 1982b: 9a), but that he has the ability 'to distinguish "better" (or "preferred") from "worse" directions of change in his behavior and to adjust continually in the direction of the "better"' (Simon 1965: 87). As he adds: 'A rational process in which the choice of a "best" is central we will call optimization; a rational process in which movement toward a "better" is central we will call adaptation' (ibid.).

11 The ambiguous use of the term 'data' in economics obliterates, as Hayek (1948: 39) supposes, the fundamental difference between 'data' in the sense of the 'objective real facts, as the observing economist is supposed to know them', and 'data' in the 'subjective sense, as things known to the person whose behavior we try to explain'.

12 Hayek (1973: 19): 'The constructivist approach denies implicitly that it can be rational to observe such rules.'

13   Though it sounds paradoxical to say that in order to make ourselves act rationally we often find it necessary to be guided by habit rather than reflection, or to say that to prevent ourselves from making the wrong decision we must deliberately reduce the range of choice before us, we all know that this is often necessary in practice if we are to achieve our long-range aims.   (Hayek 1960: 66)

14 Where the 'balance of advantage' is in favour of following a rule, 'an apparent striving after rationality in the sense of fuller taking into account all the forseeable consequences' may, as Hayek (1964: 12) argues, result in 'greater irrationality, less effective taking into account of remote effects and an altogether less coherent result.'

15 A more recent restatement of this argument by R.E. Lucas (1987: 241) reads as follows: 'To observe that economics is based on a superficial view of individual and social behavior does not ... seem to me to be much of an insight. I think it is exactly this superficiality that gives economics much of the power that it has; its ability to predict human behavior without knowing very much about the make-up and the lives of the people whose behavior we are trying to understand.'

16 Herbert Simon has similarly criticized the orthodoxy's strategy of patching 'the rationality principle with *ad hoc* assumptions' (1984: 52; also 1979a: 81, 84; 1987: 30, 39).

17 Even such a tenacious critic of the standard rationality concept as A.K. Sen (1987: 72) acknowledges that, though the inadequacies of the traditional approach have become hard to deny, it 'will not be an easy task to find replacements for the standard assumptions of rational behavior'. As Sen (1987: 71) puts it: 'What is much harder to do is to develop an alternative structure for rationality that would be regarded as satisfactory for the purpose of capturing what can be demanded of reason in human choice.'

18 It should be noted that the crucial claim of a 'process explanation' is not about the factual issue whether or not, in any particular case under investigation, design has played a role. The crucial claim is that design is *not needed* in order to generate the 'adaptiveness' in question.

19 Popper (1972: 261): 'From the amoeba to Einstein, the growth of knowledge is always the same: we try to solve our problems, and to obtain, by a process of elimination, something approaching adequacy in our tentative solutions.'

20 As P.M. Allen puts it:

In an evolutionary landscape of hills and valleys representing levels of functional efficiency of different possible organisms, it is the error-maker who can move up a hill, eventually out-competing a perfectly reproducing rival. And this despite the fact that at each and every instant it would be better not to make errors. . . . Evolution concerns not only 'efficient performance' but also the constant need for new discoveries. . . . Variability at the microscopic level, individual diversity, is part of the evolutionary strategy of survivors.

(Allen 1988: 107)

21 The *capacity to learn* is, of course, itself a product of genetic evolution and there are, therefore, genetically determined limits on what can be learned and how (Gould and Marler 1987).

22 In terms of the above discussion, all three 'learning processes' can be said to involve adopting and changing *classifications* of situations and events. Language is a most important classificatory system, produced through cultural evolution. Verbal classifications ('poison', 'fuel', etc.), and classifications in general, embody 'theories' about what are appropriate behaviours with regard to the classified phenomena.

23 J.G. Cross (1983: 183): '[W]e have no guarantee that in every case the biological determinants of behavior are consistent with self-interest in the twentieth century, however appropriate they may have been thousands of years ago.'

24 R. Frank (1987: 38) points out that man as a product 'of millions of years of evolution' has not only *cognitive* but also *motivational* limitations to his capability to rationally maximize.

25 T. Parsons (1968: 234) who rejects, as entirely mistaken, the 'economic-behaviourist' perspective, has commented on Homans' contribution: 'It is not surprising that behavioristic psychology and the more rigorous kind of economic theory have tended to form certain alliances, and that these have tended to be projected into the realm of sociology. The most prominent representative of the latter trend is George Homans.'

26 J.G. Cross describes the nature of his enterprise as follows:

'This book implements quite a different approach to the behavioural underpinnings of economic theory. Rather than assuming that individuals engage in conscious optimization and planning, we assume the existence of feedback mechanisms that use historical successes and failures as guides, directing individuals into behavioral paths that, in the light of experience, have had the greatest payoffs.'

(Cross 1983: 5)

On the relation between 'maximization theory' and 'behavioural psychology' see also Rachlin *et al.* (1981) and Archibald and Elliott (1989).

27 One of the implications of a theory of adaptive learning is, as J.G. Cross (1983: 186) points out, 'that human subjects in laboratory experiments will not react to brand new situations in newly appropriate ways, but will carry with them responses that have already been learned outside the laboratory.'

28 A detailed discussion is provided in my paper (in progress) on 'Cultural evolution as collective learning.'

29 It should also be mentioned that T. Veblen's idea of *economics as an evolutionary science* to which I referred earlier in this chapter also belongs in the 'cultural evolution' category. Veblen views economic and social change in general as a change in *routines*, as a change 'in the methods of doing things' (1919: 71). The process of cumulative change that economics is to study is, Veblen argues, 'always in the last resort a change in habits of thought, . . .

196

[the] habitual methods of procedure' (1919: 75). It is 'the cumulative growth of that range of conventionalities and methods of life that are currently recognized as economic institutions' (1919: 76).

30 Hodgson (1988a: 140) points out that this interpretation can also be found in T. Veblen's view of institutions as 'complexes of habits, roles and conventional behavior'.

31 In answer to the question of what it is 'that maintains the stability of the patterns of behavior in groups of interacting persons?', H.A. Simon (1982b: 6b) notes: 'Any one member of the group is acting rationally in maintaining his present pattern of behavior so long as others do likewise. This is not to say that all members of the group or some subset of them would not be better off if they all changed their behavior in an appropriate *synchronous* fashion.'

32 An interesting example for the collapse of an institutional order as a system of interconnected routines is provided in T.G. Buchholz's (1988) discussion of the situation in Saigon during the approach of the revolutionary forces in 1975.

33 About the use of the concept of 'perfect competition' Hayek says:

> It seems almost as if economists by this peculiar language were deceiving themselves into the belief that, in discussing 'competition', they are saying something about the nature and significance of the process by which the state of affairs is brought about which they merely assume to exist. In fact this moving force of economic life is left almost altogether undiscussed.
>
> (Hayek 1948: 92f)

34 These theoretical developments and their relevance for economics are discussed in more detail in J.M. Buchanan and V. Vanberg 1991.

REFERENCES

Alchian, A.A. (1950) 'Uncertainty, evolution and economic theory', *Journal of Political Economy* 58: 211–21.

Alhadeff, D.A. (1982) *Microeconomics and Human Behavior – Towards a New Synthesis of Economics and Psychology*, Berkeley, Los Angeles, London: University of California Press.

Allen, P.M. (1988) 'Evolution, innovation and economics', in G. Dosi, C. Freeman, R. Nelson, G. Silverberg and L. Soete (eds) *Technical Change and Economic Theory*, London and New York: Pinter Publishers, 95–119.

Archibald, R.B. and Elliott, C.S. (1989) 'Trial-and-error learning and economic models', *Kyklos* 42: 35–59.

Axelrod, R. (1986) 'An evolutionary approach to norms', *American Political Science Review* 80: 1095–111.

Biddle, J.E. (1990) 'Purpose and evolution in Commons's institutionalism', *History of Political Economy* 22: 19–47.

Buchanan, J.M. and Vanberg V. (1991) 'The market as a creative process', *Economics and Philosophy* 7: 167–86.

Buchholz T.G. (1988) 'Revolution, reputation effects, and time horizons', *Cato Journal* 8: 185–97.

Campbell, D.T. (1975) 'On the conflict between biological and social evolution and between psychology and moral tradition', *American Psychologist* 30, 1103–26.

—— (1983) 'The two distinct routes beyond kin selection to ultrasociality: implications for the humanities and social sciences', in D. Bridgeman (ed.) *The Nature of Prosocial Development: Interdisciplinary Theories and Strategies*, New York: Academic Press, 11–41.

—— (1987) 'Rationality and utility from the standpoint of evolutionary biology', in R.M. Hogarth and M.W. Reder (eds) *Rational Choice – The Contrast between Economics and Psychology*, Chicaco and London: University of Chicago Press, 171–80.

Coleman, J.S. (1987) 'Norms as social capital', in G. Radnitzky and P. Bernholz (eds) *Economic Imperialism – The Economic Approach Applied Outside the Field of Economics*, New York: Paragon House Publishers, 133–55.

Conlisk, J. (1988) 'Optimization Cost', *Journal of Economic Behavior and Organization* 9: 213–28.

Cross, J.G. (1983) *A Theory of Adaptive Economic Behavior*, Cambridge: Cambridge University Press.

Field, A.J. (1984) 'Microeconomics, norms, and rationality', *Economic Development and Cultural Change* 32: 683–711.

Frank, R.H. (1987) 'Shrewdly irrational', *Sociological Forum* 2, 21–41.

—— (1988) *Passions Within Reason – The Strategic Role of Emotions*, New York and London: W.W. Norton.

Friedman, M. (1953) *Essays in Positive Economics*, Chicago: University of Chicago Press.

Gould, J.L. and Marler, P. (1987) 'Learning by instinct', Scientific American 256: 74–85.

Hayek, F.A. (1937) 'Economics and knowledge', *Economica* 12: 33–54. (Reprinted in F.A. Hayek *Individualism and Economic Order*, Chicago: University of Chicago Press.

—— (1948) *Individualism and Economic Order*, Chicago: University of Chicago Press. (First published 1937).

—— (1960) *The Constitution of Liberty*, Chicago: University of Chicago Press.

—— (1964) 'Kinds of order in society', *New Individualist Review* 3(3): 3–12.

—— (1967) *Studies in Philosophy, Politics and Economics*, Chicago: University of Chicago Press.

—— (1973) *Law, Legislation and Liberty*, Vol. 1, *Rules and Order*, London: Routledge & Kegan Paul.

—— (1976) *Law, Legislation and Liberty*, Vol. 2, *The Mirage of Social Justice*, London: Routledge & Kegan Paul.

Heiner, R.A. (1983) 'The origin of predictable behavior', *American Economic Review* 73: 560–95.

—— (1987) 'Imperfect decisions, evolutionary stability, and predictable behavior: on the origins of rules over flexible optimizing', in M. Commons and R. Herrnstein (eds) *The Quantitative Analysis of Behavior*, Cambridge: Harvard University Press.

—— (1988a) 'The necessity of imperfect decisions', *Journal of Economic Behavior and Organization*, 10: 29–55.

—— (1988b) 'Imperfect decisions and routinized production: implications for evolutionary modeling and inertial technical change', in G. Dosi, C. Freeman, R. Nelson, G. Silverberg and L. Soete (eds) *Technical Change and Economic Theory*, London and New York: Pinter Publishers, 148–69.

—— (1990) 'Rule-governed behavior in evolution and human society', *Constitutional Political Economy* 1.

Herrnstein, R.J. (1988) 'A behavioral alternative to utility maximization', in S. Maital (ed.) *Applied Behavioural Economics*, Vol. 1, Brighton, Sussex: Wheatsheaf Books.

Hodgson, G.M. (1988) *Economics and Institutions – A Manifesto for a Modern Institutional Economics*, Philadelphia: University of Pennsylvania Press.

Hogarth, R.M. and Reder, M.W. (eds) (1987) *Rational Choice – The Contrast between Economics and Psychology*, Chicago and London: University of Chicago Press.

Homans, G.C. (1961) *Social Behavior – Its Elementary Forms*, New York: Harcourt Brace (revised edition 1974).

Klamer, A. (1989) 'A conversation with Amartya Sen', *Journal of Economic Perspectives* 3: 135–50.

Knudsen, C. (1989) 'Equilibrium, perfect rationality and the problem of self-reference within economics', this volume.

Leibenstein, H. (1980) 'Microeconomics and X-efficiency theory', *The Public Interest*, special issue on *The Crisis in Economic Theory*: 97–110.

—— (1982) 'The Prisoners' dilemma in the invisible hand: an analysis of intrafirm productivity', *American Economic Review (Papers and Proceedings)* 72: 92–7.

Lucas, R.E. (1987) 'Adaptive behavior and economic theory', in R.M. Hogarth and M.W. Reder (eds) *Rational Choice – The Contract between Economics and Psychology*, Chicago and London: University of Chicago Press, pp. 217–42.

Mayr, E. (1982) *The Growth of Biological Thought*, Cambridge, Mass: Harvard University Press.

Mitchell, W.C. (1935) 'Commons on institutional economics', *American Economic Review* 25: 635–52.

Mueller, D.C. (1986) 'Rational egoism versus adaptive egoism as fundamental postulate for a descriptive theory of human behavior', *Public Choice* 51: 3–23.

Nelson, R.R. and Winter, S.G. (1982) *An Evolutionary Theory of Economic Change*, Cambridge, Mass: Harvard University Press.

Parsons, T. (1968) 'Utilitarianism: sociological thought', *International Encyclopedia of the Social Sciences* 16: 229–36.

Popper, K.R. (1972) *Objective Knowledge – An Evolutionary Approach*, Oxford: Oxford University Press.

Rachlin, H., Battalio, R. and Green, L. (1981) 'Maximization theory in behavioral psychology', *Behavioral and Brain Sciences* 4: 371–417.

Rutherford, M. (1989) 'Introduction' to J.R. Commons, *Institutional Economics: Its Place in Political Economy*, New Brunswick: Transaction, pp. xiii–xxxvii.

Sen, A.K. (1979) 'Rational fools: a critique of the behavioural foundations of economic theory', in F. Hahn and M. Hollis (eds) *Philosophy and Economic Theory*, New York: Oxford University Press, pp. 89–109.

—— (1987) 'Rational behavior' *The New Palgrave*, 4: 68–76.

Simon, H.A. (1957) *Models of Man*, New York: Wiley.

—— (1965) 'Mathematical constructions in social science', in D. Braybrooke (ed.), *Philosophical Problems of the Social Sciences*, New York: Macmillan, pp. 83–98.

—— (1979a) 'From substantive to procedural rationality', in F. Hahn and M. Hollis (eds) *Philosophy and Economic Theory*, New York: Oxford University Press, pp. 65–86.

—— (1979b) 'Rational decision making in business organizations', *American Economic Review* 69: 493–513.

—— (1982a) 'Economics and psychology', in H.A. Simon (ed.) *Models of Bounded Rationality*, Vol. 2, *Behavioral Economics and Business Organization*, Cambridge, Mass: MIT Press.

—— (1982b) 'The role of expectations in an adaptive or behavioristic model', in

199

H.A. Simon *Models of Bounded Rationality*, Vol. 2, *Behavioral Economics and Business Organization*, Cambridge, Mass.: MIT Press.

—— (1984) 'On the behavioral and rational foundations of economic dynamics', *Journal of Economic Behavior and Organization* 5: 35–55.

—— (1987) 'Rationality in psychology and economics', in R.M. Hogarth and M.W. Reder (eds) *Rational Choice – The Contrast between Economics and Psychology*, Chicago and London: University of Chicago Press, 25–40.

Tversky, A. and Kahneman, D. (1987) 'Rational choice and the framing of decisions' in R.M. Hogarth and M.W. Reder (eds), *Rational Choice – The Contrast between Economics and Psychology*, Chicago and London: University of Chicago Press, 67–94.

Ursprung, H.W. (1988) 'Evolution and the economic approach to human behavior', *Journal of Social and Biological Structures* 11: 257–79.

Vanberg, V. (1975) *Die zwei Soziologien – Individualismus und Kollektivismus in der Sozialtheorie*, Tübingen: J.B.C. Mohr (Paul Siebeck).

—— (1983) 'Der individualistiche Ansatz zu einer Theorie der Entstehung und der Entwicklung von Institutionen', *Jahrbuch für Neue Politische Ökonomie* 2: 50–69.

—— (1986) 'Spontaneous market order and social rules: a critical examination of F.A. Hayek's theory of cultural evolution', *Economics and Philosophy* 2: 75–100.

—— (1988a) *Morality and Economics – De Moribus est Disputandun*, New Brunswick and London: Transaction Books (Social Philosophy & Policy Center, Original Papers No. 7).

—— (1988b) 'Rules and choice in economics and sociology' in *Jahrbuch für Neue Politische Ökonomie*, 7: 147–67.

—— (1989a) 'Hayek as constitutional political economist', *Wirtschaftspolitische Blätter* 36: 170–82.

—— (1989b) 'Carl Menger's evolutionary and John R. Commons' collective action approach to institutions: a comparison', *Review of Political Economy* 1: 334–60.

—— and Buchanan, J.M. (1988) 'Rational choice and moral order', *Analyse & Kritik* 10: 138–60.

Veblen, T. (1919) 'Why is economics not an evolutionary science', in T. Veblen, *The Place of Science in Modern Civilization and Other Essays*, New York: Russell & Russell, 56–81.

Winter, S.G. (1987) 'Comments on Arrow and on Lucas', in R.M. Hogarth and M.W. Reder (eds) *Rational Choice: The Contrast between Economics and Psychology*, Chicago and London: University of Chicago Press, 243–50.

Part IV

INSTITUTIONS AND
THEIR EVOLUTION

8

INSTITUTIONAL STABILITY AND CHANGE IN SCIENCE AND THE ECONOMY

Brian J. Loasby

ABSTRACT

In this chapter, Hahn's definition of equilibrium in terms of agents' theories and policies is adapted to explain stability and change in firms and markets. People are treated as scientists, who use, test, and sometimes replace hypotheses. This process must take place within a framework of rules or conventions, which is incompletely specified; but the framework itself is subject to change, which may be evolutionary or revolutionary. Nelson and Winter's conception of an organization as a cluster of routines is extended to a cluster of research programmes, which guide the interpretation of evidence and constrain conjectures. Every market, too, operates according to a set of conventional practices or institutions which may also be treated as a research programme. Attempts to innovate may then be examined in relation to the research programme of both firm and market.

THEORIES AND POLICIES

In 1973, Frank Hahn proposed a new definition of general equilibrium, which was based not on prices and quantities but on the decision-making system which produced them: 'An economy is in equilibrium when it generates messages which do not cause agents to change the theories which they hold or the policies which they pursue' (Hahn 1973: 25, 1984: 59). Hahn's purpose was clearly to extend the general equilibrium research programme; but (like Coase's extension of marginal analysis to explain why firms sometimes replace markets as the instruments of economic coordination) his proposal may also be used to justify a transformation of theory. Indeed, Hahn's own discussion suggests, unconsciously, it would seem, the need for such a transformation. In accepting 'the plausible requirement that the theory held by the agent must in some sense be simple enough to be intellectually and computationally feasible for him' (Hahn 1973: 24, 1984: 58) he implicitly accepts bounded rationality; and his commitment (if only provisional) to 'the ill-specified hypothesis that an agent abandons his theory when it is sufficiently and systematically falsified' (Hahn 1973: 26, 1984: 59) entails the replacement of optimization by a satisficing procedure. In this analytical scheme, rational expectations equilibria constitute a very special subset of cases; in general, we should expect theories and policies to work well only within a limited range and each equilibrium to be temporary; the focus of attention thus naturally shifts to the sequence of equilibria.

Hahn's conception evokes such questions as the following. What messages are generated and what messages does each agent receive? How are messages interpreted? What criteria are used to decide whether a theory or policy should be maintained, modified, or abandoned? If the decision is to modify or abandon, by what process is a new theory or policy adopted, and with what consequences? What factors tend to preserve existing theories or policies, to guide changes in particular directions, and to maintain coherence, first within the collection of theories and policies which are employed by an individual decision maker, and second, between the theories and policies which are held by different people? We should not assume successful coordination: but nor should we make coordination depend on complete theoretical coherence; for a world of bounded rationality can tolerate a great deal of inconsistency in non-crucial areas. The factors which influence such processes may be categorized as institutions: the set of conventions, customs, routines, and procedures which are such a pervasive, but too often neglected, feature of economic and social systems. We shall consider both the influence of institutions on behaviour and the evolution of institutions as the consequence (often not the intended consequence) of behaviour.

THE GROWTH OF KNOWLEDGE

Among the more obvious precursors of this approach we may mention Carl Menger and Herbert Simon. However, in this chapter we shall begin with the study of the growth of knowledge, which has become increasingly concerned with scientific conventions and procedures, and is a study of processes, not of equilibria. Instead of economic agents as rational choosers, we shall explore the concept of economic agents as scientists, attempting to predict and control, and seeking to extend their knowledge in ways that will help them to do so. This particular strategy will, it is hoped, help to preserve an adequate degree of coherence in making the change from one interpretation of Hahn's analytical scheme to another.

The proposal to consider people as scientists was made by Kelly (1963) as the basis of his theory of personality. I have discussed it more fully elsewhere (Loasby 1986); it will be sufficient here to note the features to be used in this chapter. First, people try to make sense of their world by imposing their own interpretative framework on it, and use this framework to guide their actions. (They construct theories and policies, in Hahn's terminology.) Second, because the universe is far too complex to be properly represented by any framework which human beings can understand and use, the sequel to any prediction or action is liable to call into question the framework on which it was based. Kelly emphasizes that what matters is not the event, but the construction which is placed upon it: the messages which agents receive are not simple reports of pure facts. Third, a well-ordered individual in an orderly environment modifies his or her personal framework in response to an acknowledged failure of prediction or action; but fourth, if the framework is particularly rigid, or the events unusually chaotic, satisfactory adjustment may prove impossible, and the consequence is one kind or another of personality disorder (which was Kelly's principal interest). Kelly recognizes, in unconscious agreement with Adam Smith's *History of Astronomy* (1795), the powerful attraction of a set of 'connecting principles' which link together wide areas of experience, and the corresponding difficulty sometimes experienced in making local adjustments which cannot be readily contained within the currently-accepted set.

What Kelly offers is a kind of theory which economics obviously lacks – a theory of fallible coordination. Hahn's conception provides a convenient means of introducing Kelly's ideas into economic theories of reasoned choice, and thereby permitting the analysis of fallibility. Kelly is concerned with the individual, whereas our interest in this chapter is primarily in patterns of interaction between individuals; but the standard interpretative framework in economics requires the analysis of inter-actions to begin with individuals, and Kelly's system is well suited for this purpose.

The bridge is easy to find: people are to be considered as scientists, but science is necessarily a social activity, as Ziman (1978) emphasizes. The process of conjecture, testing and criticism which leads to the growth of knowledge is hopelessly inefficient if carried on by individuals in isolation. A group of people investigating a particular problem area in collaboration – which may be informal, and even rivalrous – is likely to be much more fertile in conjecture, much more ingenious and rigorous in criticism, and to produce many more and much better validated tests than its members could produce in isolation. But if this collaboration is to be effective it must find some way of coping with what is commonly referred to as the Duhem–Quine problem (Quine 1951). Since any test of one particular hypothesis always requires us to assume the truth of many more, and since there is no way of guaranteeing the truth of any of these, then if the test results in failure we can never be absolutely certain what it is that has failed. All that we know is that there is some internal inconsistency among the set of hypotheses which we were explicitly or (very often) implicitly testing; and even the enumeration of this set may be impossible to complete.

The commonest response to such a failure, among scientists and economists as well as economic agents, is to reject, not the hypothesis, but the test result. (For neoclassical economists, everyone really is optimizing; it's just that we have not got the constraints right.) Such a response is often justified; but that is not the present issue. What needs to be emphasized is that, in the language of decision theory, which makes a sharp distinction between decisions and events, the refutation of a hypothesis is not an unambiguous event which must be accepted but a choice which is open. It therefore needs to be explained in terms of the criteria being employed and the institutional framework. Pilkington's persistence with the recalcitrant float glass process is an important example: a publicly-owned company, subject to stock-market constraints, including the possibility of takeover, might have decided that their hypothesis had been falsified.

SHARED FRAMEWORKS FOR KNOWLEDGE

If individuals are to make sense of their own experience, they must be reasonably consistent in deciding what parts of their personal structure of hypotheses is to be exempt from challenge, and what is to be modified; as Simon (1965: 97–8) observes, creativity normally flourishes most when its scope is limited. The value to the individual scientist of a ready-made framework was emphasized by Popper (1972) in 1934; and he has always insisted that an orderly process of testing requires the acceptance of a set of rules or conventions. Such conventions do not embody scientific truth, but provide the institutional framework within which scientific truth may be effectively sought. But if individuals are to collaborate, however informally, in the advance of science, it is not enough that each should work within a framework; their frameworks have to be reasonably compatible, and resistant to change. They cannot, however, be a product of rational choice, in the extreme sense of that term used by economists, but are likely to call for explanation as the unintended, or partly-intended, consequence of a series of boundedly-rational decisions.

This evolutionary process results in the kind of framework for science that Kuhn (1970) calls a paradigm and Lakatos (1970) a research programme, which sets bounds on the interpretation of messages, exempts certain general hypotheses from refutation, and limits the range of alternatives from which members of a scientific community may choose. The consequent concentration of activity on normal science, or work within the protective belt, both focuses the attention of individual researchers, or research teams, and facilitates communication between them. Rational choice theory certainly has these effects in microeconomics.

Paradigm shift, or a move between research programmes, appears to be very different, and very infrequent. It is also, especially in Kuhn's formulation, very mysterious: although the disintegration of the old paradigm under the weight of accumulated and inexplicable anomalies is clear enough, its replacement seems to be created out of nothing by some unanalysable leap of the imagination.

But perhaps the creation of a new paradigm is not so mysterious. The paradigm which is to be superseded is not completely unconnected to other scientific ideas, nor do a scientist's professional activities normally provide the only way of thinking about problems. In time of crisis recourse may be had to other frameworks, perhaps in other areas (aesthetics and religious beliefs have sometimes been very important), or perhaps more broadly defined. (The idea that the behaviour of aggregates is to be explained in terms of their component parts, for example, is extraordinarily pervasive.) Indeed, it is not easy to conceive of any change except in relation to something which has not changed. Discontinuities are never absolute.

Thus, contrary to what is often asserted or assumed, the appropriate research questions for the analysis of paradigm change are not different in principle from those which are appropriate to the analysis of normal science: what persists, what is replaced, and how are these choices affected by, and in turn affect, the institutional framework within which they are made? We might go further and observe that this distinction between normal science and paradigm change resembles the familiar economic distinction between the short and the long run. Both distinctions are intended to separate the analysis of constrained response from that of wider-ranging adjustment; and both rely on an imposed framework which is extremely convenient but, in the last resort, unsustainable.

The institutions of science are often implicit and always imperfectly specified: assumptions, conventions, and procedures are rarely free of ambiguity, or even inconsistency. It is no accident that Kuhn has given us no precise specification of any paradigm, nor Lakatos of the hard core of any research programme. The result is a great deal of inconvenience and inefficiency; many debates and disagreements concern nothing more substantial than the implicit definition of terms. But this may be a price worth paying to retain some freedom of manoeuvre: the ability to pose a problem in slightly different ways, to experiment with slightly different interpretations, and, when faced with apparent anomalies, to exercise some choice about the level, and not merely the detail, at which change might be envisaged, and therefore to trigger different kinds of imaginative response, all these liberties may encourage that tendency to variation which Marshall (1920: 355) identified as a chief cause of progress.

My conception of the research programme of the new institutional economics envisages both a theory of development within an institutional framework and a theory of the development of institutions, recognizing that the two are far from independent, though it may often be helpful to pretend that they are. Such a double theory may be applied to the growth of knowledge (including the evolution of economics), organizational behaviour, market processes, and the economy as a whole. In each setting we may observe a process of conjecture, testing, and criticism, which is both conditioned by and modifies the institutional setting, a process which is best characterized, not as impersonal but as interpersonal, not as objective but as intersubjective. In each the quality of the results appears to depend on the quality of the process which produces them. I have examined the problems of scientific method and the organization of science elsewhere (Loasby 1989). In the remainder of this chapter I propose to concentrate on organizations and markets, but not forgetting that both are systems which produce knowledge through the generation and testing of hypotheses — hypotheses about products, processes, markets, methods, organizational structures, coalitions, amalgamations, tactics and strategies. (A more extended treatment is provided in Loasby 1991.)

KNOWLEDGE AND DECISIONS

As Hahn points out, when an economy is in a state of equilibrium according to his definition, no agent, whether operating within a firm or a market, is learning. There is no development other than replication, no growth of knowledge. Yet despite the appearance of pure routine, something worth noting may be happening. Indeed, since Hahn (1973: 26–7; 1984: 80) wishes to make his equilibrium independent of market clearing, the way in which each agent handles messages is crucial. Reports or observations must be matched with theory and policy, and this process is problematic. We must remember that 'report' and 'observation' are not synonyms for 'event', since events are always observed or reported through some interpretative system: pure data is not accessible to humans. Economists have their own particular idea about what should count as evidence, and how it is to be presented: messages from the economy which do not conform to established rituals are ignored.

Whether an event produces a mismatch may therefore depend on the interpretative system used to produce the message, even if all expectations are held in common. Independent agents receive many messages which have been interpreted by others – newspaper reports, for example, or government statistics; but of especial interest are the interpretative systems of a firm, or a division, or department, of a firm, and of a market network. But expectations, too, may vary; though they are derived from the supposedly relevant network of apparently reliable knowledge, as in the sciences, this network, or research programme, can accommodate significant variety. The processes which develop, sustain, and modify the corpus of knowledge in a business may not be so clearly understood or as rigorous as in a scientific discipline, but they do not seem to be different in kind.

Let us suppose that a report or observation does not conform with the agent's expectations. That is not sufficient to signal a refutation, which, remember, is not a message from the environment, but a decision taken in response to that message. The mismatch may be dealt with in many ways. The simplest, and perhaps the commonest, is to decide that the facts are wrong; they often are. That ends the matter, unless attention shifts, as sometimes happens, to a disparity between one's expectations about the reporting system and what it is delivering: if so the problem is of redesigning the reporting system, not forgetting the incentives which are entangled in it.

Acceptance of the report implies an inconsistency somewhere within the agent's network of knowledge, but does not itself determine where an amendment should be made, and how extensive that amendment should be. But economic agents, like scientists, will rarely feel anything like as free as that statement suggests; their institutional framework (which will be influenced, but not wholly determined, by their organizational or market environment) will deter them from venturing on many kinds of change. Indeed, as in Kelly's theory of personality, their willingness to accept the evidence may depend on the attractiveness of the modifications which that framework permits. In extreme cases, accepting the evidence may threaten a substantial segment of a tightly-connected framework; for most of us, some evidence is simply incredible.

It is, by definition, impossible to predict a novel conjecture; but it may be possible, by examining the institutional setting, to predict the general area within which the conjecture will be made, or, more confidently, within which it will not be made. The institutional setting itself may change in a way which encourages or discourages particular levels of conjectures. Constraints are likely to be slackened if a set of institutions is buffeted by a multitude of recalcitrant and diverse anomalies. Individuals or organizations and markets are susceptible to paradigm crises, or the apparent disintegration of research programmes; and these are circumstances which give particular scope to imaginative conjectures. But they may not be the circumstances which actually encourage the trial of many imaginative conjectures; for, as has been noticed earlier, imagination too needs a framework, and if the institutions are in total disarray, there may be no base which seems secure enough on which to build – especially if acting on this conjecture (and we are here thinking primarily of business decisions) entails large and irrecoverable commitments.

ORGANIZATIONAL ROUTINES

Let us now consider in a little more detail the institutional arrangements of firms and markets. It is convenient to begin with the former, where one can make use of ideas which are already well known. Nelson and Winter (1982) have suggested analysing a firm as a hierarchy of routines, which include routines for making product, for collecting information, for search (in laboratory, market, or manager's office), for operating decisions, and for strategic review. Associated with each routine is a cue, or set of cues, which call it into use: these may include the arrival of a partly-finished product at a work-station, a telephone call from a customer, an unfavourable variance underlined in a monthly report, a government announcement, and many others. As these examples suggest, many routines act as cues to subsequent routines.

Some of these routines and cues may be deliberately created, though in time these may diverge substantially from the original intentions; others may emerge from a sequence of narrowly-focused decisions. They embody much of what is thought to be relevant knowledge; but this knowledge is often tacit, rarely capable of complete expression, of uncertain scope, and based on experience which can be only partially recovered. An organization's routines may be thought of as a network of theories and policies, constituting a research programme which, like the research programmes of science, is imperfectly specified. It is natural to think of such a network as fairly stable, but not in an equilibrium as precisely defined by Hahn, and that is how Nelson and Winter think of it.

Routines evolve over time, as a series of minor changes are made to accommodate experience. They comprise a large part of the organization's memory: it remembers by doing, learns by doing something new, and (a point Nelson and Winter do not stress) forgets by not doing. A flexible organization will lose flexibility if it does not have occasion to exercise its various skills. Even once-core skills may be lost, without anyone recognizing the loss. Routines are also likely to mutate (Nelson and Winter's word) with each change of personnel, in the first place because they are hardly ever clearly defined, or even definable, and in the second because each newcomer is likely to bring somewhat different routines which have been acquired elsewhere. Newcomers may also make deliberate attempts to introduce such routines, out of a desire for improvement or to gain extra recognition.

Other changes may occur in response to external forces (Pfeffer and Salancik 1978). The survival of a business depends on its ability to elicit the contributions which it needs in order to remain in business – from, among others, its customers, suppliers, workers, managers, bankers, and governmental agencies. At any one time, some of these contributors will be more difficult to satisfy than others, and there is likely to be particular attention to the routines which are intended to meet, bypass, or counterweight their demands. But the balance of pressures may change, and this is likely to lead to a switch of emphasis.

Adam Smith drew attention to the way in which the division of labour facilitated the introduction of new techniques; Marshall (1920) extended this observation to include the promotion of all kinds of knowledge relevant for business by appropriate organization. It is often the case that different departments or divisions of a firm can operate, and learn, most effectively by following very different research programmes, and attending to very different kinds of messages; and these differences may pose serious potential problems of coordination. However, it often happens that most of the theories, policies, and messages which are the focus of interest in one part of the organization have little or no relevance to other parts; its research programme can therefore be very different, and only needs to fit the research programmes of other groups where it touches. This may well be the most efficient way of running a business and of gaining knowledge; but there are two dangers. First, the evolution of knowledge, or changes in the environment (especially when either of these influences changes the linkages between technology and markets) may bring into close contact groups which had previously had no need to accommodate each other, and which now find their juxtaposed theories and policies extremely discordant; second, a deliberate reorganization may force a conjunction which rapidly and unexpectedly turns into a confrontation.

Some organizations make great efforts to improve coherence; but there are dangers here too. Simon has argued that the need for coherent and stable expectations sometimes makes it 'more important . . . to have *agreement* on the facts than to be certain that what is agreed upon is really fact' (1982, 2: 399). At this point he has apparently forgotten his warning that 'the decision-maker's . . . perceived world is fantastically different from the "real world"' (1982, 2: 306); for the price of coherence, in particular of the institutions designed to preserve it, may be a growing divergence between the organization's theories and policies and the reality which it faces. Such a phenomenon is not unknown.

The problem may be aggravated by the importance of routines as preservers of organizational truce, on which Nelson and Winter place some emphasis. The factors enumerated by Cyert and March (1963) as protectors of the organizational coalition – local rationality, the practices and procedures which result in sequential attention to goals, the use of budgets to define protected space – are among the routines which serve more than one purpose. The preservation of a truce may facilitate change in some dimensions; but Nelson and Winter choose to draw attention to the ways in which it may inhibit change. Since the terms of the truce, like so much else, are not explicitly agreed, all parties are likely to be sensitive to possible breaches; thus a proposed change which is, in itself, perfectly acceptable to one group may be opposed by them for fear of giving the impression that they will tolerate other changes which would harm them; and if the beneficiaries of such a change put a high value on preserving the coalition they may forbear proposing it. Such protective measures may, of course, contribute to later collapse. But this prospect may not be enough to avoid them: indeed the desire to maintain present stability, even against the odds, may be strongest in an organization whose members fear it is not resilient (to borrow an argument from my former colleague, M.S. Common). The attitude of printing workers in Britain to new technology has provided an especially prominent example.

Particular attention should be given to those routines which link other routines, since these may be especially significant in determining the possibilities of adaptation. Reliance on formal control systems may be expected to have different effects from 'management by walking about'; dining arrangements and physical layout are among the factors likely to condition the pattern of informal relationships which support or impede adjustments. Networks which do not rely on daily work patterns may be particularly helpful in bridging discontinuities, provided that the new system allows them to survive. The trust between W.H. Smith's Father of the Chapel and key members of the firm's management was an indispensable element in the effective handling of the transfer of the firm's book and stationery warehouse from London to Swindon (Loasby 1973): this trust rested not only on formal negotiations, but also on freedom of private conversation, and a shared interest in football.

If we are to consider people as scientists, then a formal organization is a visible college of scientists, operating within a shared research programme. This conception of a firm is readily assimilated to that proposed by Coase (1937), for whom the firm offers a means of creating a structure which will reduce the transactions costs of particular kinds of future decisions. A research programme economizes on the costs of intellectual transactions between the scientists who accept it; and, like the contract which links each individual to the firm, it is imperfectly specified. The purpose, from either perspective, is to combine flexibility and coordination.

Except for very simple organizations, the conception needs to be modified from a single research programme to a cluster of programmes; the advantages of the division of labour among boundedly rational human beings lead to the evolution of different research programmes for those working within different disciplines, departments, or divisions. With organizational design, as with academic enquiry, markets, or any other field to which the division of labour applies, there is a double problem: how to divide, and how to integrate what has been divided. This chapter is written in the belief that there is no single best solution to either part of the problem, but that different structures produce different consequences. The structures, and the routines which evolve within them, condition the generation of conjectures, the criticisms to which they are subjected, the internal tests to which they are exposed – and we should not forget that most new ideas are rejected within the firm without ever being tried in the market – and, if they survive to that stage, the form in which they are tested in the market, and the way in which the messages which the market sends back are interpreted.

MARKET PROCESSES

For business organizations, the market test is crucial, but it should not be simply equated with a test of truth, for two reasons. First, we must always remember that what is tested is a combination of hypotheses, and if the result is an admitted failure, it is still necessary to determine what has failed. The messages generated by the economy are ambiguous, unless we are prepared to immunize the greater part of our presumed knowledge against refutation. However, it is the second reason which now deserves attention. If the organization is a visible college, then the market participants constitute an invisible college, which, like the invisible college of academic science, can function effectively only within a research programme of its own. This research programme provides the environment within which a firm must survive.

A market system is a means of organizing the search for knowledge, and operates by a system of conjecture, criticism (voice, as well as exit) and testing, which is interpersonal rather than impersonal, and inter-subjective rather than objective. It is an experimentally organized economy (Eliasson 1987). As with the progress of science itself, the reliability of the results depends on the process (Ziman 1978). What is tested in the market, and according to the routines by which a particular market operates, is not only the set of conjectures offered by a particular organization, but, indirectly and over a longer period, the capacity of that particular organization to offer conjectures which meet with corroboration. Both kinds of test (as in any scientific community, or in Darwinian competition) are tests of fitness relative to what else is on offer at the time, both as substitute and as complement. No test of global optimality is available.

The working of the market will affect not only what sets of conjectures survive, but what new sets are created; for the interpretations placed on market success and failure will influence decisions on how to structure new organizations and restructure the old. Variety is a product not just of mutation and selection, but of conscious design. It is an open, and important, question whether the addition of design to this process will tend to increase or reduce the range of conjectures, and conjecture-generating structures, on offer. If there were one best organizational form, then conscious design might be expected to accelerate convergence; but if that is not so, then alternative designs may each have peculiar merits, and changing circumstances may entail changing requirements. In such circumstances, agreement on a tightly-defined research programme for all organizations, which is so often attractive to academics, politicians and consultants, is potentially dangerous; on the contrary, it is important that markets, like scientific communities, should be open to criticism and to novel conjectures.

Economists have been greatly impressed by the supposed welfare benefits of perfect competition. But perfect competition is quite inappropriate as a structure for promoting the growth of knowledge – as the difficulties encountered by economists who have tried to discuss innovation in this framework indicate. Indeed, Richardson (1960, 1990) has shown that it is not even capable of generating the expectations needed to promote the smooth adjustment which is assumed in the standard comparative equilibrium analysis of response to demand or cost changes. The economist can calculate the impact on a firm of a change which he or she has specified, and knowing (or asserting) all the relevant facts in the market, can calculate the optimal response; but the firm experiencing the impact cannot so simply and confidently identify its cause, nor, by the very conditions which define a perfectly competitive firm, does it have access to all the relevant facts of the market. Messages from the economy need to be interpreted within an appropriate research programme; a perfectly competitive market does not provide it. Neither in a scientific community nor in an economy is total anonymity helpful. Both require confidence that their members are operating on shared assumptions.

MARKET RELATIONSHIPS

Marshall had no doubt that economic development was encouraged by each firm's knowledge of the market experiments made by its rivals, who were also (like rival scientists) collaborators in the advance of knowledge; he even draws attention to the advantage of localization in promoting the active discussion of new ideas (1920: 271). Theory and policy are continually tested and revised by a process of continued, and varied, experimentation within a framework which is clearly recognized, but imperfectly specified.

The current fascination with game theory (in which neither discovery nor invention is permitted) has kept economists' minds away from such relationships – thus exemplifying the negative aspects of a research programme. Relationships between a firm and its customers and suppliers (what Marshall called its external organization) have similarly been treated as potential sources of conflict, and used – notably and effectively by Williamson (1985, 1986) – to explain the extent of vertical integration, to the neglect of their effect in structuring the growth of knowledge, which Marshall thought important. These relationships have recently, under the label of 'networks', been attracting some attention among writers on management; they have also been investigated by a group of Swedish economists, whose work deserves mention (Mattson 1987).

Instead of arm's-length exchanges, mediated by contract, firms may be joined, in twos, threes, or larger numbers, by a variety of technical, planning, social, or legal links, which evolve over time. A contract may provide a framework, but a relationship which is governed strictly by contract will not suffice for many of the needs of business (Richardson 1972). It will cope neither with production complementarities nor with the coordination of responses to changes in the market. It will rarely accomplish the transfer of technology, because it is almost impossible to convey all the relevant knowledge in documents. (None of us believe that we can transfer even the well-digested basic analysis of supply and demand that way.) Firms invest in these relationships, building up market assets, which they do not own but which can certainly yield a return. Reputation and goodwill are important in a market and in an organization – and particularly important in both when circumstances are changing. Any attempt to explain the choices made must attempt to describe the network as envisaged by the relevant decision makers, for this determines the perception of opportunities and constraints, not least through the information which is likely to be systematically sought. However, these perceptions, though subjective, are not incapable of analysis; the transactions within a network, whether this is a market, a firm, or a scientific community, both depend upon and generate shared assumptions about knowledge.

The concept of markets as networks may be redefined and extended to incorporate the study of market institutions. Some economists have already taken the first step by distinguishing between flexprice and fixprice markets, but seem satisfied to explore the implications for microeconomic and macroeconomic equilibrium. Even the question of who quotes prices is barely considered. In accordance with tradition, it seems to be assumed that in flexprice markets no economic agent has any price-setting role. Hicks, exceptionally, has drawn attention to the price-setting rôle of merchants, and linked their declining importance to the increasing prevalence of fixprice markets. Not all flexprice markets need to be merchants' markets, but a market network in which merchants are important is likely to have a very different set of institutions from one in which they play little or no part.

Fixprice markets are sometimes called producers' markets, the assumption being that the producer sets the price (perhaps of inputs as well as outputs). Why should producers behave differently from merchants? Notice what the difference is. Both quote a price, and observe how much is bought: they make a conjecture, and expose it to test. But the merchant is much quicker to decide that his conjecture has been refuted, and to adjust his price up or down to clear the market. The producer is much slower to revise his conjecture, because his opportunity costs are much higher. The relevant costs are not simply those of compiling and issuing new price lists, or sending new instructions to salesmen – which might be quite small; the usual problem is that the producer's prices, unlike the merchants, are typically embedded in a marketing strategy, or network of conjectures, which cannot be adequately tested if the price conjecture is not maintained – if necessary, despite the evidence – for what appears to be an adequate period.

As marketing textbooks emphasize, and a few economists, notably Marshall, have appreciated, what any firm offers to its customers is a complex package of characteristics and surrounding services, associated with a price which may itself be quite complex because of conditions of payment, links to complementary goods, adaptations, replacement parts, and so on. How is a firm to interpret the customer's response unless it can confidently assume that most of the elements in the package comply with the shared assumptions of the market, and how can it increase its knowledge unless it holds these elements constant to permit controlled experiments with a few others? In many, though certainly not all, situations, a refusal to change price is not a refusal to compete or a sign of failure to maximize profits but a necessary condition for gaining knowledge about the profitability of other elements in the firm's offering. One especial merit of Casson's (1982) analysis of the entrepreneur is its demonstration of the value, to the very person who is seeking to promote change, of sticking to a quoted price.

In a reasonably stable market network, many aspects of marketing policy become fairly standardized as market institutions: customers come to expect say, twelve-month guarantees, equipment which will accept additional features (possibly from other suppliers), and replacement parts in stock. There are ways of doing business which appear to define the framework within which any business must operate. But stability does not exclude evolution. Like the routines which characterize a firm, the institutions of a market are likely to drift over time, in large part for similar reasons. Sequential changes in technology may increase or reduce the importance of particular complementary links; an equally-balanced relationship may gradually turn in favour of one party; changes in demand, consequent on changes in income, may create interdependencies between previously separate networks. Over a long time span, a market, like a firm, or an academic discipline, may be transformed by a cumulative process of incremental adjustment.

INNOVATION

Innovations provide some striking examples of the importance of institutions. Drucker (1964: 94–103) invites managers to challenge their own theories and policies by asking such questions as: who are not our customers, and why not? Who are not our competitors, and why not? What other networks might we enter? An entrepreneur may thereby conjure up new opportunities. But the opportunity may be a mirage unless the institutional framework is capable of accommodating it. We might therefore expect innovation to be more likely within frameworks which tolerate a greater range of conjectures. This certainly seems to be a popular view about the kind of organizational structure and procedures which facilitate innovation; it is, however, notable that in the most popular of all expositions, Peters and Waterman (1982) insist on the simultaneous necessity, in large businesses, of constricting themes in order to maintain coherence. Freedom in one dimension apparently needs to be complemented by constraint in another: people can be allowed to do as they like if we are confident that they will like to do compatible things. Williamson (1985: 247) notes the benefits offered by a closely-integrated relational team (in which objectives and attitudes are widely shared) in attaining efficient governance structures when human assets are highly specific to the organization and contributions to effective performance are not readily separable. If linked to a generous or amendable framework of business-related knowledge (a link which is by no means automatic) such conformity appears to provide a promising setting for innovation.

Another possibility may be noted. One area of business, like one area of enquiry, may be amenable to alternative frameworks, each of which may encourage conjectures of a different kind; and at any one time, one set of conjectures may be peculiarly apt to initiate successful innovations. Of particular interest is the possibility that a framework may be transferred from one context to another, and open up new lines of enquiry. The realization of this possibility is well recognized in scientific research; it appears to be quite common in business. Marketing policies, technologies, or operating procedures may be imported on the basis of success in other contexts (often with the aid of consultants); or successful policies may be applied in other market areas. Either transfer, of course, may fail.

On the basis of this analysis, one would expect innovations which embody substantial novelty to be associated, out of proportion to their numbers, with people who have not become habituated to the current institutional networks of firm and market. Such people will generally have easier access to other frameworks, and be less deterred by the apparent consequences of accepting the refutation of large parts of the prevalent structure. The expectation is well-corroborated: major innovations often come from outsiders. Hannah (1984) has drawn attention to the continuing prominence of immigrants among the builders of successful British businesses; and surely no-one was surprised by Casson's (1982) choice of a typical entrepreneur.

Innovations always change the systems into which they are introduced. They begin by changing the firm which introduces them (unless they are incorporated into a new firm), and may fail if the firm's institutions are recalcitrant, or some of its members withhold the cooperation which is essential. If a satisfactory system for delivering the innovation can be achieved, there remains the problem of introducing it into the external network. Compatibility with existing practices, procedures, and ways of thinking, is as important an issue in the market network as in the innovating organization.

If the network is not receptive, one possibility may be to internalize part of it, as Courtaulds did in order to develop the market for their fibres. It is possible to construe such a move as an example of vertical integration to reduce transactions costs, by focusing on the difficulty of writing a contract which would adequately specify the operating practices, and the knowledge, required of the downstream partner. But it may be better to consider directly the problems of achieving compatibility. Can practices and assumptions be aligned across a market boundary? Can they be aligned better within a single organization, without destroying its effectiveness? Activities which are closely-complementary may not be similar, as Richardson (1972) has pointed out; and dissimilar activities, disconnected theories and policies, may be very hard to handle. Indeed, the information-impactedness which gives rise to opportunism in Williamson's theory is very likely to be the product of such disjunctions.

If alignment is possible within the enlarged firm, will that disrupt the compatibility between the newly-acquired business and the remainder of its network? In the process of securing increased attention for one's own products by the firm taken over, may one, for example damage that firm's ability to market effectively at the next stage? Many firms are very wary of any action which might be interpreted as competing with their customers. Their attitude may be misconceived, but one should seek to understand the institutional pattern which encourages the conception. Transaction cost analysis is not irrelevant to the study of firm and market structures; but it is not complete. Attention to theories, policies, and the institutional framework within which they are maintained, revised, or supported, can enlarge our understanding.

CONCLUSIONS

The analytical structure proposed in this chapter may be summarized in the following six propositions:

1 Choices are made in response to (theory-laden) evidence which is judged incompatible with some element within a set of conjectures: current theory or policy is deemed inadequate.
2 The choice will be conditioned, but in general not fully determined, by both the characteristics and the degree of discretion permitted by the institutional framework within which it is made.
3 Decision makers in different parts of one organization, in different organizations, or in different market networks, may operate within different institutional frameworks, and may therefore reach different decisions; some decision makers may have access to more than one framework.
4 The effects of the decision will be influenced by the responses of other people, each operating within their own frameworks.
5 A decision, or its effects, may change the set of institutions within which it was made: this change may or may not be intended by the decision maker.
6 Institutional changes will tend to modify the set of options which appear to be available at the next time of choice.

Three corollaries perhaps deserve mention:

1 In the development of well-established research programmes, technologies, or ways of doing business, those who conform to the dominant institutions are likely to have a significant advantage over those who do not; if these research programmes, technologies, or ways of doing business lose their effectiveness, the advantage is likely to pass to those who are less conformist, or who conform to some other (not *any* other) institutional pattern.
2 Particular policies, and the businessmen who design and apply them, may be very successful in certain conjunctures, but may fail in others; one should be wary of attributing general applicability to any policy, or general competence to any individual, though the attribution may

219

sometimes be merited. In particular, the success of a policy may destroy the basis of success: this is the crucial element in Schumpeter's analysis, and is not uncommon in the story of entrepreneurs (the first Lord Leverhulme may stand as an example) who build an empire which they are unable to control. Any policy which depends on gaining market share is vulnerable, as many chemical and fibre businesses have discovered, and as supermarket operators may soon find out.

3 It is common practice among economists to conclude with an implication for public policy: that implication is the need to preserve, and perhaps encourage, alternative institutions. Even if we are quite certain that there is at present one identifiable best way of doing things (or one best person to do them) there is no reason to believe that this way (or person) will be capable of adaptation to whatever new conditions may arise. At the least, we should consider how to provide access, and to allow for the dismantling, with tolerable speed and comfort, of outmoded systems and structures.

REFERENCES

Casson, M. (1982) *The Entrepreneur*, Oxford: Martin Robertson.

Coase, R.H. (1937) 'The nature of the firm', *Economica*, N.S., IV: 386–405.

Cyert, R.M. and March, J.G. (1963) *A Behavioral Theory of the Firm*, Englewood Cliffs, New Jersey: Prentice-Hall.

Drucker, P.F. (1964) *Managing for Results*, London: Heinemann.

Eliasson, G. (1987) *Technological Competition and Trade in the Experimentally Organized Economy*, IUI Research Report No. 32, Stockholm: IUI.

Hahn, F.H. (1973) *On the Notion of Equilibrium in Economics*, Cambridge: Cambridge University Press.

—— (1984) *Equilibrium and Macroeconomics*, Oxford: Basil Blackwell.

Hannah, L. (1984) 'Entrepreneurs and the social sciences', *Economica*, 51: 219–34.

Kelly, G.A. (1963) *A Theory of Personality*, New York: W.W. Norton.

Kuhn, T.S. (1970) *The Structure of Scientific Revolutions*, Chicago: University of Chicago Press. (First published 1962.)

Lakatos, I. (1970) 'Falsification and the methodology of scientific research programmes', in I. Lakatos and A. Musgrave (eds) *Criticism and the Growth of Knowledge*, Cambridge: Cambridge University Press, pp. 91–196.

Langlois, R. (ed.) (1986) *Economics as a Process: Essays in the New Institutional Economics*, Cambridge: Cambridge University Press.

Loasby, B.J. (1973) *The Swindon Project*, London: Pitman.

—— (1986) 'Organisation, competition and the growth of knowledge', in R. Langlois *Economics as a Process: Essays in the New Institutional Economics*, Cambridge: Cambridge University Press.

—— (1989) *The Mind and Method of the Economist*, Aldershot: Edward Elgar.

—— (1991) *Equilibrium and Evolution*, Manchester: Manchester University Press.

Marshall, A. (1920) *Principles of Economics*, eighth edition, London: Macmillan.

Mattson, L.G. (1987) 'Management of strategic change in a "markets-as-networks" perspective', in Andrew Pettigrew (ed.) *The Management of Strategic Change*, Oxford: Basil Blackwell.

Nelson, R.R. and Winter, S.G. (1982) *An Evolutionary Theory of Economic Change*, Cambridge, Mass.: Harvard University Press.

Peters, T.J. and Waterman, R.H. (1982) *In Search of Excellence*, New York: Harper & Row.

Pfeffer, J. and Salancik, G.R. (1978) *The External Control of Organizations*, New York: Harper & Row.

Popper, K.R. (1972) *The Logic of Scientific Discovery*, sixth impression, London: Hutchinson. (Originally published in German, in 1934.)

Quine, W. van O. (1951) 'Two dogmas of empiricism', *Philosophical Review*, 60: 20–43. (Reprinted in W. Quine (1961) *From a Logical Point of View*, New York: Harper & Row.)

Richardson, G.B. (1960) *Information and Investment*, Oxford: Oxford University Press.

—— (1972) 'The organisation of industry', *Economic Journal*, 82, 883–96; reprinted in G.B. Richardson (1990). *Information and Investment*, Oxford: Oxford University Press.

—— (1990) *Information and Investment*, with a new Foreword by David J. Teece, a new introduction, and two new chapters, Oxford: Clarendon Press.

Simon, H.A. (1965) *The Shape of Automation for Men and Management*, New York: Harper & Row.

—— (1982) *Models of Bounded Rationality*, 2 vols, Cambridge, Mass: MIT Press.

Smith, A. (1795) 'The principles which lead and direct philosophical enquiries: illustrated by the history of astronomy', reprinted in A. Smith (1980) *Essays on Philosophical Subjects*, edited by W.P.D. Wightman, Oxford: Oxford University Press.

Williamson, O.E. (1985) *The Economic Institutions of Capitalism: Firms, Markets, Relational Contracting*, New York: Free Press.

—— (1986) *Economic Organization: Firms, Markets and Policy Controls*, Brighton: Wheatsheaf.

Ziman, J.M. (1978) *Reliable Knowledge*, Cambridge: Cambridge University Press.

9

EVOLUTION AND INSTITUTIONAL CHANGE

On the nature of selection in biology and economics[1]

Geoffrey M. Hodgson

ABSTRACT

This chapter addresses some problems involved in the application of an evolutionary perspective to the theory of economic and institutional change. First, does evolution, in biology or society, lead to some optimal or ideal outcome, as has been suggested in the past? It is argued in this chapter that such Panglossian interpretations of evolutionary theory are ill-founded in both biological and economic terms. Second, if socio-economic development is evolutionary, what is the level at which evolutionary selection and innovation operate? Furthermore, while many biologists propose that the unit of biological selection is the gene, what is the analogous unit of selection in socio-economic systems? There are two prominent answers to these questions in the literature. The first is the idea of 'group selection' in the work of Friedrich Hayek, and the second is based on the notion of habits and routines as genes, as in the work of Thorstein Veblen, Richard Nelson and Sidney Winter. In surveying these issues, this chapter proposes a non-reductionist theoretical framework, involving a hierarchy of selective and replicating units, and the coexistence of both habitual and purposeful behaviour.

INTRODUCTION

From the natural sciences, the major influence on economic thought has been from physics (Mirowski 1989; Ingrao and Israel 1990). However, ever since the inception of modern economics there has been some transfer of ideas to and from biology. For instance, it is well known that Charles Darwin was inspired by the picture of 'the struggle for existence' in the writings of Thomas Robert Malthus (Jones 1989). But also, it is

222

clear that the influence of Adam Smith and the Scottish School was also highly significant (Schweber 1977).

Furthermore, economists have occasionally borrowed from biology, typically by presuming some congruence between biotic evolutionary selection and capitalist competition. Consequently, a slight but significant interaction between biology and economics has been established for over two hundred years. On the economics side it has involved prominent figures such as Alfred Marshall and Thorstein Veblen.[2] Notably, the policy consequences of this interaction have been diverse, as evolutionary ideas have been utilized to reinforce both radical interventionists and Panglossian free marketeers. However, modern economists are not so well-appraised about recent debates in biology over the nature and units of the process of evolutionary selection, or even of the decline of the idea that evolution represents some kind of progressive or optimizing procedure.

In this chapter three relevant themes are addressed. The starting point here, in the second section, is some of the Panglossian uses of the evolutionary analogy in both biology and economics. It is argued that they are ill-founded in both biological and economic terms and consequently some prominent conceptions of institutional and economic evolution have to be amended. The third section addresses the question of the unit of selection in biology, with an eye to applications to economics. This conveys a hierarchical and non-reductionist approach to analysis which is worthy of development and application to economics. In the fourth section a basis for a future theory of socio-economic evolution is suggested, involving a hierarchy of selective and imitating units, and incorporating habits and routines as replicating elements in the evolutionary scheme. The fifth section concludes the chapter.

IS EVOLUTION AN OPTIMIZER?

Critiques of evolutionary optimality in biology

Although Darwin reluctantly adopted Herbert Spencer's 'survival of the fittest' phrase in later editions of *The Origin of Species*, it is misleading. As Theodosius Dobzhansky *et al.* (1977: 88) point out, natural selection does not lead to the superlative fittest, only the tolerably fit. But even in a weaker sense, evolution is not necessarily a grand or natural road leading generally towards perfection. Change can be idiosyncratic, error can be reproduced genetically, and an obscure or tortuous path to improvement can elude discovery. Evolution thus does not provide us with a supreme moral arbiter.[3]

Clearly, an evolutionary process cannot be an optimizing one, at least in the strict sense, because for evolution to work there must always be a variety of forms from which to select. Indeed, without variety there would be no evolution. Furthermore, for selection to work there must be rejection, and the process must thus involve ceaseless error-making as well. In an evolutionary process, error is more than a stochastic perturbation, it is the very source of evolutionary change.

'Survival of the fittest' is additionally an ill-conceived slogan. Indeed, the mechanism of 'natural selection' in modern biology does not even necessarily lead to survival. Consider the evolution of tendencies to either 'selfish' or 'altruistic' behaviour. While universal altruism may be most beneficial for all members of the species, the possible existence of a 'prisoners' dilemma' — where individual selfishness is the best one-off individual response to prevailing cooperation — can lead to the break-down of the arrangement of universal altruism with its advantages for all. There is not necessarily any universal mechanism 'by which natural selection tends to favour the survival of the species or the population. The population, in fact, may "improve itself to extinction"'. (Elster 1983: 54)[4]

Thus the mere fact of survival, even to a numerous and sustained extent, need not always imply efficiency at all. The conclusion here concurs with the one of Elliott Sober (1981: 99): 'The so-called tautology of the survival of the fittest is no tautology at all; the fitter do *not* always turn out to be more successful'.

Panglossian modes of thought often involve the assumption, one that Darwin himself was sometimes keen to avoid, that evolution always means increasing progress and efficiency, a beneficient journey from the lower to the higher form of organization of life, and from the inferior to the superior. Within biology such progressionist themes are now widely disputed (Dupré 1987; Nitecki 1988).

If evolution is to lead to improvements or greater efficiency in some sense, as proposed by Panglossian writers, then the environment must be sufficiently stable for selection to take place. Improvement must be accomplished before any major or disruptive environmental change occurs. In the socio-economic context, however, improvements may not become established before there is such a disturbance in the environment.

Further undermining the idea of natural selection as a universally optimizing agent, Gould and Lewontin (1979) point out that selection and adaptation could be decoupled, as in the case of a mutation which doubles the fecundity of individuals. As natural selection always favours greater fecundity, a gene promoting it would sweep through a population rapidly, but it need not imply greater survival value. This argument suggests that selection does not simply depend on considerations of fitness of given units but also on the capacity of the type of unit to procreate.

Gould and Lewontin (1979) also gives examples of adaptation without selection, and of adaptation and selection with 'multiple adaptive peaks' (Wright 1959). In these circumstances the selection process may lead to the congregation of units around a local, rather than the global, maximum, and a journey to the global maximum may be ruled out by the distance involved and the depth of the valleys in between. In the latter case we often have no reason for asserting that one solution is better than another. The solution followed is path dependent: a result of history.

Finally, and most importantly, the environment in which selection proceeds includes not simply the climate, soil, etc., but also other species and even sometimes the 'social relations' or 'culture' of the subject species itself. Consequently, as pointed out by Conrad Waddington (1975: 170), organism behaviour is not simply a result of environmental change but also in part its cause.

As a result the fitness surface may not be static. Consider a favourable adaptation that may take place in relation to a given environmental situation. Further adaptations take place along similar lines. However, while the first few adaptations may be favourable, the accumulation of such adaptations may alter the environment itself, and the result is that the same adaptation no longer yield beneficial results for the individual unit.

PANGLOSSIAN CONCEPTIONS OF EVOLUTION IN ECONOMICS

The Panglossian idea of evolution as some kind of optimizer is very common in economics, and has taken a variety of forms. In 1950 Armen Alchian published his famous argument that maximizing behaviour by economic agents does not have to be justified in terms of their explicit or implicit objectives, but by the 'evolutionary' contention that maximizing and thus 'fit' firms and individuals are the ones more likely to survive and prosper. In his famous methodological essay Milton Friedman (1953) went one step further and argued that this 'evolutionary' argument constituted a justification of the maximization hypothesis, whether or not firms and individuals actually aimed to maximize.

A related argument is found in Hayek's work. He argues that:

Competition will make it necessary for people to act rationally to maintain themselves . . . a few relatively more rational individuals will make it necessary for the rest to emulate them in order to prevail. In a society in which rational behaviour confers an advantage on the individual, rational methods will progressively be developed and spread by imitation.

(Hayek 1982, 3: 75)

Further, although the outcomes of social or cultural evolution are given no automatic accolade in terms of economic efficiency or social justice, the thrust of Hayek's argument is to suggest that attempts to guide or direct the evolutionary process will subvert the complex 'spontaneous order'.

The assumption that evolution leads to optimal or near-optimal behaviour by individuals is closely related to the idea that evolution leads to the more efficient organizational forms. Thus Oliver Williamson (1975, 1985) asserts that because hierarchical firms exist, then they must be both more efficient and most suited to survival. Especially in Friedman's and Williamson's hands, therefore, an appeal to evolutionary theory takes a distinctly Panglossian turn.[5]

However, an error in this manner of thought, as explained above, is the assumption that what is selected tends to be the better or best, in some absolute sense. Biologists have argued convincingly that the selection process is not necessarily in accord with some absolute standard of 'fitness', and that a gene can confer high fitness in one environment and be disadvantageous in another. What is true for a gene in biology is true for a given type of organization, relation or structure in a socio-economic system. Even if the 'selected' firms, routines or institutions were the 'fittest' then they would be so in regard to a particular, economic, political, and cultural environment only; they would not be the 'fittest' for all circumstances and times.

Furthermore, the Friedman–Williamson versions of the evolutionary metaphor fail to specify any plausible and detailed mechanism for the evolution of economies and firms. More specifically, as Sidney Winter (1964) has made clear, there is no clear mechanism to show how a firm that happens to be maximizing profits will continue to do so through time, and how other firms are to acquire this behavioural characteristic. Some writers follow Alchian by suggesting that other firms will 'imitate' the profit maximizers. Not only does this contradict the Alchian–Friedman view that intentional behaviour has to be disregarded in the theoretical explanation, but also it leaves open the question as to how other firms know what characteristics to look for and to imitate.

Friedman and Williamson take it for granted that survival means efficiency. Edna Ullmann-Margalit (1978) shows that this is invalid. Strictly, in order to explain the existence of a structure it is neither necessary nor sufficient to show that it is efficient. Inefficient structures do happen to exist and survive, and many possible efficient structures will never actually be selected. As Gregory Dow (1987: 32) observes: 'it is all too easy to abuse economic selection arguments by simply declaring that surviving forms of organization are efficient *ipso facto*'.

The issue of fecundity, raised above, relates directly to Williamson's mistaken 'evolutionary' argument. He alleges that the relatively low density of worker cooperatives in modern capitalism indicates that they are less efficient than the normal firm based on individual ownership. In a famous work, Mancur Olson (1965) analyses the difficulties of forming collective organizations where individual benefits do not seem to justify the trouble and expense of organizing. Referring to this in their study of the rise of the modern industrial system, Nathan Rosenberg and Luther Birdzell point out that:

> By comparison, the promoter of an investor-owned enterprise can, by retaining part or all of the ownership interest, profit handsomely if the enterprise succeeds. So one might expect more investor-owned enterprises, small or large, to survive simply because far more of them are likely to be born.
>
> (Rosenberg and Birdzell 1986: 316)

Consequently, even if in a rational-choice framework, such as that employed by Olson, there is good reason to doubt that preponderance necessarily means efficiency.

The principal arguments used by modern biologists against the idea of evolution as an optimizer, also, with slight modification, contradict the type of Panglossian thinking that has been noted above. For instance, if firm payoffs are dependent on the nature of the industry as a whole then the selected characteristics are likewise depend on the overall environment. Here 'natural selection' does not necessarily favour the most efficient unit, nor always the optimal outcome. In particular, there is no guarantee that firms exhibiting some kind of maximizing behaviour or efficiency-related characteristic will actually be selected in the evolutionary process.

For example, a firm may find a market niche involving the manufacture of a new type or variety of product. Initially, the firm may make large profits from the venture. Indeed, it may initially be at a global maximum on the fitness or profits surface. However, if a large number of other firms perceive and grasp the same opportunity, the market may become flooded and the produce may no longer be profitable. The 'environment', that is the state of market demand, itself may alter as other firms seek out buyers. What was profitable for one or a few may not be profitable for many. Being placed in this deteriorating situation, it may then be difficult for the firms congregating in the niche to move elsewhere, because of the specificity of their assets or skills.

This important possibility, deriving from cybernetic or 'feedback' relationship between a unit and its environment, is as significant in economic evolution as it is in the biological sphere. The neglect of this eventuality would be another example of the 'fallacy of composition'; the erroneous presumption that the selection of fitter individuals always leads to the selection of fitter populations. The repetition of this type of error in economics can likewise have damaging consequences for theory and policy.

The idea of a multiplicity of adaptive peaks also has relevance, with the possibility of agents or firms congregated around a local profit or efficiency maximum. In this way an economic system can get locked into given paths of development, excluding a host of other, perhaps more 'efficient' or desirable possibilities. This is redolent of Waddington's (1972) idea of a 'chreod': that is a relatively stable trajectory of development for a species. Norman Clark and Calestous Juma (1987) argue that there are technological trajectories each which develops a hierarchical control sequence very similar to the chreod. Once a technological 'paradigm' is adopted, this predetermines a general direction or path of development. This is not necessarily optimal and it is difficult for individual agents to change or move far away from this path.

In some respects the idea of chreodic development is similar to the biological idea of 'hyperselection'. Hyperselection emerges from strong positive feedback effects that 'freeze' a given attribute or structure, making further amendment difficult, even if the initial configuration is imperfect. One of the most famous technological analogues is the emergence of the immutable but sub-optimal 'QWERTY' typewriter keyboard (David 1985). A similar phenomenon has been described as 'lock-in' (Arthur 1989). In the case of chreodic development, hyperselection and lock-in, the outcomes have an arbitrary quality, depending much on initial conditions.

In the economic context the possibility is thus raised of some form of government intervention to set out or change the contours of chreodic development, or to initiate a more desirable hyperselective scenario. This does not establish that state intervention or economic planning are necessarily superior to *laissez-faire*. It does suggest, however, that there is a possibility that they may be, in certain modes or circumstances. Furthermore, the nineteenth-century idea of unhampered evolution necessarily reaching optimal outcomes is misconceived. Both in the biological and the economic context, evolution is not a grand optimizer, nor a perfectionist. To improve economic circumstances we may well require the judicious intervention of the visible hand.

UNITS OF EVOLUTIONARY SELECTION

Group versus gene

In his best-selling book, Richard Dawkins (1976) sustains a forceful polemic against the idea of biological 'group selection' advanced by V.C. Wynne-Edwards (1962) and others. The relevance of this issue for socio-economic evolution is shown by the fact that Dawkins's arguments have been used by Viktor Vanberg (1986) to undermine theories of cultural group selection and to promote methodological individualism. Vanberg's main target of criticism is actually Friedrich Hayek, who strangely supports the principle of group selection with simultaneous allegiance to methodological individualism (Hayek 1982, 1988).

The prominent argument against group and cultural selection is that there is no clear mechanism to ensure that an advantageous pattern of behaviour for the group will for some reason be replicated by the actions of the individuals concerned. In particular, such a mechanism must ensure that 'free riders' do not become dominant in the groups that exhibit socially useful altruistic behaviours. Free riders would have the benefits of being members of a group whose other members perform socially useful and self-sacrificial acts, but bear no personal costs or risks in terms of self-sacrificial behaviour themselves. Consequently, in the absence of any compensating mechanism, it is likely that free riders within the group will expand in numbers, crowd out the others, and alter the typical behaviour of the group as a whole.

Thus, despite the possible benefits to the group of self-sacrificial behaviour, it appears that there is no mechanism to ensure that groups with these characteristics will prosper above others. What seems crucial is the selection of the constituent individuals and not the groups as a whole. Vanberg (1986: 97) thus concludes that the 'notion of cultural group selection is theoretically vague, inconsistent with the basic thrust of Hayek's individualistic approach, and faulty judged on its own grounds'.

However, as argued elsewhere (Hodgson 1991a), the arguments of Dawkins and others against the group selection are not entirely satisfactory. A number of biologists now propose that there are levels of selection other than the gene. Biologists such as Niles Eldredge, Stephen Jay Gould, Richard Lewontin and Ernst Mayr have all taken issue with such single-level or 'genetic reductionist' explanations in which it is assumed that animal behaviour can be explained exclusively in terms of the appropriate genes. It is proposed that selection operates simultaneously on different types of unit, depending on the time scale and the type of selection process. Such ideas reflect a widespread, but non-universal, acceptance of non-reductionist and hierarchical views of selection in biology.

When group selection occurs, all the organisms in the same group are bound together by a common fate. Although members of the group may not have identical fitness values, group selection works via a uniform effect. It may be that all such information about ostensible group selection may be reduced to and represented by selection coefficients of organisms or genes. But, contrary to Dawkins, such a formal reduction does not imply that the concept of group selection is invalid or that it is individual or genic selection which is occurring. 'In particular, the computational adequacy of genetic models leaves open the question whether they also correctly identify the causes of evolution' (Sober and Lewontin 1982: 158).

Genetic reductionists respond that the gene is the single unit of replication. However, as Sober argues, group selectionists:

> Do not deny that the gene is the mechanism by which biological objects pass on their characteristics . . . this shared assumption about the unit of replication simply cuts no ice. That genes are passed along leaves open the question as to what causes their differential transmission.
>
> (Sober 1981: 113)

David Sloan Wilson and Elliott Sober (1989) go so far as to argue that to settle on the individual as the unit of selection involves an inconsistency. Simple reduction to the individual level is unacceptable because the same arguments concerning reduction from groups to individuals apply equally to reduction from individual to gene. To avoid this 'double standard' one must either accept multiple levels of selection, or reduce everything to the lowest possible level: the gene or even below. Thus Vanberg's attempt to support methodological individualism by citing the genetic reductionist is open to objection.

Some of the major detailed arguments against group selection emanate from the mathematical work of John Maynard Smith (1964, 1976) and his collaborators. However, mathematical expressions of evolutionary dynamics are highly complex and notoriously intractable. In order to build Maynard Smith's 'basic selection model' a number of necessary simplifications had to be made, excluding several non-linearities and environmental interdependencies. Michael Wade (1978) demonstrates that the mathematical selection models in the literature are based on over-simplifying and restrictive assumptions. He argues that when these assumptions are relaxed, group selection is much more plausible.

D.S. Wilson (1983) points out that all such models assume a spatial homogeneity in the genetic composition of populations. Although this assumption is mathematically convenient, it is neither necessary nor realistic. Once again, the assumptions upon which the basic selection model is founded are shown to be over-restrictive and over-simplified.

The possibility of multiple levels of selection is considered by a number of biological theorists. For instance, foreshadowing Eldredge (1985), Anthony Arnold and Kurt Fristrup write:

> It is self-evident that evolutionary theory has acknowledged the utility of hierarchical structure in *describing* biological phenomena.

However, this body of evolutionary theory does not incorporate hierarchical structure in its conventional modes of *explanation*.

(Arnold and Fristrup 1982: 113)

Selection between species is considered in Leigh Van Valen (1975) and between ecosystems in M.S. Dunbar (1960). Arnold and Fristrup elaborate:

If we step back and look at the hierarchy as a whole, a picture emerges of a highly interrelated system, in which selection at a given level can be opposed, reinforced, or unaffected by processes operating at other levels. If this concept emphasizes the complexity of interrelations in the evolutionary process, it also underscores the essential unity of its theoretical structure: no single level can be fully understood except in the context of its position in the evolutionary hierarchy.

(Arnold and Fristrup 1982: 128)

Thus a view has been developed that selection mechanisms are hierarchical, involving culls at higher levels that favour groups or whole species, rather than simply genes or individuals. In other words, selection operates simultaneously on different types of unit, depending on the time scale and the type of selection process.[6]

What is different at each level is the fidelity of the reproductive process; in general, reproductive accuracy declines as the hierarchy is ascended. Correspondingly, the longevity of the reproductive unit, but not necessarily of its embodied information, increases. Although the information in genes is in a sense 'immortal', individual genes do not outlast organisms, and organisms certainly do not outlast the species to which they belong.

HIGHER-LEVEL SELECTION IN SOCIO-ECONOMIC EVOLUTION

Given the possibility of group selection in biology, it may be conjectured that a similar phenomenon occurs in the socio-economic sphere. Considerations of institutions, rules, norms and cultures are apposite. Assume that a particular characteristic affects all members of a group equally, such as the enforcement of different modes of diet, dress or behaviour. Assume further that this characteristic affects the future growth and prosperity of the group. Then there may be grounds for considering that group selection is at work. Thus, for example, the Shakers as a religious sect have approached demise because of their internal law of celibacy. In earlier times, as Max Weber (1978) argues, Protestant communities or nations prospered relative to the Catholic, partly because of their relatively individualistic culture and their disposition to accumulate worldly wealth.

231

Arguably, economic evolution could work through the selection of habits, individuals, routines, institutions and even whole socio-economic systems and sub-systems. Accordingly, there is no reason why selection should be confined to agents or entities within the framework of the market. Markets are also institutions, and selection will operate on types of market framework as well as the agents and organizations operating within them. It is also necessary to consider selection both between different types of market, and between market and non-market forms of allocation. A selection process in this context would involve a mixed economy, of whatever type or hue.

Given this, Hayek should be criticized, not for embracing group selection and eschewing a consistent individualism, but for failing to incorporate additional processes of selection above the group level. Such processes must involve a variety or plurality of different types of economic system and not simply a plurality of economic agents. To work at such higher levels, evolutionary selection must involve different types of ownership structure and resource allocation mechanisms, all coexisting in a mixed economy. The rehabilitation of group selection, based on modern work in biology, thus rebounds on the free market ideas of Hayek himself.

There is another important reason for group selection which seems to be barred by Hayek's liberal and individualistic outlook. Although he stresses the importance of tacit knowledge, he seems to relate this exclusively to individuals. However, experience suggests that it may in a sense reside in groups as well. An example is suggested by Sidney Winter who argues that the capabilities of an organization such as a firm are not generally reducible to the capabilities of individual members. He points out that:

> The coordination displayed in the performance of organizational routines is, like that displayed in the exercise of individual skills, the fruit of practice. What requires emphasis is that ... the learning experience is a shared experience of organization members. ... Thus, even if the contents of the organizational memory are stored only in the form of memory traces in the memories of individual members, it is still an organizational knowledge in the sense that the fragment stored by each individual member is not fully meaningful or effective except in the context provided by the fragments stored by other members.
>
> (Winter 1982: 76)

Winter's argument suggests that although tacit or other knowledge must reside in the nerve or brain cells of human beings, its enactment depends crucially on the existence of a structured context in which individuals interact with each other. Otherwise, no such knowledge can become manifest. Given the critical nature of the impulses that are dependent upon the existence of the organization, and the fact that they affect the behaviour of all its members, here is a clear case of the fate of a group of individuals being bound together in a single whole. Such 'organizational learning' is thus feasibly associated with group selection.

An evolutionary theoretical framework with multiple levels of selection provides an alternative to the prominent reductionism of modern economics. Neoclassical economics is preoccupied with the attempt to found macroeconomics on 'sound microfoundations'. In this effort it mimics the reductionism of classical physics, in trying to build up models from the allegedly fundamental particles of the system. But biology is developing hierarchic and non-reductionist modes of thinking in which entities at several levels can be considered. This suggests both the possibility and the legitimacy of a macroeconomics that enjoys some autonomy from microeconomics and does not have to be based exclusively on the axiom of the maximizing individual.

PROCESSES OF EVOLUTION IN SOCIO-ECONOMIC SYSTEMS

Habits and routines as genes

An emphasis on relevance of habits and routines to economic science is a key feature of the institutionalism of Veblen and others. Within such a perspective, organizational structures, habits and routines play a similar evolutionary role to that of the gene in the natural world.

Habits are essential to deal with the complexity of everyday life; they provide us with a means of retaining a pattern of behaviour without engaging in global rational calculations involving vast amounts of complex information. Fortunately, human agents have acquired habits which effectively relegate particular ongoing actions from continuous rational assessment. The processes of action are organized in a hierarchical manner, facilitating monitoring at different levels and rates, and with different degrees and types of response to incoming data.

The capacity to form habits is indispensable for the acquisition of all sorts of practical and intellectual skills. At first, while learning a technique, we must concentrate on every detail of what we are doing. Eventually, however, intellectual and practical habits emerge, and this is the very point at which we regard ourselves as having acquired the skill. Thereafter, analytical or practical rules can be applied without full, conscious reasoning or deliberation.

Work itself involves a degree of practical knowledge or know-how which is both acquired and routinized over time. Indeed, the industrial skill of a nation consists of a set of relevant habits, acquired over a long time, widely dispersed through the employable workforce, reflective of its culture and deeply embedded in its practices (Veblen 1914; Dyer 1984).

Institutions involve congealed habits. As Veblen (1919: 241) puts it: 'institutions are an outgrowth of habit. The growth of culture is a cumulative sequence of habituation, and the ways and means of it are the habitual response of human nature to exigencies'. Thus institutions are at a different level from habits in multi-tiered hierarchy, and are themselves subdivided by the degree to which they have become ingrained or ossified.

Consequently, to a greater or lesser extent, habits and institutions have a stable and inert quality and tend to sustain and thus 'pass on' their characteristics through time, and from one institution to another. For example, the skills learned by a worker in a given firm become partially embedded in his or her habits. Thus these act as carriers of information, 'unteachable knowledge', and skills. Likewise, the structures and routines of the firm are durable institutions, and may be more difficult to alter than the skills of a single worker. In this respect habits and institutions have a quality analogous to the informational fidelity of the gene. Clearly, however, the reproductive accuracy of the gene is much the greater.

Habits and routines thus preserve knowledge, particularly tacit knowledge in relation to skills, acting through time as a transmission belt of information and knowledge. There is also another sense in which institutions supply information, by establishing more or less fixed patterns of human action upon which decision making can take place. Such inflexibilities or constraints suggest to the individual what other agents might do, and the individual can then act accordingly. Institutions, other than acting simply as rigidities and constraints, enable decision and action by providing more-or-less reliable information regarding the likely actions of others. Consequently, in a highly complex world, and despite uncertainty, regular and predictable behaviour is possible.

The idea that routines within the firm act as 'genes' to pass on skills and information is adopted by Nelson and Winter (1982: 134–6). Being concerned to show how technological skills are acquired and passed on within the economy, they argue that habits and routines act as repositories of knowledge and skills. In their words, routines are the 'organizational memory' (ibid., p. 99) of the firm, and act as the unit of selection for the organization. As Nelson and Winter make clear, routines do not act as genes in the neo-Darwinian sense because the inheritance of acquired characteristics is possible. Thus the evolutionary process in society is not Darwinian but essentially Lamarckian, in that acquired characteristics can be inherited.

It is important to note that social evolution can be regarded as Lamarckian in another sense, in that there is a case for assuming a degree of intentional or purposeful behaviour. I have suggested elsewhere (Hodgson 1988) that it may be possible to combine the notions of purposeful action with the more determined and routinized aspects of human behaviour in a multi-levelled conception of human consciousness.

Although intentional behaviour – other than of the kind which could be associated with automata – is excluded from Darwinian theory, it is possible to integrate it in a conception of socio-economic evolution (Hodgson 1991d). While at the strategic sense we may be rational or free, much of our activity is governed by habit and routine over which there is no more than occasional intervention by conscious deliberation. Consequently, actions have both deliberative and non-deliberative elements.

Notes on the evolution of habits and institutions

It has already been pointed out, quoting Winter (1982: 76) that the 'knowledge' purveyed by habits is not only tacit and often uncodifiable, but it is also context dependent in a particular sense. Individual pieces of information often make sense only when fitted together into the whole. Thus in the case of socio-economic evolution, context dependence is not simply relevant in regard to the development of the phenotype, as in the case of biology, but also in regard to the survival and replication of the socio-economic analogues of the genotype, that is, institutional routines and rules, and the habits and preferences of the individual.

Partly for this reason a fully-fledged view of institutional evolution contrasts somewhat with the mainstream view of economics as 'the science of choice', with individual preferences taken as given. Orthodox economists take such factors for granted, concentrating simply on the forward-looking analysis of decision and choice. This view is incompatible with a fully, phylogenetic, evolutionary perspective, because one of the major features of such an approach is to examine the impact of the past on present and future development and the possibilities of mutation or change. Thus we must not only accept but incorporate into the analysis the reasonable assumption that individual tastes and preferences are malleable and will change or adapt.

In this case the objectives and behaviour of agents can be moulded or reinforced by institutions. This is partly because institutions have an important cognitive function (Douglas 1987; Hodgson 1988). The information they provide is not transmitted raw; it is affected by the structures of those institutions themselves. Such structures do not simply provide information, they influence the processes through which information is selected, arranged and perceived by agents. For this and other reasons: 'The situation of today shapes the institutions of tomorrow through a selective, coercive process, by acting upon men's habitual view of things, and so altering or fortifying a point of view or a mental attitude handed down from the past' (Veblen 1899: 190–1).

However, institutions in the social world are not eternal, and it is a major task of evolutionary theory in the social sciences to consider the manner of their mutation and change as well as their aspects of continuity. The Lamarckian process of inheritance in a multi-tiered social system occasionally leads to conflict, creating the possibility of change. Stephen Edgell summarizes Veblen's view in these terms:

> Institutions that emerge during one era may persist into another and the resulting cultural lag is likely to give rise to 'friction' between the habits of thought generated by the new material conditions and the habits and institutions more appropriate to an earlier period of cultural development.
>
> (Edgell 1975: 272–3)

Institutional development and change can be likened to strata shifting slowly at different rates, but occasionally causing seismic disturbance and discontinuities.[7]

For several reasons the 'genetic' character of habits, routines and institutions is different from the role of the gene in genetic reductionist biology, in particular because the transmission of 'genetic information' that supposedly programmes future action does not take place at one level. Most obviously, a distinction has to be made between habits, which relate to the individual and constitute his or her 'genotype', on the one hand, and routines, which form the genotype for institutions, on the other. Each level of hierarchy and sub-hierarchy has its own genotypical forms. Thus in some respects social evolution is similar to biological evolution in non-reductionist accounts such as those of Eldredge or Gould.

The replication processes concerning habits, routines and institutions are very different from those of the gene. Habits reproduce themselves mainly by training and practice, and possibly by imitation through personal contact or example. Individuals may copy the actions or acquire the ideas of others, thereby becoming habituated to new ways of thinking and doing. Social mobility facilitates this process, as do a cultural and institutional environment that is receptive to change.

In fact, the processes of learning and imitation may be more important than direct selection in some cases. Effective evolutionary selection requires not simply a degree of environmental stability but also some continuity or stability in the entity to be selected. Unlike biological evolution, evolution in the socio-economic context may involve rapidly-changing units of selection at some levels. For instance, individual agents may be learning and changing rapidly, while institutional structures are relatively stable. Consequently, the processes of learning and imitation may be more important at some levels of the developmental process than the processes of sifting and selection resulting from environmental tests.

CONCLUDING REMARKS

It has been argued here that even if the genetic reductionist view was valid in biology, there are many reasons for abandoning an individual or similar reductionism in social science. Even if there was one level of selection in biology, there are good reasons to assume that socio-economic evolution operates on a number of levels. The idea of a hierarchy of levels and units of selection seems to be eminently transferable to economics and social science through the incorporation of hierarchies of habits, routines and institutions.

In other respects, evolution in socio-economic systems goes beyond evolution in modern biological theory. First, socio-economic evolution is Lamarckian in that acquired characters can be inherited. As well as changes in the distribution of habits and routines, and their possible 'mutation', evolution in society may work more dramatically through cumulative inheritance in a Lamarckian manner.

Furthermore, on another Lamarckian theme, socio-economic evolution encompasses both habitual and purposeful behaviour. Both coexist in the evolutionary process, ensuring that its dynamics reflect both expectations of the future and cumulative influences from the past. An exclusive emphasis on either the former or the latter, in respectively either a subjectivist or a determinist manner, would be unwarranted.

Above all, however, there is no reason to assume that socio-economic evolution leads to optimal or near-optimal outcomes. This is despite many assertions from economists to the contrary. While analogies should always be employed with discrimination and care, this is a clear instance where economists can learn a great deal from modern biology. While biology offers no ready-made solutions, it certainly seems to provide a more appropriate metaphor for economics than that of nineteenth-century physics. Furthermore, biology no longer seems to sustain the kind of *laissez-faire* or Panglossian thinking in social theory as presumed in the past. Recognition of the common degrees of complexity in both biotic and economic systems should dissuade us from ready-made or simplistic policy stances or theoretical conclusions.

NOTES

1 The author is grateful to the participants of the SCASSS conference in Friiberg, Sweden in August 1989, including Richard Langlois, Hans Lind and Pavel Pelikan, and particularly to the three editors of this volume, for helpful comments on early drafts of this chapter, and for the support of a SCASSS fellowship for some of the later work or revision.
2 The omission of Joseph Schumpeter here is deliberate. I have shown elsewhere that he explicitly rejected an analogy with evolutionary biology and defined evolution in a different way. For an evaluation of the evolutionary theory of Marshall see Thomas (1991). Also, Karl Marx praised Darwin but did not take Darwinism on board (Hodgson 1992). For a discussion of the 'evolutionary' ideas of all the aforementioned writers, as well as those of Veblen, see Hodgson (forthcoming).
3 This point has been argued and illustrated extensively in the works of Stephen Jay Gould (1978, 1980, 1989). For a critique of Panglossian ideas in economic evolution see Hodgson (1991b).
4 Nevertheless, the evolution of so-called 'altruistic' behaviour is still explicable in neo-Darwinian terms. On this see E.O. Wilson (1975) and Dawkins (1976, 1982), as well as the work of Axelrod (1984) on 'the evolution of cooperation'.
5 In response to criticism, Williamson brushes aside the charges of Panglossian excess raised by Mark Granovetter (1985) among others. While he does not hold to the stronger proposition 'that all is for the best in this best of possible worlds' (Williamson 1988: 178), Williamson still holds to the view that competition performs some kind of sort and shifts resources in favour of the more efficient forms of organization. This article of faith is juxtaposed with an observation that a 'more fully developed theory of the selection process' (ibid., p. 174) is lacking. However, modern and developed evolutionary theory in biology does not give universal or unqualified support for the kind of proposition Williamson wishes to entertain.
6 Contributions to the 'units of selection' controversy are found in Brandon and Burian (1984). See also Sober (1984a,b).
7 For elaborations and similar ideas see Hodgson (1989, 1991c) and Mokyr (1990, 1991).

REFERENCES

Alchian, A.A. (1950) 'Uncertainty, evolution and economic theory', *Journal of Political Economy* 58 (June): 211–21.
Arnold, A.J. and Fristrup, K. (1982) 'The theory of evolution by natural selection: a hierarchical expansion', *Paleobiology* 8: 113–29. (Reprinted in R.N. Brandon and R.M. Burian (eds) (1984) *Genes, Organisms, Populations: Controversies over the Units of Selection*, Cambridge, Mass.: MIT Press).
Arthur, W.B. (1989) 'Competing technologies; increasing returns, and lock-in by historical events', *Economic Journal* 99 (March): 116–31. (Reprinted in C. Freeman (ed.) (1990) *The Economics of Innovation*, Aldershot: Edward Elgar.)
Axelrod, R.M. (1984) *The Evolution of Cooperation*, New York: Basic Books.
Brandon, R.N. and Burian, R.M. (eds) (1984) *Genes, Organisms, Populations: Controversies over the Units of Selection*, Cambridge, Mass.: MIT Press.
Clark, N.G. and Juma, C. (1987) *Long-Run Economics: An Evolutionary Approach to Economic Growth*, London: Pinter.

David, P.A. (1985), 'Clio and the Economics of QWERTY', *American Economic Review* 75 (May): 332–7.

Dawkins, R. (1976) *The Selfish Gene*, Oxford: Oxford University Press.

—— (1982) *The Extended Phenotype: The Gene as the Unit of Selection*, Oxford: Oxford University Press.

Dobzhansky, T., Ayala, F.J., Stebbins, G.L. and Valentine, J.W. (1977) *Evolution*, San Francisco: Freeman.

Douglas, M. (1987) *How Institutions Think*, London: Routledge & Kegan Paul.

Dow, G. & K. (1987) 'The function of authority in transaction cost economics', *Journal of Economic Behaviour and Organization* 8 (March): 13–38.

Dunbar, M.S. (1960) 'The evolution of stability in marine environments: natural selection at the level of the ecosystem' *American Naturalist,* 94: 129–36.

Dupré, J.A. (ed.) (1987), *The Latest on the Best: Essays on Evolution and Optimality*, Cambridge, Mass.: MIT Press.

Dyer, A.W. (1984) 'The habit of work: a theoretical exploration', *Journal of Economic Issues* 18 (June): 557–64.

Edgell, S. (1975) 'Thorstein Veblen's theory of evolutionary change', *American Journal of Economics and Sociology* 34 (July): 267–80.

Eldredge, N. (1985) *Unfinished Synthesis: Biological Hierarchies and Modern Evolutionary Thought*, Oxford: Oxford University Press.

Elster, J. (1983) *Explaining Technical Change*, Cambridge: Cambridge University Press.

Friedman, M. (1953) 'The methodology of positive economics', in M. Friedman *Essays in Positive Economics*, Chicago: University of Chicago Press.

Gould, S.J. (1978) *Ever Since Darwin: Reflections in Natural History*, London: Burnett Books.

—— (1980) *The Panda's Thumb*, New York: Norton.

—— (1989) *Wonderful Life: The Burgess Shale and the Nature of History*, London: Hutchinson Radius.

—— and Lewontin, R.C. (1979) 'The spandrels of San Marco and the Panglossian paradigm: a critique of the adaptationist programme', *Proceedings of the Royal Society of London, Series B* 205: 581–98. (Reprinted in E. Sober (ed.) (1984) *Conceptual Issues in Evolutionary Biology: An Anthology*, Cambridge, Mass.: MIT Press.

Granovetter, M. (1985) 'Economic action and social structure: the problem of embeddedness', *American Journal of Sociology* 91 (November): 481–510.

Hayek, F.A. (1982) *Law, Legislation and Liberty*, (three-volume combined edition), London: Routledge & Kegan Paul.

—— (1988) *The Fatal Conceit: The Errors of Socialism*, Vol. 1, *Collected Works of F.A. Hayek*, London: Routledge.

Hodgson, G.M. (1988) *Economics and Institutions: A Manifesto for a Modern Institutional Economics*, Cambridge Polity Press/Philadelphia: University of Pennsylvania Press.

—— (1989) 'Institutional rigidities and economic growth', *Cambridge Journal of Economics* 13(1) March: 79–101. (Reprinted in A. Lawson, J.G. Palma and J. Sender (eds) (1989) *Kaldor's Political Economy*, London: Academic Press; and in G.M. Hodgson (1991) *After Marx and Sraffa*, London: Macmillan.)

—— (1991a) 'Hayek's theory of cultural evolution: an evaluation in the light of Vanberg's critique', *Economics and Philosophy* 7 (April): 67–82.

—— (1991b) 'Economic evolution: intervention contra Pangloss', *Journal of Economic Issues* 25 (June): 519–33.

—— (1991c) 'Socio-political disruption and economic development', in G.M.

—— (1991d) 'Evolution and intention in economic theory', in J.S. Metcalfe and P.P. Saviotti (eds) *Evolutionary Theories of Economic and Technological Change*, Reading: Harwood Academic Publishers.

—— (1992) 'Marx, Engels and economic evolution', *International Journal of Social Economics*.

—— (forthcoming) *Economics and Evolution*, Cambridge: Polity Press.

—— E. Screpanti (eds) *Rethinking Economics: Markets, Technology and Economic Evolution*, Aldershot: Edward Elgar, pp. 153–71.

Ingrao, B. and Israel, G. (1990) *The Invisible Hand: Economic Equilibrium in the History of Science*, Cambridge, Mass.: MIT Press.

Jones, L.B. (1989) 'Schumpeter versus Darwin: In re Malthus', *Southern Economic Journal* 56 (October): 410–22.

Maynard Smith, J. (1964) 'Group selection and kin selection', *Nature* 201: 1145–47.

—— (1976) 'Group selection', *Quarterly Review of Biology* 51: 277–83. (Reprinted in T.H. Clutton-Brock and P.H. Harvey (eds) (1978) *Readings in Sociobiology*, Reading: W.H. Freeman, and also in R.N. Brandon and R.M. Burian (eds) (1984) *Genes, Organisms, Populations: Controversy over the Units of Selection*, Cambridge, Mass.: MIT Press.)

Mirowski, P. (1989) *More Heat Than Light: Economics as Social Physics, Physics as Nature's Economics*, Cambridge: Cambridge University Press.

Mokyr, J. (1990) *The Lever of Riches: Technological Creativity and Economic Progress*, Oxford: Oxford University Press.

—— (1991) 'Evolutionary biology, technical change, and economic history', *Bulletin of Economic Research*, 43(2) (April) pp. 127–49.

Nelson, R.R. and Winter, S.G. (1982) *An Evolutionary Theory of Economic Change*, Cambridge Mass.: Harvard University Press.

Nitecki, M.H. (ed.) (1988) *Evolutionary Progress*, Chicago: University of Chicago Press.

Olson, M. Jr (1965) *The Logic of Collective Action*, Cambridge, Mass.: Harvard University Press.

Rosenberg, N. and Birdzell, L.E. Jr (1986) *How the West Grew Rich: The Economic Transformation of the Industrial World*, New York: Basic Books.

Schweber, S.S. (1977) 'The origin of the *Origin* revisited', *Journal of the History of Biology* 10: 229–316.

Sober, E. (1981) 'Holism, individualism and the units of selection', in P.D. Asquith and R.N. Giere (eds) *Philosophy of Science Association 1980* vol. 2: 93–121, East Lansing, Michigan: Philosophy of Science Association. (Reprinted in E. Sober (ed.) (1984) *Conceptual Issues in Evolutionary Biology: An Anthology*, Cambridge Mass.: MIT Press.)

—— (1984a) *The Nature of Selection: Evolutionary Theory in Philosophical Focus*, Cambridge, Mass.: MIT Press.

—— (ed.) (1984b) *Conceptual Issues in Evolutionary Biology: An Anthology*, Cambridge, Mass.: MIT Press.

—— and Lewontin, R.C. (1982) 'Artifact, cause, and genic selection', *Philosophy of Science*, 49(2): 157–80. (Reprinted in E. Sober (ed.) (1984) *Conceptual Issues in Evolutionary Biology: An Anthology*, Cambridge, Mass.: MIT Press.)

Thomas, B. (1991) 'Alfred Marshall on economic biology', *Review of Political Economy*, 3 (January): 1–14.

Ullmann-Margalit, E. (1978) 'Invisible hand explanations', *Synthèse* 39: 282–6.

Van Valen, L.M. (1975) 'Group selection, sex, and fossils', *Evolution* 29: 87–94.

Vanberg, V. (1986) 'Spontaneous market order and social rules: a critique of

F.A. Hayek's theory of cultural evolution', *Economics and Philosophy* 2 (June): 75–100.

Veblen, T.B. (1899) *The Theory of the Leisure Class: An Economic Study of Institutions*, New York: Macmillan.

—— (1914) *The Instinct of Workmanship*, New York: Augustus Kelley.

—— (1919) *The Place of Science in Modern Civilisation and Other Essays*, New York: Huebsch. (Reprinted 1990 with a new introduction by W.J. Samuels, New Brunswick: Transaction Publishers.)

Waddington, C.H. (ed.) (1972) *Towards a Theoretical Biology*, (4 vols), Edinburgh: Edinburgh University Press.

—— (1975) *The Evolution of an Evolutionist*, Ithaca, New York: Cornell University Press.

Wade, M.J. (1978) 'A critical review of the models of group selection', *Quarterly Review of Biology* 53: 101–14. (Reprinted in R.N. Brandon and R.M. Burian (eds) (1984) *Genes, Organisms, Populations: Controversies over the Units of Selection*, Cambridge, Mass.: MIT Press.)

Weber, M. (1978) *The Protestant Ethic and the Spirit of Capitalism*, London: Allen & Unwin.

Williamson, O.E. (1975) *Markets and Hierarchies: Analysis and AntiTrust Implications*, New York: Free Press.

—— (1985) *The Economic Institutions of Capitalism: Firms, Markets, Relational Contracting*, London: Macmillan.

—— (1988) 'The economics and sociology of organization', in G. Farkas and P. England (eds) (1988) *Industries, Firms, and Jobs: Sociological and Economic Approaches*, New York: Plenum Press, pp. 159–85.

Wilson, D.S. (1983) 'The group selection controversy: history and current status', *Annual Review of Ecology and Systematics* 14: 159–88.

—— and Sober, E. (1989) 'Reviving the superorganism', *Journal of Theoretical Biology* 136: 337–56.

Wilson, E.O. (1975) *Sociobiology*, Cambridge, Mass.: Harvard University Press.

Winter, Sidney G., Jr (1964) 'Economic "Natural selection" and the theory of the firm', *Yale Economic Essays* 4(1): 225–72.

—— (1982) 'An essay on the theory of production', in S.H. Hymans (ed.) (1982) *Economics and the World Around It* Ann Arbor, Michigan: University of Michigan Press, pp. 55–91.

Wright, S. (1959) 'Physiological genetics, ecology of populations, and natural selection', *Perspectives on Biological Medicine* 3: 107–51.

Wynne-Edwards, V.C. (1962) *Animal Dispersion in Relation to Social Behaviour*, Edinburgh: Oliver & Boyd.

10

INSTITUTIONS AND ECONOMIC PERFORMANCE[1]

Douglass C. North

ABSTRACT

Institutions provide the incentive structure of an economy and therefore the way they evolve shapes long-run economic performance.

Institutions, composed of rules, norms of behaviour, and the way they are enforced, provide the opportunity set in an economy which determines the kinds of purposive activity embodied in organizations (firms, trade unions, political bodies, and so forth) that will come into existence. If the institutions reward productive activity then the resultant organizations will find it worthwhile engaging in activities that induce economic growth. If, on the other hand, the institutional framework rewards redistributive and non-productive activities then organizations will maximize at those margins and the economy will not grow.

This chapter provides an analytical framework to explore the interrelationship between institutions, organizations, and the performance of economies over time.

INTRODUCTION

From the most primitive tribes to modern societies, human beings have always devised ways to structure human interaction. Institutions, whether solutions to simple problems of coordination (conventions), or to more complex forms of exchange such as those that characterize modern societies, provide a set of rules of the game that (together with other constraints) define and limit the choice set. They are the humanly devised constraints that shape human interaction so that when we wish to greet friends on the street, drive an automobile, buy oranges, borrow money, form a business, bury our dead, or whatever, we know or can learn how to do these things. It is easy to observe that institutions differ when we attempt to do the same things in a different country – Bangladesh for example.

That institutions affect the performance of economies is hardly controversial. That the differential performance of economies over

242

time is fundamentally influenced by the way institutions evolve is also not controversial. Yet neither current economic theory nor cliometric economic history shows much sign of appreciation of the role of institutions in economic performance. What has been missing is the development of an analytical framework to integrate institutional analysis into economics and economic history. This chapter and the larger study from which it is derived are an attempt to, at least partially, fill this void.

[The central argument of this chapter is that institutions structure incentives which shape the way economies evolve over time.] Specifically the institutional framework (of rules, norms, and enforcement characteristics) together with the traditional constraints (budget, technology) of economic theory determine the opportunities available at any moment of time. This opportunity set determines what kind of purposive organizations (firms, trade unions, farm groups, political bodies) will find it worthwhile (given wealth maximizing or other objectives of the organization) to come into existence. As these organizations acquire the skills and knowledge that will enable them to survive they will gradually alter the institutional framework. The kinds of knowledge and skills it is worthwhile acquiring will shape the evolution of the economy. If those skills lead to productivity improving outcomes the economy will grow but if, in fact, the knowledge and skills that pay off are those that make organizations more efficient at redistributive or rent seeking activities, then the economy will fail to grow. The process is incremental, an ongoing ceaseless result of myriads of decisions by the entrepreneurs of political and economic organizations that shape the long-run direction of societal change.

Institutions exist because it is costly to structure exchange and I therefore begin by examining the relationship between institutions and the costs of exchange. But as briefly noted above institutions are more than formal rules and therefore I explore the various dimensions of institutions. The central puzzle of institutional analysis is to account for the existence and persistence of 'inefficient' institutions which entails examining political institutions. Then I am ready to develop the model of institutional change briefly outlined above. Finally I summarize the contribution that institutional analysis can make to an understanding of economic performance over time.

INSTITUTIONS AND THE COSTS OF EXCHANGE

Ever since Adam Smith, economics has been built on the firm bedrock of the gains from trade. Until very recently, however, economists have assumed that exchange is costless; and even with the introduction of transaction cost analysis the implications of the costliness of transacting have not been understood by the profession. Let me state baldly the implications of transaction analysis for economics. The transaction sector (that part of transaction costs that goes through the market and therefore can be directly measured in monetary terms) made up approximately 45 per cent of United States GNP in 1970 (North and Wallis 1986). Those transaction costs are a large part of the total cost, the sum of the production and transaction costs, of operating an economy or an individual enterprise. Since institutions play a critical role in the cost of transacting (and also help determine production costs) their success in reducing total cost has been and continues to be a critical determinant of economic performance.

Why is it so costly to transact? The short answer is that it takes resources to define and enforce exchange agreements. Even if everyone had the same objective function (e.g. maximizing the firm's profits) transacting would take substantial resources; but in the context of individual wealth maximizing behaviour, and asymmetric information about the valuable attributes of what is being exchanged (or the performance of agents), the costs arising from transacting are a fundamental influence on economic activity.

A longer explanation of the costliness of transacting requires a more thorough examination of the nature of exchange. We owe to Lancaster (1966) and Becker (1965) the insight that a good or service is composed of a bundle of valuable attributes. It is only a short additional step to recognize that some attributes are physical (size, shape, colour, location, taste, etc.); others are property rights attributes (the right to use, to derive income from and to exclude others). To the extent that these attributes are separable they must be defined, that is measured, in order to be transferable in exchange. It is costly to measure and protect the rights over them (Barzel 1982). This argument holds equally for the performance of agents in hierarchical organizations. It is also costly to enforce agreements. If exchange consisted of the transfer of a uni-dimensional good at an instant of time (implicit features of neoclassical theory) then these issues would be of trivial importance. But enforcing the exchange of multidimensional goods across space and time poses fundamental dilemmas of cooperation.

Let me illustrate the problems involved in complex exchange by briefly summarizing in very oversimplified fashion some of the implications derived from game theory. Wealth maximizing individuals will usually find it worthwhile cooperating with other players when the play is repeated, when they possess complete information about the other players' past performance, and when there are small numbers of players. Such a crude summary disguises the richness (and ingenuity) of the results of an army of game theorists who have extended, elaborated, and modified (as well as found exceptions to) each of those qualifications to squeeze a great deal more out of them.

But let me turn the game upside down. Cooperation is difficult to sustain when the game is not repeated (or there is an end game), when information on the other players is lacking, and when there are large numbers of players. Now these polar extremes do in fact reflect real life contrasts. We do usually observe cooperative behaviour when individuals repeatedly interact, when they have a great deal of information about each other and when small numbers characterize the group. But at the other extreme, realizing the economic potential of the gains from trade in a high technology world of specialization and division of labour characterized by impersonal exchange is rare because one does not necessarily have repeat dealings, know the other party, nor deal with small numbers. In fact the pure essence of impersonal exchange is the antithesis of the conditions for game theoretic cooperation. The reason is that the costliness of measurement and enforcement as described above forecloses complex forms of exchange. Successful solutions have entailed the creation of institutions that in game theoretic terms raise the benefits of cooperative solutions or raise the costs of defection; and that in transaction cost terms lower transaction plus production costs per exchange so that the potential gains from trade become realizeable. Regardless of the approach, the key is institutions.

WHAT ARE INSTITUTIONS?

Institutions consist of informal constraints and formal rules, and of their enforcement characteristics. Together they provide the rules of the game of human interaction. As I have defined institutions they could include organizations since organizations also provide a structure to human interaction. Indeed when we are examining the costs that arise as a consequence of the institutional framework, they are the result of both the basic institutional framework and the organizations that arise in consequence of the institutional framework. A great deal of this chapter will blur the distinction between them. But conceptually they must be separated for reasons that are essential to understanding institutional change and will be elaborated below.

Let me illustrate my definition by analogy with the rules of the game of a team competitive sport. They too consist of formal written rules and typically informal unwritten codes of conduct that underlie and supplement formal rules, such as not deliberately injuring a key player on the opposing team. These rules and informal codes are sometimes violated and punishment is enacted. Therefore, an essential part of the game is the likelihood of ascertaining violations and the severity (costliness) of punishment. Taken together the formal and informal rules and the effectiveness of enforcement shape the whole character of the game. Some teams are successful as a consequence of (and therefore have the reputation for) constantly violating rules and thereby intimidating the opposing team. Whether that strategy pays off is a function of the effectiveness of monitoring and the severity of punishment. Conversely sometimes codes of conduct, good sportsmanship, constrain players even though they could get away with successful violations. It should be noted that it is one thing to analyse the rules that define the way the game is played but it is something else to model the organization and strategy that the team will develop as a response to the rules. Now let me return to institutions to elaborate on these common elements.

Informal constraints include conventions that evolve as solutions to problems of coordination and that all parties are interested in having maintained; norms of behaviour that are recognized codes of conduct; and self-imposed codes of conduct such as standards of honesty or integrity. Conventions are self-enforcing. Norms of behaviour are enforced by the second party (retaliation) or by third party (societal sanctions or coercive authority) and their effectiveness will depend on the effectiveness of enforcement. Models of such exchange structures make up a large share of the game theory literature.

Self-imposed codes of conduct, unlike conventions and norms of behaviour, do not entail wealth maximizing behaviour but rather the sacrifices of wealth or income for other values. Their importance in constraining choices is the subject of substantial controversy – for example in modelling voting behaviour in the United States Congress – (see Kalt and Zupan 1984). Most of the controversy has missed the crucial reason of why such behaviour can be and is important. And that is, that institutions, frequently deliberately, sometimes accidentally, lower the cost to individuals of such behaviour and can make ideas matter a great deal. Votes may not matter individually but in the aggregate they matter and they cost the voter very little; legislators commonly find enough ways by strategic voting to vote their personal preferences rather than those of the electorate; and judges with lifetime tenure are deliberately shielded from interest group pressures. In each of the above illustrations the institutional framework has altered the cost to the individual of expressing his or her convictions. In each case the choices that were made may be different than they would be if the individual bore the full cost that resulted from those actions. The lower the cost we incur for our convictions (ideas, dogmas) the more they contribute to outcomes (see Nelson and Silberberg 1987, for empirical evidence).

Formal rules differ in degree from informal constraints. On a continuum from taboos, customs, traditions at one end to written constitutions at the other end of the scale the gradual transition in history has been uneven but unidirectional. Most conspicuously, both the sources and the rate of change are different as between formal rules and informal constraints. Formal rules are altered by deliberate action of political, judicial or economic bodies. While informal constraints are certainly influenced by alterations in formal rules the sources of change are much more complex, much less understood, and the rate of change very different. This difference has important implications for institutional change.

Formal economic rules are typically nested in a hierarchy, from constitutions to statute and common law to specific contracts and by-laws of organizations; they are more costly to alter as we go higher on the ladder. Formal political rules specify the hierarchy of the polity from basic decision rules to agenda control. Economic rules define property rights, that is the bundle of rights over the use and the income to be derived from property, and the rights of alienation. Both political and economic rules are devised as a consequence of the bargaining strength of those making the decision rules; marginal changes occur with changes in bargaining strength (to be discussed below). But given the initial bargaining strength of the parties the function of the rules is to facilitate exchange, both political and economic.

It is the effectiveness of the enforcement of agreements that is the single most crucial determinant of economic performance and the key difference that separates First from Third World economies. The ability to enforce contracts across time and space is the central underpinning of 'efficient' markets.

The costliness of defining and enforcing agreements reflects the effectiveness of the institutions. The ability at low cost to measure what is being exchanged and to enforce agreements across time and space requires complex institutional structures; conversely, the inability at low cost to measure and enforce agreements has been a consequence of institutions that make it costly to transact (or produce). Successful economic growth is the story of the evolution of more complex institutions that make possible cooperative exchange relations extending over long periods of time, among individuals without personal knowledge of each other. Institutional reliability means we can have confidence in outcomes increasingly remote from our personal knowledge. The combination of formal rules, informal constraints, and enforcement characteristics of institutions defines the humanly devised constraints and, together with the traditional constraints of standard theory, the choice set. The property rights literature has long since demonstrated that different property rights produce different outcomes; but because it has not taken into account both the effectiveness of enforcement and informal constraints, that approach is incomplete and at least partly misleading. The choices as reflected in contracts between exchanging parties actually will reflect not only formal constraints, but also the uncertainties arising from the effectiveness and costliness of enforcement. Equally conventions, informal community sanctions, will play a part in the exchange. Therefore, to understand the choices available in

247

an exchange one must take into account all the dimensions that make up an institution.

INSTITUTIONS AND TRANSACTION COSTS

Let me illustrate the relationship between institutions (formal rules, informal constraints, and enforcement characteristics) and transaction costs in a specific example – the exchange of a residential property in modern United States.

In the seller's utility are the price, terms, and security of the contractual obligation; that is, the likelihood that the buyer will live up to the contract *ex post*. The value of the residence to the buyer is a function not only of price and credit terms but also of the attributes that are transferred with the sale. Some, such as the legal rights that are and are not transferred, the dimensions of the property and house, are easily measured; others, such as the general features of the property, are readily observed on inspections. But still others, such as the maintenance and upkeep costs and the characteristics of neighbours, may be far more difficult to ascertain. Equally, the security of property against default, expropriation, uncertain title, or theft will vary according to the difficulty of ascertaining the likelihood of each and therefore its importance.

Now in the traditional neoclassical paradigm, with perfect information, i.e. zero transaction costs, the value of the asset that is transferred assumes not only perfect information but perfectly secure property rights. In that case, since both buyer and seller have been able to costlessly ascertain the value of all the attributes (both physical and property rights) and there is no uncertainty or insecurity of property rights, the standard supply and demand models of housing with zero transaction costs would define the value of the asset. In fact, because all of the above-mentioned attributes influence the value of the residence to the buyer and seller, the smaller the discount (i.e. the smaller the transaction costs incurred) from the idealized neoclassical model, the more perfect the market. It is institutions in the aggregate that define and determine the size of the discount, and it is transaction costs that the buyer and seller incur that reflect that institutional framework.

The transaction costs of the transfer are partly market costs, such as legal fees, realtors fees, interest charges, title insurance, credit rating searches; and partly the costs of time each party must devote to gathering information, the costs of searching, etc. Obtaining information about crime rates, police protection, security systems entail search costs for the buyer. To the degree that the buyer's utility function is adversely affected by noisy neighbours, pets, etc. it will pay to invest time in ascertaining neighbourhood characteristics and the norms and conventions that shape neighbourhood interactions.

The particular institutional matrix of this housing market consists first of all of a hierarchy of legal rules, derived from the US Constitution and the powers delegated to the states. State laws defining the conveyance characteristics of real property, zoning laws restricting which rights can be transferred, common and statute law undergirding, defining, or restricting a host of voluntary organizations: all of these influence transaction costs. Realtors, title insurance, credit bureaus, savings and loan associations that affect the mortgage market all will be influenced. The efficiency of these organizations is a function of the structure of property rights and enforcement (such as title insurance costs) and the structure of the capital market (including both voluntary organizations and governmental organizations, guarantees, and subsidies). Equally important are a range of informal constraints: conventions, norms, and codes of conduct that broadly supplement and reinforce the formal rules. They range from conventions of neighbourhood conduct to ethical norms defining degrees of honesty in information exchange between the variety of parties involved.

My description has emphasized institutions that lower the costs of transacting but some – such as rules that restrict entry, require useless inspections, raise information costs, or make property rights less secure – in fact raise transaction costs. Institutions everywhere are a 'mixed bag' of those that lower the costs and those that raise them. The US residential housing market is a relatively efficient market in which on balance the institutions induce low cost transacting.

The fundamental implication of the foregoing illustration is that the discount from the frictionless exchange envisioned in economic theory will be greater to the degree that the institutional structure allows third parties to influence the value of attributes that are in the utility function of the buyer. These could be the behaviour of neighbours, the likelihood of theft, the possibility of changes by local authorities in zoning ordinances that may affect the value of the property, etc. The greater the uncertainty of the buyer, the lower the value of the asset. Likewise, the institutional structure will equally determine the risks to the seller that the contract will be fulfilled or that the seller will be indemnified in case of default. It is worth emphasizing that the uncertainties described above with respect to security of rights are the critical distinction between the relatively efficient and secure markets of high income countries and the insecure and costly nature of these transactions in economies both in the past and in the present Third World.

INSTITUTIONS AND TRANSACTION AND PRODUCTION COSTS

Institutions play an even more decisive role in the production of goods and services since institutional structures affect both production and transaction costs; the latter via the direct connection between institutions and transaction costs as described in the above illustration; the former by influencing the technology employed. All the usual problems of measurement and enforcement obtain; that is institutions shape the consequent transaction and production costs via the structure of property rights, the effectiveness of the courts and the judicial system, and the complementary development of voluntary organization and norms.

Specifically the firm's entrepreneur must be able to ascertain the quantity and quality of inputs and outputs. Since in the neoclassical firm these can be obtained costlessly, the contrast between a hypothetical neoclassical firm and a real firm is striking. The former was little more than a production function without any costs of organization, supervision, coordination, monitoring, metering, etc. However a real-life firm must purchase inputs that constantly require measurements and metering if it is to produce output of constant quality since variability in quality will, *ceteris paribus*, adversely affect demand for its product. Otherwise consumers (or if it is an intermediate good, producers) must (when quality is variable) devote resources to ascertaining quality; hence producers who can guarantee constant quality will be favoured.

These conditions (i.e. costless measurement and enforcement) are implicitly assumed in what we call efficient factor and product markets but their existence entails a complex set of institutions that encourage factor mobility, the acquisition of skills, uninterrupted production, rapid and low cost transmission of information, and the invention and innovation of new technologies. Realizing all these conditions is a tall order never completely filled since, as with the institutions of exchange described above, the actual institutional framework is a mixed bag of those institutions that promote productivity raising activities and those that provide barriers to entry, encourage monopolistic restrictions, and impede the low cost flow of information.

We have only to contrast the organization of production in a Third World economy with a First World economy to be impressed by the consequences of overall poorly defined and/or ineffective property rights. Not only will the institutional framework result in high costs of transacting in the former but also insecure property rights will result in using technologies that employ little fixed capital and do not entail long term agreements. Firms will typically be small (except those operated or 'protected' by the government). Moreover such mundane problems as an inability to get spare parts or a two-year wait to get a telephone installed will necessitate a different organization of production than in an advanced country. Now it is usually true that a sufficient bribe may exist that will get quick delivery of spare parts through the maze of import controls or get rapid telephone installation but the resultant 'shadow' transaction cost does significantly alter relative prices and consequently the technology employed.

Even with the relatively secure property rights that exist in high income countries it is frequently the case that a technical combination that involves costly monitoring may be less 'efficient' than a technique that has lower physical output but less variance in the product quality or lower costs of monitoring the worker. Because much of the recent transaction cost literature implies that institutions only determine transaction costs and techniques only determine production costs let me illustrate three different choices arising from the interplay between techniques, institutions, production costs and transaction costs to make clear that the relationship among them is more complex.

1 A contention of Marxist writers such as Edwards, (1979) is that deliberate deskilling of the labour force occurred during the early twentieth century in the United States. That is, employers adopted capital intensive techniques which eliminated the demand for highly skilled workers and replaced them with semi-skilled or unskilled workers. The explanation for this choice is that the bargaining power of skilled workers enabled them to strategically disrupt the production process, which given the 'high speed throughput' (Chandler's term, 1977) of modern technology was enormously costly. Long-run total cost could be reduced by using less skilled workers who were without the bargaining power to disrupt production. In this case a new technique was introduced to lower transaction costs.

2 Unitizing an oil field, that is creating an organization with the coercive power and monitoring authority to allocate the output of the oil field, raises transaction costs (because of the resources that must be devoted to creating and maintaining an organization and then to monitoring compliance). At the same time it reduces production costs (the result of more efficient pumping and recovery) to an extent that more than offsets the rise in transaction costs (Libecap and Wiggins, 1985). In this case an institutional change raised transaction costs which were more than compensated by lower production costs.

3 Andrea Shepard (1987) describes the deliberate policy of a semi-conductor manufacturer who licenses the design of new chips to competitors, so that customers can be assured that the chip manufacturer will not be able to hold up customers who adopt the new design. By alleviating customers' concerns, this policy enhances demand for the product. While this policy lowers transaction costs, it does so at the sacrifice of productive efficiency, since both scale economies and 'learning curve' effects are lost to competing firms.

Informal institutional constraints frequently play a major role with respect to the quantity and quality of labour output. While Marxists long

251

ago recognized that the quantity of labour input could not be mechanically transformed via a production function into the quantity and quality of output, this subject has only recently become a major focus of economists' concern (at least partially a consequence in recent years of the quality difference in labour output between Japanese and American automobile manufacturers). Conventions about output, forms of organization designed to encourage worker participation and cooperation, and attempts to select labour with an ideological commitment to hard work have all become recent research agendas in industrial organization. The unique feature of labour markets is that institutions are devised to take into account that the quantity and quality of output is influenced by the attitude of the productive factor (hence investing in persuasion, morale building, etc. is a substitute at the margin for investing in more monitoring).

THE SOURCES OF INSTITUTIONAL INEFFICIENCY

The major focus of the literature on institutions and transaction costs has been on institutions as efficient solutions to problems of organization in a competitive framework (Williamson 1975, 1985). Thus market exchange, franchising, or vertical integration are efficient solutions to the complex problems confronting the entrepreneur in various competitive environments. Valuable as this work has been, it leaves out the most important contribution which institutional analysis can make to economics: to explain the diverse performance of economies. How do we account for the poverty of nations, the failure of some economies to grow, or for that matter the differential performance of sectors in an economy? Institutions structure incentives, which in turn determine the performance of economies. The formal economic constraints (property rights) are specified and enforced by political institutions and the literature described above simply takes those as a given. While there is a large literature on regulation and even modelling political outcomes (for example Becker 1983, 1985), it is essentially a-institutional and therefore fails to recognize that different political institutions will affect the efficiency of political exchange and hence economic outcomes.

In an earlier study (North 1981) I argued that there were two basic reasons why rulers typically produced inefficient property rights (defined here simply as rules which do not produce increases in output). First, the competitive constraint on the ruler means that a ruler will avoid offending powerful constituents with close access to alternative rulers. He will agree to a property rights structure favourable to those groups regardless of its effects on efficiency. Second is a transaction cost constraint. While efficient property rights would lead to higher societal income they may not lead to more tax revenues because of higher costs of monitoring, metering and collecting. Granting guilds monopolies in Colbert's France may not have been efficient but it did improve tax collecting as compared to an unregulated decentralized economy.

The same two constraints have obtained throughout history (and continue to obtain). Inefficient (as defined above) economic institutions are the rule not the exception. It is not that political entrepreneurs would not like to have economic growth; it is that the institutions that have evolved do not create conditions of credible commitment that makes low-cost transacting possible. Moreover the process of institutional change does not result in evolutionary competition weeding out inefficient institutions in favour of efficient ones (or at least the tendency is so weak and diffuse as to permit the persistence of inefficient economies for very long periods of time). Let us see why.

HOW DO INSTITUTIONS CHANGE?

Understanding institutional change entails an understanding of (1) the stability characteristics of institutions, (2) the sources of change, (3) the agents of change, and (4) the direction change.

A basic function of institutions is to provide stability and continuity by dampening the effects of relative price changes. It is institutional stability that makes possible complex exchange across space and time. A necessary condition for efficient markets which underlie high income societies are channels of exchange, both political and economic, which make possible credible agreements. This condition is accomplished by the complexity of the set of constraints that constitute institutions; by rules nested in a hierarchy, each level more costly to change than the previous one. In the United States the hierarchy moves from constitutional rules to statute law and common law to individual contracts. Political rules are also nested in a hierarchy even at the level of specific bills before Congress. Both the structure of committees and agenda control assure that the status quo is favoured over change. Informal constraints are even more important anchors of stability. They are extensions elaborations and qualifications of rules that 'solve' numerous exchange problems not completely covered by formal rules and hence have tenacious survival ability. They allow people to go about the everyday process of making exchanges without the necessity of thinking out exactly at each point and in each instance the terms of exchange. Routines, customs, traditions and culture are words we use to denote the persistence of informal constraints. It is the complex interaction of rules and informal constraints, together with the way they are enforced, that shapes our daily living and directs us in the mundane activities that dominate our lives. It is important to stress that these stability features in no way guarantee that the institutions are efficient (as defined above).

Stability is a necessary condition for complex human interaction but it is not a sufficient condition for efficiency.

One major source of institutional change has been fundamental changes in relative prices (see North and Thomas 1973, for illustration) but another has been changes in preferences. I know of no way to explain the demise of slavery in the nineteenth century in an interest group model. The growing abhorrence on the part of civilized human beings of one person owning another not only spawned the anti-slavery movements but through the institutional mechanism of voting resulted in its elimination. It is not that interest groups did not use the abolitionist movement to further their interests. They did. But the success of the interest groups did entail the ideological support of the voter. The voter paid only the price of going to the polls to express his conviction and the slave owner had no feasible way to bribe or pay off voters to prevent them from expressing their beliefs. As noted earlier, institutions make ideas matter.

The agent of change is the entrepreneur – political or economic. So far I have left organizations and their entrepreneurs out of the analysis and the definition of institutions has focused on the rules of the game rather than the players. As noted at the beginning of this chapter this separation of the institutions from organizations was deliberate. Left out was the purposive activity of human beings to achieve objectives which in turn result in altering constraints. Organizations and learning alter outcomes, but how?

Let me begin with organization. More than half a century ago Coase (1937) argued that transaction costs are the basis for the existence of the firm. That is, if information and enforcement were costless, it is hard to envision a significant role for organization. What is it about transaction costs that leads to organization? The answers have ranged from the firm being a form of exploitation (Marglin 1974), to a response to asset specificity (Williamson 1975, 1985) to a response to measurement costs (Barzel 1982). Whatever the merits of these alternatives (and they are not altogether mutually exclusive), they all focus on the trees but not the forest. Organizations are a response to the institutional structure of societies, and, in consequence, the major cause of the alteration of that institutional structure.

The institutional constraints together with the traditional constraints of economic theory define the potential wealth maximizing opportunities of entrepreneurs (political or economic). If the constraints result in the highest pay-offs in the economy being criminal activity, or the pay-off to the firm is highest from sabotaging or burning down a competitor, or to a union from engaging in slowdowns and makework, then we can expect that the organization will be shaped to maximize at those margins. On the other hand if the pay-offs come from productivity enhancing activities then economic growth will result. In either case the entrepreneur and his or her organization will invest in acquiring knowledge, coordination and 'learning by doing skills' in order to enhance the profitable potential. As the organization evolves to capture the potential returns it will gradually alter the institutional constraints themselves. It will do so either indirectly, via the interaction between maximizing behaviour and its effect on gradually eroding or modifying informal constraints; or directly, via investing in altering the formal rules. The relative rate of return on investing within the formal constraints or devoting resources to altering the constraints will reflect the structure of the polity, the pay-offs to altering the rules, and the costs of political investment.

INSTITUTIONAL CHANGE ILLUSTRATED

Let me briefly expand on this model of institutional change by reframing a familiar story in American economic history – the growth of the economy in the nineteenth century. The basic institutional framework that had been carried over from England had not only encouraged decentralized and local political autonomy but also provided low cost economic transacting through fee-simple ownership of land (with some early exceptions in proprietary colonies) and secure property rights. The post revolutionary enactments of the Northwest Ordinance and the Constitution codified, elaborated, and modified colonial institutions in the light of contemporary issues (and the bargaining strength of the players) but created an institutional environment that broadly induced the development of economic and political organizations that promoted increased productivity and economic growth (both directly and indirectly by an induced demand for education, for example). But it should be carefully noted that this institutional framework also spawned some organizations and policies that raised transaction costs and hence reduced efficiency (the Know-Nothing party or tariffs for example). Moreover as these political and economic organizations evolved to take advantage of profitable opportunities they gradually altered the basic institutional framework. Sometimes these alterations made the basic institutional framework even more conducive to productive activity; sometimes however they raised the rate of return to unproductive activity; sometimes the results were unanticipated by the entrepreneurs (political or economic). Exogenous forces such as changes in political or economic conditions in the rest of the world induced changes in the American economy by altering relative political or economic prices to domestic political and economic entrepreneurs and their organizations and hence leading them to actions that altered the institutional framework. The story is familiar, but, by focusing on the interaction between the rules and the players, this approach has, I believe, the promise of telling a far more interesting history than before. More interesting because it can account for the path of historical change.

Institutional change therefore is an incremental process in which short-run profitable opportunities cumulatively create the long-run path of change. The long-run consequences are often unintended for two reasons. First, the entrepreneurs are seldom interested in the larger (external to them) consequences but the direction of their investment influences the extent to which there is investment in adding to or disseminating the stock of knowledge, encouraging or discouraging factor mobility, etc. Second, there is frequently a significant difference between intended outcomes and actual outcomes. Outcomes frequently diverge from intentions because of the limited capabilities of individuals and the complexity of the problems to be solved. The path of institutional change that determines the long-run evolution of societies is shaped by constraints derived from the past and the (sometimes unanticipated) consequences of the innumerable incremental choices of entrepreneurs which continually modify those constraints. Path dependence means that history matters, that it is a consequence of incremental institutional change and that it can account for the divergent paths of economies. Moreover given the tendency of polities to produce inefficient property rights, economic decline or stagnation can persist since there will not typically develop a feedback that will create organizations with the incentive to invest in productive activity. Instead the 'perverse' incentives will generate organizations and hence entrepreneurs with economic and political bargaining strength who will find it profitable to pursue economically inefficient paths. Indeed it is the increasing returns characteristic of an institutional matrix that produces path dependence. The network externalities that arise from the symbiotic relationship between the institutions of an economy and polity and the consequent organizations makes fundamental alterations of economic paths difficult. The contrasting histories of England, its North American colonies and their subsequent development (briefly outlined above) with Spain (and Portugal) and subsequent Latin American development is striking.

In the former the institutional framework that evolved was broadly conducive to the creation of organizations that induced political democracy, stability and economic growth. In the latter, centralized bureaucratic political controls and detailed regulation of the economies carried over to the colonies and persisted even after independence. The long-run consequences were not only political instability but the relatively poor economic performance that has characterized two centuries of Latin American history. Typically the opportunities that were open to political and economic entrepreneurs were policies that reinforced the existing strictures. This was so because the opportunities consisted of marginal changes that were shaped by an overall institutional framework that overwhelmingly favoured such institutional policies. But this is not the whole story. With the revolutions, formal rules were instituted to alter the polities and economies. The ideological winds from the American Revolution did induce laws patterned after the US Constitution and economic legislation was enacted to reduce or eliminate regulatory constraints. Yet the consequences were radically different. It is the complex of formal rules, the way they are enforced and the informal constraints that together define the institutional framework. In the Latin American institutional environment, changes in the formal rules alone were not sufficient to redirect polities and economies in a new direction in the context of the persistence of the historically derived informal constraints.

While the contrasting 'path dependent' stories are clear enough, the incremental institutional and organizational evolutions are far from being well understood. It is relatively easy to trace the specific evolution of organizations and the way by which their development influenced the institutional framework (see, for example, North and Rutten 1987 on the evolution of US land policy). But the organizational consequences were not unidirectional (as I have stressed above) and the aggregate effects on economic and political performance were almost always a complicated multidimensional story.

Institutional change is overwhelmingly incremental; but discontinuous institutional change does occur in the form of revolution. It would take me far beyond the limits of this essay to deal properly with this topic, but one important point follows from the preceding analysis. That is that revolutionary change is seldom as revolutionary as it appears on the surface (or in the Utopian vision of revolutionaries). The reason is not just that the 'half-life' of ideological commitment tends to be short but that the formal rules change while the informal constraints do not. In consequence there develops an ongoing tension between informal constraints and the new formal rules, many of which are inconsistent with each other. The long-run resolution tends to be some restructuring of both and an outcome that retains or even recreates some of the pre-revolutionary formal constraints.

INSTITUTIONS AND ECONOMICS

I shall not elaborate on the already rich literature that has sprung up from institutional and transaction cost analysis in industrial organization, public finance, public choice but instead focus on the broader contribution that is still to be undertaken.

Institutional modelling

The most general contribution that institutional modelling can make to economic theorizing is to make clear and explicit the institutionally specific context within which the model holds. Implicit in most economic models are specific political rules, property rights and enforcement characteristics that are critical to the outcomes. Changes in these would produce different outcomes. Economists, however, seem seldom to be aware of just how specific their model is to the institutional constraints (how would it work in Bangladesh for example).

Even more important is that specific institutional constraints dictate the margins at which organizations operate and hence make intelligible the interplay between the rules of the game and the behaviour of the actors. If organizations – firms, trade unions, farm groups, political parties, regulatory agencies to name a few – devote their efforts to unproductive activity, it is the institutional constraints that have provided the incentive structure for such activity. Third World countries are poor because the institutional constraints define a set of pay-offs to political/economic activity that do not encourage productive activity. Socialist economies are just beginning to appreciate that the underlying institutional framework is the source of their current poor performance and are attempting to grapple with ways to restructure the institutional framework to redirect incentives that will in turn direct organizations along productivity increasing paths.

Behavioural models

A self-conscious incorporation of institutions into economic theory will force economists to question the behavioural models that underlie the discipline. If neoclassical economics has no institutions in the models, it is because the behavioural assumption, which incorporates characteristics about human behaviour as well as about the information that the players have, does not require it. But since institutions really exist, it is incumbent on the economist to ask searching questions about the implications of institutions for the behavioural model that the economist employs. The role of ideology, for example, plays an important part once we recognize that people have subjective perceptions about the world around them and that expressing convictions in various institutional contexts frequently can be done at negligible cost to the individual. Likewise when our behavioural models incorporate the incompleteness of our information and our limited ability to process that information, then we will understand why we need to develop the regularized patterns of human interaction that we call institutions and why they may be very inadequate or far from optimal in any sense of the term. The nascent cooperation between psychologists and economists offers the promise of enriching our behavioural models (see Hogarth and Reder 1986).

Institutions and economic models

Incorporating institutions in their models should make economists aware that ideas matter. Institutions structure human interaction so that we frequently and in many critical choice contexts can express our ideas, ideologies, and dogmas at little or no cost to ourselves. The result is to frequently produce different outcomes than those derived from interest group models in economics and public choice.

Integration

The integration of political and economic theory is essential in a world where government plays such an immense role in choices. The key to such integration is the modelling of political and economic institutions that will permit us to explore in theoretical terms the interaction between these two institutional structures and to derive in consequence real political economy models in macroeconomics and other areas in which government plays a critical role.

Understanding institutions and change

If an understanding of the nature of institutions can make an important contribution to redefining the parameters and choice set in economic theory, an understanding of institutional change offers the prospect of getting a handle on long-run economic change – something that has so far eluded traditional economics. The central role that institutions play in connecting the past with the present and the future, the incremental character of institutional change and the path-dependent process together provide an opening wedge to undertake a meaningful exploration of economic performance over time.

The implications for economic history are, I believe, clear. The wedding of institutional analysis with cliometric economic history makes possible a far richer history than previously. The contribution of cliometrics has been the use of sophisticated quantitative methods, price theory, and the underlying assumption of neoclassical theory of scarcity and hence competition. But the result was fundamentally ahistorical. History must explain the way by which societies, polities and economies evolve through time. It is institutional analysis that connects change in economies over time, ties the past to the present and future, and relates the separate parts of an economy to each other.

259

The implications are equally fundamental to an understanding of economic development. Certainly one of the failures of the social sciences in the post-World War II era has been its inability to develop useful models that would account for the poor performance of Third World economies and in consequence provide a policy guide to deal with economic development. Neoclassical economic theory was not intended to account for such poor performance and it does not. It simply assumes away all the relevant issues. It is institutions that provide the key constraints and therefore shape incentives, and it is the interaction between the institutional framework and the organizations that are a response to that framework that shapes the evolution of economies. Institutional theory focuses on the critical problems for development of human organization and the problems of achieving cooperative solutions to human interaction.

It is only appropriate that an economic historian should conclude this chapter by making what should by now be an obvious point. Institutional analysis should place history in a more central role in economics, not only because it sheds light on a critical parameter held constant by the economist – institutions, but also because the constraints within which choice-making occurs are derived from the past, and with an appreciation of the way those constraints have evolved, we can have a far better understanding of the choice set today and the institutionally specific context within which the economists's model holds.

NOTE

1 This chapter is drawn from, and is a drastic condensation of, parts of a book by the author entitled, *Institutions, Institutional Change and Economic Performance* (1990). An earlier version of this chapter was prepared for a conference on 'Government and Economic Growth and Development' held at the State University of New York at Buffalo under the auspices of the Institute for the Study of Free Enterprise Systems.

REFERENCES

Barzel, Y. (1982) 'Measurement cost and the organization of markets', *Journal of Law and Economics* 25: 27–48.

Becker, G.S. (1965) 'A theory of the allocation of time' *Economic Journal* 75: 493–517.

—— (1983) A theory of competition among pressure groups for influence', *Quarterly Journal of Economics* XCVIII: 371–400.

—— (1985) 'Public policies, pressure groups, and dead weight costs', *Journal of Public Economics* 28: 329–47.

Chandler, A. (1977) *The Visible Hand*, Cambridge, Mass. Belknap Press.

Coase, R.H. (1937) 'The nature of the firm', *Economica* 4, 386–405.

Edwards, R. (1979) *Contested Terrain*, London: Heinemann.

Hogarth, R.M. and Reder, M.W. (eds) (1986) 'The behavioral foundations of economic theory', *Journal of Business* Volume 57, special issue.

Kalt, M.A. and Zupan, M.A. (1984) 'Capture and ideology in the economic theory of politics', *American Economic Review* 75: 279–300.

Lancaster, K. (1966) 'A new approach to consumer theory', *Journal of Political Economy* 74: 132–57.

Libecap, G.C. and Wiggins, S.N. (1985) 'The influence of private contractual failure on regulation: the case of oil field Unitization', *Journal of Political Economy* 93: 690–714.

Marglin, S. (1974) 'What do bosses do?', *Review of Radical Political Economy* 6: 33–60.

Nelson, D. and Silberberg, E. (1987) 'Ideology and Legislator shirking', *Economic Inquiry* 25: 15–25.

North, D.C. (1981) *Structure and Change in Economic History*, New York: W.W. Norton.

—— (1990) *Institutions, Institutional Change and Economic Performance*, Cambridge: Cambridge University Press.

—— and Rutten, A. (1987) 'The Northwest Ordinance in historical perspective' in D. Klingerman and R. Vedder (eds) *Essays on the Old Northwest*, Athens, Ohio: Ohio University Press.

—— and Thomas, R.P. (1973) *The Rise of the Western World: A New Economic History*, Cambridge: Cambridge University Press.

—— and Wallis, J. (1986) 'Measuring the transactions sector in the American economy, 1870–1979', in S.L. Engerman and R.E. Gallman, (eds) *Long-Term Factors in American Economic Growth*, Chicago: University of Chicago Press.

Shepard, A. (1987) 'Licensing to enhance demand for new technologies', *Rand Journal of Economics* 18: 360–68.

Williamson, O.E. (1975) *Markets and Heirarchies: Analysis and Antitrust Implications*, New York: Free Press.

—— (1985) *The Economic Institutions of Capitalism*, New York: Free Press.

Part V
CONCLUSION

11

MODELLING RATIONALITY, INSTITUTIONS AND PROCESSES IN ECONOMIC THEORY

Christian Knudsen

ABSTRACT

This chapter argues that the renewed interest in institutions and the emergence of neo-institutionalism within economic theory can mainly be attributed to different fields of applied research. In these fields it has been necessary to look far more closely at institutional relations, as well as at those processes which have resulted in the equilibria that are the central object of study in pure economic theory. Institutions and processes have traditionally held the status of *ad hoc* models which were intended to supplement the formal equilibrium theory. In recent decades, however, these *ad hoc* models have developed into independent 'neo-institutionalist' theories and research programmes. A typology of the most important of these contributions is set up in order to clarify how the concepts of rationality, institution, and process are modelled in each individual case. In this way we can attempt to clarify the differences between the individual neo-institutionalist contributions, along with their relation to orthodox theory.

1 THE REDISCOVERY OF INSTITUTIONS IN ECONOMIC THEORY

Over the last two decades economic theorists have been increasingly absorbed with analysing the origins of institutions and their significance for economic and technological development. Descriptions such as 'new' institutionalism or 'neo-institutionalism' are often seen used in connection with analyses of this kind. The renewed interest in institutions does not though appear to be directly associated with a revival of 'older' or 'classical' institutionalism. These descriptions are normally used in reference to the German historical school, known from the so-called

'*Methodenstreit*' at the end of the last century, or to American institutionalism, associated with names such as Thorstein Veblen, John Commons, Wesley Mitchell, etc. Despite the frequent use of the term 'neo-classical institutionalism' in this connection, it does not appear to have been any innovations in orthodox neoclassical theory which are behind this.

On the contrary, the revived interest for institutions within economics appears to originate within fields of applied research. The use of formal equilibrium models in a practical and empirical context has therefore made it necessary to supplement formal theory with what Benjamin Ward (1972) described as 'storytelling' and what Richard Nelson and Sidney Winter (1982) described as 'appreciative theory'. This is a form of theorizing in which the very abstract and formal equilibrium analysis is supplemented with *ad hoc* structures and 'storytelling' so that it can be applied in concrete empirical contexts. In this way it has been attempted to remedy the lack of institutional detail within orthodox equilibrium analysis and its consistent suppression of the very disequilibrium processes which produced the equilibria studied in formal theory.

As an example of this kind of 'storytelling', we can just call attention to the frequent use by economists of arguments concerning selection processes as grounds for the extensive study of states of equilibrium, instead of studying the processes themselves. That is to say, the question of selection has held the status of a story which should have been regarded as an *ad hoc* model alongside the formal theory in order to encourage its application, and not as a part of it. The argument was simply this: the states of equilibrium which were under examination could be regarded as a summary of a processes of selection, which had as its result the state of equilibrium which was being studied. When the process therefore came to be regarded as a 'story' alongside the formal model, the main reason for this was that the story was not open-to formal analysis in the same way that the equilibrium was.

Still, over recent decades there has been an increase in attempts to develop these *ad hoc* 'stories' – concerning disequilibrium processes and concrete institutional details – into autonomous models and in some cases even into separate research programmes. It is therefore the thesis of this chapter that the renewed interest in institutions is due to breakthroughs in applied fields of research – where converting 'stories' into independent models and in some cases into entirely new research programmes is concerned. This thesis seems also to be confirmed by the widespread use of terms such as 'new economic history', 'new industrial organization', 'new comparative economic systems', 'law and economics', etc., whenever this more recent institutionalist literature is referred to.

2 COMMON THEMES BEHIND NEO-INSTITUTIONALIST CONTRIBUTIONS

Precisely because neo-institutionalism has its origins in such seemingly separate fields of research, we may consider what the integrating force behind these relatively diffuse contributions is. In a much-quoted essay, Richard Langlois asserts (1986a) that there are common themes behind some heterodox theories and traditions in economics (for instance the Austrian school, evolutionary theory, behaviouralism, transaction cost theory, post-Keynesianism, neo-institutionalists within game theory, etc.), which motivates him to speak of a movement or a 'programme' within economics for which he suggests the term 'new institutional economics'. These common themes, which are claimed to give such a programme some intellectual structure, are:

1 A broadening of the behavioural foundations of orthodox economic theory.
2 A greater emphasis on the study of economic processes in preference to the preoccupation with equilibrium analyses in orthodox theory.
3 The traditional emphasis of economics on studies of market institutions should be expanded to include other types of institution.

Theme 1

It is attempted to indicate below how these three themes are related. Where the first theme is concerned, most neo-institutionalists are meant to be united in their efforts to replace the maximization concept of orthodox theory with a broader concept of rationality. Langlois (1986b) suggests that the common, unifying feature of the various new institutionalist economists is their use of what Karl Popper refers to as the method of situational analysis – assuming that the agents take action which is reasonable in or appropriate to the situations in which they find themselves. However, in this contribution (1986b) Langlois is not very specific as to how this method of situational analysis encompasses the different alternatives to maximization rationality that have been used as the behavioural foundations of different 'neo-institutionalist' theories. For example, Oliver Williamson bases his theory of transaction cost on Herbert Simon's assumption of *bounded rationality*. That is to say, the decision-making competence of economic agents will usually be seen as a scarce resource in relation to the relatively complex decision-making problems they are confronted with. Other neo-institutionalist theories have diverged from orthodox maximization hypothesis not only in their acceptance of bounded rationality, but also in their belief that behaviour is determined by *rules*, *routines*, or *ideologies*. In this case the maximization principle is not merely replaced with a *bounded*, but also with a *procedural* concept of rationality. This involves not linking the question of rationality to an evaluation of individual actions, instead it becomes a question of whether the procedures or rules that agents apply in order to reach decisions are sensible or rational.[2] The question is now, whether these two concepts can be encompassed under the method of situational analysis and how this method is related to the concept of maximization rationality. In their contribution to this volume Richard Langlois and Lázló Csontos have made some progress in answering these questions.

Theme 2

The second theme which, according to Langlois, characterizes neo-institutionalists as opposed to more orthodox economists, is their commitment to viewing economic phenomena from a 'process perspective'. In economic research, large resources have traditionally been devoted to the purely logical or axiomatic study of states of equilibrium. However, only few resources have been devoted to analysing the process *per se*, through which these states might have emerged. This unequal distribution of resources for research has actually gone so far, that many economists have perceived the two questions to be more or less independent of one another. However, in a textbook on microeconomics the game theorist David Kreps (1990) asserts that these two questions cannot and must not be completely isolated from each other. Without a 'story' of how the equilibrium in question has arisen, the purely axiomatic analysis of the state of equilibrium cannot be justified. As an example of how such stories can be employed to justify equilibrium analyses, R. Lucas (1987) can be named in his defence of rational expectation theory. Contrary to what might be expected, Lucas regards rational expectation equilibria as states which are the result of a process of adaptation. That is, the steady state of a trial-and-error process where the agents can no longer learn anything new in the sense of being capable of replacing existing decision-making rules with even better ones. In the same way, however, as Walras's auctioneer is simply 'tacked onto' general equilibrium theory, so can Lucas's 'story' be criticized as a similar *ad hoc* story with regard to rational expectation theory. When the above way of handling processes in economics is criticized as *ad hoc*, the main reason is that the adjustment process is not integrated and analysed in the formal model, but is only included as an *ad hoc* structure 'tacked onto' the formal model.

What part, then, does neo-institutionalism play in relation to the above *ad hoc* models or stories? As indicated in the introduction it is the central thesis of this chapter, that neo-institutionalism emerged as an attempt to create independent theories or models from these stories. In order to grasp the character of these stories and indeed how they differ in relation to the formal neoclassical models, we can consider what assumptions are employed, respectively, in the formal model and in the *ad hoc* stories. The decisive difference here is what assumptions can be made concerning the individual decision maker. In the *ad hoc* stories the agents are typically confronted with highly uncertain situations where they experiment with different decision-making rules, and where in some cases they eventually learn their equilibrium strategies. As opposed to this, the individual in the equilibrium analysis is modelled as a perfectly rational agent who is able to find the optimal strategy in each situation without any learning process. That is to say, the ambition to incorporate these *ad hoc* stories into formal models necessitates a broadening of the behavioural foundations of economic theory. The connection between theme 1 and theme 2 should hereby be established.

Theme 3

The third theme which, according to Langlois, characterizes the neo-institutionalist research programme is its attempt to expand the domain of economics beyond studies of market institutions. It should be emphasized here, however, that the difference between neoclassical and neo-institutional theory does *not* consist in the former not studying institutions at all, while these form the focus of the latter. R. Langlois puts it as follows: 'what we ... really want is ... not only pure economic theory informed by the existence of specific institutions, but also an economic theory of institutions' (Langlois 1986a: 5). In other words, neoclassical theory has treated institutions mainly as exogenous variables focusing on what effect given institutions have. On the other hand, unlike in neo-institutionalist theory, there has been little interest both in studying the political, social and legal institutions that are pre-supposed in neoclassical theory as well as the process whereby institutional arrangements or organizations emerge in response to different problems of social interaction.

So what *is* a social institution? In the contributions examined in this chapter, social institutions are linked to rule-following behaviour. That is, institutions are defined as formal and informal social rules (as opposed to personal rules) that may solve various problems of social interaction. By following certain social rules the agents have either voluntarily restricted or been restricted through sanctions in choosing whatever strategy they like. Social institutions therefore reduce the social uncertainty in the system by making the actions of the agents more predictable and stabilizing their expectations as to what strategies the other agents may choose.

269

3 ARE THERE ONE OR MORE NEO-INSTITUTIONALIST PROGRAMMES?

The identification of these three themes formed the basis of Richard Langlois' (1986c) proclamation of the existence of a neo-institutionalistic research programme which would unite a range of heterodox schools. In a review of Langlois (1986c), Uskali Mäki (1987) maintained that too high a degree of programmatic unity has been read into the individual heterodox schools, and that the heterogenity of neo-institutionalists had in this way been underestimated.

In this chapter I will try to characterize neo-institutional economic theory by formulating a typology of contributions to this field. The purpose of this is to avoid reading too great a degree of programmatic unity into a range of heterodox contributions. In this way it should be possible to clarify on which points the different contributions diverge in relation to orthodox economic theory as well as to account for the differences that exist between the individual contributions. After this mapping and evaluation of the relations between the 'neo-institutionalist' models, we will have a better base for evaluating how individual contributions can supplement each other and perhaps even merge in the future. By following such a procedure it should be easier to ascertain whether a unified institutionalist research programme can be established in the future, firmly rooted in existing models.

In Figure 11.1 it is attempted to set up a typology of contributions which have been labelled 'neo-institutionalist'. The typology is set up with the following two dimensions:

Perspective/ unit of analysis / Type of explanation and concept of rationality	Contractual focus: 'Transaction'	Technological focus: 'Decision maker'
Equilibrium models & Maximization Rationality	Principal Agency Theory	Neoclassical Theory/ Game Theory
Functionalist Explanation & Bounded Rationality	Property Rights Theory Williamson's Transaction Cost Theory	Information Economics (Akerlof-Stiglitz) 'Institutional game theory'
Models of Economic change and Procedural Rationality	D. North's Transaction Cost Theory	'Austrian' institutionalism Path-dependency Theory Evolutionary Economics (Nelson & Winter)

Figure 11.1 'Neo-institutionalist' research programmes

1 The first dimension distinguishes between which 'unit of analysis' is the focus of the contribution or research programme concerned: the 'transaction' as opposed to the 'decision maker'.
2 The second dimension distinguishes between which explanatory type the contribution or research programme concerned employs, including the concept of rationality. More specifically, there is a distinction below between: (a) equilibrium explanations and the maximization principle, (b) functional explanations and bounded rationality and (c) explanations of economic change and procedural rationality.

In order to structure our discussion of the individual 'neo-institutionalist' contributions, I will make use of Lakatos's methodology of scientific research programmes and its division of a programme in an invariable part consisting of the hard core (as well as a positive and a negative heuristic) and a variable part consisting of its protective belt. Before applying these concepts to economics in general and neo-institutional economics in particular, we must notice that most of the programmes concerned operates on two different levels of analysis: the decision-making level and the system level. A full characterization of a programme must include a characterization of both these levels.

Starting with the decision-making level the distinction between the 'hard core' of a research programme and its 'protective belt' corresponds to a distinction between, respectively, the 'basic behavioural assumptions' and the 'situational assumptions' including the 'informational assumptions' by which the decision-making problem of the individual agent is specified. Theoretical development within a programme at this level can, then, be described as follows. The decision maker, acting from an invariable principle for action, is presented with successive new decision-making situations. These situations are specified by the auxiliary hypotheses in the protective belt. As was pointed out above, in this chapter we distinguish between three different and independent principles of rationality: maximization rationality, bounded rationality and procedural rationality, which together form the 'hard core' of three classes of research programme. A more detailed characterization of these three principles of rationality follows, indicating the differences between them.

A complete definition of a specific research programme should include some description of how the system level is handled in addition to the individual analysis, as well as how these two levels are bound together. It is in this connection that the type of explanation upon which the programme in question is placed, plays a central role.

The ambition of the neo-institutionalists to gradually broaden the behavioural foundations of economic theory can, as indicated in section 2, be regarded as linked to a need to directly incorporate the study of

271

processes into the economic models, rather than treat them as separate *ad hoc* constructions. In Lakatos's methodology of scientific research programmes he denounces these so-called *ad hoc₃* hypotheses, and insists that 'additional assertion must be connected with the original assertions *more intimately* than by mere conjunction' (Lakatos 1970: 136). The purpose of this methodological rule is to secure the 'organic unity' of a research programme, and by so doing protect it against disintegration and fragmentation. More specifically, this involves the direct incorporation into the formal economic models of, for example, those processes which might be assumed to produce equilibrium, rather than just 'tacking them onto' the model as *ad hoc* hypotheses. Almost the same requirement has, in terms of 'formal' and 'appreciative theory', been formulated in the following way by Nelson and Winter:

> In a well-working scientific discipline, the flow of influence is not only from formal to appreciative theory, but in the reverse direction as well. Phenomena identified in applied work that resist analysis with familiar models, and rather causal if perceptive explanations for these, become the grist for the formal theoretical mill.
>
> (Nelson and Winter 1982: 47)

In a well-working discipline the formal or pure theory should not only develop autonomously, but the theoretician should also be able to incorporate diverse empirical phenomena in his formal models, which an applied researcher has treated as separate *ad hoc* hypotheses or stories. In the theory sketched here this will, however, require a broadening or generalization of the behavioural basis of economic theory.

4 RESEARCH PROGRAMMES BASED ON EQUILIBRIUM MODELS AND THE MAXIMIZATION PRINCIPLE

In sections 4 to 6 the research programmes mentioned in the typology above are presented. The most important methodological problems associated with the programmes are discussed. In this section we will start with those programmes which are based on unbounded rationality or maximization as their 'hard core', and at the same time use equilibrium models. By pointing out some of the weaknesses in these models in section 5 (p. 275) it is hoped to clarify why a range of 'neo-institutionalist' research programmes have replaced the concept of maximization with a concept of bounded rationality, and replaced the comparative static form of analysis with a functionalist type of explanation. Finally, it is explained in section 6 which criticisms of the functional type of explanation are behind the attempts of some 'neo-institutionalists' to introduce a more change-oriented type of explanation, as well as replace the bounded rationality concept with a procedural concept of rationality.

Orthodox, neoclassical economics

We may now try to use the Lakatosian concepts introduced above to account for the orthodox, neoclassical research programme. This account will be used later on as a point of reference in a discussion of how different neo-institutionalists' contributions diverge from it. The first characteristic we notice about the orthodox tradition is that it operates on two different levels of analysis: the decision-making level and system level. Several economists, including John Hicks (1939) and Fritz Machlup (1967) argue, however, that 'although economics has been concerned with the behaviour of single individuals, in the end, its main concern is with the behaviour of groups'. That is, the 'level of analysis' of the programme of research is *a* system rather than an individual. But it is a system in which the single decision-making units form 'logical atoms'. When we characterize mainstream economics as a scientific research programme both these levels must be included in the description.

There are two central concepts characterizing orthodox economic theory: the concept of an optimizing agent and the equilibrium concept. These two concepts have been applied when studying optimizing agents interacting in different kinds of systems – which is claimed to be the main 'level of analysis' in this programme. When studying such systems of interaction, orthodox economics has used almost all of its intellectual resources on solving the logical problem of whether equilibria exist that may coordinate the activities of the optimizing agents, and if they exist, what efficiency properties they may have.

In modelling single decision makers orthodox economists keep the *maximization principle* as an invariant, irrefutable hard core, while *situational assumptions* (specifying the type of situational constraints the agents face as well as what type of information they have about the situation) form the programme's more flexible and revisable *protective belt*. By adjusting and readjusting these situational assumptions the orthodox economist has been able to identify a whole sequence of decision problems facing the agent. The starting point of this sequence is the model of decision making under perfect information. This model has gradually been modified by attempting to add more and more uncertainty.

If the principle of maximizing rationality constitutes the hard core at the individual level, the equilibrium concept may be said to have a similar methodological role at the system level. As a result the programme has committed itself to an analysis of only those systems that display rather stable and well coordinated behaviour, while dismissing, for instance, systems with no or several equilibria as anomalous and uninteresting cases. At this level of analysis the theoretical development of the programme may be characterized as a study of systems of interaction that have become less and less anonymous starting with the theory of perfect competition, through different theories of oligopoly theory and non-cooperative game theory before finally coming to a very direct form of interaction in cooperative game theory.

In studying these different systems of interaction, orthodox economics has used almost all its intellectual resources to solve the problem of the existence of equilibrium. How a state of equilibrium may have emerged in the first place from the causal interaction between agents has, however, not attracted an equal amount of attention. In fact, it is only in equilibrium that the model of optimizing agents really works, since it does not tell us anything about the procedures used by the agents to acquire the knowledge required to make the optimal choices. The concept of maximizing may therefore be limited to a formal and static type of analysis.

It does not seem that the orthodox programme can adequately answer the question of how equilibrium comes about. By insisting on working within an optimizing-cum-equilibrium framework, economists have introduced *ad hoc* hypotheses of a more and more elaborate kind. However, as I have argued in Chapter 6 of this volume finding a *non-ad hoc* solution to this conceptual problem seems to require a broadening of the behavioural foundation of orthodox economics. Analysed from this perspective the emergence of several non-orthodox programmes can probably be explained as responses to exactly this conceptual problem within the orthodox theory.

What makes most of these solutions *ad hoc* in orthodox theory is, that the proposed adjustment mechanism has not been linked to the analysis of the single individual decision makers in disequilibrium positions. So by postulating an adjustment mechanism without a foundation in individual behaviour, the orthodox programme has been restricted to make the rather extreme and unsophisticated assumptions:

Namely that the only institutions existing in the economy are markets of the competitive type in which all information on the economy must be transmitted through the prices formed in these markets. The economy is, therefore, assumed to have no money, no property rights, no legal system, no banks – in short none of the many social institutions that are created by societies to help coordinate their economic and social activities by offering information not available in competitive prices.

(Schotter 1983: 675)

The principal–agency theory

While the neoclassical paradigm took the 'decision maker' as its basic analytical unit, and, as a strategy of theory development analysed the interaction between firms in different types of market, the principal–agency theory is a research programme which takes the individual economic 'transaction' as its basic analytical unit. A principal–agency relationship can be characterized generally as a contractual relationship between two parties: a person called a *principal*, who employs another party, called an *agent*, to take a whole range of decisions on his behalf. Such relationships will be characterized with *asymmetrical information*, in that the principal has less information about the actions of the agent than the agent himself. As a result, the agent can pursue his own interests without being discovered by the principal. The problem that this theory seeks to resolve is how a so-called *incentive compatible contract* can be drawn up. That is to say, a contract in which it is in the agent's own interests to act in accordance with the interests of the principal.

The principal–agency model is placed in the top column of the typology above with a clear kinship to orthodox, neoclassical theory. The reason for this is that the model is built on a traditional behavioural foundation, within which an optimal solution may be found. This results from the modelling of uncertain events in the principal–agecy theory as pure risk decisions: the probability distribution of the uncertain event is assumed to be known to both the principal and the agent. According to Richard Langlois (1984) there is a widespread preoccupation with 'parametric' and not 'structural uncertainty', in that uncertainty about *what* contingencies might possibly occur cannot be presumed to exist. Structural uncertainty will arise in decision-making situations where the agent might be confronted with unforeseen contingencies or genuine surprises. As opposed to the principal–agency theory for instance, a contingent contract cannot therefore be specified *ex ante*, but an incomplete contract may solve unforeseen problems *ex post* as they arise, through previously agreed methods. We shall return to this in the next section.

5 FROM EQUILIBRIUM MODES OF EXPLANATION TO THE FUNCTIONALIST EXPLANATIONS OF NEO-INSTITUTIONALISM

In the following section a number of institutionalist research programmes are discussed which replace the equilibrium-cum-maximization mode of explanation found in orthodox theory with a functionalist or quasi-functionalist mode of explanation. In order to explain how activities can be coordinated in a decentralized system, these programmes argue that

275

the research strategy followed by orthodox theorists should be inverted. Instead of starting the analysis by proving the existence of an equilibrium with the institutional structure of the economy fixed exogenously, and then formulating a dynamic adjustment mechanism, economists should from the very start study a much wider variety of systems than merely those with a unique and stable equilibrium. Institutionalists therefore focus from the start on systems in which there are either no or several equilibria, or on systems with different kinds of coordination failures such as market failures, organizational failures, etc. The rationale behind this research strategy is that it is as solutions to these kinds of problems that institutions including norms, conventions, standards, etc. have evolved, either to supplement the market or to replace it.

When neoclassical economists gave reasons for their interest in systems with stable states of equilibrium, they normally insisted that it was only in those kinds of systems that comparative static theorem or conditional predictions could be deduced. As we noted in the previous section, the cost of this was that only an *ad hoc* solution could be provided for the problem of equilibrium adjustment. When on the other hand neo-institutionalism proceeded to study all conceivable forms of systems, it was, according to Herbert Simon, due to the fact that qualitative and structural questions were more of a preoccupation than the quantitative questions of traditional price theory:

> What is characteristic of the exemplars of functional analysis cited in the last section, . . . is that they are not focused upon, or even much concerned with, how variables are equated at the margin, or how equilibrium is altered by marginal shifts in conditions. Rather they are focused on qualitative and structural questions, typically, on the choice among a small number of discrete institutional alternatives. . . . As economics expands beyond its hard core of price theory, and its central concern with quantities of commodities and money, we observe in it this same shift from a highly quantitative analysis, in which equilibrium at the margin plays a central role, to a much more qualitative institutional analysis, in which discrete structural alternatives are compared.
>
> (Simon 1978: 6)

In contrast to the comparative static form of analysis which is used to explain and predict empirical *events*, functional explanations have *persistent features* such as institutions, norms or behavioural rules as their *explananda*. In functional explanations it is therefore the 'beneficial consequences' to which an institution, norm, or behavioural rule leads – or the functions served by 'the phenomenon we wish to explain' – which are meant to explain its existence. However, criticisms have been raised against this reversed order of cause and effect. Whereas in

276

traditional causal explanations, *explanans*/cause comes before the *explanandum*/effect, it seems that in functionalist explanations persistent features are explained by the 'beneficial consequences' provided or the function served. In biology such an explanation would not be seen as problematic because it would normally be assumed that a natural selection mechanism had been involved. When biological features are explained with reference to their 'beneficial consequences', therefore, this should merely be regarded as a simplifying 'as if' explanation of another, far more complex explanation based on Darwin's mutation and selection mechanism. According to Jon Elster (1983) this is not acceptable within the social sciences. Whenever we try to explain an institutions or a behavioural pattern X by its function Y for a group Z it will, according to Jon Elster, only be a legitimate explanation, if it satisfies the following five criteria: (1) Y is an effect of X; (2) Y is beneficial for Z; (3) Y is unintended by the actors producing X; (4) Y, or at least the causal relation between X and Y, is unrecognized by the actors in Z; (5) Y maintains X by a causal feedback loop passing through Z.

Jon Elster's main argument in regard to functionalist explanation in the social sciences is, that they must in each single case be provided with a specification of the mechanism or feedback loop by which an institution is maintained because of its 'beneficial consequences'. Or as Elster formulates it:

> I want to argue that many purported cases of functional explanation fail because the feedback loop of criterion (5) is postulated rather than demonstrated. . . . Functionalist sociologists argue *as if* (which is not to argue *that*) criterion (5) is automatically fulfilled whenever the other criteria are. Since the demonstration that a phenomenon has unintended, unperceived and beneficial consequences seems to bestow some kind of meaning on it, and since to bestow meaning is to explain, the sociologist tends to assume that his job is over when the first four criteria are shown to be satisfied.
>
> (Elster 1983: 58–9)

According to Jon Elster the social researcher must specify the causal mechanism through which an institution is reproduced, and not merely indicate it. Elster can though be criticized for not clearly specifying precisely what is meant by 'demonstrated'. Elster appears to accept simply 'tacking' the feedback loop onto the functional explanation as a detached *ad hoc* model, in the same way that the auctioneer model was tacked onto general equilibrium theory without being integrated into it.

More specifically, Elster recommends both a natural selection mechanism and a reinforcement mechanism as two possible examples of feedback loops which can justify the use of functionalist explanations.

277

The former mechanism was used for instance by Armen Alchian (1950) as an argument for why apparently adaptive or teleological behavioural patterns do not necessarily involve any form of foresight or 'intention', but can emerge from a market selection process. As opposed to optimization theory, Alchian characterizes a theory based on this mechanism in the following way:

> By backing away from the trees – the optimization calculus by individual units – we can better discern the forest of impersonal market forces. The approach directs attention to the interrelationships of the environment and the prevailing types of economic behaviour which appear through a process of economic natural selection.
>
> (Alchian 1950: 213)

While this selection mechanism takes place at the population or industry level, the reinforcement mechanism takes place at the level of the single decision maker. The reinforcement mechanism means that behaviour that is rewarded is reinforced, while behaviour that is punished is discouraged. The individual 'becomes aware' of the relationship between a certain behaviour and its 'beneficial consequences', and works out a rule from this 'learning process'.

However, Elster (1983: 58) works with a relatively narrow definition of what he considers to be genuinely functionalist explanations. It appears from the above quotation that the 'beneficial consequences' produced by an institution or behavioural pattern should be both 'unintended' and 'unperceived'. In his requirement that the consequences should be 'unintended', he seeks to separate the functionalist form of explanation from the intentional. Furthermore, in his requirement that the consequences should be 'unperceived', Elster shows that he only regards latent-functionalist and not manifest-functionalist explanations as genuine functionalist explanations. The latter division is also, of course, the reason why Elster prefers to use the term 'filter explanation' rather than functionalist explanation in the case of an explanation that is based upon a reinforcement mechanism.

It can also be questioned whether such a rigid division should be maintained between intentional explanations on the one hand, and functionalist explanations on the other. It appears reasonable to link the use of functionalist explanations of institutions together with the concept of satisfying or bounded rationality, as does Herbert Simon:

> In these analyses aimed at explaining institutional structure, maximizing assumptions play a much less significant role than they typically do in the analysis of market equilibria. The rational man who sometimes prefers an employment contract to a sales contract

need not be a maximizer. Even a satisfier will exhibit such a preference whenever the two arrangements are sufficiently large and evident.

(Simon 1978: 6)

It is even possible to go a step further than Simon to assert that a traditional maximization model cannot generally be employed in connection with explaining institutions, since these models do not allow for the possibility of the occurrence of unforeseen contingencies. The orthodox model of decision making under uncertainty assumes that individuals are capable of foreseeing any conceivable future events, even though they are uncertain about the probability of their occurring. The rationale behind an institution such as the employment contract is precisely that the parties cannot anticipate all conceivable future events and must therefore enter into incomplete contracts. This does not however imply that the parties to such a contractual relationship are irrational or acting blindly. Even though they cannot agree *ex ante* about what will happen in every single instance, they can anyway come to an agreement in advance to determine a procedure for tackling unforeseen contingencies. In employment contracts it is established from the start that employees have the right to terminate an employment contract whenever they wish. In return, the employer has the right to adapt or adjust working relationships within reasonable limits, whenever unforeseen circumstances arise.

The parties to an incomplete contract will not therefore be able to make optimal calculations *ex ante*, because unforeseen contingencies might occur. However, the replacement of the principle of unbounded rationality does not mean that we are compelled to accept Alchian's market selection model, where all behaviour is stochastic, and where it is the environment alone that determines behaviour. This will also be apparent from the following survey of 'neo-institutionalist' research programmes, which are based upon a functionalist type of explanation and combined with the principle of bounded rationality as their 'hard core' assumption.

From the property rights programme to Akerlof–Stiglitz's theory of imperfect information and institutions

The 'property rights' tradition starts with situations arising from various forms of market failure, as do most research programmes discussed in this section. However, as opposed to classical welfare theory à la Pigou – who argues that market failures can almost always be resolved by means of taxation and subsidies – the main thesis of the property rights school has been formulated as follows, by Harold Demsetz:

279

Property rights develop to internalize externalities when the gains of internalization become larger than the cost of internalization. Increased internalization, in the main, results from changes in economic values, changes which stem from the development of new technology and the opening of new markets, changes to which old property rights are poorly attuned.

(Demsetz 1967: 350)

Demsetz (1967) himself uses this theory to explain the introduction of the concept of land as private property to Canadian Indians in the beginning of the 1700s. Previously the Indians had lived for centuries *without* a system of private property rights, which meant that the right to hunt or trap animals for their furs had remained unspecified. With immigration from Europe followed a rapid increase in the demand for furs. The vagueness of property rights resulted in the 'tragedy of the commons' type of problem, which threatened the hunted animals with extinction. A similar problem exists with other exhaustible resources such as common fishing rights. Where resources were 'not exclusive', wrote Demsetz, there was a tendency to introduce a system of private property rights to solve the problem. Like the other 'functionalist' research programmes examined in this section, however, Demsetz did not specify the process or mechanism whereby the institution *private property rights* came about and solved the problem of the 'tragedy of the commons'. Nor was it specified what role a state would play in the establishment and maintenance of such property rights. As Furubotn and Pejovich (1972) have commented: 'A theory of property rights cannot be truly complete without a theory of the state. And, unfortunately, no such theory exists at present' (1972: 1140). As it is pointed out in section 6, Douglass North's transaction cost theory can, as can James Buchanan's constitutional political economy, be said to partly cover this gap.

It may be interesting to point out in this context that, although the thesis of the property rights school was that market failures will mostly lead to a redefinition of property rights, Kenneth Arrow (1963) went a step further. He maintained that in certain circumstances market failures would also produce institutions as a substitute for, and not merely as a support for the market institution. Certainly, Arrow had been primarily occupied with the study of what he called 'invisible institutions' such as ethics, morals, trust, etc. and their significance for the efficiency of the market system. However, in the book *The Limits of Organization* of 1974, Kenneth Arrow also sought an answer to the question of whether internal organization would be a suitable solution to market failures, and found that:

The possibility of using the price system to allocate uncertainty, to insure against risks, is limited by the structure of the information

280

channels in existence. Put the other way, the value of non-market decision making, the desirability of creating organizations of a scope more limited than the market as a whole, is partially determined by the characteristics of the network of information flows.

(Arrow 1974: 37)

In other words, it was in situations marked by 'structural uncertainty', and where it was impossible to formulate contingent contracts that the market was replaced with internal organization as a more suitable allocation mechanism.

George Akerlof (1970, 1980) and Joseph E. Stiglitz's (1974) theory that institutions are created on the basis of imperfect information had almost the same starting point. They were particularly concerned with institutions in the developing countries, such as the tenure system and other types of leasing arrangements for cattle and arable land, credit rationing, means through which landowners can bind the labour force to them, etc. The research strategy behind this school has involved looking at the origins of institutions as solutions to various types of information problems, such as incomplete markets, asymmetrical information, problems with moral hazards, etc. Just as in the other research traditions presented in this section, the theories or models have been mostly based upon a functionalist mode of explanation. After revealing a specific information problem and discovering an institution which had the 'beneficial consequences' required to solve this, it was almost automatically assumed that the institution concerned would emerge, so it was not considered necessary to demonstrate the process.

Game theory and institutions

According to one traditional viewpoint, the purpose of game theory is to prescribe a strategy for each player through rational analysis. The theory assumes that none of the players knows anything more about the others than the fact that they are rational and what preferences they have. It is then up to the game theorist to deduce from this what strategies perfect rational agents will choose and what outcome the game will have.

Seen against this background, games such as 'chicken' and pure 'co-ordination games' appear anomalous, since it is in general impossible to prescribe a rational strategy for each player. More than one Nash equilibrium solution can be pointed out in these games, so that the perfectly rational player will not have sufficient information to decide what to do.

It is because of such 'anomalous' game situations where there are

281

either no, several, or exclusively suboptimal equilibria, that many economists consider that we can understand the emergence and existence of different forms of 'institution' as solutions to these problems. The origins of using game theory to analyse institutions can be traced back to Thomas Schelling's studies of pure coordination games at the end of the 1950s. It was a central thesis of Schelling's (1960) work that many day-to-day coordination situations were solved without any real difficulty. This was paradoxically due to the fact that real-life players were far less rational than the perfectly rational players we know from abstract game theory. According to Schelling this was a result of games theorists 'discarding' information when formulating their formal models, information which real-life players used to coordinate their strategies. Schelling therefore maintained that, even in situations without the possibility of communication, real people are often capable of solving pure coordination problems by drawing on common experiences, culture and general 'background knowledge'. The ability to coordinate our activities in different ways appears obvious and natural. Schelling calls it *'prominence'* or *'salience'*. He describes the coordination solution as a *'focal point'* solution.

With Schelling's analysis in mind we might expect that the emergence of institutions would be explained and modelled as the result of an evolutionary process. However, the earliest versions of the neo-institutionalist tradition within game theory were based upon a relatively 'ahistorical' and functional explanatory model. Here the philosophers David Lewis (1969) and Edna Ullmann Margalit (1978) can be included. They both used game theory as a tool in order to make typologies of the situations which *might* lead to the formation of institutions. It was not until the works of Andrew Schotter (1981, 1983), Robert Axelrod (1984) and Robert Sugden (1986, 1989) that attention was focused away from the purely functionalist explanatory model and it was attempted instead to model the processes whereby different institutions emerged as a solution to such 'repeated' social problems. This 'process perspective' means that these contributions can be seen as a kind of formalization of the Austrian school, as well as of Carl Menger's programme for economics as 'the study of how individual economic agents pursuing their own selfish ends evolve institutions as a means to satisfy them'. We shall return to these contributions in section 6 under the heading 'Austrian' institutionalists.

Consensus has not been reached among neo-institutionalists concerning what type of recurrent situations might generate institutions. On a very general level a distinction can be made between *coordination* and *cooperative* institutions as a response to, respectively, *common aversion* and *common interest dilemmas*. In the first of these dilemmas the actors find themselves in a situation in which they have a common interest in avoiding one or more aggregated, but unintended results of their behaviour. The function of the institution in these cases will be to counteract those processes of change which are threatening to unravel the social structure, producing a stabilizing effect. There are other examples of this than institutions which emerge as responses to co-ordination games and chicken games. These include those 'property rights institutions' which emerge as responses to the 'tragedy of commons' type of dilemma. The solution to problems involving asymmetric information also falls into this category. On the other hand, an institution that solves a recurrent common interest dilemma will have the function of bringing the social system out of a stable, but suboptimal situation, and it will therefore initiate a process of social change. The paradigm example of this is of course the prisoner's dilemma type of situation.

Oliver Williamson's transaction cost theory as a scientific research programme

Transaction cost theory is the paradigm founded by Ronald Coase in his article on 'The nature of the firm' of 1937, it was later developed extensively, particularly by Oliver Williamson (1975, 1981, 1985). The central idea behind this programme is that there are different ways of organizing transactions (or different 'modes of governance' for trans-actions) and that these ways of organizing differ in cost. The main hypothesis of this research programme – what I would argue to be part of the hard core of Williamson's research programme – may then be said to be that: 'transactions are assigned to and organized within governance structures in a discriminating (transaction-cost economizing) way.' (1981: 1564). In accordance with the functionalist mode of analysis, 'observed' ways of organizing transactions are therefore explained by their 'beneficial consequences' that is, their ability to economize on transaction costs. Thus Williamson does not explain 'observed governance structures as the result of a rational plan, intention or design, but as the final result emerging from some unspecified evolutionary process. As in most functionalist explanations, this process is just assumed, rather than demonstrated and built into central concepts of the transaction cost theory. I shall return to this later in my appraisal but it is first necessary to give a full account of this research programme.

According to Williamson, any systematic account of the existence of transaction costs would necessitate their reduction to a number of basic human and environmental conditions. By exploring Arrow's (1969) classic analysis of different market failures – the paradigmatic example of situations with positive transaction costs – Williamson (1973) suc-ceeded in identifying the common human and environmental conditions behind these costs. In his book *Markets and Hierarchies* Williamson argued that the key behavioural assumptions of his programme consisted of (1) bounded rationality and (2) opportunism. By giving these two assumptions methodological status as the behavioural foundation of his programme, he made them irrefutable by definition. As in other research programmes in economics, the transaction cost programme also consisted of a set of variable and exchangeable *situational* assumptions. It was changing by these assumptions that the 'contractual man' of Williamson's theory could be confronted with successively new transactional and contractual problems. Thus, by disclosing a set of critical dimensions for describing transactions and letting these vary in degrees from low to high, Williamson has succeeded in specifying the protective belt of his programme. These dimensions of a transaction were: (1) degree of uncertainty, (2) the frequency with which transaction recurs, and (3) the degree to which asset-specific investments are involved in the transaction.

In presenting his theory, Williamson (1975, 1985) never makes it quite clear whether it should be interpreted in an 'intentionalist' or a 'functionalist' way. In some cases he seems to favour an intentionalist explanation, according to which observed governance structure is said to be consciously chosen by the parties in a transaction after deliberating (calculating) the transaction costs in each case. However, such an interpretation seems to conflict with Williamson's emphasis on bounded rationality and incomplete contracting. Or as Greg Dow (1987) formulates it: 'If transaction costs incorporate the value of adaption to future circumstances, then the parties cannot know the objective transaction costs they face' (ibid., p. 27).

In most cases, however, Williamson (1987, 1988) seems to prefer a functionalist interpretation, according to which observed governance structures exist or have evolved, not because they have been fully anticipated, but because they have beneficial, and partly unintended consequences (i.e. they economize on transaction costs). As is the case with functionalist explanation in the social sciences in general, Williamson may justify such 'consequence laws' either by using (1) a market selection mechanism, or (2) a reinforcement mechanism as the causal feedback mechanism. Using a market selection mechanism would imply that firms with more efficient governance structures will in the long run eliminate firms with less efficient structures. Using a reinforcement mechanism, meanwhile, would imply that an organization would be able to converge to an efficient adaptation to its environment – confronted with recurrent transactions.

Williamson (1988) even argues that the account given by transaction cost theory of the emergence of the multidivisional structure is one of the few examples of a 'functionalist explanation' which satisfies Elster's requirements.

However, this does not seem to remove the fundamental tensions within the transaction cost paradigm. Tensions exist between the more formal and static part of the theory and the wider 'processual' rhetoric used by Williamson to justify its use. It seems that these tensions can only be removed if the behavioural foundation of transaction cost theory is broadened. That is, the hard core of bounded rationality, apparently suited to comparative institutional analysis, must be replaced by what Williamson (1985: 46–7) himself calls a process or an organic rationality (we prefer the term: *procedural rationality* introduced by Herbert Simon 1976) – which is better suited to evolutionary explanations. According to Williamson (1985), such an organic concept of rationality can be associated with modern evolutionary approaches (Nelson and Winter 1982) as well as with Austrian economics (Menger, Hayek and Kirzner). We shall return to these two research programmes in the next section.

NEO-INSTITUTIONALIST THEORIES BASED ON EXPLANATORY MODELS WHICH FOCUS ON SOCIAL CHANGE

Research programmes based on a traditional equilibrium analysis, and programmes which employ a functionalist mode of explanation share a common characteristic. They both give priority to the study of stable states at the expense of the processes which are meant to have produced these conditions. The reason is often that it is much more difficult to study social processes *per se* than it is to study the results or outcome of the processes in question. In this section a range of programmes will nevertheless be presented which have the opposite priority, in that they place greater emphasis on processes than equilibria.

Those researchers who focus on social processes are usually unwilling to accept a theory or model as an explanation unless a 'causal account' is provided of how an equilibrium or a permanent social pattern has arisen. They are not therefore satisfied with theories which do not explicitly account for the conceivable origins of a state of equilibrium or a relatively enduring social pattern. This means that they are usually critically inclined towards both equilibrium analyses and functionalist explanations since no explicit model is provided for how these states emerge – except in loose *ad hoc* terms. Those who focus on processes and explanations of social change therefore require that the dynamic analysis be integrated into the actual model on a *non-ad hoc* basis.

As indicated by Sidney Winter (1987), the choice between an 'equilibrium perspective' and a 'process perspective' is often founded in the 'ontological assumptions' we make about reality:

To be willing to limit the aspirations of economic science to the study of steady states of adaptive processes is presumably to view vast realms of apparent social change as either unimportant or illusory; it is to join with the writer of Ecclesiastes in maintaining that 'there is no new thing under the sun'. I, on the other hand, side with Heracleitus [sic] in arguing that 'you could not step twice into the same river, for new waters are ever flowing on to you'.

(Winter 1986: 245–6)

If the 'equilibrium perspective' is taken as a starting point, a commitment is made to 'see' the world in a certain way, so that no allowance is made for fundamentally new and unforeseen contingencies. Those who take the 'process' perspective will argue in face of this, that certain empirical phenomena – as for example innovations of a technological and organizational nature – could not be 'understood' within such a framework. For this a theoretical framework or ontology is required, which permits the occurrence of essentially new and consequently unforeseeable contingencies.

From this perspective the question can be raised of which metaphor best captures this way of 'looking at' social phenomena? As an indication of this Hayek (1978) proposed, for instance, that we consider social processes as analogous with processes of 'scientific discovery'. The result of such processes of discovery can by their very nature not be foreseen. If this had been possible, there would by definition have been no scientific discovery involved in it. In the same way, Hayek maintains that market processes are characterized by joining together the 'private' and 'local' information of single agents into a combined result, in the form of a set of market prices which could not have been foreseen in principle by any agent.

It can nevertheless be argued that the metaphor 'the market as a discovery procedure' is not as far-reaching as might be assumed. The most serious objection is though that, on closer examination, it does not break fundamentally with an ontology according to which the world is always considered to be unchangeable in principle. 'Scientific discovery' does not necessarily refer merely to the uncovering of deeper layers of the same unchangeable reality. In order to allow for explanations of social change it could be argued that a constructive element should be incorporated in the metaphor employed. From this perspective it can therefore be proposed that economic processes be seen as analogous with biological processes – which constantly produce 'evolutionary novelties' to use Mayr's (1976) expression.

For instance, these processes can consist of the birth of new organizational structures which can undertake completely new and more complex functions. They can also consist of behavioural patterns which permit the practice of entirely new areas of competence. By emphasizing the constructive side of the social process in this way it is also stressed that social processes should be seen as non-deterministic, open and

286

irreversible. Only when this happens has a clear break taken place with the idea of anchoring orthodox theory in an ontology which sees the world as essentially unchangeable and deterministic.

Another common characteristic of the theories which are built upon models of social change is that they have necessitated a broadening of the behavioural foundations of economic theory. This mainly involves the replacement of both the concept of unbounded rationality in equilibriun analyses and the concept of bounded rationality in functionalist models with a procedural concept of rationality. As opposed to both equilibrium models and functional models, this involves incorporating the procedural elements within the theory, so that they are not merely 'tacked onto' a model as a more or less detached *ad hoc* structure. According to Viktor Vanberg (see Chapter 7, this volume), this does not mean we can assume that an agent only treats a sequence of repeated decisions separately, that is, acts on a case-by-case basis by finding the optimal strategy in each individual instance. Rather, the individual must be assumed in such cases to be a genuine rule-follower by binding himself to a specific rule of decision making. In this way he voluntarily abandons his flexibility to find the optimal solution in each individual case.

There are several arguments for why it could be sensible to 'bind one's self' to rules. The first argument is associated with Ronald Heiner (1983) and is based on the assumption that economic agents are 'imperfect' decision makers. It is assumed that a decision maker is normally confronted with a so-called 'competence-difficulty gap'. That is to say, a gap between the competence of the decision maker and the degree of complexity of the problem. The greater this gap is, the harder it will be to identify the best solution in each individual situation, in that he will tend to make more and more mistakes. It would therefore also appear more and more reasonable to make decisions on the basis of a rule which reduces complexity. There is, however, another argument concerning the rationale of rule-following behaviour. This argument was originally put forward by the game theorist Thomas Schelling (1960) and assumes that it can be better for an agent to 'bind himself' to a rule rather than acting freely on a case-by-case basis. This would be the case if in binding his own future behaviour to a specific rule he could also influence his opponent's expectations towards his own future behaviour. One of the examples Schelling gives is of an army which burns the bridges over which it has advanced. In this way it signals to its opponent a commitment to fight to the last man.

'Austrian' institutionalism

The section on game theory (p. 281) was concerned with whether institutions could be explained within this framework. It was emphasized that the earliest versions of this research programme were often based upon a functionalist mode of explanation. That is to say, it was first attempted to uncover various types of recurring situations of social interaction, for example, coordination games and the prisoner's dilemma game. After that it was attempted to point out a social institution which had the 'beneficial consequences' to be able to solve the problem or dilemma concerned, and in this way the existence of these institutions was thought to have been explained. As examples of this a number of institutions can be named such as the 'give way' traffic rule, various standardized measurements for distance, weight, and time, the use of money in modern economies, the use of a common language, the use of various technical standards, etc.

When, however, we try to explain the existence of an institution by reference to its 'beneficial consequences', we employ an illegitimate functional explanation, according to Jon Elster. The fact that an institution has 'beneficial consequences' does not necessarily mean that it will emerge. It has especially been pointed out, that in social situations which are structured like a finitely repeated 'prisoner's dilemma' game, it would be highly improbable that an institution or behavioural rule would emerge which solves such a dilemma by bringing the agent out of the suboptimal but stable Nash equilibrium. The reason for this is that the optimal state is not individually, but only collectively achievable. It is first necessary to specify the mechanism whereby the institution emerged if we are to claim that an explanation of the institution has been given. In this case we must employ a 'group-selection mechanism', which many economists regard as highly problematic.

It is to this background, for instance, that a range of new game theorists like Andrew Schotter (1981, 1983) and Robert Sugden (1986, 1989), taking their starting point in the Austrian 'process perspective', have sought to model the process whereby an institution – understood here as social rules for behaviour – might arise. Sugden maintains that convention and other social rules cannot be understood within the framework of traditional game theory with its assumption of perfect rationality. It would be far more productive if we placed less emphasis on the importance of individual rationality, examining social institutions as the unintended result of an evolutionary process. Sugden therefore introduces agents who learn their behavioural rules from a simple reinforcement mechanism in order to replace the perfectly rational agents of game theory: 'I shall assume that individuals tend to adopt those strategies that have proved most successful over a long sequence of games'. That is to say, those strategies which have been shown to have 'beneficial consequences' in a process of trial-and-error are reinforced, while strategies with less beneficial consequences are abandoned. This theory therefore assumes a kind of intermediary position between the traditional preoccupation of economists with perfectly rational agents and the study by biologists of natural selection as a blind mechanism without any individual intentionality. Although Sugden bases his theory on biologist John Maynard Smith's model of 'stable evolutionary strategies', he does however point out the following distinction:

> My concept of utility is quite different from the Darwinian concept of fitness, because learning by experience is quite different from natural selection. I am concerned with social evolution and not with genetic evolution, with economics and not with sociobiology.
>
> (Sugden 1986: 26)

In his process-analysis of how institutions as behavioural rules arise, the starting point is often taken from asymmetrical games. These are games in which importance is attributed to whether the agent has the 'role' of either A or B player. It is now maintained that a social institution will arise when an individual is in a position to decide – on the basis of previous experience – that *one* strategy is better than the others when they have *one* of the roles, and that another strategy is preferable when they have the opposing role. Sugden does however emphasize that it would typically be random events that led to the emergence of a social institution. In order to explain what institution would be the outcome of such a process, we cannot therefore merely focus on the final state, but must also study the process *per se* which produced the institution.

When the above explanations from game theory of the origins of institutions are termed 'Austrian', the reason is that they can be seen as an attempt to formalize Carl Menger's theory of the 'organic' origins of institutions. Menger argued that 'The solution of the most important problems of the theoretical social sciences in general and of theoretical economics in particular is thus closely connected with the question of theoretically understanding the origin and change of "organically" created social institutions' (Menger 1985: 4). For Menger, an 'organically created' institution like money should be reconstructed with an 'invisible hand' explanation. Such an explanation involved accounting for the stages whereby the institution of money was produced as the unintended result of the actions of individuals.

In the above account, invisible hand explanations have mainly been identified with explanations of how institutions and social patterns emerge spontaneously from a state of nature. Edna Ullmann-Margalit (1978) describes these explanations as 'invisible-hand-explanations-of-the-aggregate-mold'. She places this form of explanation opposite to 'invisible-hand-explanation-of-functional-evolutionary-mold', which focuses more on the reasons why already established institutions exist and how they are perpetuated. As noted by Richard Langlois (1986b), these two forms of explanation are complementary and may thereby supplement each other. While the former explains how a new institution emerges or is 'discovered', the latter tries to account for how these institutions are subsequently maintained, and, by analogy to biological transmission mechanisms, passed on from one generation to the next through socialization.

F.A. Hayek (1978, 1988) has attempted to formulate such a theory of how institutional rules are transmitted culturally through time. This theory has, however, been criticized by 'Austrian' institutionalists such as Viktor Vanberg (1986) and John Gray (1984), since it does not satisfy the principle of methodological individualistism. This is because Hayek's theory is based on a 'group selection' mechanism which considers that 'rules of conduct . . . have evolved because the groups who practised them were more successful and displaced others'. Group selection therefore provides the feedback mechanism (process) which should explain how social rules with beneficial social consequences have emerged and later been reproduced. The main objection to such a group selection mechanism is that each social rule, praxis or institution should benefit a group as a whole; but within the group the greatest advantages will fall to 'free riders' at the expense of the person or persons who make sacrifices in order to maintain the expedient social praxis. Such rules can therefore only be developed 'to the extent that the intergroup advantage from self-sacrificing behaviour outweighs the intragroup disadvantage' (Viktor Vanberg 1986: 86). This is a condition which, it is often maintained, will almost never be met.

Path-dependency theory

The theorists behind the 'path-dependency' approach are noted for two reasons in relation to 'Austrian' institutionalism. The first is that they have concentrated on explanations of how technical standards emerge as solutions to recurrent coordination problems. Here they clearly represent a development of 'Austrian' institutionalism in the sense that they have focused on *one* institution as a solution to coordination games, namely the choice of technical standards. The second reason is *the modelling of self-reinforcing mechanisms* (cf. B. Arthur 1988). This is probably the main reason why the 'path-dependency' theorists have aroused such interest among institutionalist economists.

In the coordination game the agents have a common interest in avoiding uncoordinated actions. Each individual sees it as being in his own interest to choose a behavioural pattern which conforms to that chosen by the other individuals. If for example an agent expects other motorists to drive on the right, it is also in his own interests to follow the same rule. If the others speak a certain language, it is also in the interests of the agent to learn the same language. If the other owners of network technology (such as telephone or computer) use a specific standard, it is also in the interests of the user concerned to choose equipment which is based on the same standard.

What distinguishes the above examples is that it would be impossible to anticipate a priori which of several possible institutions or conventions would provide the solution to the coordination game. It is not possible to simply point out one institution as for example the most efficient, and say that it is the solution to or result of the game. In this kind of situation the path-dependency theorists insist that it is of decisive importance to explicitly model the process from which the institution emerges. Apparently unimportant events can arise early on in such a process and start a 'snowball' effect, leading the system towards a particular institutional solution from which it is no longer possible to escape. Processes of this kind are known as *path-dependency processes*. They can in many cases account for the existence of inefficient institutions.

There are many examples in the technological field of how social systems become 'locked into' a technical standard or institution early on, which later proves to be inefficient and provides no opportunity of switching to more efficient solutions. A well-known example of this is the standard QWERTY typewriter keyboard (cf. David 1985). Once the system is set in motion towards a specific solution, the tendency is soon reinforced because the number of decision makers choosing the same solution rises, because of increasing return to scale due to network externalities: the more agents who choose a specific standard, the more attractive it becomes. This is a cumulative process where random events in the opening phase of the process determine the outcome in the long term. It is therefore with good reason that these processes are termed 'historical' (cf. David 1988).

A good example of such a 'path-dependent' process is the *Polya distribution*. Assume that we start with an urn containing one red and one white ball. If we pull out a red ball, the rule is that we put it back in together with another red ball. If we pull out a white ball we put it back together with another white ball. The question is now whether the relative number of red and white balls will infinitely vary between 0 and 1, or whether the number of red or white balls will reach a limit value, thereby producing a specific pattern? If such a pattern emerges, what limit value will then be reached?

In practice the relative proportion of red to white balls stabilizes after only a few draws, and does not diverge from the value achieved. If the balls are drawn again, they soon converge to a new limit value, and another distribution of red and white balls. It is characteristic of this process, then, that a stable pattern is produced every time (in terms of distribution), and that this pattern (the limit value) is stochastically determined and therefore a priori unpredictable.

Nelson and Winter's evolutionary research programme

While Oliver Williamson's transaction cost paradigm had its origin in Ronald Coase's article 'The nature of the firm' of 1937, the theoretical roots of Nelson and Winter's evolutionary research programme can be traced to Armen Alchian's classical article 'Uncertainty, evolution and economic theory' of 1950. It was in this article that the selection argument was first presented. The argument was basically that it is often necessary to assume the existence of 'maximizing' agents in economic theory which could freely adapt to new circumstances. Alchian on the other hand argued that the market acted as a kind of selection mechanism which 'formed' the behavioural pattern of the firm in the long term, so that only the more profitable firms survived at the expense of the less profitable.

Starting with this article, Milton Friedman produced his classical defence of economic theory, based on instrumentalist methodology. The main thesis of this was that economic theories should only be evaluated in accordance with the accuracy of their predictions, not according to whether they were based on realistic assumptions or not. Friedman introduced Alchian's selection argument in order to underpin this methodological maxim. If we are to explain the observable behavioural patterns of firms, a number of different theoretical models can be used to explain the same empirical phenomena. Orthodox maximization theory can be used, which assumes that firms 'consciously' try to maximize their profits. Alchian's thesis may also be used to maintain that it is the environment or market which selects the more profitable firms at the expense of the less profitable. These two theories would lead to the same empirical predictions, which led Friedman to conclude that '. . . the process of "natural selection" thus helps to validate the hypothesis [of profit maximization] or, rather, given natural selection, acceptance of the hypothesis can be based on the judgement that it summarizes appropriately the condition for survival' (1953: 35). Thus, Friedman used the selection argument as an *ad hoc* defence of what he regarded as the 'unrealistic' profit maximization theory, which was claimed to give a correct 'summary' of the selection process which had produced the observed behavioural pattern. Alchian's argument was, therefore, paradoxically used to justify the prevailing research strategy, whereby economists were meant to concentrate on studying equilibria, the result of a selection process, but *not* to study the adaptive process itself.

It was Friedman's basis in an instrumentalist methodology that led him to use Alchian's selection argument as an *ad hoc* model or 'appreciative theory' as a supplement to the formal equilibrium and profit maximization theory. Economists with a basis in *realist* methodology drew a completely different conclusion from Alchian's article. It was important to them that we strive to present theories which are as true as possible. If we had some independent evidence that it was mechanism A (market selection) and not mechanism B (conscious profit maximization) that had brought about an observed phenomenon, then we should base our theory on mechanism A and not B. It was from such a *realist* position that Winter (1964, 1975) and later Nelson and Winter (1982) attempted to develop an evolutionary research programme with the argument that 'if the auxiliary defenses are valid and the true explanation for the success of optimization theories, why should they not be considered as the appropriate foundation for the theory of the firm, while the optimization theories are treated as approximation schemes?' (Winter 1975: 95). With this argument Nelson and Winter (1982) tried to establish an independent research programme based on Armen Alchian's selection arguments, which in Friedman's (1953) case had only been used as an *ad hoc* model or 'story' in order to defend the profit maximization theory.

As a consequence of this realist methodology, the evolutionary research programme has undertaken to analyse long-term processes of change. It has in this way tried to get round the limitations of traditional equilibrium analyses and functional explanations where conceptualizing processes of change are concerned. Especially the evolutionary models of biology have been used pragmatically to establish a conceptual framework which could cope with the study of processes of economic change.

In Nelson and Winter's (1982) evolutionary theory a behavioural study of a firm or organization is said to be analogous with biological genetics. Where genes transmit the information that influence, if not determine, the behaviour of an individual, *routines* are said to be their equivalent in a firm. *Routines* are repositories of knowledge concerning how a firm can 'do' different things. In order to survive, a firm must therefore continually reproduce its routines. In describing the firm as a collection of routines which need to be continuously reproduced, the evolutionary theory diverges on several counts from neoclassical theory. Neoclassical theory 'sees' the firm mainly as a production function which transforms input to output in the most efficient way. When a firm is characterized in this way, however, the characterization is ahistorical. In face of this, evolutionary theory attaches great significance to viewing the firm as a 'historical' entity. Seen in this way, it would be of decisive importance that the specific history of the firm can be reconstructed – along with the development of its capabilities – if we are to understand its present behavioural patterns. In evolutionary theory, a firm will be able to continue doing what it always has without problems, but it will encounter great problems if it tries to 'do' something completely new.

Nelson and Winter (1982) are though aware that the transmission of routines is quite different from the transmission of genes. While the transfer of genes takes place during reproduction, the transmission of routines takes place continuously through imitation, social learning, etc. This means that 'acquired features' can be inherited and passed on, unlike biology. The social transmission of routines can thus be characterized as 'Lamarckian'.

In Darwinian evolutionary theory the variation mechanism results from errors in genetic codes known as *mutations*. They are assumed to take place stochastically, which is the reason why the variation mechanism in biology is described as 'blind'. The analogy in Nelson and Winter's theory to the concept of mutation is shifts or changes in the behavioural patterns and technical routines – also known as *innovations*. Just as in the case of mutations, a number of innovations occur stochastically as errors in the transmission of routines. This applies to all the innovations that occur accidentally. Still, it is important to emphasize that the variation mechanism in economics involves far greater intentionality and conscious control than within the biological sphere.

The final mechanism in evolutionary theory is natural selection. This mechanism is very general and is probably active in every system of inherited features. It functions quite differently within the economic as opposed to the biological field, however, because the transmission of routines happens much faster than the transmission of genes. Sidney Winter (1964, 1975) has shown that economic environments change too quickly to eliminate all inefficient firms – or firms with inadequate routines. Both efficient and inefficient firms can therefore be found living side by side.

North's transaction cost theory

So far the term 'institution' has been used with a number of different meanings. In the property rights tradition institutions were almost synonymous with the rules of the game which defined existing opportunities for action. The concept had quite a different content in Oliver Williamson's transaction cost theory. Here institutions were regarded as efficient ways of organizing transactions, that is to say, as governance structures. As a result, North and Thomas (1973) feel that it is of decisive importance to distinguish between what they call 'institutional environments' and 'institutional arrangements':

> The *institutional environment* is a set of fundamental political, social and legal ground rules that establish the basis for production, exchange and distribution. Rules governing elections, property rights, and the right of contract are examples. . . . An *institutional arrangement* is an arrangement between the economic units that govern the ways in which these units can cooperate and/or compete.

It ... [can] provide a structure within which its members can cooperate ... or [it can] provide a mechanism that can effect a change in laws or property rights.

(North and Thomas 1973)

North's contribution to neo-institutional theory was not limited to accounting for the distinction: 'institutions as rules' and 'institutions as organizations'. Instead, his main contribution is that he has attempted to unite these two separate trends within neo-institutionalist theory in his latest book *Institutions, Institutional Change and Economic Performance* (1990). It is North's thesis, that institutions (as rules of the game) determine which opportunities are open to the individual agent in a society. It is these institutions that determine both production and transaction costs. Within these rules, a range of institutions-as-organizations are then created in order to exploit these opportunities. When they develop, they have a feedback effect on existing institutions. North presumes that institutional changes take place within 'path-dependent' trajectories, where the incentive structure of the institutional rule is of great importance to the later course of development. North's purpose was to establish an explanatory model which could account for the radically different long-term growth patterns observed in different economies.

It can hardly come as a surprise after this very short presentation of North's model of institutional change that he considers the maximization hypothesis in orthodox economic theory as an inadequate behavioural foundation of his own neo-institutional theory: 'The behavioural assumptions of economists are useful for solving certain problems. They are inadequate to deal with many issues confronting social scientists and are the fundamental stumbling block preventing an understanding of the existence, formation and evolution of institutions' (North 1990: 24). North is of the opinion that human behaviour is based on a more complex foundation than can be perceived from the utility maximization models of economists. He considers that this model is not capable of accounting for behaviour which is controlled by norms and ideology, just as actions based on voluntary constraints of a moral or ethical nature can substantially change behaviour. North also points out – in reference to Herbert Simon's and Ronald Heiner's works – that the actors will almost always have limited decision-making competences in relation to the complex environments they are confronted with. North emphasizes that a major reason for this is that there will always be *behavioural uncertainty* in any system of interaction, concerning what decisions the other actors will make.

CONCLUSION

The thesis has been argued in this chapter, that the development of the neo-institutionalist theory within economics has brought with it a development away from the maximization concept through the bounded rationality concept and on towards a procedural rationality concept. It has been argued that this development originated in problems which existed within orthodox equilibrium theory concerning the possibility of incorporating processes of economic change into the central behavioural assumptions of the theory, and in this way establishing a *non-ad hoc* solution to the equilibrium adjustment problem. This led in the first instance to the introduction of the functionalist type of explanation, which has greatly played down the degree of rationality that can be attributed to the single decision maker. There are also a number of difficulties involved in the functionalist type of explanation, which are associated with consistently incorporating both adjustment processes and processes of change into the central behavioural assumptions of the theory. Only when theories emerged which were based on a procedural concept of rationality was any real attempt made to explicitly model processes of change.

Although these models still appear relatively incomplete, a foundation has been created during the last twenty years for the formation of *a* theory of institutions within economics. Developments over the next twenty years should show whether a more coherent institutionalist research programme can be created on the basis of the contributions outlined in this chapter.

NOTES

1 I am indebted to Thráinn Eggertsson and Uskali Mäki for their helpful comments.
2 There are even differences between the supporters of this procedural concept of rationality. On the one hand we have the consequentialists who argue that rules of behaviour should be evaluated in accordance with the consequences the rules might have for the agent concerned. On the other hand, we have the deontologists, who argue that rules of behaviour should be evaluated in accordance with ethical or moral standards, without reference to the consequence (cf. Amartya Sen 1987).

REFERENCES

Akerlof, G. (1970) The market for 'Lemons': qualitative uncertainty and the market mechanism', *Quarterly Journal of Economics* 84: 488–500.
—— (1980) 'A theory of social custom, of which unemployment may be one consequence', *Quarterly Journal of Economics* 94: 749–75.
Alchian, A. (1950): 'Uncertainty, evolution and economic theory', *Journal of Political Economy* 58 (3): 211–21.
Arrow, K. (1963) 'Uncertainty and the welfare economics of medical care', *American Economic Review*, 53: 941–73.
—— (1969) 'The organization of economic activity: issues pertinent to the choice of market versus non-market allocation', in Joint Economic Committee,

The Analysis and Evaluation of Public Expenditure: The PPB system, Vol. I: pp. 59–73.

—— (1974) *The Limits of Organization,* New York: W.W. Norton.

Arthur, B. (1988) 'Self-reinforcing mechanism in economics', In P.W. Andersen, K.J. Arrow, and D. Pines (eds), *The Economy as an Evolving Complex System* Reading, Mass.: Addison-Wesley.

Axelrod, R. (1984) *The Evolution of Cooperation,* New York: Basic Books.

Bardhan, P. (1989) *The Economic Theory of Agrarian Institutions,* Oxford: Clarendon Press.

Coase, R. (1937) 'The nature of the firm', *Economica,* N.S. 4: 386–405.

David, P.A. (1985) 'Clio and the economics of QWERTY'. *American Economic Review* 75: 332–7.

—— (1988) 'Path-dependency: putting the past into the future of economics' Stanford University, unpublished paper.

Demsetz, H. (1967) 'Toward a theory of property rights', *American Economic Review* 57 (2): 347–59.

Dow, G. (1987) 'The function of authority in transaction cost economics' *Journal of Economic Behavior and Organization* 8: 13–38.

Elster, J. (1983) *Explaining Technical Change, A Case Study in the Philosophy of Science,* Cambridge: Cambridge University Press.

Friedman, M. (1953) 'The methodology of positive economics', in M. Friedman (ed.) *Essays in Positive Economics,* Chicago: University of Chicago Press.

Furubotn, E. and Pejovich, S. (1972) 'Property rights and economic theory: a Survey of recent literature', *Journal of Economic Literature* 10 (4): 1137–62.

Gray, J. (1984) *Hayek on Liberty,* New York: Basil Blackwell.

Hayek, F.A. (1948) 'Economics and knowledge' in F.A. Hayek (ed.) *Individualism and Economic Order,* London: Routledge.

—— (1978) 'Competition as a discovery procedure' in F.A. Hayek (ed.) *New Studies in Philosophy, Politics, Economics, and the History of Ideas,* London: Routledge and Kegan Paul.

—— (1988) *The Fatal Conceit,* London: Routledge.

Heiner, R. (1983) 'The origin of predictable behavior' *American Economic Review,* 73: 560–95.

Hicks, J. (1939) *Value and Capital,* Oxford: Oxford University Press.

Hodgson, G.M. (1991) 'Hayek's theory of cultural evolution: an evaluation in the light of Vanberg's critique', *Economics and Philosophy* 7 (1): 67–82.

Kreps, D. (1990) *A Course in Microeconomic Theory,* London and New York: Harvester Wheatsheaf.

Lakatos, I. (1970) 'Falsification and the methodology of scientific research programmes' in I. Lakatos and A. Musgrave (eds) *Criticism and the Growth of Knowledge,* Cambridge: Cambridge University Press, pp. 91–196.

Langlois, R. (1984) 'Internal organization in a dynamic context: some theoretical consideration', in M. Jussawalla and H. Ebenfield (eds) *Communication and Information Economics,* Amsterdam: Elsevier Science, pp. 23–49.

—— (1986a) 'The new institutional economics: an introductory essay', in R. Langlois (ed.) *Economics as a Process, Essays in the New Institutional Economics,* Cambridge and New York: Cambridge University Press, pp. 1–25.

—— (1986b) 'Rationality, institutions, and explanation', in R. Langlois (ed.) *Economics as a Process, Essays in the New Institutional Economics,* Cambridge and New York: Cambridge University Press, pp. 225–55.

—— (ed.) (1986c) *Economics as a Process, Essays in the New Institutional Economics,* Cambridge and New York: Cambridge University Press.

Lewis, D. (1969) *Conventions: A Philosophical Study*, Cambridge, Mass.: Harvard University Press.

Lucas, R.E., Jr (1987) Adaptive behavior and economic theory' in R. Hogarth and M. Reder (eds) *Rational Choice: The Contrast between Economics and Psychology*, Chicago: Chicago University Press.

Machlup, F. (1967) 'Theories of the firm: marginalist, behavioral, managerial, *American Economic Review* 57: 1–33.

Mäki, U. (1987) 'A review of "Richard N. Langlois, ed, *Economics as a Process*', *Economics and Philosophy*, 3 (2): 367–73.

Mayr, E. (1976) *Evolution and the Diversity of Life*, Cambridge Mass.: Harvard University Press.

Menger, C. (1985) *Investigations into the Methods of the Social Sciences*, (Translation of: *Untersuchungen Über die Methode des Socialwissenschaftens*) New York: New York University Press.

Nelson, R. and Winter, S. (1982): *An Evolutionary Theory of Economic Change*, Cambridge, Mass.: Harvard University Press.

North, D. (1990) *Institutions, Institutional Change and Economic Performance*, Cambridge: Cambridge University Press.

—— and R.P. Thomas (1973) *The Rise of the Western World: A New Economic History*, Cambridge: Cambridge University Press.

Schelling, T. (1960) *The Strategy of Conflict*, Cambridge, Mass.: Harvard University Press.

Schotter, A. (1981) *The Economic Theory of Social Institutions*, Cambridge: Cambridge University Press.

—— (1983) 'Why take a game theoretical approach to economics? Institutions, economics, and game theory' *Economie Appliqué* 36: 673–95.

Sen, A. (1987) *On Ethics and Economics*, Oxford: Blackwell.

Simon, H. (1976) 'From substantive to procedural rationality', in S. Latsis (ed.) *Method and Appraisal in Economics*, Cambridge: Cambridge University Press.

—— (1978) 'Rationality as a process and as a product of thought', *American Economic Review* pp. 1–16.

Stiglitz, J.E. (1974) 'Incentives and risk sharing in sharecropping', *Review of Economic Studies* 41: 219–55.

Sugden, R. (1986) *The Economics of Rights, Co-operation and Welfare*, Oxford: Blackwell.

—— (1989) 'Spontaneous order', *Journal of Economic Perspectives* 3: 85–97.

Ullmann-Margalit, E. (1977) *The Emergence of Norms*, Oxford: Clarendon Press.

—— (1978) 'Invisible-hand-explanations' *Synthèse* 39: 263–91.

Vanberg, V. (1986) 'Spontaneous market order and social rules: a critical examination of F.A. Hayek's theory of cultural evolution', *Economics and Philosophy* 2:

Ward, B. (1972) *What's Wrong with Economics*, New York: Basic Books.

Williamson, O.E. (1973) 'Markets and hierarchies: some elementary considerations', *American Economic Review* 63: 316–25.

—— (1975) *Markets and Hierarchies: Analysis and Antitrust Implications*, New York: Free Press.

—— (1981) 'The modern corporation: origins, evolution, attributes' *Journal of Economic Literature* 19: 1537–68.

—— (1985) *The Economic Institutions of Capitalism: Firms, Markets, Relational Contracting*, New York and London: Free Press.

—— (1987) 'Transaction cost economics. The comparative contracting perspective' *Journal of Economic Behavior and Organization* 8: 617–25.

—— (1988) 'The economics and sociology of organization. Promoting a dialogue' in G. Farkas and P. England (eds) *Industries, Firms, and Jobs, Sociological and Economic Approaches*, New York and London: Plenum Press, pp. 159–85.

Winter, S. (1964) 'Economics, "Natural Selection", and the theory of the firm', *Yale Economic Essays* 4: 225–72.

—— (1975) 'Optimization and evolution in the theory of the firm', in R.H. Day and T. Groves (eds) *Adaptive Economic Models*, New York: Academic Press.

—— (1987) 'Comments on Arrow and on Lucas', in R.M. Hogarth and M.W. Reder (eds) *Rational Choice: The Contrast between Economics and Psychology*, Chicago: University of Chicago Press.

INDEX

300